JANE AUSTEN AND OTHER MINDS

Jane Austen's fiction is itself philosophy, a fact to which Stanley Cavell attested when he honored his philosophical teacher, J. L. Austin, through homage to her and her work. Engaging equally in criticism and in philosophy, *Jane Austen and Other Minds* demonstrates the standing of Austen's fiction as a philosophical investigation, both in its own right and as a resource to ordinary language philosophy in the twentieth and twenty-first centuries. Eric Reid Lindstrom addresses a long-standing shortcoming of Austen scholarship by locating in her fiction a linguistic phenomenology available to the novelistic everyday but not afforded her in intellectual history. He simultaneously advances recognition and understanding of J. L. Austin and Stanley Cavell, and of ordinary language philosophy, within Austen scholarship and the broader field of contemporary literary studies. This book argues compellingly for Cavell's choice of Austen as a means to pursue "passionate exchange," reimagining her common association with restriction and confinement.

ERIC REID LINDSTROM is the author of *Romantic Fiat: Demystification and Enchantment in Lyric Poetry* (2011), and editor of *Stanley Cavell and the Event of Romanticism* (2014). His essays on Jane Austen, Romantic and modern poetry, ordinary language, and philosophical poetics have appeared widely in academic journals. He lives in Vermont and Louisiana.

CAMBRIDGE STUDIES IN ROMANTICISM

Founding Editor
Marilyn Butler, *University of Oxford*

General Editor
James Chandler, *University of Chicago*

Editorial Board
Claire Connolly, *University College Cork*
Paul Hamilton, *University of London*
Claudia Johnson, *Princeton University*
Essaka Joshua, *University of Notre Dame*
Nigel Leask, *University of Glasgow*
Alan Liu, *University of California, Santa Barbara*
Deidre Lynch, *Harvard University*
Jerome McGann, *University of Virginia*
David Simpson, *University of California, Davis*

This series aims to foster the best new work in one of the most challenging fields within English literary studies. From the early 1780s to the early 1830s, a formidable array of talented men and women took to literary composition, not just in poetry, which some of them famously transformed, but in many modes of writing. The expansion of publishing created new opportunities for writers, and the political stakes of what they wrote were raised again by what Wordsworth called those 'great national events' that were 'almost daily taking place': the French Revolution, the Napoleonic and American wars, urbanization, industrialization, religious revival, an expanded empire abroad, and the reform movement at home. This was an enormous ambition, even when it pretended otherwise. The relations between science, philosophy, religion, and literature were reworked in texts such as *Frankenstein* and *Biographia Literaria*; gender relations in *A Vindication of the Rights of Woman* and *Don Juan*; journalism by Cobbett and Hazlitt; and poetic form, content, and style by the Lake School and the Cockney School. Outside Shakespeare studies, probably no body of writing has produced such a wealth of commentary or done so much to shape the responses of modern criticism. This indeed is the period that saw the emergence of those notions of literature and of literary history, especially national literary history, on which modern scholarship in English has been founded.

The categories produced by Romanticism have also been challenged by recent historicist arguments. The task of the series is to engage both with a challenging corpus of Romantic writings and with the changing field of criticism they have helped to shape. As with other literary series published by Cambridge University Press, this one will represent the work of both younger and more established scholars on either side of the Atlantic and elsewhere.

See the end of the book for a complete list of published titles.

JANE AUSTEN AND OTHER MINDS

Ordinary Language Philosophy in Literary Fiction

ERIC REID LINDSTROM

University of Vermont

Shaftesbury Road, Cambridge CB2 8EA, United Kingdom

One Liberty Plaza, 20th Floor, New York, NY 10006, USA

477 Williamstown Road, Port Melbourne, VIC 3207, Australia

314–321, 3rd Floor, Plot 3, Splendor Forum, Jasola District Centre, New Delhi – 110025, India

103 Penang Road, #05–06/07, Visioncrest Commercial, Singapore 238467

Cambridge University Press is part of Cambridge University Press & Assessment, a department of the University of Cambridge.

We share the University's mission to contribute to society through the pursuit of education, learning and research at the highest international levels of excellence.

www.cambridge.org
Information on this title: www.cambridge.org/9781009206952

DOI: 10.1017/9781009206976

© Eric Reid Lindstrom 2023

This publication is in copyright. Subject to statutory exception and to the provisions of relevant collective licensing agreements, no reproduction of any part may take place without the written permission of Cambridge University Press & Assessment.

First published 2023
First paperback edition 2025

A catalogue record for this publication is available from the British Library

Library of Congress Cataloging-in-Publication data
NAMES: Lindstrom, Eric Reid, author.
TITLE: Jane Austen and other minds : ordinary language philosophy in literary fiction / Eric Reid Lindstrom.
DESCRIPTION: Cambridge ; New York, NY : Cambridge University Press, 2022. | Series: Cambridge studies in Romanticism | Includes bibliographical references and index.
IDENTIFIERS: LCCN 2022022844 | ISBN 9781009206990 (hardback) | ISBN 9781009206976 (ebook)
SUBJECTS: LCSH: Austen, Jane, 1775–1817 – Language. | Austen, Jane, 1775–1817 – Literary style. | Austen, Jane, 1775–1817 – Criticism and interpretation. | English language – 19th century – Usage. | Romance fiction, English – History and criticism. | English fiction – 19th century – History and criticism. | Ordinary-language philosophy. | BISAC: LITERARY CRITICISM / European / English, Irish, Scottish, Welsh
CLASSIFICATION: LCC PR4038.L33 L56 2022 | DDC 823/.7–dc23/eng/20220728
LC record available at https://lccn.loc.gov/2022022844

ISBN   978-1-009-20699-0   Hardback
ISBN   978-1-009-20695-2   Paperback

Cambridge University Press & Assessment has no responsibility for the persistence or accuracy of URLs for external or third-party internet websites referred to in this publication and does not guarantee that any content on such websites is, or will remain, accurate or appropriate.

Contents

Acknowledgments	*page* vi
List of Abbreviations	ix
Introduction: On Criticism and Other "Middle Subjects"	1
1 Austen and Austin	22
2 Intelligible Community	50
3 *Sense and Sensibility* and Suffering	72
4 *Pride and Prejudice* and the Comedy of Perfectionism	96
5 Perlocutionary Entailments	131
6 *Emma* and Other Minds	161
7 *Persuasion*, Conviction, and Care: Jane Austen's Keeping	200
Notes	232
Bibliography	264
Index	278

Acknowledgments

In order to reach something closer to its best form, this book has required many years longer than I had initially planned for it, when it took shape out of my talk "Austen and Austin," at the 2009 New Directions in Jane Austen Studies Conference at Chawton. I had a summer cold at that conference, and I think it cost me a chance for a timely meeting with Linda Bree; thanks should go, I suspect, to Linda and to the whirligig of time at a much later date for bringing Cambridge University Press back into the picture as the ideal home for this book. At CUP, Bethany Thomas's commitment to this project has seen it through more than one dire strait over the past couple years. Her support and flexibility have been in every sense decisive. George Paul Laver has seen it through production with alacrity. The final study has benefitted greatly from the comments of three anonymous press readers of the script, all of whom insisted on needed elements of structure, clarity, and concision that have strengthened my aim and made it possible to find an audience at all. They gave me some well-deserved pains and saved me many more. Five other anonymous external readers of the manuscript – this time serving in the cause of a promotion review in 2020 – sharpened, validated, and challenged much that is here too. In the person behind two of these reports, especially, I found precious community. Jim Chandler's and Bethany Thomas's suggestion to bring the book into the Cambridge Studies in Romanticism series was unexpected and professionally gratifying. I am honored to have *Jane Austen and Other Minds* enter and be in the world within this distinguished line of studies.

For her supportive and pointedly helpful initial response to its proposal as a first communication, I wish to thank and remember Helen Tartar. Valerie Rohy and Todd McGowan, colleagues at the University of Vermont, responded with readiness and insight to an in-house version of that initial proposal back in 2013. At Vermont, thanks also to Tony Magistrale, Val Rohy, Dan Fogle, and John Gennari: Each of these

Chairpersons of English during the decade-plus spent on this project have given it, and me, critical support.

In very different forms and much compacted, portions of Chapters 1 and 2 have appeared in print in my article "Austen and Austin" at *European Romantic Review* (2011). Much of Chapter 3 appeared as "*Sense and Sensibility* and Suffering; or, Wittgenstein's Marianne?" in *English Literary History* (2013). A small slice of Chapter 5 was taken, further divided, and revised from my essay "Perlocution and the 'Rights of Desire': Cavell, Nietzsche, and Austen (and Austin)," published online in *Conversations: The Journal of Cavellian Studies* (2016). A group of eight students and myself "lab" composed the essay "Lady Catherine, Out of Order," which now has appeared in *Persuasions On-Line* (2021). This essay expands a subject touched on at the end of Chapter 4 here, without strict overlap, in my own solo voice. The students in that 2019 Masters seminar "Austen and the Ordinary" contributed to my thinking and reading during a key push toward a view of the finish. Lively, generative panels at the American Comparative Literature Association conference in 2016, 2019, and 2021, and at the North American Society for the Study of Romanticism conference in 2015, 2016, and 2018 were resources to my exploration of Romanticism, Austen, and ordinary language philosophy and criticism.

For their friendship and further perspectives at Vermont, I am keen to thank Dale Jaffe, Ellie Miller, Mark Usher, Tyler Doggett, and Katie Gough. Sabbatical periods granted in 2012–2013 and in Fall 2019 enabled my writing and rewriting. The University of Vermont Humanities Center, led by Luis Vivanco, stepped in with perfect timing to offer a generous subvention to pay for the production of this book's index. The opportunity to think about Austen and philosophy as a presenter (twice) in the affable context of Burlington's Public Philosophy Week (created by Tyler) was a gift. When we met after his talk at St. Michael's College, Christopher Ricks generously shared his then-scarce Austin audio lecture file with me and recharged my sense of purpose.

Among many friends, colleagues, and fellow travelers in Romantic Studies, Emily Sun, Eric Walker, Nancy Yousef, Anne-Lise François, and (crossing into philosophy) Richard Eldridge have most nourished this book, in equal parts through their conversation, shared work, and example as writers. I've concluded that Paul Fry seeded this book with wise inadvertency, sometime back in the early 2000s, when he once let pass that my dissertation was smart to bring up Cavell only at the end, because it clearly was too indebted to dig out. I think Paul rightly surmised I only learn by being spiritually behind-hand. (And if I'm making all this up, there are a dozen other reasons to thank Paul.)

An awaited acknowledgment of Stanley Cavell himself could be done very simply – I never met him in person – and also could be rightly understood to take nothing less than the scope of the work itself. I have learned to think productively and even joyfully, not back in regret, about this, from Cavell's own stories about the intimacy of a major acquaintance he made too late to force. His words in print do plenty. It is enough to eat from the gleaning. A talk I gave at Harvard in Spring 2013, "Stanley Cavell and (British) Romantic Perfectionism: Godwin, Austen, Keats," found its way into his hands. Warm thanks to Andrew Warren for inviting me.

A short-term fellowship at Trinity College, Cambridge, in late 2019 just before the global-health curtain fell, enabled me to conduct research on the unpublished writings of D. W. Harding, held in the Library of Emmanuel College. (See the largesse there?) I am particularly grateful to Anne Toner as a truly thoughtful and gracious host for this period and to Cambridge for providing a range of sociable atmospheres for me and Kira, and (not least) a wonderful audience for hearing about the *next* project.

My parents, Esther Hartzheim and Steve Lindstrom, have given not only unconditional love to me but a respect for each other that makes the thinking in this book possible. This book is dedicated to Veronica Lindstrom and Maren Lindstrom, for their warmth of intelligence, and their distinctively individual measures of enthusiasm and dubiety toward my schemes. I feel known because they do really know me. For companionship, comradeship, and endless conversation, my biggest thanks beyond thanks are to Kira Braham, and to our shared life of pleasurable labor and eventful rest.

Abbreviations

CH	B. C. Southam, *Jane Austen: The Critical Heritage*. 2 vols. London: Routledge & Kegan Paul, 1968.
Claim	Stanley Cavell, *The Claim of Reason: Wittgenstein, Skepticism, Morality, and Tragedy*. New York: Oxford University Press, 1979.
CM	Gilbert Ryle, *The Concept of Mind*. London and New York: Hutchinson's University Library, 1949; London: Penguin, 1990.
CT	Stanley Cavell, *Contesting Tears: The Hollywood Melodrama of the Unknown Woman*. Chicago: University of Chicago Press, 1996.
E	Jane Austen, *Emma*. George Justice. Ed. New York: W.W. Norton, 2012.
How to Do Things	J. L. Austin, *How to Do Things with Words*; 2nd ed. J. O. Urmson and Marina Sbisà. Eds. Cambridge, MA: Harvard University Press, 1975.
In Quest	Stanley Cavell, *In Quest of the Ordinary: Lines of Skepticism and Romanticism*. Chicago: University of Chicago Press, 1988.
MP	Jane Austen, *Mansfield Park*. Claudia L. Johnson. Ed. New York: W.W. Norton, 1998.
Must	Stanley Cavell, *Must We Mean What We Say? A Book of Essays*. Cambridge: Cambridge University Press, 1976.
NA	Jane Austen, *Northanger Abbey*. Susan Fraiman. Ed. New York: W.W. Norton, 2004.
P	Stanley Cavell, *Philosophy the Day after Tomorrow*. Cambridge, MA: Harvard University Press, 2005.

Per	Jane Austen, *Persuasion*. Patricia Meyer Spacks. Ed. New York: W.W. Norton, 2013.
PI	Ludwig Wittgenstein, *Philosophical Investigations*. Trans. G. E. M. Anscombe. Malden, MA: Blackwell, 2001.
Pitch	Stanley Cavell, *A Pitch of Philosophy: Autobiographical Exercises*. Cambridge, MA: Harvard University Press, 1994.
PP	J. L. Austin, *Philosophical Papers*; 2nd ed. J. O. Urmson and G. J. Warnock. Eds. London: Oxford University Press, 1970.
P&P	Jane Austen, *Pride and Prejudice*. Donald Gray and Mary A. Favret. Eds. New York: Norton, 2016.
Scandal	Shoshana Felman, *The Scandal of the Speaking Body: Don Juan with J. L. Austin, or Seduction in Two Languages*. Catherine Porter. Trans. Stanford: Stanford University Press, 2003.
Secret of Style	D. A. Miller, *Jane Austen, or The Secret of Style*. Princeton: Princeton University Press, 2003.
Senses	Stanley Cavell, *The Senses of Walden*; an expanded edition. Chicago: University of Chicago Press, 1981.
SS	J. L. Austin, *Sense and Sensibilia*. London: Oxford University Press, 1962.
S&S	Jane Austen, *Sense and Sensibility*. Claudia L. Johnson. Ed. New York: W.W. Norton, 2002.

Introduction
On Criticism and Other "Middle Subjects"

A work of literary criticism and philosophical theory in equal parts, *Jane Austen and Other Minds* demonstrates the standing of Jane Austen's fiction as a philosophical investigation in its own right, as well as a resource to ordinary language philosophy in the twentieth century. The book locates in Austen's fiction a kind of "linguistic phenomenology" available to the everyday world of the novelist, but not permitted her in intellectual history. The study also strives to honor the thought and teaching of Stanley Cavell (1926–2018). Though these two primary goals are inextricably bound together, the event of reading Cavell (reading Austen, and others) necessarily irrupts into the middle of a neater and all-English Jane Austen with J. L. Austin pairing that also concerns me at length. I take up the charge found at a relay-point in Cavell's late book, *Philosophy the Day After Tomorrow* (2005), where Cavell connects the "passionate exchanges" and rational play found in Jane Austen's novels to the figure of J. L. Austin, his mentor in the field of ordinary language philosophy, in the following way: "Because it is not to my hand here, or perhaps ever, to lay out a fuller geography of the courses that 'endless' passionate exchanges can take in satisfying the conditions of perlocutionary utterance, and because I think of myself here as wishing to honor Austin's work, I cite one brilliant source of such passionate exchanges that I imagine Austin would feel quite happy to be associated with, indicated in his announcing one of his once famous courses of lectures at Oxford, the one on the foundations of empirical knowledge, in roughly the following form: SENSE and SENSIBILIA. J. AUSTIN" (*P*, 188). This book seeks to answer a question raised for Cavell by the play of endless passionate exchanges within the constraints both of manner and time: Why would Cavell honor his philosophical teacher through homage to Jane Austen and in terms of the critique of the "foundations of empirical knowledge"?

This is a question that requires dealing with various modes, moods, and levels of performativity: literary and philosophical; intimate and public.

The inset question about the foundations of knowledge, of course, is not to be easily answered; surely not in any final way by a work of literary criticism. But the reassessment of our education in foundational knowledge occasions less ultimate registers of "passionate exchange." These are properly in reach. From the midst of things, such relations press meaningfully upon philosophical concerns as Austin understood them in *How to Do Things with Words*. Where the alliance with Jane Austen signaled by J. L. Austin's choice of the title *Sense and Sensibilia* may be imagined as acerbic, authoritatively witty, and coolly cultured in his own terms, Cavell's complex homage to Austin is more earnestly warm and more generous – if tortuous – in its involvement. It offers to make Austin posthumously happy by fully welcoming passionate (perlocutionary) utterance into classic illocutionary speech-act theory, and by extending Austin's range and circle of association beyond the lectures and famous Oxford Saturday mornings. Explaining why Cavell chooses Jane Austen as the means to make this enlargement around "passionate exchange" – when her writing and person have for so long been taken as examples of various confinements: Regency manners, heteronormativity, country estates – is equally this book's argument and performative task.

"Moderate-Sized Dry Goods"

J. L. Austin argues that sense data and material things "live by taking in each other's washing" (*SS*, 4). It is an image drawn from domestic life, though class-distanced from Jane Austen, the writer from whom he adapts the title of his 1947–1948 lecture series on modern sense-perception philosophy, *Sense and Sensibilia*. According to Austin, the ideas of both "sense-data" and "material things" trade on preoccupations found repeatedly in western theory of knowledge from Berkeley to Hume (on one track of this tradition from the eighteenth century), and from Bertrand Russell to A. J. Ayer (in another related line from the twentieth century). Austin thinks these ideas thrive insidiously by their pairing. "What is spurious," he claims, "is not one term of the pair, but the antithesis itself. There is no *one* kind of thing that we 'perceive' but many *different* kinds, the number being reducible if at all by scientific investigation and not by philosophy" (*SS*, 4).[1] In parallel with his contention that "[t]here is no one kind of thing that we 'perceive'," there is no one act of perception but a manifold of perceiving, sensing, and receptive activities: a plurality that is indicated but hardly exhausted by Austin's careful attention to the differences of usage among words like looks, appears, and seems.

One of Austin's most winning papers is entitled after the event of a small upset in the study, "Three Ways of Spilling Ink."[2] (The three ways and dimensions of ordinary-language analysis are: intentionally, deliberately, and purposefully/on purpose.) In *Sense and Sensibilia*, Austin objects to the narrow use of the "moderate-sized specimens of dry goods" that so often serve as the constituents of a small rotating cast of "material objects" when philosophy presents narrative examples. Austin sharply criticizes the furnishings both as philosophical exempla and as language use. He also targets the metonymic thinking behind them, countering the picture of the world of things as a dry-goods store from an affirmatively critical vantage *within* the same "moderate" world (the world of William Wordsworth's "spousal verse" of "common day").[3] In doing so, Austin harkens back to one of John Locke's foundational metaphors for the mind and ideation, less famous only than the *tabula rasa*, and linked to it by Locke's own slippage of metaphor: "Let us then suppose the mind to be, as we say, a white paper, void of all characters, without any ideas; how comes it to be furnished? Whence comes it by that vast store"?[4] How indeed is a flat sheet of white paper furnished? Austin contrasts to the prop-like dry goods an alternate middle range of experiential entities that we would not usually call "material things" – a liquid grouping of streamy, fuzzy, and re-mediated phenomena. Austin contends that sense-data philosophy in general, and Ayer's approach in *The Foundations of Empirical Knowledge* in particular, employs an impoverished and hollowly tasked concept of the "material thing," as he reflects on the experiential omissions from the day's standard philosophical list of objects (chairs, tables, pens) that "the ordinary man" is said to perceive:[5] "We may think, for instance, of people, people's voices, rivers, mountains, flames, rainbows, shadows, pictures on the screen at the cinema, pictures in books or hung on walls, vapours, gases."

I will back up for a full run through the extraordinary passage at hand:

> 1. It is clearly implied, first of all, that the ordinary man believes that he perceives material things. Now this, at least if it is taken to mean that we would *say* that he perceives material things, is surely wrong straight off; for "material thing" is not an expression which the ordinary man would use— nor, probably, is "perceive." Presumably, though, the expression "material thing" is here put forward, not as what the ordinary man would *say*, but as designating the general way the real *class* of things of which the ordinary man both believes and from time to time says that he perceives particular instances. But then we have to ask, of course, what this class comprises. We are given, as examples, "familiar objects"— chairs, tables, pictures, books,

flowers, pens, cigarettes; the expression "material things" is not here (or anywhere else in Ayer's text) further defined.⁶ But *does* the ordinary man believe that what he perceives is (always) something like furniture, or like these other "familiar objects"— moderate-sized specimens of dry goods? We may think, for instance, of people, people's voices, rivers, mountains, flames, rainbows, shadows, pictures on the screen at the cinema, pictures in books or hung on walls, vapours, gases—all of which people say that they see or (in some cases) hear or smell, i.e., "perceive." Are these all "material things"? No answer is exactly vouchsafed. The trouble is that the expression "material thing" is functioning *already*, from the very beginning, simply as a foil for "sense-datum"; it is not here given, and is never given, any other role to play, and apart from this consideration it would surely never have occurred to anybody to try to represent as some single kind of things the things which the ordinary man says that he "perceives." (*SS*, 8)

The passage transitions from the genre of comic philosophical satire to something like the lyric arts of performative attention. When Austin thinks of "familiar objects," he presents not a static, disconnected list of "material things," but a dynamic association moving from people to their voices to the flowing river to the mountain through which it cuts, to flame, to shadows and the flickers of cinema.

What the so-called "ordinary man" perceives and experiences is best made available when sourced in the resources of ordinary language. It is a world of moderately vibrant materialism and of the variously medium-scaled. We might call it a garden-variety Romanticism. This notion of the garden draws on its ordinary idiomatic phrasing, though it does make reference to the thought-picture of the garden as a picture of mind, as in the privileged setting of the "other minds" problem in an English backyard: "There is a goldfinch in the garden" (*PP*, 77). Despite the role Cavellian perfectionism will play in this book, this is not the garden of the William Godwin-Erasmus Darwin-Percy Bysshe Shelley line of Romantic perfectibility, where kings, priests, and statesmen eliminated, "A garden shall arise, in loveliness / Surpassing fabled Eden."⁷ For Austin, the garden is a locale and figure of an original – not sin – but ordinary mistake, where one encounters a songbird misrecognized. Lecture II of *Sense and Sensibilia* begins: "Let us have a look, then, at the very beginning of Ayer's *Foundations* – the bottom, one might perhaps call it, of the garden path" (6).

The likely allusion to the English popular author Beverley Nichols is a hint. In the English phrase, to lead someone down (or up) the garden path is to mislead, to deceive them. But, redoubling the play of the idiom and its allusion, Austin's philosophical dispute with Ayer's *Foundations* is precisely over the role of deception as providing a key of misguidance in the theory of knowledge. For Austin, "at the very beginning" of Ayer's theory and at the "bottom" of the garden is not a truth about the perception of objects (indirect and misperception), but an intellectual muddle and social mistake, a philosophical education in misleading (6). Austin's ready-to-hand garden metaphor preserves the sense of entanglement in the history of philosophy, but denies inherent philosophical profundity to Ayer's tradition. The beginning, the origin, is the root of the problem, its bottom. The garden here is not the mythic site of transcendental origin or utopian recovery, but of immanent, though fraught and even mysterious, communication. The garden path denotes a place of daily discovery and error. Knowledge in the garden is ready-to-hand and available. To cite from the everyday and conversational narrative poetics of the overlooked modernist novelist Henry Green, "[t]he argument ... is that we cannot go outside everyday life to create something between reader and writer in narrative. The communication between the two will be on a common or garden plane." But, as Green goes on to note, in its premise of immanent exchanges of contact, "the common or garden plane" of communication is not free of mysteries and miracles. Rather, he wonders at the prior fact of language as an asset and means of exchange: "the mere exchange between two human beings in conversation is a mysterious thing enough. The mere fact that we talk to one another is man's greatest asset. That we talk to one another in novels, that is between complete strangers ... is nothing less than miraculous if you once realise how much common experience can be shared."[8]

Cavell's major early essay "Knowing and Acknowledging" asks what we are doing to the precondition of embodiment by giving the standing of myth to this version of "other minds" skepticism. Cavell also thinks through the metaphor of accessing another's mental life as that of contemplating a garden (*Must*, 260–261; *Claim*, 368). He cites John Cook and the analogy that we may not be able to see our neighbor's crocuses (*Must*, 259). Indeed, there is a wider motif of thinking about flowers and about what we might call living walls and their fissures in ordinary language philosophy, including in John Wisdom's symposium on *Other Minds* (*In Quest*, 68–70). Cavell reconsiders the garden analogy so as to gain a clearer vantage upon the human "abilities" and "inabilities" of knowing that this picture of thought may help us to grasp, when Cook calls it a "circumstance" that conditions our knowledge, that we are not the other in pain. Cavell ponders what may count as the meaning of such a "permanent circumstance" as embodiment. In his most identifiably

Romantic and lurid mood regarding the thorns of life, Cavell invests in a Shelleyan allusion to the garden space, as he offers a kind of lyric paradigm of suffering transposed into the philosophical third person of Jamesian narrative: "the analogy captures the impression that I am sealed *out*; but it fails to capture the impression (or fact) of the way in which *he* is sealed *in*. He is not in a position to walk in that garden as he pleases, notice the blooms when he chooses: he is *impaled* upon his knowledge" (*Must*, 261). At a closely related moment in Part 4 of *The Claim of Reason*, Cavell writes amidst discussion of various thought pictures: "[a]nother such description which arises in thinking about other minds is that of a garden which I can never enter. But this expression is really (mythologically) about a particular quality of the other's mind (it is not, say, a jungle, or dump yard or haunted house), and about a particular position I am in relative to it (say one of envy or disgust or fear). Such descriptions emphasize that I do not enter another's mind the way I enter a place. This is so far not much help; it does not distinguish either from entering, say, into marriage" (*Claim*, 368). Here the various locutions of *entering into* (a mind, a place, a marriage) serve as a relay of metaphors we live by in the metaphor of mind as location. They may structure alternatively dramatic or comedic possibilities of relation and insight. But more often they go unregarded. An additive troping declines into a subtractive trope, then hardens. Syllepsis is one of the resources of "the fierce ambiguity of ordinary language" (*Claim*, 180).

Admittedly rough-cast, these working concepts of the middle subject and the garden plane carry significant philosophical implications for the phenomenologies of reading and writing. Cavell's arrestingly melodramatic Romanticism departs from J. L. Austin's tone but draws from his tenacity in making distinctions. The dryly satirical mode of Austin contrasts to his colleague Gilbert Ryle's harangue on the "Myth of Descartes" as a wholesale "category mistake" in *The Concept of Mind*, the work (Austin says) of a "*philosophe terrible*" who "has chosen therefore to cast his work in the form almost of a manifesto."[9] Austin – who describes his method as "linguistic phenomenology" in the essay "A Plea for Excuses" (*PP*, 182) – offers something like a phenomenologically attuned list to counter his chagrin for positivist nomenclature: "pens are in many ways though not in all ways unlike rainbows, which are in many way though not in all ways unlike after-images, which in turn are in many ways though not in all ways unlike pictures on the cinema-screen – and so on, without assignable limit" (*SS*, 4). Austin makes such distinctions without limiting dualities. He advances by a plurality that finds its method through examples and distinctions that search past pseudo-metaphysical binaries (including the insurgent opposition to binaries). After reading Austin at any length, one wonders why one, two, and three are the only philosophical numbers. Despite his "installing monogamous heterosexual dyadic church- and state-sanctioned marriage at the definitional center" of *How to Do Things with Words* at both a rhetorical and social level, in this way Austin's work throughout evinces the reformist's challenge to entrenched intellectual practices.[10] His non-dualistic project in linguistic philosophy and social performativity anticipates the ampler spatial poetics found throughout Eve Sedgwick's late work – a positionality of the "beside": "Beside is an interesting proposition also because there's nothing very dualistic about it; a number of elements may lie alongside one another, though not an infinity of them. Beside permits a spacious agnosticism about several of the linear logics that enforce dualistic thinking: noncontradiction or the law of the excluded middle, cause versus effect, subject versus object."[11] In J. L. Austin's writings beyond *How to Do Things with Words*, we often find a companionable interest phrased differently. His important paper, "A Plea for Excuses," makes use of a Sedgwick-like nonce concept or "weak theory" to trace a bushy "ramiculated branch of philosophy" into the "coverts of the microglot." Here Austin bridles even at excuses as his announced subject beyond the title, since it is "unwise to freeze too fast to this one noun and partner verb." He voices his sometime preference for "'extenuation' instead" (*PP*, 175).

Austin's philosophical writings contain no sustained literary criticism and very few direct references to novels, beyond the allusion to Jane Austen's *Sense and Sensibility*. But an aside in "A Plea for Excuses" – "[a] course of E. M. Forster and we see things differently" (*PP*, 194) – casually indicates Austin's sense that the English novel may provide a resource to philosophical quandaries, serving at what he calls, with the tactical caginess of one who has served in intelligence during war, "the stage of appreciation of the situation." In his 1950 paper, "Truth," Austin urges philosophers at once to quit bullying their subjects and "take something more nearly their own size to strain at" (*PP*, 117). If perception, sizing things up, is an implicitly warlike act in this idiom, right-sizing philosophical observation may be irenic. In giving such focused critical attention to the compelling and problematically rendered middle scale, Austin may be seen to draw philosophical resources from the critical history of the modern novel and its imagined interdisciplinary courses. An enriching preoccupation with experience, perception, and an associative "life" beyond just the sense of sight runs from Henry James (whom Max Beerbohm parodied in "The Mote in the Middle Distance") to Virginia Woolf ("The Mark on the Wall," "Solid Objects").[12]

Austin demonstrably owes something to the I. A. Richards of *Practical Criticism*: "There are subjects – mathematics, physics and the descriptive sciences supply some of them – which can be discussed in terms of verifiable facts and precise hypotheses. There are other subjects – the concrete affairs of commerce, law, organization and police work – which can be handled by rules of thumb and generally accepted conventions. But in between is the vast *corpus* of problems, assumptions, adumbrations, fictions, prejudices, tenets; the sphere of random beliefs and hopeful guesses; the whole world, in brief, of abstract opinion and disputation about which civilized man cares most." The history of criticism, summarizes Richards, is a history of "middle subjects."[13] William Empson, Richards's precocious student, says this about the interaction of "Sense and Sensibility" in *The Structure of Complex Words*: "A mathematician will often take an absurdly small context —'me seeing a stick'— and argue from what is inherent in that to a theory of continuity; a philosopher commonly takes 'my seeing my table' and finds inherent in it his theory of knowledge. You do not know his real context till you know what he has to say. It is the distinguishing mark of the expert of sensibility that he does the same; from the small specimen he leaps to the universal truth, commonly with references to infinity, and when he is wrong you do not want to introduce a larger context but a middle-sized one such as the human creature really knows about."[14] The challenge to bring dynamic, unscripted forms of thought to the shuttling acts we perform as literary theorists and critics, between theory of knowledge and the "small specimen," is the task of criticism outright. For Austin, the reductions of sense-data philosophy traffic in a world of moderately sized dry goods scripted into roles as "material thing" dummies. Yet the importance of consulting ordinary language is, as Cavell maintains, pursued *In Quest of the Ordinary*, that is, in recognition of the uncanniness and strangely receding distance of the ordinary.

"We may think, for instance, of people, people's voices, rivers, mountains, flames, rainbows, shadows, pictures on the screen at the cinema, pictures in books or hung on walls, vapours, gases." In the generativity of excess understanding, Empson's enthusiastic "expert of sensibility" stands not in contrast to but aligned with the mathematician and philosopher. All stand in need not of a new "larger context" but of the re-introduction of "middle-sized one[s]" such as other human creatures experience and about which "material objects" themselves may afford knowledge, through greater working intimacy with their capacities, constraints, and limits.[15]

Austin's brilliant debunking of typecast "material things" is phrased at once in the form of a critical countermand, a kind of poetic reverie, and a list. It is offered in *Sense and Sensibilia* to remind readers of what they already practice as their knowledge of the world, grasped through ordinary natural language, delivered from the world-as-undertaken. Austin's critique of the positivists' rendering of "material things" offers a prescient challenge to the philosophical habits of phrase – but also of thought and exemplification – that evoke such concepts as "matter," "objects," and "things." His stubborn persistence in not allowing the convenient reduction of the "material thing" as a token of discourse is especially noticeable in light of the recent critical turn to new and vibrant materialisms of many stripes. In this instance, Austin fashions a type of sentence found increasingly in writings by new formalist literary scholars and by practitioners of object-oriented ontology: an ontologically level, syntactically straight, but philosophically careening list of disparate objects.

At their best, such lists generously distribute agency. Acknowledging entities as "autonomous forms," Graham Harman says these irreducible entities exist "all the way up and down the ladder of the cosmos." Then Harman enumerates the entity-forms of "lemon-meringue, popsicles, Ajax Amsterdam, reggae bands, grains of sand."[16] With comparable heterogeneity, Caroline Levine writes in a definitional passage of *Forms*:

> To capture the complex operations of social and literary forms, I borrow the concept of *affordance* from design theory. *Affordance* is a term used to describe the potential uses or actions latent in materials and designs. Glass affords transparency and brittleness. Steel affords strength, smoothness, hardness, and durability. Cotton affords fluffiness, but also breathable cloth when it is spun into yarn and thread. Specific designs, which organize these materials, then lay claim to their own range of affordances. A fork affords stabbing and scooping. A door-knob affords not only hardness and durability, but also turning, pushing, and pulling.[17]

There is something at once delightfully ingenuous and soliciting of criticism about these lists that include "things" like reggae, soccer teams, popsicles, transparency, fluffiness (a predicate found in both meringue and in cotton), breathability, pushing and pulling. The total effect depends upon defamiliarization, but not simply to make us feel the primitively obdurate or hard modernist version of things – to "*make the stone stony*," as Viktor Shklovsky once memorably claimed.[18] These lists of one-off "things," and increasingly the listicles in which they appear, might put us in mind, as Jacques Lezra recently notes, of the polyamorous love of all things in a poetic effusion like Pablo Neruda's "Oda a las Cosas" ("Ode to Things"). Yet affordances assume their human usage. When such concepts of objecthood or materiality are misapplied to the scope of today's "matters" without a critical sense of how things are mediated, material*ized* in forms of philosophical, cultural, and economic exchange, the amassed things and their essences or affordances can well cause the concept-laden feeling Lezra calls "deep dissatisfaction."[19]

Austin identifies the philosopher's original sin in the thought-picture that sacrifices ordinary language to sensa as the basis of an account of perceptual knowledge. That move amounts to the abandonment of the world as a garden. Throughout the *Sense and Sensibilia* lectures he pursues this case, most philosophers think unsuccessfully, as "the illusion of the so-called 'argument from illusion'" (*SS*, 4), and casts the world it has lost in the storied shape of a garden. Sandra Laugier observes of this passage in her summary of the lectures:

> At the beginning of *Sense and Sensibilia*, Austin takes issue with the notion of "sense datum," which Moore and Russell introduced in order to avoid the problems raised by the notion of sensation, by thus specifying its "content" (an absolute premise that would, in a way, except the relativity of sensation). The idea that we can examine our sensations (or strip them down in such a way as to be able to obtain sense data, which for Austin amounts to the same thing) is "the original sin (Berkeley's apple, the tree in the quad) by which the philosopher casts himself out from the garden of the world we live in." The illusion Austin condemns is twofold: first, it is the illusion that I have a better chance of reaching "the real" by speaking about sense data than by speaking about objects and following the ordinary rules of language, and second, the illusion that there is a univocal definition of "real."[20]

In the substitution of sense data theory for the plurality of midsized and medium-zoned experiences, Austin laments not the loss of the Garden of Eden (he mentions the quad, keeping in mind he is a professor at Oxford). Rather, he laments the ruse of a knowledge production-and-validation by means of an exile from human scaled receptivities of knowing. The sense data account alienates what Austin imagines to be the very donation of knowing.

Unknowing, too, can be a distributed and inflected position. Austin alleges of the tradition of indirect perception that it utilizes and bequeaths a diminished jargon of analytical language that hedges against an appropriate boldness in ordinary language. Against that picture, he invokes the variously lush but still scrutable, finite, multiple and yet specifiable – and pleasurable – garden world. Austin deploys garden variety types of ordinary language knowing. If we accept Jonathan Kramnick's argument on anti-representational philosophy and eighteenth-century poetry, an argument with aims very much compatible with Austin's work, and mine here, "perceptual acquaintance employs a kind of everyday skill or homely style."[21] With Kramnick, we can ask, what if our picture of knowledge isn't constructed in that usual way, as the product of the multipart mechanism, or modular story, of external/internal/external: an impression made upon a camera-like inlet through the senses followed by an image formed of the object by internal mental representation, finally articulated by expressive externalization?[22] Part 2 of Wittgenstein's Brown Book contrasts the "feeling of familiarity" with "familiar objects" not with skepticism or doubt, but instead with *surprise*.[23] By contrast to the presentation of ideas of sense data and the framing of a theory of perception based on painterly impressionism – and carrying through to the study of literature the argument that perception as such is not a major theoretical problem – the focus in *Jane Austen and Other Minds* is not on the epistemology of Austen's fiction, but on its relation to Austin's mode of performative felicity and Cavell's insistence on finding the place of acknowledgment. What if everything one wants out of knowledge is available, "fully sensible of its mysteries and fully open about them"? (*Senses*, 4). Plenty of limits, conflicts, and failures remain, but the machinery of Eden and hollow skepticism both move to the wings after this readjustment (which is also, à la philosophical satire in early Marx, a radical philosophical critique of the discourse of most everything that is said to exist).[24]

Austin commends not rest but *fieldwork* in his invocation of the garden site. This means not origin work but bottom work, requisite work in the language thicket: "drawing the coverts of the microglot"; "forget[ting] for a while about the beautiful and get[ting] down instead to the dainty and the dumpy" (*PP*, 175, 183). As opposed to the sublime and the beautiful, he thinks we are more likely to "get going on agreeing about discoveries" on that more modest and particular pairing of terms.

Though we encounter the garden of this world as a bewildering tactical situation, and it must be *made* public and available, there is a thread to follow from Austin's investigations of linguistic phenomenology to Austen's fictional garden plane of conversations. Despite the apparent contempt of her object world of fabrics and furniture (the world Paula Byrne deploys to organize Jane Austen's historical writing life as "a life in small things")[25] – and in the face of the widely supported notion that Austen's philosophical background lies with the eighteenth-century British empiricists – J. L. Austin's satirical mode in *Sense and Sensibilia* shares with the fictions of Jane Austen an inalienable possession in language and a distaste for the premise that knowledge must be routed through an idiolect of indirect perception. Another way to say this – which Stanley Cavell labors to claim for himself as a practitioner of ordinary language philosophy in his early essay "Must We Mean What We Say?" – is that Jane Austen is entitled to philosophy, through nothing more than her position in the contested community of English as a natural language.

What I think of in this book as J. L. Austin's unexpected Romanticism is enabled as a challenge and a resource in this moment from "The Meaning of a Word"; the method it provisions contrasts ordinary language to an anticipatory defensive structure characterizing "doing physics" and "ideal" language: "Ordinary language breaks down in extraordinary cases. (In such cases, the cause of the breakdown is semantical. Now no doubt an *ideal* language would *not* break down, whatever happened. In doing physics, for example, where our language is tightened up in order precisely to describe complicated and unusual cases concisely, we *prepare linguistically for the worst*. In ordinary language we do not: words fail us. If we talk as though an ordinary must be like an ideal language, we shall misrepresent the facts" (*PP*, 68). This openness to failure – *availingness* to failure, even, given the non-ideal nature of all contexts – represents dialogue with failure as a possible outcome that is nonetheless more resourceful and less damaging than any insurance taken out against its possibility. The culmination of Austin's argument in *Sense and Sensibilia* is that, by seeking a single kind of statement about knowledge that is *incorrigible* (not subject to doubt or to further challenge, incapable of being proved wrong *in any context*), the sense data theory of perception seeks not so much knowledge as the elimination of risk. Its form Austin calls "not a maximally certain, but a minimally adventurous form of words" (*SS*, 103, 112, 139). For Cavell and Wittgenstein in related ways, it is this availability of felicity and failure alike that constitutes the possibility to go on (and go on well enough), to inherit, succeed, and take part; and occasionally to reach felicity.[26]

J. L. Austin once claimed that importance isn't important, truth is. Since its initial critical reception, the consensus of critical commentary on Jane

Austen's work has praised it for "small truths," contributions which one anonymous review (in 1854) made clear to distinguish from "half-truths" (*CH* I, 147). Walter Scott's famous review of *Emma* is only one example of how Austen's middlingness has long been taken to represent her commitment to realism in artistic production.[27] A century later, George Saintsbury found in *Emma* "the absolute triumph of that reliance on the ordinary."[28] Yet, by underwriting the ordinary with a canned and stabilized version of empiricism, in the dominant history of bourgeois realism and the scenario of the rise of the novel, we forget the intimate relation of this middle zone to unintelligibility and failure. Austen's history of middle subjects is precarious. The most sanguine of her Victorian admirers knew this at the level of style and characterization: "One degree less felicitous, and failure begins!" (*CH* 1, 130).

Cavell's remarks upon Jane Austen in *Philosophy the Day after Tomorrow* are framed by a discussion of Wittgenstein that draws from the latter a philosophical method and set of aspirations that counter the idea of "philosophy as a chapter of science" (*P*, 112). As opposed to positivist scientific method, "philosophy's task is to assemble reminders" rather than necessarily add to knowledge (*P*, 112). In Cavell's eponymous chapter – and in the study before you – this prompt leads to a perspective on Austen as a writer who helps us assemble reminders of everyday life not in complacency or complicity but in the critique of the ordinary. Austen confronts "everyday life with itself" (*P*, 123). This book doubles down on the importance and multiplicity of the living entailment of reading Austen's work precisely because we understand her as a writer from whom we do not learn anything too much that is empirically new.

In *Philosophy the Day after Tomorrow*, Cavell adverts to Jane Austen's novels in the effort to honor and praise J. L. Austin, and in so doing, extend Austin's account of the institutional performative to improvised "passionate exchanges." Cavell relates a proleptic course of explanation by way of an insight into Austin, Austen and "the courses that 'endless' passionate exchanges can take in satisfying the conditions of perlocutionary utterance." Recounting why it took him so long to come to a serious engagement with Austen's novels – and outlining a course of study we must imagine now – Cavell describes the very late blooming of an "unconstrained fascination" with Austen (*P*, 126), one that begins with a recognition of her "narrator's renowned surface of containment" (*P*, 124). In the lecture version of "Philosophy the Day after Tomorrow," Cavell stunningly calls the "surface" of Austen's prose a "lethal calm."[29] He accounts for his late fascination with Austen's novels as a response not to the "elation" and "thrill" of identificatory participation in the main marriage plots, but in response to "the stupidity, the silliness, the empty-headedness, the quality of being worn-out...of so many of her supporting players" (*P*, 126). No examples of the worn-out lives, or schticks, of Austen's "supporting players" are immediately provided. But any reader of the novels can conjure some names, from the relatively lively and famous (Mr. Collins, Mrs. Norris, Mrs. Elton) to the burnt-out far reaches of the Austen character system (Mrs. Allen's rain-forecasting tautologies; the itch to act past the death of his host that characterizes the bit player Mr. Yates). To play this dispiritingly fun game yourself, read any stretch of the character entries found in Part 2 of Paul Poplawski's *Jane Austen Encyclopedia*.[30] Did Cavell associate these unforgettable caricatures with Thoreau's sense of lives led in quiet desperation?

The fascination with the ongoing non-life of Austen's "worn-out" characters is, of course, especially salient when read against the constitutionally optimistic, "exceptionalist" mood of Ralph Waldo Emerson's American perfectionism. In his engagement with Jane Austen, the dimensions of nation, genre, and gender all shift for Cavell, who thereby acknowledges powerfully (if so late) a fascination with Austen's novels as zones of decline and of oddly fruitful depletion.[31] The shift, I argue in the middle chapters of this book, reflects not simply an expansion of topic in Cavell's career but a re-disposition toward the material foundations of public feelings – one based in predicaments of thought and affect, as well as geopolitical structures that have bearings in and on gender and power. These new dimensions in Cavell's writing can be shown not only to have taken on, but to have been inspired with, disorganizing displacement. Cavell in this sense thinks with gender and genre in *Philosophy the Day after Tomorrow*, to respond implicitly to the disorganization and decline of Anglo-American prestige that has unfolded globally in the years during which he published books (1969–2010). That paradoxically "new" yet entropically declining mood is appropriate not only to a cultural response to the challenge of envisioning a philosophical future in the already "filled" imaginations and positional spaces of Anglo-European high culture, as the old story goes (it is the dominant account from Emerson and Whitman and Hawthorne to Henry James – and one still very much alive to Cavell);[32] it is further appropriate to the contemporary scene of the ordinary in disinvested, now often-crazed British and American life, intimacies, and public space. Cavell's project in *Philosophy the Day After Tomorrow* has many more commonalities than differences with the field of twenty-first century affect theory (by Lauren Berlant, Kathleen Stewart, Sianne Ngai and others) on the dysphoric ordinary and public feeling. "The ordinary is a circuit that's always tuned in to some little something somewhere," writes Kathleen Stewart. "It can take off in flights of fancy or go limp, tired, done for now." In a passage evocative of Cavell's resonantly tired fascination with Austen's downstage characters, Stewart continues: "The ordinary throws itself together out of forms, flows, powers, pleasures, encounters, distractions, drudgery, denials, practical solutions, shape-shifting forms of violence, daydreams, and opportunities lost or found."[33]

This effort to reorient our understanding of what Cavell means, makes, and leaves to us in *Philosophy the Day after Tomorrow* finds its partner in a long-overdue reset of our comprehension of the aims, mood, and methods of J. L. Austin. Austin is often taken to task for seeming to make both normative assumptions and undue claims about ordinary language, though in the essay "A Plea for Excuses," he cheerfully acknowledges that ordinary language "has no claim to be the last word, if there is such a thing" (*PP*, 185). "[I]t is necessary," Austin goes on, "first to be careful with, but also to be brutal with, to torture, to fake and to override, ordinary language" (*PP*, 186). Ordinary language in Austin's hands neither promotes a recourse to authoritarian "last words," nor does it supply any defense from brutalities of method, or provide refuge from violence both as a risk and as an occasional tactic. Cavell's interest in Jane Austen as a novelist of the ordinary responds with sensitivity to what he calls "the little deaths of everyday life" in her fiction, "the slights, the grudges, the clumsiness, the impatience, the bitterness, the narcissism, the boredom, and so on (variously fed and magnified and inflamed by standing sources of social enmity, say, racism, sexism, elitism, and so on)."[34] Cavell's work on the philosophy of film and in the genre he calls the "melodrama of the unknown woman" in *Contesting Tears* (1996) is one source of the #Metoo Movement's use of the term "Gaslighting."[35]

On the same page of the same text just quoted (his foreword to a 2007 book by the anthropologist Veena Das), Cavell reports:

> A decisive turn in my own studies in skepticism came from the realization that a skeptical process toward other human beings (others like myself, Descartes says) results not in a realization of my ignorance of the existence of the other, but in my denial of that existence, my refusal to acknowledge it, my psychic annihilation of the other.

Cavell himself presents the great theme and "decisive turn" of his work as the recognition – a recognition leading to many writing acts of intensive redescription – that the problem of knowledge ("ignorance") displaces an even prior skepticism towards acknowledgment ("denial," "psychic annihilation"). Cavell presents this autobiographical description also as a datum of literary history in *The Claim of Reason*: "romanticism opens with the discovery of the problem of other minds, or with the discovery that the other is a problem, an opening of philosophy" (467). The present book seeks an audience in Romantic studies, but all the more engages with Cavell's theme of skepticism and acknowledgment via Jane Austen as an insecurely Romantic author. My Austen is one of Isaiah Berlin's "restrained" rather than "unbridled" Romantics.[36]

Jane Austen and Other Minds, too, begins from the further recognition of what we might call a second turn in Cavell's writing on Romantic writing.[37] An event takes place in Cavell's thought in the interval between the publication of *In Quest of the Ordinary*, with its tour de force accounts of English Romantic Poetry by Wordsworth and Coleridge (among others – Kant, Emerson, Poe), and *Philosophy the Day After Tomorrow* with its expression of a new interest in Austen, concerning dynamics of a vulnerable conformity and resistance to the ordinary, in the medium of literary fiction. This expression of Romanticism by prose, on my reading, is not so much a discursive or communicative grounding of the poetic leaps as an attentive grinding – an aversive frictional thought being worked beside some form of community of acknowledgment and experience of being known. The empiricism Cavell values is an abrasive retention of that skeptical-sociable rhythm, an adhesion that takes both sides, rather than the kind of "impress" that sinks into the subject unilaterally from without. We can glimpse something of this eventual (and evental) shift in another text Cavell published in conversation with Veena Das, almost a decade after the publication of *In Quest of the Ordinary*: "My knowledge of myself is something I find, as on a successful quest; my knowledge of others, of their separateness from me, is something that finds me. I might say that I must let it make an impression upon me, as the empiricists almost used to say."[38]

With the exception of the first, chapters to follow take the common path of six chapters, each focusing on one of Jane Austen's six completed novels. The traditional format is meant both to help orient the reader who comes to the book for case studies in Austen, and to license philosophical departures. These risks can take a variety of shapes, large and small: sections that dwell with known information in a novel so as to weigh its acknowledgment differently (Chapters 3 and 6); chapters that push outward from a major starting premise or structural feature of a novel, which do not return to offer a comprehensive textual reading of the fiction as a whole (Chapters 4 and 5); and intensive digressions on apparently minor interactions in the novels, where my hope is to revalue the fiction's philosophical standing and redistribute our attention as critical readers and teachers (Chapters 2, 3, 7). My sense of the common zone of the hopeful readerships of *Jane Austen and Other Minds* makes for a wide territory – including Austen scholars and scholars of Romanticism, colleagues and students of Cavell, and those committed to the history and contemporary role of ordinary language philosophy in literary studies. The last is a growing body; but I am also aware that the disciplinary engagements within such a project can feel crosscutting. The book overall might be judged to present Cavell and ordinary language philosophy *via* Jane Austen – using Austen's novels as a repository – and to share readings *in* Austen rather than *of* her works. But the book, and each chapter individually, also displays how Austen's prose fiction is a repertoire, in its acts and in its potentials, for a mode of doing ordinary language philosophy in its own right, and not simply a common stock for philosophy's later use. Every chapter, and almost every segment or section, has been developed and tried out in classrooms where it was Jane Austen who brought us there and held the collective attention.

Chapter 1, "Austen and Austin," presents the details of the book's central proposition that Jane Austen's novels are not conduct books sharing preset values but philosophical studies of conduct more in the J. L. Aust*i*nian sense. The chapter claims that Austen – in common with the grouping of ordinary language philosophers I engage in this book: Austin, Wittgenstein, and Cavell (most of all) – does not view perception itself as a philosophical problem of major interest. My approach departs from the widespread view that Austen's fiction reflects the mitigated skepticism of eighteenth-century empiricists and anticipates modernist literary impressionism. In the words of her Victorian critic G. H. Lewes, Austen's epistemological project includes her cultivation of a prose style not hyper-realized as visuality but "content to make *us know*" through the testing and textures of dialogue and character.[39]

Chapter 2, "Intelligible Community," reads Austen's first novel accepted for publication, *Northanger Abbey*, in terms of a zero-degree of intelligibility in communicative social exchange. *Northanger Abbey* presents Catherine Morland's entry not just to Bath society but into the linguistic public. Throughout the novel, Catherine is subject to stratagems of deceit by her false friends, Isabella and John Thorpe. The latter even makes a coercive (and dishonorably deniable) marriage proposal that Catherine, in a state of absent-minded imaginative distraction, does not so much as uptake as information. J. L. Austin once identified untruth and unclarity as "the birthright" of all speakers. This mock birthright is the arrogation and entitlement of Thorpe. In a striking alignment of this kind of threat with its obverse – a critical investment of interest, if not fascination – Cavell explains his renewed reading of Austen only late in life as an exhausted intimacy with minor characters. In the tedious, packed rooms of Bath where nothing meaningful may happen, or originate, the main couple, Catherine and Henry, broach the possibility of intimacy through the precondition of the apartness of other minds.

Chapter 3, "*Sense and Sensibility* and Suffering," begins from the experimental philosophical writings of Ludwig Wittgenstein on the problem of other minds. Wittgenstein, like Adam Smith, positions suffering and pain as the paradigmatic experiences in discussion of other minds. (Austin's paradigmatic feeling is anger.) This chapter deploys a flattened point of view in terms of what it means to be "insensible," particularly in relation to the non-human paper and ink fictional characters in an "early" Austen novel. It reads *Sense and Sensibility* through a Cavellian exploration of the philosophical problems of skepticism and acknowledgment. Cavell presents his own reading of late Wittgenstein as one of an intimate frustration with the workings of criteria. The chapter uses that experience to model a necessarily and potentially productive frustration that modern novel readers often report with the main character/trait pairings of *Sense and Sensibility*. The chapter promotes the interest of otherwise flat writing as modeling forms of resiliency. Wittgenstein remakes philosophy as an opportunity for working out criteria while letting stand the dissatisfaction that is internal to the way criteria differ from the thing itself; he shares grammatical limits in relation to human experience even where there is nothing else to take over from linguistic practices, to get us "inside" them. These critical practices are especially vital to reading Austen's fiction written before her great success in writing novels of inwardness.

Chapter 4, "*Pride and Prejudice* and the Comedy of Perfectionism," interprets Austen's enduring, beloved comedy of marriage in dialogue with Cavell's philosophy of the perfectionist comedy of remarriage. In its first half I consider the charismatic art of *Pride and Prejudice* as a form of the conversational "sequel," as *Pride and Prejudice* the cultural phenomenon comprises an unbounded event of uncontainable circulation and exchange. The second half of the chapter gives visibility to Cavell's omission of the philosophical genealogy of the European concept of perfectibility from his Emersonian inflection of moral perfectionism. Cavell's version of Emersonian "moral perfectionism" has never explicitly laid out or paid homage to the trajectory, tensions, and implications of perfectibility as a concept found in European philosophy and literature of the late Enlightenment. The omission impacts a Cavellian reading of *Pride and Prejudice* by laying new stress on how Austen uses comic style to articulate her own fictional stance against the disembodiment and rhetorical rigidity of much thinking on "perfectibility" – especially William Godwin's. Positioned at the center of *Jane Austen and Other Minds*, and (along with the next) one of two chapters that break out of their Austen frame, the chapter enacts a key argumentative hinge-movement regarding philosophy's historical and material conditions and gender as topics of emergent interest in the later works of Cavell.

Chapter 5, "Perlocutionary Entailments," engages with a larger transhistorical discourse of female personhood. Following Lionel Trilling, I consider how the challenges that accompany Austen's public status are echoed in the reading and enlarged reception history of *Mansfield Park*. I move this discussion back to the 1772 Mansfield Decision, and forward to consider the controversy surrounding the less momentous twenty-first century decision to place Austen on a British bank note. The open-ended, improvisatory, and finally uncontrollable nature of feelingly impactful speech links cultural and critical conversations to what J. L. Austin calls the perlocutionary realm of performative language. Perlocution, the dimension of language that most signals organizational breakdown, bogging down the progress of J. L. Austin's official illocutionary speech-act theory, is also the dimension or capacity of language through which paratextual literary encounters – allusions, conversations, revisions, and eventful readings – persist. This concern with the embodied but unbounded effects of language (doing things *by* our words as well as *in* them) evokes a central feature of the enterprise of literary criticism altogether, I argue. Thus a section of the chapter, "The Problem of Praise," engages with Cavell's post-Kantian adaptation of the very mood and project of criticism as praise open to rebuke.

One of the book's main goals is to read and put forward for attention a wider range of J. L. Austin's writings than is typically found in works of literary studies, given the outsized impact of *How to Do Things with Words* in literary and cultural theory. Chapter 6, "*Emma* and Other Minds," discusses Austin's critique of certainty in "Other Minds," and his account of the pluralities of verbal action in the essays "Pretending" and "A Plea for Excuses." Austin's arguments in these essays possess not only cognitive and epistemological dimensions; they are supremely rich investigations of moral thought and sociality: dimensions of life that produce endless opportunity for mistake. Illuminating Austen's *Emma*, Austin's rejection of the exclusive dimension of certainty driving so much modern theory of knowledge goes hand in hand with his recognition of the epistemological character of social responsibility.[40] Rather than seeing presumption in Emma's matchmaking, this transmissible sociolinguistic form, I argue, is the serious sphere of implication at risk in *Emma*, where "expressions and behavior *place a claim on others*."[41] The novel's famous scene at Box Hill enacts these dynamics in a tour de force of recursive layers. The gap between what words say and what words do has seldom been so richly explored as in *Emma*. The ordinary-language philosophical topics treated in this chapter include moral luck, pretending, and the self-problematizing division (made famous by Paul de Man's reading of Rousseau) between exculpatory confessions and pleasure-taking excuses. The chapter begins with Austin's and Austen's joint critique of certainty alike as a philosophical and narrative goal. It ends by dislodging omniscience as a placeholder of philosophical value.

Chapter 7, "*Persuasion*, Conviction, and Care: Jane Austen's Keeping," develops from Cavell's striking interest in Michel Foucault's final works on "care of the self" (*Le souci de soi*). Cavell finds in Foucault an alternate version of the potential forms of life taken by moral perfectionism. Cavell in his autobiography *Little Did I Know* marks his engagement with Foucault's concept of *parrhesia*, or truth-telling, as it developed from a seminar Cavell co-taught with Arnold Davidson at The University of Chicago in 1999. As a fictional investigation of the conviction-persuasion distinction, *Persuasion* suggests rethinking the idea of being convinced through a practice of reason-giving whose grounds are to provide advance rationale for their validity of support. Rather, in Foucauldian practice Cavell finds "a place and an instrument of confrontation" (*P*, 155). Anne Elliot, the protagonist of *Persuasion*, undertakes a turn from the obedient subject of persuasion to a linguistic and social agent of conviction. This example of a late-Foucauldian reading of Austen in rapport with the ordinary, everyday, and *quotidienne* departs markedly from earlier influential Foucauldian readings of Austen which understand sociolinguistic and formal narrative features in terms of surveillance in the dispersed power/knowledge framework. I conclude the book's reading of Cavell's Austen under the aegis of "vulnerable conformity" by underlining a shift in the meaning of conformity as such. Drawing from language in George Saintsbury's 1894 essay on Austen, the chapter presents a curative and durational practice of "keeping" as an alternative to heroic investment. A term of art drawn from such diverse practices as landscape painting and fruit and vegetable canning, "keeping" is a communitarian and haptic practice (a care of touch), a custodianship, not a relation of epistemological mastery or ideological debunking.

The chapter, finally, returns to the famous claim that Jane Austen is a "prose Shakespeare." It reconceives the comparison in terms of an uncomfortable affinity of physical comedy between Austen and Shakespeare, and specifically in the irruptive violence of *Persuasion*. In the image of a character's head as a broken hazelnut, the chapter also provides an exemplary object lesson for what it looks like to hold the wrong picture of other minds.

CHAPTER I

Austen and Austin

In Jane Austen's youthful manuscript writings ("Volume the Second") appears a short fragment entitled "The female philosopher." In *The Cambridge Edition of the Works of Jane Austen*, Peter Sabor characterizes the title as an "oxymoron."[1] Austen has seldom been claimed as a philosophical writer on her own terms – that is, without sponsoring her claim to philosophical thought by the comparison of her self-described fine brush to, say, the big bow wow of a major philosophical figure such as Aristotle, Descartes, Adam Smith, or David Hume.[2] Yet this book presents Jane Austen as a resolutely philosophical novelist. I develop this claim through a set of interfacing readings of Austen's works with major texts and figures in (mostly) twentieth-century "ordinary language" philosophy, especially J. L. Austin and Stanley Cavell. In taking this approach, though, my hope is not simply to substitute one regulating philosophical construct over literature for another. Instead – as the blur of the proper names in the first chapter's title insinuates – I think Austen *does* philosophical work in her language as prose fiction. Anachronistically from the points of view of the histories of literature and of philosophy, ordinary language philosophy provides the appropriate means to analyze and honor this quality of Jane Austen's writing.

To Swynk as Austyn Byt

Chapter 1 begins outside of the discipline of close reading with the premise that an exciting way to engage philosophically in Jane Austen's work is also, given her surname, likely to be the most available to us as twenty-first century readers across fields of literary and cultural production. In comparing aspects of Austen's novels to the philosophy of J. L. (John Langshaw) Austin (1911–1960), I imagine myself taking a step many scholars have thought about before, but for whatever reason have chosen not to take in print. Of course there are the surnames. A gift from the realm of the everyday, the connection has seemingly always been there for the taking. What should we make of this happy contingency? On at least one occasion, Jane Austen received and – we can assume – deposited and enjoyed a royalty check from her published novels, made payable to the name "Jane Austin." Paula Byrne is convinced that a portrait that recently came into her possession in fact depicts the author. (Excitingly, she is surrounded by the objects of her craft, and situated in London.) That portrait's subject also is inscribed as "Miss Jane Austin."[3]

Such initial examples of authorial empowerment conflict, however, with the mode of extraction in which the name performs an act of displacement. First, there is a redirection from the person of Austen to her exemplary traits. From the beginning of her afterlife as a series of texts, the public attempt to honor Jane Austen's literary genius upon her death in 1817 served at once to elevate and elide her person. Her brother Henry Austen's Biographical Notice promotes the memory of Jane Austen as a steady Christian, a "[f]aultless" family member, and a rare genius of "unpretending" gifts. Henry's account does celebrate the literary stature of Austen's burial place in Winchester Cathedral. But the novels themselves are submerged in the focus on Jane Austen's "polished" wit and her "happy" manners and temper. At the end of the nineteenth century, this decorously managed testimonial was raised in a very public association with the name Austin. In *Jane Austen's Cults and Cultures*, Claudia Johnson recounts how through "a widely advertised public subscription," and in the wake of J. E. Austen-Leigh's *Memoir* (1869–1870), Austen belonged not only to a circle of "family witnesses," but thereafter to "all of England," a national community that in turn sought to memorialize its author by commissioning a three-panel stained-glass window to be installed above her grave in Winchester Cathedral.[4] To honor "Austen's status as a public figure," the very top center panel of the window represents St. Augustine – or *Austin*, as was once commonly rendered in contracted English. Johnson writes of the substitution: "[t]hrough the mediation of an English pun, then, Austen gets represented at the pinnacle, but in St. Augustine's body rather than in her own. The window thus demonstrates that Austen's bodily effacement is the condition of her apotheosis."[5] Apparently, to "swynken with his hands and labour, / As Austyn byt" – to quote the scornful words of the Monk in Chaucer's Prologue to *The Canterbury Tales* (ll. 186–187) – in the case of Jane Austen requires the effacement of both an embodied self and the signs of her professional labor as a writer.

Henry Austen's "Biographical Notice" (1818) has often and understandably been read as a document anxious to establish Jane Austen's good standing as a pious Christian and a contented member of her immediate family – an author withdrawn from the public spotlight, "unpretending" of any claim to fame, and almost of any claim to more modest recognitions, such as payment, for her writings. The gender and professional authority of Austen's authorship are everywhere at stake. The tone and aims of the Notice are perhaps best taken in light of the short interval of time between its composition and Jane Austen's death. The genre of this text lies somewhere in between a personal eulogy and an author introduction. Yet the narrow and idealizing, or alternately prudential, aspects of Henry's account aren't the only tendencies worth noticing in this document, which repeatedly adverts to "happiness" in the environment fostered by Jane Austen's company. If it does not address them by name – indeed, it cannot, given the larger horizon of her mass future readership and public[6] – the Notice yet speaks to "those who knew their happiness to be involved in her existence" (*NA*, 192). This domestic company has exploded, illimitably it would seem, to the community of her readership in the two centuries since Austen's death.

The above sense of Austen's swynk – labor without the recognition for it in her own person – differs from Christopher Ricks's stylistic sense of "swink" in J. L. Austin, as the performance of recurrent dry wit.[7] A second level of the relay of names does not seek to manage Austen's biographical personhood, but to locate it – intimately though impersonally – in her prose style. In an unexpected merging of necessity with aesthetics, the swynk or work not only denotes a field of toil in the post-Edenic state, but the care and craft of literary styling. It deserves remark that Henry Austen notes the "charms of style," of a prose body, in the "cultivation of her own language" through conversation and writing. The continuation of Henry Austen's proto-Victorian testimonial to Jane Austen's domestic virtues shifts mid-sentence and takes an interesting turn back to the start of her writing life in a culture of eighteenth-century prose authorship. Henry records Jane's sensibility from youth onward "to the charms of style" in "the cultivation of her own language." Henry's terms of praise raise for only the first time the difficult question of whether prose style is expressive or dissolving of Austen's personhood.[8] But certainly not for the last time. In 1859, the Victorian critic G. H. Lewes said of Austen that she "has made herself known without making herself public" (*CH* I, 150) – thus reversing a judgment that Samuel Johnson had cuttingly shared "of somebody, 'Sir, he managed to make himself public without making himself known'."[9] Redirecting Doctor Johnson's stentorian judgment, Lewes anticipates this book's central Cavellian theme of knowing versus acknowledgment. Where Johnson's remark calls on a distinction between the achievement of public reputation and the knowledge of private moral character, Lewes's terms for Austen can be felt to activate something other than a simple public/private inversion. Harkening to Judith Butler's account of the institution of gender as the *stylized repetition of acts,* the stylistic knowing of Austen is in the mode of extimacy, the kind of intimately external and impersonal making known that nonetheless registers the production of the effects of selfhood and inwardness. In Austen's sentences and not in her fantasized company do we find her most intimate and public appearance: "the *treasures* we might cherish for their power to conjure Austen's presence can also bewilder us into a false sense of the fullness of her being," writes Claudia Johnson, "which, if we are able to feel it at all, we will find only in reading her novels."[10]

Since Austen's ability to make herself known is not a function of information and publicity, it can gesture strikingly to the Cavellian treatment of acknowledgment and the making (here a narrative poetics) of transpersonal intimacy. Lewes himself shares a critical anecdote regarding Austen's underacknowledged legacy, an intimate jest perhaps, because it may involve an implicit reference to his own scandalous partnership with George Eliot, another translator "from the German":

> We have met with many persons who remember to have read *Pride and Prejudice,* or *Mansfield Park,* but who have altogether forgotten by whom they were written. "Miss Austen? Oh, yes; she translates from the German, doesn't she?" is a not uncommon question—a vague familiarity with the name of Mrs Aust*i*n being uppermost. From time to time also the tiresome twaddle of lady novelists is praised by certain critics, as exhibiting the "quiet truthfulness of Miss Aust*i*n." (*CH* I, 148–149)[11]

The contention that Austen is known through her language, and by works like *Pride and Prejudice* and *Mansfield Park*, while she is subject to personal misrecognition, could not be further from the truth today. Beyond need of stating, Austen is ubiquitous in contemporary media, where film and web adaptations anticipate and often supersede the experience of reading her books. In the cases of mistaken identity or conjunctive pairing, now it is Jane Austen's name that subordinates and triggers the Aust*i*ns. And on another level, that of literary history, it is nearly all *other* novelists, especially female novelists, of Austen's time that have been subject in the phrase of Clifford Siskin to "The Great Forgetting."[12]

Nevertheless, I rely on Lewes 1859 "Great Appraisal" as a touchstone assessment of the way in which Austen's authorial figure is dispersed through her writings. A common practice, submersing the personal into the impersonal by performances of style, links Austen to ordinary language philosophers. Both Jane Austen's and J. L. Austin's names are now tokens of the way in which a decided manner – style as not distinct from meaning and substance[13] – aligns with mastery and highly specific achievement in a discipline of writing. Austen's and Austin's writings are each independently known for their spirit of exuberant rigor and daunting play: to bring them together first by the link of their names only intensifies the challenge of responding to either author's complex individuality. In the interdisciplinary zone of philosophy and literature, we are driven to areas where long-standing disciplinary conventions are put in question, in order to respond adequately to the prompt of the parataxis, "Austen and Austin."

I will show in this and the next chapter how Austen's early fiction in particular responds to a philosophical impulse: that of addressing the grounds of intelligibility between persons from within the socialized field of language. This project does not accord with the typical scheme for relating philosophy to literature, in which literature deals in metaphors, figures, or alternately in realist particulars that eschew rational concepts. The central argument of the chapter here is that Austen – in common with the grouping of ordinary language philosophers I engage – does not view perception itself as a philosophical problem. She is not that kind of a skeptic.[14] Austen is not "perfect" as her brother Henry and many Janeites insist. But she writes committed, if (therefore) revisable, characters and conversations, in bold lines. She seldom devotes her artistic energies to a project of "physiological moment-to-moment intensity" (an exception here being the densely sensitive remediations of the past that characterize Anne Elliot in *Persuasion*).[15] And she only rarely and ironically writes passages that describe sensation through proto-impressionist mists or sense envelopes: the two examples I know of being the "something white and womanish" seen through a fence paling near the breakoff point in Austen's unfinished last work, *Sanditon*; and this passage from *Mansfield Park*, which provides moral judgment through a stunning report of Maria Bertram's turpitude: "It was a gloomy prospect, and all that she could do was to throw a mist over it, and hope when the mist cleared away, she should see something else" (*MP*, 76). Instead of problematizing and solving mysteries of sensation, Austen's philosophical energies address problems of (mis)recognition and acknowledgment – the threat to and hopeful securing of linguistic sensible community.[16]

***

My joint subject of Austen and Austin in this chapter risks belaboring a chance event of names bearing little weight beyond Cavell's allusive autobiographical investments. Yet Cavell's own self-adoptive act of naming, recounted in *Little Did I Know*, leads us to pause further over the depths and intricacies of the kinds of affiliation that are fostered by style. This project may confuse, but perhaps to good ends, the clear line keeping names free of connotations and entirely fixed in the possessive person, in the proper name's index (*PP*, 61). In its aspiration, familiar to twentieth-century American myth, Stanley Goldstein's renaming can be read as self-authorizing and self-disidentifying at once (the result of an "inward leave-taking").[17] His choice of self-given name, Stan Cavell, draws from an alternate branch of the family bearing the Anglicized analogue Cavalier, but with its extravagant economy more than hints at the pivoting edge of a cavil.[18] Some of this book's key verbal and conceptual lines of development – for example, the place of form in the performative; the difference between an entailed consequence and a communicative sequence; or the distinction between improvisation and improvement – will take some of their authorization to construct main arguments through verbal play from the much greater boldness toward names shown by Cavell.

Beside the verbal play, *Jane Austen and Other Minds* throughout its pages means to demonstrate the adhesiveness of writerly aspects of the Austen/Austin pairing. The more conspicuously shared cultural, perhaps national, elements of this duo are mixed and easy to oversimplify. They are both English comedic writers who use irony for enriched rhetorical purposes in order to show the prevailing environment – beyond descriptive and persuasive functions – of language's manifold activity. There is an ideologically English component to this virtue of un-single-minded attunement.[19] In "Imperfect Sympathies," one of his *Essays of Elia* (1823), Charles Lamb writes of his efforts to try to "like Scotchmen" and of the insuperable difficulty he experiences in doing so, as a result of the perceived rigidity of Scottish habits of speech and thought: "Above all, you must beware of indirect expressions before a Caledonian. Clap an extinguisher upon your irony, if you are unhappily blest with a vein of it. Remember you are on your oath." There are situations, like the shop and the marketplace, Lamb argues, in which more "latitude is expected," and "[s]omething less than truth satisfies." For the English "imperfect intellects" among whom Lamb counts himself, the linguistic dimensions of understanding must be taken, "speaking or writing, with some abatement."[20]

Lamb's essay might be judged a special plea for comedy, irony, evasiveness, and irreducible metaphoricity in language. These writerly qualities resist the reduction of communication to truth. But it would not be right to say they resist the communicative function, since in context these acts of "abatement" – latitude given and taken – are precisely about getting things done in the shop and marketplace. In Lamb's Elia's rendering, satisfactions and (plural) sympathies provide the requisite "latitude" of full exchange. Against this value of mobility, Lamb's essay, however, is certainly nativist in considering the provisions of "latitude" and "abatement" to be definitionally "English" linguistic habits. The title of his essay comments on a disparity between Scottish and English sensibilities, humorously but seriously suggesting discrepant modes of linguistic action and being. An impasse of dislike reigns over the practical language politics of British union. There are asymmetries of language use, at least, that make community and the perfect sympathy between English Elia and the Caledonian appear impossible. What emerges instead is a kind of plural sympathy of multiple identity from within the essay's speaking voice. Thus a response to "Imperfect Sympathies" might be angled to address the idea of the ironist's sympathy. Not the fully explicit spoken contracts of oath, but imperfect communications, allow sympathy to be laterally nourished. Even the prime linguistic virtue, shared by Austen and Austin, of calling things by their names might depend on a fuller understanding of context, a larger remit for sensibility, than the truth-telling Caledonian affords.[21] Against a rigid truth teller's point of view, imperfections make for the inflected social space and complex habitus of language that promote irony and sympathy together. As they move from shop and marketplace to spaces of domestic exchange, such imperfect communications likewise appear in passages of Austen that generously stipulate the incompleteness of all acts of exchange, even the most intimate and privileged. Examples from Austen's novels include Emma withholding Harriet Smith's secret ambitions for Mr. Knightley (*E*, 324); or Elizabeth Bennet reserving the full impact of her judgment and knowledge in the restorative company of her sister Jane (*P&P*, 146).

By contrast, the wariness of Elia's speaker toward Caledonian directness of speech and thought responds to his discomfort with the idea that one truth standard governs all exchange. For Lamb, this antipathy has regionalist and nationalist bearings, religious underpinnings, and competing trajectories in the history of Enlightenment and taste (so that David Hume might count as English linguistically here). In terms of our own contemporary critical practice, Elia's allowance of "some abatement" in speaking or writing suggests an affinity to Tim Milnes on the philosophical tradition of "essayism," and to what Andrew Miller has explored as the difference between "implicative" and "conclusive" modes of criticism.[22] Miller too discusses J. L. Austin, connecting implicative criticism to the perlocutionary dimension of speech acts; that is, to eliciting responses "not sheltered by conventions" fixed in advance. Such exchanges are "ended typically not by refutation, but by recession" and a "withdrawal" for which conclusiveness often means unhappy failure.[23]

Lamb's (and Elia's) "abatement" as a provision of inflected or deflected standards of truth invites a move between national discourses and ordinary language criticism.[24] His abatement of Scottish truth-telling pieties will be turned, later in this study, toward an idea of the comedic abatement of skepticism. Propriety, impersonality, humor, and irony are all qualities characteristic of Austen's and Austin's written voices. Nonetheless, both write with unusual and undeniable authority. Both give the study of conduct a philosophical standing, as they make of philosophy or the novel something "at once more serious, and more fun."[25] Neither discounts the important role of manners. And yet the patent character of shared Englishness between Austen and Austin may largely be the projection at a distance of American criticism and theory. Looking more closely than the nation and even region they share – the southern Home Counties of Hampshire and Oxford – Austin's early linguistic experience may well place him more in the region of Lamb's Caledonian exemplar. He was born in Lancaster and raised in St. Andrews, Scotland, until leaving for Oxford in 1933. Isaiah Berlin in his account of Austin's early career remembers a thinker who deployed "rational" as his highest term of praise, but who was "not doctrinaire" and "treated problems piecemeal."[26] G. J. Warnock presents Austin's life and thought by stressing a similar balance and tension between philosophy as a rationally zealous cooperative pursuit, and a different kind of intelligence that knows "[t]here is a lot more to language than 'the meaning' of its words and phrases."[27]

In the face of this acknowledged variousness in the fields of social intelligence and linguistic action, the monolith looms: Austen and Austin on marriage. Quite obviously, if not oppressively, there is the ubiquitous role played by marriage in all of Austen's novels and in J. L. Austin's most influential philosophical work. What should we call this feature? It seems inadequate to say it's a topic, example, or theme. Interestingly, the philosophical community as a group tends to situate J. L. Austin on marriage at a commensurate level to his concerns for excuses, pretending, and expressions about knowledge of other minds; no more privileged or sustained than the well-known (but not world famous) articles collected in *Philosophical Papers*. Fiona Brideoak remembers that "[i]t was not until the 1960s that marriage and romantic love became identified as the structurally and thematically defining element of [Austen's] 'six perfect novels."[28] Before that time, it was much more common to remark on Austen's seemingly perfunctory, bored, or wholly formal relation to the marriage plot – especially insofar as the marriage plot beyond Austen (but never within her pages) demands children.

One thinks of Eve Sedgwick on the "bare choreographies of procreative sex." Or of Sedgwick's further comment that *How to Do Things with Words* might have been more accurately entitled *"How to say (or write) 'I do' hundreds of times without winding up any more married than you started out."*[29] If *How to Do Things* undertakes a clothes-pins replication of "hundreds" of cited unactualized marriage rites, each of Austen's novels presents several unenviable existing marriages while driving the protagonist toward the fulfillment of her own arrangement, at the verge of which narrative halts. In discussing the "strange, disavowed but unattenuated persistence of the *exemplary*" in *How to Do Things with Words*, Sedgwick's essay on the "periperformative" in *Touching Feeling* arrives at this analysis of Austin's "at least … triple gesture":

> *How to Do Things with Words* thus performs at least a triple gesture with respect to marriage: installing monogamous heterosexual dyadic church- and state-sanctioned marriage at the definitional center of an entire philosophical edifice, it yet posits as the first heuristic device of that philosophy the class of things (e.g., personal characteristics or object choices) that can preclude or vitiate marriage. And it constructs the philosopher himself, the modern Socrates, as a man—presented as highly comic—whose relation to the marriage vow will be one of compulsive, apparently apotropaic repetition and yet of ultimate exemption.[30]

Jane Austen's life and work are similarly structured by marriages and the tension between a heteronormative *exemplary* realm and a queer or celibate register of *exemption*.[31] Her relation to marriage too may be "apotropaic," while her relation to pleasure gives "overplus" for so many.[32]

J. L. Austin is often and understandably seen as a figure of (institutional, conventional) law and order. Indeed, even Cavell outlines Austin's contribution as a form of participation in the order of law. Following Cavell directly, I work to contrast this historically and conceptually pre-existing version of the couple in "point of law" and the notion of a "perfectionist" couple, as constructed through and known by their mutual education, interest, and conversation. But Austin's reliance on *contextualization* rather than definition as a philosophical method provides one key means of better understanding this pervasive association as less rigidly normative. Without seeking to deflect Austin's close reliance on the "normal case," it is illuminating to note what Austin himself categorizes as "in order" and "out of order" in his view of philosophy. What is marked "out-of-order" is "making statements about somebody else's feelings" (*PP*, 249). This call-out, however, does allow the making of statements of a kind about another person's thoughts; that is, concerning assumptions and priorities of thought as demonstrated by behavior or conduct in speech or writing, even if the other may not agree (or not be alive to consent). In *Sense and Sensibilia*, Austin has no reservations in stating his view that the conduct of A. J. Ayer's discussion of the "argument from illusion" shows that he does not believe his own conclusion. Austin's judgment about "the official state of play" of making in-order and out-of-order statements does not preclude such a claim about what Ayer's line of thinking shows him in practice to believe (*SS*, 84). Despite this bold commitment to a claim on another's "belief" – made manifest in a testable, professional, and public conduct of his own thought – Austin remains keenly aware that appropriating the feelings of another by second- or third-person statement is not "in order" linguistically and ethically. He reserves the term nonsense almost uniquely for this kind of assertion, which allows the senses both of a logical fallacy and of bullying. Thus while it is reasonable at first to take Austin's position as a formal, logical judgment on "out of order" grammars of statement, his own conduct gives permission for including lived dynamics.

One has only to think of an Eliot or Empson, however, to realize the hard division between thought and feeling – hence between philosophy and literature – cannot hold as a schematic for criticism. Queer theory in particular has often merged these formal and affective dimensions, offering divergent perspectives with regard to the criteria of "intelligibility" and the philosophical sense collectively made or denied by the claims to reproductive community, including the radical critical project (articulated most clearly by Lee Edelman) to reject its terms outright. In her Introduction to *Touching Feeling*, Sedgwick (mindful of "oversimplif[ication]") posits, accurately and usefully but on a broad level, "that both deconstruction and gender theory have invoked Austinian performativity in the service of an epistemological project than can roughly be identified as anti-essentialism. Austinian performativity is about how language constructs or affects reality rather than merely describing it."[33]

Though important specialized differences may be observed and argued over down the line, Sedgwick of course is right to position deconstruction and gender theory foremost as allies to Austin's program to go beyond "the descriptive fallacy" – that is, to expose and redress the error in thinking that all language exists in the mode of (falsifiable) statement, or else is nonsense. Cavell insists that his mentor wrote on many other topics besides the performative, yet Austin's most famous and influential work remains the theory of "performative utterance," which dates from as early as 1939 and was gathered posthumously in 1962 as *How to Do Things with Words*. When it has been capacious enough to own his contributions, philosophy after Austin has had to cope with his demonstration that statements are seldom "constative" merely.[34] Literary theory has instantiated the rich complex of performativity in which "*truth is only an act*," as Shoshana Felman in a paradigmatic rhetorical reading once drew on Austin's "Don Juanism" – his ineluctable bent toward methodological promise-breaking, and promise-repeating in cheerful good faith – to conclude (*Scandal*, 111).[35]

Jane Austen and Other Minds traces no single departure from the form of the statement, but a reticulated sequence of performative functions, institutions, and affects: marriage, to be sure, but also promises and a broader array of promissory behaviors and structures, including judging, teaching, honoring, commemorating, inviting, seducing, praising, pretending, excuse-making, persuading. Taking philosophical aspects of Jane Austen's novels seriously leads us toward a fuller awareness of kinds of experience that ordinary language philosophy exists to honor and critically inherit. Jane Austen's novels are not conduct books but philosophical studies of conduct in the J. L. Aust*i*nian sense. The Austen and Austin pairing emerges with a special clarity once we note J. L. Austin's statement of interest in a "latter-day" philosophical study of conduct (*PP*, 177, 180). In his meditations on the voice of the nineteenth-century novel in the philosophical project of the ordinary in *Philosophy the Day after Tomorrow*, Cavell asks to be understood not only as explaining his formative relationship with the work of J. L. Austin, but as honoring Austin – the homosocial bond is evident – by extending and newly improvising upon the model of ordinary language philosophy to which Cavell had long before engaged himself in early essays including "Austin at Criticism," a review essay on *Philosophical Papers*.

Institutions of Form and Forms of Life

While *Jane Austen and Other Minds* works from Cavell, some of its interventions are positioned against Cavell's premises and their uses. This is particularly true of the book's engagement with the "New Formalism." Cavell, along with many other commentators, associates the role of form in Austen's fiction with narrative and social constraint. By contrast, this book pursues a more flexible model of thinking (Cavellian in itself) via Garrett Stewart's notion of "formative" poetics and Wittgenstein's "forms of life." The latitude of this conception of form allows me to address the philosophical contribution of Austen's prose style more fully than in previous scholarship, and to do so through a critical aesthetics that engages social and formal dimensions together.

This section presents a kind of annotated cento of the plural and proliferating variations of work on form now. Frances Ferguson's influential 2000 essay on the jointly formal and social implications of free indirect style, "Jane Austen, *Emma*, and the Impact of Form," represents a good place mark of the intersectional points of Romantic studies and study of Austen under that critical trend. Less a movement than a networked set of inflections, new formalist reading practice has largely focused on poetry. Nonetheless, an important strain of formalist commentary on the novel draws its examples from free indirect style and thus from the breakthrough example of Austen. Ferguson urges the pursuit of formal and social/ideological shapes of argument perspicaciously as a joint effort. Value, after all, manifests as forms of value. Ferguson demonstrates the braiding of these two apparently opposed strands, taking her argument to the final (delightfully blasphemous) view that marriage for Austen "might be the ultimate social game," subject to both formalist and ideological analysis. Her essay's synthetic but not necessarily harmonious conclusion is that marriage is "genuinely communal [at least in *Emma*], because the most desirable partners would look the most desirable not just to one person but to all."[36] Ferguson thus dissolves the methodological problem of how to situate a formal "object" within a contextual "frame": here, the problem of whether the performativity of marriage in Austen's novels acts on the level of formal structure, or if marriage furnishes the content that drives a reproductive ideological agenda. This opening of critical attention to the formal patternings of social forces rejects the old New Critical warhorse of a formalism that would construct spatial, structural enclosures through the architectures of form and content, poetic figure and prose sense or primary meaning. *Emma*'s marriage economy plays out its meanings through the quotidian formal occupations of the novel's many games, while it yields for Ferguson an uncontainable cultural imperative. All of Highbury should recognize an image of perfect union when Knightley and Emma end up together. The villagers formally recognize this as the impersonal endgame, one in which narrative, stylistic, and moral economies all coalesce.[37]

While I am interested in form as a means by which Jane Austen's novels are associated with constraint, this book pursues a more restive model of thinking – mostly in Wittgensteinian terms but also associated with philosophical and historical poetics – based in the concept of "forms of life."[38] Against the New Critics' exclusive modeling of a closed spatial form, the modes of formal (and formative) analysis have diversified unboundedly. In terms of narrative forms alone, one counts: characterological space and ontology; social networks; aggregate and individual agencies; omniscience and focalization; free indirect style and ironic distance; free indirect style as the guided discourse of a "close writing" that flexes between the enactment and recording of thought; as well as bibliography and publication. Constructing his own idiosyncratic tradition out of the unexpected pair of Stanley Cavell and the early writings on poetics of Giorgio Agamben, in *The Deed of Reading* Garrett Stewart lays down tracking loops in theory and practice with regard to the conduct of prose as the formative dimension of language. Stewart draws a strong distinction between the formative and a formalist, "let alone form*alistic*" approach.[39]

Another formalist strain, best exhibited by Daniel Stout's *Corporate Romanticism*, translates the forceful techniques and critical allegories long known within lyric reading practice to the analogous but distinct terms of the nineteenth-century novel and its distributions of personhood.[40] Contrary to the scholarly history of the novel, there is no generic bar to poetic theory of narrative prose. Under the aegis of narrative form too, we encounter many of the rhetorical devices and figures of institutional modernity: poetic tropes of address, personification, and prosopopoieia (tropes of personhood itself as social form); of biopoetics (as Sara Guyer renews the genealogical depth and present urgency of our critical entanglement with form not as the dress of content, but knotted into rhetorical tropes of personhood in social life);[41] forms of representation alongside those of morphology; epigenetic form – a biology taking shape under social pressure. In his 1994 book, *The Community of Those Who Have Nothing in Common* (a study predating the New Formalisms, but cited in the background of the work of object-oriented ontologists), anthropologist Alphonso Lingis melds the concerns of performative utterance with an awareness of human neurological and biological plasticity: "Beyond the communication with another through signals, abstract entities, in the community allied against the rumble of the world, we make contact with inhuman things by embracing their forms and their matter. We also make contact with one another by contracting another's form, by transubstantiating our own material state."[42]

Franco Moretti's quantitative formalism brings back the argument of D'Arcy Wentworth Thompson in *On Growth and Form* (1917; second edition 1942) that "[w]e rise from a conception of form to an understanding of the forces which gave rise to it" – revealing the "the direct, almost tangible relationship between social conflict and literary form"; here we encounter "form as a diagram of forces; or perhaps, even, as *nothing but force*."⁴³ Forms elsewhere for Moretti serve by functional definition as "devices in the marketplace," and morphologically as "*the repeatable element in literature*."⁴⁴ And to go further back: what about Wollstonecraft and Godwin on conventional social forms, including the institution and rites of marriage; or Malthus's calculus of the "various forms of misery"? The latter raises forms of larger quantitative precarity. In *The Great Derangement*, Amitav Ghosh details "the peculiar forms of resistance that climate change presents to what is now regarded as serious fiction."⁴⁵ Ghosh offers an important ecological critique of the triumph of uniformitarian expectations, the way the global nineteenth-century "realist" novel in English installed a discourse of probability at odds with the weird of the real and emergent. Ghosh supports his book's critique of the "concealments" effected by the terms of realist intelligibility by an odd allusion to the legacy of Jane Austen within a broader narrative of exurban extractive modernism, one in which a certain style of consumption is allowed to remain safe, coherent, and – until catastrophe hits – uninterruptedly expected: "When we see a green lawn that has been watered with desalinated water, in Abu Dhabi or Southern California or some other environment where people had once been content to spend their water thriftily in nurturing a single vine or shrub, we are looking at an expression of a yearning that may have been midwifed by the novels of Jane Austen."⁴⁶ By presenting "literary forms and conventions" rigidly, as a "grid," and setting Austen's narration of cultural desires in terms of the consolidation of human social interests and consumerist wants, Ghosh implies a profound cost in ecological dimensions of the ordinary.⁴⁷ He assumes, as Walter Scott does of Jane Austen, that her project involves "the banishing of the improbable [in] the assertion of the everyday."⁴⁸

Henri Lefebvre's *Rhythmanalysis* preserves the old terms of the form/content distinction but creatively notes that rhythms are an embodied measure of sociopolitical form: "Social times disclose diverse, contradictory possibilities: delays and early arrivals, reappearances (repetitions) of an (apparently) rich past, and revolutions that brusquely introduce a new *content* and sometimes change the form of society"; a transformation such that, "[b]etween 1789 and 1830 were not bodies themselves touched by the alterations in foods, gestures, and costumes, the rhythm of work and of occupations?"⁴⁹ Such formal alterations of aesthetic concepts, immersed historical affect, are not decisively changed once and for all but further transformed under the pressures of neoliberalism and globalization. As seen in Sianne Ngai's books *Ugly Feelings* (2005) and *Our Aesthetic*

Categories (2012), for instance, forms are the means through which the disorientations and suspensions of agency that confuse the subject-object relationship are experienced and may be critically reencountered.[50] For the child psychotherapist D. W. Winnicott, the goal of analysis is to return the subject to the possibility of creative play in the conviction that play is "a basic form of living."[51]

Under the broad aegis of political aesthetics as the distribution of the sensible, Caroline Levine's *Forms* (and the ensuing discipline-wide discussion) has made formal inquiry freshly available by identifying form and formativeness not with New Critical tensile unities but with multiplicities of interaction, by exploring an unbounded overlap of literary and political, aesthetic and sociological, form and arrangement. In a recent essay on the criticality of mood work, published in the journal *New Formations*, Kathleen Stewart and Jennifer Carlson attend to the "legibilities" of "emergent forms…[of] worlds being thrown together."[52] Ordinary language philosophy recommends itself to this renewed plural interest in form as emergent, even when it is not so headily contemporary. J. L. Austin's installation of marriage at the center of *How to Do Things with Words* entails problems of institution and example. Jane Austen didn't herself enter marriage as a compulsory step. She nonetheless composed and packaged books according to its logic and availed herself of its literary opportunities. What can troubling the position of J. L. Austin as a formal theorist and Jane Austen's text as a socially conservative template do for us? The questioning of Austen's heteronormative marriage plots has in large part been the contribution of queer Austen studies of the last several decades. The capacity even to name heteronormative fulfillment as an interpretive stake is the accomplishment of queer theory and its allies. Through her use of the "Don Juan conflict," Felman addresses a mode of excess that challenges the logic of straight institutional fulfillment, as is visible in a quotation Felman pulls from Moliere's play in her own discussion of "The Promise of Marriage": "He gets married all the time [he is a marrier on every hand]" (*Scandal*, 20).

At once broken down and revealed as constitutive in its fractals, marriage is the model of promising, and promising sets the model for the entire dimension of performative meaning in Austin – with performative meaning in the end proving impossible to seal off from all other ("constative," informational and descriptive) functions of language. Perhaps because of this metonymic displacement of the performative altogether to marriage, *Sense and Sensibilia* and its focus on theory of knowledge remains in the wings of Austin's achievement. It imparts no main example to compare to marriage in *How to Do Things with Words*. *Sense and Sensibilia*'s recurrent example, the supposed "argument from illusion" invoked with the experience of seeing a "bent" stick in water, does not saturate our cultural life. (Though I was once chilled and fixed when coming upon the phrase, "the thing in the water," without the frame of narcissistic reflection.) Marriage connotes the promise of happiness in Austin's language universe – of the felicity that is set off by the fall into "infelicitous" speech – and may even be taken to secure the conditions of meaning entirely. In the introduction to a special issue of *Diacritics* on "Literature and the Right to Marriage," Steven Miller and Sara Guyer develop a forceful, critically and philosophically inclusive version of this argument, joining Hegel's *Philosophy of Right* to Austinian speech-act theory. They judge that "[m]arriage makes...trust possible because it is the ritual that establishes the credibility of the word as the basis for trust."[53] Cavell observes in his foreword to the new English edition of Felman's *Scandal of the Speaking Body* (originally published in English as *The Literary Speech Act* in 1983), that "promising – even especially the promise to marry – is somehow privileged in Austin's view, naming as it were the fact of speech itself"; "as if it were a condition of speech itself" – its "lining" much as Kant held of "I think" (xiii).

This stimulating profusion of new formal analysis brings fresh reminders not only of imbrication of the aesthetic and the social, but of the formative opportunities associated with constraint.[54] This constraint at something like its zero degree bears on the problem of other minds intimately and pervasively, due to the givenness of our separate bodies. We are at the same time creative, relational, pleasure-taking and pleasure-giving, and knowing, only *from* that enabling condition of limits. Form is dynamic and constitutive constraint. Elsewhere I have argued that Austen's celebrated use of free-indirect style, for instance, cannot be classified as an ontologically stable feature "of" or "in" the discursive enclosure of her fictional texts. It is at best (to use a phrase typical of making a concession affirmatively) an ongoing critical description of emergent form. Sedgwick's three-part description of the performative centrality, preclusion, and irony concerning the role of marriage in J. L. Austin is apposite too for his "namesake." Free indirect style may be understood as a narrative means to practice illimitable irony and distance in the social spaces of an ongoing closeness in Austen's character-based fictions.

Jane Austen herself did not marry for the form of it, whatever the resulting material benefits of the proposal – accepted for just one night in November of 1802, then refused the next morning – to marry Harris Bigg-Wither. Deirdre Le Faye shows her characteristic mastery over the details of Austen's world to conjure a dry kind of sympathy with the duties of clergyman brother James (the logistics involve some inconvenient weekend travel between Steventon and Bath to fetch his sisters).[55] The verbal commitment that Austen took back decisively enabled her career as a writer. Had she not annulled this commitment in all its bearing on the speech-act category of the "commissive" engagement, there would be no Austen the writer. Without this undoing, the retraction of her consent, there would be no novelistic production. In her remarks upon this story of consent given and then withdrawn, and upon the juxtaposition of this scene with the (take-back) aside of Austin, Anne-Lise François writes that the (non-) event "de-dramatize[s] a consent no sooner given than withdrawn, where the consent and its withdrawal constitute a single, finished non-drama, and not an invitation for further courtship."[56] The non-drama of Austen's withdrawn consent to marriage is an event as lightly borne as her night's sleeping. Based on whatever motives, Austen's acceptance one day, then rejection the next, of Bigg-Wither, his sisters who were already friends, and the family's considerable estate at nearby Manydown, signaled the choice of an Elizabeth Bennet over a Charlotte Lucas. But the indecision first shown by accepting him also leads us to ask – had she not come to this resolution before? That messy act of clarification begins and anchors the somber biopic, *Miss Austen Regrets* (2008). More importantly, it appears to have lifted an obstruction from Austen's novelistic career. Her promise-breaking was an annealing experience.

J. L. Austin's promise-making, promise-exempting practice is a Don Juanism, for Shoshana Felman. Jane Austen declines marriage and allows a possible space for her authorship. *Northanger Abbey*, to which Austen returned in 1803 in the months just after her acceptance-rejection of marriage, is a text of broken engagements at many levels, with marriage not necessarily among the book's reparations. In Cavellian terms, Austen's rejection of Bigg-Wither sealed a remarriage to her fiction and the life of a writer, day by day. Revision and the initial sale of *Northanger Abbey*, still titled *Susan*, came just months later.[57] Unpublished a decade on, that novel too was something she had to take back. Austen did just this in her 1809 "M.A.D." letter to the publisher Crosby, who had bought the manuscript of *Susan* for ten pounds, but never brought it forward to the public (*NA*, 215).

Undoing is itself a form of doing things that can express various attitudes, from responsible to evasive. Illocutionary acts may be annulled, retracted, or amended by their speaker under controlled rites and certain conditions; but not so with perlocutionary effects.[58] J. L. Austin's aside in

Sense and Sensibilia, "(There's the bit where you say it and the bit where you take it back)" (*SS*, 2), applies to the insincerity of a non-commitment he sees in skeptical doctrine. It mimics and makes visible the behavior of the skeptic who does not want others to take seriously the practical consequences of holding skeptical views; who does not wish fully to mean them. At a crucial moment in his earliest major essay, "Other Minds" (1946), Austin writes:

> It is fundamental to talking (as in other matters) that we are entitled to trust others, except in so far as there is some concrete reason to distrust them. Believing persons, accepting testimony, is the, or one main, point of talking. We don't play (competitive) games except in the faith that our opponent is trying to win: if he isn't, it isn't a game, but something different. So we don't talk with people (descriptively) except in the faith that they are trying to convey information. (*PP*, 82–83)

This entitlement to trust and belief has been dubbed the "hyper-protected cooperative principle."[59] A ready means to contextualize Austin's later writings on the performative is to say they move against this notion that language exists only to "convey information," the condition referenced by his stipulating, "(descriptively)." While the passage implies a default precondition of sociable meaning, requiring "some concrete reason" to distrust language users who might be *neither* competitive nor cooperative, *How to Do Things with Words* has the opposite tendency in its striking passages, and suggests that meaning is constructed by promising as a violable act. Cavell draws from this side of Austin in treating the intelligibility of our language as a vulnerable premise.[60] One has this sense, for example, at the emphatic moment where Austin proclaims, "[a]ccuracy and morality alike are on the side of the plain saying that *our word is our bond*" (*How to Do Things*, 10). Always and already related by language, we have engaged terms for our bonds with one another; however inevitable this process, analysis cannot take it for granted. But the univocally serious, cleaving to moral clarity, forget this is the motto of the London Stock Exchange.[61] Neither transparency nor communicative intent can be taken as given, only exchange. And the "non-serious" issuance of language that Austin views as a sideline concern which brings "a sea-change in special circumstances" – but is yet "intelligibly" special and readable – pertains in no clear-cut way to the modes of poetry and fictionality (*How to Do Things*, 22–23).[62] Austin's exclusion of literary performativity as (intelligibly) non-serious does not actually shore up the bounds of a pre-known world of non-literary seriousness. It depends not upon an opposition between the fictional and the "real," but rather upon a recognition of the signaling within social poetics and forms of life, inviting us to think about distinctions between the contexts of fiction and *other* ritual contexts.[63] Forms are both various and ubiquitous.

Honoring Austen

> So far then we have merely felt the firm ground of prejudice slide away beneath our feet. But now how, as philosophers, are we to proceed? One thing we might go on to do, of course, is to take it all back: another would be to bog, by logical stages, down. But all this must take time.
> —J. L. Austin, *How to Do Things with Words*

A stylistic satire on the presumption of the ascent of "logical stages," Austin's dry comment about what to do next after the loss of "prejudice" gestures in addition to a difference between narrative (literary) and argumentational (philosophical) time. Austin thus calls into question not only the ways in which a narrative poetics may ground the operations of philosophical system-building, but the progress of a narrative view of history, perhaps even its intelligibility. Whereas narrative is understood to be constituted by deferral and obstacles, the genre of the philosophical treatise is supposed to progressively clarify: "to proceed." It is not immaterial that the kind of philosophical papers Austin wrote are published as "proceedings," quite as if such a theory of causality were internal to them. Austin's witty observation shifts us off customary grounds for understanding how philosophy and literature relate, and interanimate. (Again, he might be tapping his experience in wartime intelligence and logistics.) Conventionally, the novel's relation to philosophy contrasts imagination to concepts, asking: What philosophical schema does a novelist evince, or test her way through? That scheme assumes art's perspective, but largely by means of assuming its debt. It is seldom in more than a trivializing subset of this question that we ask what novels philosophers read and find generative.[64] An anecdote circulates that when Gilbert Ryle – the British ordinary language philosopher and author of the essay "Jane Austen and the Moralists" – was asked if he read novels, he replied something like, "Yes, all six, every year."[65] In this honoring of Austen, via a joke, the six completed novels stand in for all novels and are literary fiction's stand-out example. Ordinary language philosophers repeatedly use Austen's fiction as a touchstone in arguments about affective responsiveness and emotive intelligence. While these examples admittedly show the use of Austen as a currency of honor for a male homosocial culture of bruising and bonding, they indicate the grounds and leave suggestions for how to explore a performative philosophical conduct pioneered in Austen's own writing.

Because of the unique position she is seen to embody in the realms of the sociable, of wish, and the everyday, the example of Jane Austen in particular shows how this intellectual gift-giving gesture may be returned. We can thus complement abstract philosophy's relevance to everyday life by presenting it with the annual gift book of kinship to "Aunt Jane." But are we honoring Austen and the tradition of Austen scholarship if we suggest her novels achieve some kind of fullness in a philosophical context not yet provided? Doesn't that risk condescension? Throughout much of this study I pursue a methodology of juxtapositionality and of what Jacques Derrida calls "consignation" – an archive fever that gathers together divergent, asynchronous, outmoded vectors of thought and phenomenological experience.[66] Mary Ann O' Farrell calls a similar method "conjugation," noting in the "'Austen and …' phenomenon" a humming industry in the production of supplementary knowledges.[67] My splicing of Austen with ordinary language philosophy deliberately resists both the usual approaches to situating Jane Austen's work in the history of social thought and ideas, as well as the tendency of the "conjugation" study to explore empirically contextual aspects of Austen's contemporaneous world. Instead, this study follows other resonant features of available conjugation: foremost, Cavell's headings of conversation and remarriage. Making space for an anachronistic conversation in philosophy inside the industry of Austen conjugations, I place Cavell with O'Farrell to stress the recurrent way in which many "Austen and" conjunctions press on the issue of her and our unknowing.

O'Farrell discusses this dynamic of Austen's availability to "conjugational" rhetorics as a sexual rhetorical practice. With insight and provocation she writes of the heretofore safe topic of manners.[68] O'Farrell identifies an "aggression against manners that construes them as removed and remote, protected rather than protecting, unknowing and unworldly"; an "aggression of juxtaposition and conjugality [that] envies manners and, in so doing, would deprive them of their protected status, forcing on them as though carnally a knowledge of the world that manners might be imagined not, in advance of such forcings, already to possess."[69] At the essay's most disturbing moment, this rehearsal of Austen as a fantasy of the subject that does not know beyond such protected status involves "a fantasy of conjugality as a violent conjoining with Jane Austen that would fuck her, unknowing, into knowledge, a fantasy that satisfies itself in exchanging for violent laughter the smug aggressions that inform the old familiar 'I know something you don't know'."[70]

It is notable that even in a field where male critics are a minoritarian culture, male sexual fantasies may thus still structure the philosophical and political terms of unknowing in Austen, and of knowing Austen. Jarringly, O'Farrell merges sexual and epistemic versions of "knowing." Her terms and tone dispel the notion that playing *did-Austen-know-x-if-she-never-did-it* is an anodyne pastime. O'Farrell's boldness encompasses the turn from epistemological fantasies to something already very near to Cavell's lifelong theme of knowing versus acknowledgment. The question is not just if Austen knew certain thinkers and topics at the time of writing; but also, whether she had the exposure or not, is it necessary to stage that scene of initiating experience as a force of indoctrination and intrusion? Why reflect the attitude of the biopic, *Becoming Jane* (2007), that an Austen lacking experience needs the right man to teach her about the kinds of encounter necessary to write? This loop is figured in the film by the mis- and reassigned use of young Jane Austen's actual references to the novels of Henry Fielding, whose protagonist Tom Jones (his words insinuatingly placed in the mouth of James McEvoy, the actor playing Tom LeFroy), knows all about the genitality of birds and rutting animals, matters about which Jane is supposed not to have known, or not to have empowered knowing.

My point, modeled by Lewes's claim that Austen can be known without ever becoming a subject of public knowledge, is that competencies such as this film underlines need no forbidden reaching to gain and no particular introduction; and further, that Austen's writing performs and manifests knowing without the addition of a superlevel of visual proof to confirm how it ever got to be so. This is not to argue that empirical source research on what she actually read does not matter, or fails to deepen understanding.[71] There are of course numerous philosophically oriented individual essays on Austen that do this.[72] Nevertheless, the most developed book-length philosophical account of Austen's intellectual background – Peter Knox-Shaw's *Jane Austen and the Enlightenment* – stabilizes the field of her knowledge by dampening the play of philosophical energies in the novels.[73] By referring her approach to the mixed motives and common sense "low road" of the trio of Adam Smith, David Hume, and Samuel Johnson, Knox-Shaw takes a sensible line on what we can reconstruct of Austen's philosophical temperament. But by implication he downplays the idea that connections more widely afield (and less historically determined by the example of a mitigated British skepticism and Enlightenment) can be in dialogue with her novels.[74] A salutary shift can come by thinking of her novels as prose. Tim Milnes argues that in the long Romantic century "between the skeptical naturalism of David Hume and the inductivism of John Stuart Mill," British and Scottish philosophy undergo a paradigm shift and "swerve away from systematic epistemology and towards a form of essayism, involving a corresponding change in philosophical style and vocabulary."[75] Essayism, intersubjectivity and the sociability of knowing all together do philosophical work (and play) in the apparent absence of determinate ties to systemic philosophy in Romantic-era Britain. In contrast to the overlapping plurality and multi-sidedness of ordinary language, Knox-Shaw's account of Austen's relation to Enlightenment thought takes its headings a faculty at a time. He pairs *Sense and Sensibility* with the sympathetic investments of empiricist thought; *Mansfield Park* and religious historiography; *Emma* and political sovereignty. By contrast to such an isolating seriality, J. L. Austin lays stress on how language always is doing many things. Gilbert Ryle says this about Jane Austen and *Pride and Prejudice* in *The Concept of Mind*: "When Jane Austen wished to show the specific kind of pride which characterized the heroine of *Pride and Prejudice*, she had to represent her actions, words, thoughts, and feelings in a thousand different situations. There is no one standard type of action or reaction such that Jane Austen could say 'My heroine's kind of pride was just the tendency to do this, whenever a situation of that sort arose'" (*CM*, 44).

The restriction of scholarly commitment to historically available influences and causal routes can impart a staggered tempo to realizations of what interests us, making such learning possible only in the psychoanalytic temporality of hindsight. Slavoj Zizek maintains in a section titled "Hegel with Austen" from *The Sublime Object of Ideology*, his first book published in English: "Aust*e*n, not Aust*i*n: it is Jane Austen who is perhaps the only counterpart to Hegel in literature: *Pride and Prejudice* is the literary *Phenomenology of Spirit*; *Mansfield Park* the *Science of Logic* and *Emma* the *Encyclopedia*.... No wonder, then, that we find in *Pride and Prejudice* the perfect case of this dialectic of truth arising from misrecognition."[76] Zizek's unacknowledged forerunner in this Hegelian Reading of Jane Austen is Lionel Trilling, who in *Sincerity and Authenticity* discusses Hegel with Austen (and Rousseau), and concludes that Austen's novelistic depiction of "the new consciousness" is more like Hegel's critique: "she judges not as Rousseau does, categorically, but as Hegel does, dialectically."[77]

With just a few words in his 2005 book *Philosophy the Day After Tomorrow*, Cavell breaks ground to literary scholars, in flagging the Austin/Austen connection. In a passage I have already cited, but here want to unfold further, Cavell unabashedly frames his reference to the novels as an act of homage, making it a richly performative act that does more than one thing with its brief intensity of words. He honors J. L. Austin, his teacher, in a paragraph-length sentence that not only executes an explicit, or "illocutionary," performative which does things *in* language – but also acts by means of "perlocutionary" force (impacting others *by* and *through* our utterances) held at the affective margins of Austin's official theory. Cavell writes:

> Because it is not to my hand here, or perhaps ever, to lay out a fuller geography of the courses that "endless" passionate exchanges can take in satisfying the conditions of perlocutionary utterance, and because I think of myself here as wishing to honor Austin's work, I cite one brilliant source of such passionate exchanges that I imagine Austin would feel quite happy to be associated with, indicated in his announcing one of his once famous courses of lectures at Oxford, the one on the foundations of empirical knowledge, in roughly the following form: SENSE and SENSIBILIA. J. AUSTIN. The source I have in mind is Jane Austen's *Emma*.
>
> Jane Austen's world is one her namesake John would have cause to cherish. It is one in which love talk is referred to benignly, even lovingly, as talking nonsense, and in which those who require this talk also crave and are capable of the daily exchanges necessary to what they call rational society. (*P*, 188–189)

The discussion of Austin with Austen, proleptically marked ("I cite") and exempted ("not to my hand here, or perhaps ever"), refers back to and yet transforms, decenters, Cavell's interest in the specific kind of "moral perfectionism" he calls "rational transformation" (*P*, 189). *Philosophy the Day after Tomorrow* discusses Austen's heroines "as in a state of convalescence with respect to…a new way" (*P*, 122), living "from within some place in this state of vulnerable conformity" (*P*, 123). The linkage – an "undertak[ing] to criticize *that* ordinary" (*P*, 123) – troubles the perfectionist philosophical narrative of joyful becoming, and is framed by demands for "lurid … compromises with an imperfect … society" (*P*, 126).

Cavell's allusive homage draws attention to Austin's prior allusion and homage, hearing new measures of nonsense and reason, taking up weightier stakes for the verbal play he savors than simply dry wit. Cavell deepens the seriously playful performance that Christopher Ricks calls "Austin's Swink." Ricks remarks of J. L. Austin that "his witticism is not cheaply at the expense of Jane Austen, being itself a tribute" – that word again – "to the wit that she was and that she mustered. *Sensibilia* emends *Sensibility* as little, and yet as much, as Austin emends Austen."[78] Following the punning example set by his World War II invasion handbook, *Invade Mecum* (after *vade mecum*, "go with me"),[79] Austin puns on *Sense and Sensibility* in a manner that mobilizes the novel's equivocal pairing – firming it up into a charge of what's right (sense) and what's wrong (sensibilia, the derivative jargon of the data theory of logical positivism). At the same time, wordplay establishes parity between his Oxford lecture's sure polemic and Austen's more dialogical view of the distinctions. Ricks points out that in the "famous joke" of Austin's title, sensibilia not only presents the challenge to interpret its puzzling conjugation with sense, but displaces the word sensibility, which thereby "enters, not into the equation, but into the opposite of equation": "[t]he gap between the obdurately professional term 'sensibilia' and the flexibly personal word 'sensibility' (cognate, to boot) is wide enough to challenge any spark."[80] Where to find sensibility in *Sense and Sensibilia*? I wish to provide answers to Ricks's question.

Remarking that "[a]ll of Jane Austen's novels express a profound epistemological interest, and their plots are sustained adventures in modes of knowing," Margaret Anne Doody continues in her Oxford World Classics Introduction to *Sense and Sensibility*:

> Sense and Sensibility together promise perceptive activity, apprehensions, synthesis, recombinations—i.e. mind, thought, consciousness. A modern philosopher, J.L. Austin, paid tribute to Austen's philosophical title and concerns when he named his own book *Sense and Sensibilia*. The adventures in a world presumed to be knowable are, however, fraught with tormenting problems in Austen's second novel.[81]

Doody gestures toward the epistemological cruces in Austen's fiction not only to gain true knowledge, but to assess the scope of the "knowable" – a realm "fraught with tormenting problems" that lie just beneath socialized control of "mind, thought, consciousness." I am stimulated by Doody's observation that Austen's novels are a site of philosophical scrutiny, trouble, and adventure. *Jane Austen and Other Minds* nonetheless departs from the exclusively epistemological program suggested by this passage, to address a broader array of possible "modes of knowing." Insofar as Doody appears to place J. L. Austin plumbly in line with the eighteenth-century British empiricists, there is cause for redress and a need for elaboration. Especially as *Sense and Sensibilia* frames philosophical history, the mitigated skepticism of eighteenth-century empiricists would estrange our knowledge claims about the world while leaving experiential psychology itself untouched by estrangement. Does this form of skepticism adhere to, or live within, the people who think it? Austin's satire of philosophy and of a certain heritage of understanding Hume opens to these approaches, calling out (as a form of intellectual insincerity) the disjunct between philosophical procedures and linguistic and social behaviors. One hears not just playful mimicry but the accusation of disavowal under Austin's philosophical breath, "(There's the bit where you say it and the bit where you take it back.)" He airs a serious joke about the academic philosopher who brackets a professional view of reality by confiding in the next moment, "take it easy – really it's just what we've believed all along" (*SS*, 2). Such a statement indicates its critical target is a wider culture of quasi-philosophical complicity in maintaining the status quo.

For her part, Jane Austen engages "tormenting problems" without this professional safety, in which a disciplinary conviction is held apart from what, we are reassured, remains the perfectly ordinary state of affairs; as if "we all know" the way things work anyhow. Austen is neither so sure, nor this condescending, toward philosophical consequences of skepticism. Austen's marriage novels detour through provocations of skepticism. While Austen's typical train of thought can be judged a mitigated skepticism, as Hume's was, it is without Hume's ease of dismissal of skepticism's implications in an "ordinary" world. Her work instead aligns with the Kantian genre of Critique.[82] Austen's novels as a group identify what Kant calls the power of "reflecting judgment" – judgment without a set rule or fixed concept – and place at stake a fundamental and unique *mode of human intelligibility*.[83] As in the thought of Hegel on the role of the novel and the prose of everyday life, Austen's plots are "sustained adventures in modes of knowing"; they subtend not a narrative arc toward certainty but one straining toward recognition: the shareability of embodied, sensible meaning in a linguistic community.[84]

If we are to limit knowledge to experience, we at least need to let all experience in.[85] Cavell wishes to honor his mentor though the linkage of male philosopher and female novelist. It is worth noticing that Doody too identifies Austin's relevance in a form of "tribute." The addition of gift exchange to a narration of what might be thought a chapter in intellectual history demands comment. But Doody and Austin draw different conclusions from referencing mainstream philosophical tradition: Doody, that the novels absorb and reflect the major Enlightenment project concerning doubt of the senses that are also the source of all ideas; Austin, that we are better off not to have had our reality processed and returned to us upon the alienated terms of sense data, which provide for no way "back" to the ordinary through knowledge once we have granted their currency. Austin's final word on the subject, the end of his lectures, is a clearing root-and-branch, perhaps even a bombing run. He recommends that "[t]he right policy is to go back to a much earlier stage, and to dismantle the whole doctrine before it gets off the ground" (*SS*, 142).

If Austin complements his "namesake," it is likely in his judgment that she hadn't been "bamboozled" by the doctrine of indirect knowledge (*SS*, 142). From the start, Austen practices good prose "policy." Austen's fictions are *conduct* novels – philosophical conduct novels – in this Aust*in*ian sense. Austen does not position access to knowing as a major philosophical problem. She is bolder than a proto-modernist. It is rare to find Jane Austen writing as a sense-impressionist who seems really to bother about the data of perception as a theoretical problem. An isolated example occurs within a page of the end of *Sanditon*, the text D. A. Miller points to as the end of her art in the *a*syndetonic erosion of language:[86]

> These entrance gates were so much in a corner of the grounds or paddock, so near one of its boundaries, that an outside fence was at first almost pressing on the road—till an angle *here*, and a curve there threw them into a better distance. The fence was a proper park paling in excellent condition; with clusters of fine elms, or rows of old thorns following its line almost everywhere.—*Almost* must be stipulated—for there were vacant spaces—and through one of these, Charlotte as soon as they entered the enclosure, caught a glimpse of something white and womanish in the field on the other side;—it was something which immediately brought Miss Brereton into her head—and stepping to the pales, she saw indeed—and very decidedly, in spite of the mist—Miss Brereton seated, not far before her, at the foot of the bank which sloped down from the outside of the paling and which a narrow path seemed to skirt along;—Miss Brereton seated, apparently very composedly—and Sir Edward Denham by her side.[87]

With her access so carefully hedged (as if the picket fences Brontë so hates had been arranged as a view finder), Austen's narrator tracks in Charlotte Heywood's visual observation "something white and womanish in the field on the other side." The passage and the secret interview glimpsed here are staged. These impressionistic effects are so atypical of Austen that most readers take *Sanditon* to be unfinished in its style as well as in its mere sum of pages, a symptom of her lack of time under the conditions of approaching death. The exception of "something white and womanish in the field" of vision proves the rule of Austen's boldly drawn lines of women and men.[88]

Hedging and circumlocution can become "occulted" magic, as Ryle says in the broader tone of his anti-Cartesian polemic in *The Concept of Mind*. Right up to this selectively blurred and angled end, Austen is not a literary impressionist even from within the domain of her skeptical epistemological fieldwork. Because as we see at the end of Virginia Woolf's *To the Lighthouse* with Lily Briscoe's final bold "line there, in the centre,"[89] or like William Blake in his art of energetically undeceived bold edges – or in the writings of William Cobbett, the Rural Rider and fellow Hampshire resident, for that matter – Austen refuses to exchange the clear outline of a thing named for the idiolect of indirect perception.[90]

"Content to Make Us Know"

As one of Austen's greatest nineteenth-century critics, as well as a philosopher himself, a Goethe scholar, and the (married) partner of George Eliot, G. H. Lewes noticed that Austen's indifference at providing visual description in her fiction is so sustained that it elicits both aesthetic and non-aesthetic explanations. Lewes wrote in 1859: "So entirely dramatic, and so little descriptive, is the genius of Miss Austen, that she seems to rely upon what her people say and do for the whole effect they are to produce on our imaginations. She no more thinks of describing the physical appearance of her people than the dramatist does who knows that his persons are to be represented by living actors" (*CH* I, 158).[91] This observation supplies one basis of the celebrated and oft-repeated link between Austen and Shakespeare on the art of characterization: a comparison made in the mid-nineteenth century by Lewes himself as well as by Macaulay and others, and continued a century later by Harold Bloom.[92] It also leads Lewes to postulate a "defect" in Austen's art – if not in her physiological person. Lewes wonders if Austen was near-sighted: "As far as any direct information can be derived from the authoress, we might imagine that this was a purblind world, wherein nobody ever saw anybody, except in a dim vagueness which obscured all particularities. ...Balzac or Dickens would not have been content without making the reader *see* this Mr. Collins. Miss Austen is content to make us *know* him, even to the very intricacies of his inward man. It is not stated whether she was shortsighted, but the absence of all sense of outward world – either scenery or personal appearance – is more remarkable in her than in any writer we remember" (*CH* I, 158–159).

Austen is "content to make us *know*" her characters rather than have her readers *see* them. Worth noticing in this remarkable response is how Lewes switches indiscriminately between faulting Austen as an individual for her non-standard or aging body – much as Hume had done in ruling out defective sensibilities from the model of the true judge in "Of the Standard of Taste" – and pronouncing upon Austen's fictional world. It is a "purblind world, wherein nobody ever saw anybody, except in a dim vagueness." This, written in celebration! Lewes already identifies the crucial value of Austenian knowledge not with sensory perception, but with dynamics of knowing and acknowledgment: "Miss Austen is content to make us *know* [Mr. Collins]"; as, earlier, she "has made herself known without making herself public" (*CH* I 158, 150). I show later how Cavell takes up something of the position of Lewes in *Philosophy the Day After Tomorrow*, in his choice to select and compare George Eliot and Jane Austen from all the available choices in the Leavisite great tradition of the nineteenth-century novel. Against the empiricist focus on the primacy of perception (especially visual perception) and the logical positivists' later exaggerated attention to problems of access in the production of certainty out of sensa, Cavell weighs the knowing and unknowing already embedded in seeing (as do his teachers in ordinary language philosophy, Austin and Wittgenstein). Cavell attends in *The Claim of Reason* to what he calls the condition of "soul blindness" as a condition not to be dispelled by clearer sight (*Claim*, 378–380).

Austen avails herself of language as her entitlement to philosophy. Though readings in the "Austen and Philosophy" subfield are by no means new, in this chapter my interest has been to show that areas of affinity with Austin indicate just how Austen is *not* best considered a novelist in the empiricist stamp, or a precocious modern literary impressionist. *Jane Austen and Other Minds* instead pursues Cavell's embattled romantic considerations of the ordinary and the rejection and discounting of the ordinary. I begin reading individual novels in the next chapter with *Northanger Abbey* and Catherine Morland's fraught introduction to a linguistic sensible community. I trust already that readers will play with the book's argument more freely, test it perhaps against Mary and Mr. Bennet, those apparent but false philosophers in *Pride and Prejudice*, as Cavell himself extends the reach of his approach immediately to *Emma*.

CHAPTER 2

Intelligible Community

> Me?—yes; I cannot speak well enough to be unintelligible
> —*Northanger Abbey*

⁂

In their theoretical scholarship on J. L. Austin, Shoshana Felman and J. Hillis Miller each individually argue that breaches of promise open unsanctioned possibilities within the official conduct of the languages of the ordinary. Austin's bogging down of the system allows, if with a good measure of irony, for the multiform ways in which language is always *doing many* things and also *not quite doing* things.

Jane Austen's *Northanger Abbey* – a novel in which the protagonist receives an unwelcome, dangerously semi-actionable marriage proposal *she does not even hear* (and which readers might do a double-take to process as having occurred [*NA*, 85–86]) – has the charm of a work whose main functionality is to allow for the fullness of play so as to regulate better the smooth reproductivity of gaming: the marriage game, the novel game. The promise here too is the crucial linguistic institution. At one point in Volume II of *Northanger Abbey*, Henry Tilney exclaims about Isabella Thorpe's declaration that she would write to Catherine Morland: "'Promised so faithfully!—A faithful promise!—That puzzles me.—I have often heard of a faithful performance. But a faithful promise—the fidelity of promising!'" (*NA*, 135). As is typical for this character, Henry's point is "arch" and multiple. Yet in Henry's analytical hilarity there is also more than a little of the ordinary language philosopher. He is a kind of young J. L. Austin (say, holding forth on the differences among the implications of the words "looks," "appears," and "seems" [*SS*, 36]), cast as male romantic lead. Henry insinuates here that all promises necessarily come with the unstated precondition that they are "faithfully" made. They must be taken on faith or have no value at all. He contends that Isabella's exaggeration adds nothing to her communication and costs her nothing. Further, Henry implies that Isabella behaves as though to have made her promise is already by itself to have achieved its end. The act of promising faithfully executes its end with no commitment of the promise-bearer to anything further. Promising becomes professing, and the redundancy of Isabella's words shows her hollowness twice over in deeds. Henry is actually responding to and turning over Catherine Morland's own language in report about her friend's promise-making and breaking ways in this interchange; so there is an element of his mocking Catherine's generous solecism along with his judging disapproval of the absent Isabella. From all this unpacking of conversation we get the idea that for him, engagements are seriously undertaken, so as implicitly to carry out (and carry on with; he's always a dash charismatic, a bit tedious) a linguistic and social general theory. But also, throughout the novel, Henry remains inconstantly explicit in the play of his own speech.[1] The style of Henry's conversation, what Lefebvre in his critique of the ordinary might call the "dressage" of his iterative training, contrasts to how Mr. Darcy and Mr. Knightley in later Austen novels admit no risks with spilled meaning.

Isabella Thorpe's abuse of promising calls to mind two etymologies with critically rich implications: "*épouser*," which in French means both to marry and to promise; and (as Felman notes strikingly) the "constative" as derived from constancy (*Scandal*, 20, 21).[2] Compare Henry Tilney's satire of Isabella to another instance from one of Austen's "early" novels. Near the beginning of *Sense and Sensibility* occurs one of those impersonally turned phrases for which Austen Style is heralded. It's the Johnsonian line, "that sanguine expectation of happiness which is happiness itself" (*S&S*, 7). This phrase suggests that happiness is in fact enjoyed, not deferred, by its promissory condition. *Northanger Abbey* the printed novel can physically promise its "hastening" toward "perfect felicity" merely by "the tell-tale compression of the pages" (*NA*, 172). In the plot line featuring Marianne and Willoughby, *Sense and Sensibility* plays out the ordinary language notion of a promise of happiness in its most risk-laden terms. With the plot featuring Brandon's two Elizas in the background, acting as a lightning rod and a warning, Marianne suffers exposure to the pledge of the male body: Felman's "speaking body." Austen juxtaposes the implicitness of a promising feeling with Willoughby's cagey omission ever to state explicit terms for their relationship. (In novels written after the 1857 Matrimonial Causes Act, the binding power of an inexplicit promise becomes stronger than Willoughby's casuistry allows, and it can be enough simply to *incite* belief in, and dependency upon, an engagement.[3])

To take up a different context positioned in the gap between contract and promise, in *Sense and Sensibility*, one might consider the manner in which all the dying Dashwood men in Chapter 1 only make recommendations for the care of the surviving Dashwood women. On his deathbed, Henry Dashwood engages for all he can legally execute in drawing a mere promise from John, which under Fanny Dashwood's influence in the next chapter John travesties. Compared to a binding legal document, was this a more or less serious trust to have violated? (In response to John and Fanny Dashwood's violation of the mere offer to perform "neighbourly acts," the narrator suggests it is more serious in the final Christian judgment, but not as a legal matter [*SS*, 11].) Are we to understand Henry Dashwood's weak provisions as a personal failure, or as an allegory for how most social meaning really gets produced and maintained? Is it Austen's way of suggesting that we don't formally "contract" for the most necessary of social supports? Impatient with contract theory and willing to grant that violent power is at the origin of all governments, David Hume had argued instead (in line with evolutionary social theory today) that we don't fear breaking our word so much as the discontinuance of society altogether. In modern societies with large groups of potentially unknown and anonymous people, individuals are not bound by promises made explicitly, but by the social forms articulated through them, maintained on the basis of general belief or credit.[4] That there are no written wills on the Norland estate anticipates Willoughby's later dodge of an explicit pledge to Marianne.

I adduce these examples to suggest that it is not marriage alone, but the category that J. L. Austin named "commissives," and indeed the dominant conditions for the whole promissory structure of experience (entailments, engagements, dance cards, rents, Christ's evangelical promise, the weather, money and credit), that occupy Austen's narrative field.[5] In such a reading, the engrossing speculations of the unfinished *Sanditon* may need no culmination in marriage, because the plot's convergence of desire and opportunity has already transpired on an economically speculative plane. Suggestive of bigamy, Mr. Parker's schemes are conceptually already "a second wife and four children to him."[6] To move further out along this arc from the marriage act to a broader promissory social structure, while it is obvious that Austen and Austin share the subject of marriage, it is equally evident that in Jane Austen's novels no marriage ceremonies are directly undertaken. Even the ceremonies that happen offstage in the midst of books – Robert Ferrars and Lucy Steele, Mr. Collins and Charlotte Lucas, Wickham and Lydia – involve relatively minor figures whose constrained lives are easy to reject both for the heroines and for readers. Austen rarely acknowledges the speaking "I"/"you" circuit that is essential to Austinian performative language and all its ritual scenarios, most archetypally marriage. Thus Jane Austen keeps silent about the premise of a cohesive and self-willing "I" that for some commentators makes J. L. Austin's theory complicit with the powers of "the fantasy of sovereign action that sponsors the threat."[7] Even a robust character like Elizabeth Bennet is represented as saying "I feel so ashamed" as a way of assenting to marriage, rather than "I do, I will." By contrast, Judith Butler's concern with "linguistic vulnerability" indicts Austin as the enabler of injurious speech, due to her view that his theory presupposes the subject as sovereign. Wherever Austin's position sifts out exactly in this important exchange – does he reinforce the hegemonic fiction of a sovereign "I"? enlist Humean skepticism toward our mere habit for saying "I" without foundational grounds? or unfold, as Felman argues, from the essentially Lacanian position that "the only knowledge is knowledge of languages," and the referent itself is an effect? (*Scandal*, 50) – it is to this sense of a language at once constitutive and vulnerable that we turn.

Fiction and Other Minds

Frances Ferguson has summarized how "[f]ree indirect style carries with it the implicit claim that characters have what Dorrit Cohn has called 'transparent minds'."[8] Margaret Doody, by contrast, in an account that argues for one of Austen's "greatest techniques" as having "nothing to do with interiority," maintains that "*Style indirect libre* is not exactly 'free'," but "a brilliant device with which to express complex limitation"; for Doody, free indirect style "lets us in on the limitations of freedom, the comic inadequacy of consciousness trying to make terms with the rest of everything that is."[9] My focus in this chapter remains anterior to that stylistic revolution, directed toward what is still unforthcoming or opaque about the problem of "other minds" and the technical stylistic innovations used both to annotate and address it. Cavell's *Claim of Reason* redoubles this problem as one also of literary history in its conversation with philosophy: "romanticism opens with the discovery of the problem of other minds, or with the discovery that the other is a problem, an opening of philosophy" (467). Cavell's scheme for perfectionist thinking, the form of life and mode of thought which comes, as he often says, after religion and before philosophy, never mounts a full philosophy of history. But it carries consequences for his engagement with the history of the novel as the emergent genre (in Hegel, Lukacs, etc.) established precisely in, and expressive of, this self-consciously dilated moment of the prose of life.

Northanger Abbey – with its obtrusive narrator and its close parodic commitment to convention as both a matter of generic expectation and as a form of the heroine's own adolescent self-involvement – opens by demonstrating a healthy disrespect for the other minds problem: "No one who had ever seen Catherine Morland in her infancy, would have supposed her born to be an heroine" (*NA*, 5). Not so famous as the first sentence of *Pride and Prejudice*, this opening is a rewarding puzzle from the point of view of eighteenth-century fictional awareness. Terry Castle highlights its negative entailments in her observation that *Northanger Abbey* "might be described, in a number of senses, as an experiment in negation." The phrasing of the novel's opening move is of course ambiguous. We're being told either that the novel has no typical heroine; or that Austen's novel, which needless to say has destined Catherine Morland to be its heroine (as a matter of generic and characterological choice that could be called an install of form), is playing with readers' expectations about what kind of young woman she is to be. A "thinking woman's heroine," Castle eventually decides, "she makes her way out of mental slavishness to a kind of liberation."[10] Showing that she really can "go back to a much earlier stage" of fundamental thinking (as Austin directs philosophical inquiry in *Sense and Sensibilia*), Austen here undoes some of the eighteenth-century work of naturalizing a fact/fiction divide in the genres of specialized writing.[11] She toys with and obtrudes the philosophical problem her immersive reader would like to forget, the problem of fiction's position within reality and yet intransitively suspended beside "real life." From Burney to Radcliffe, many novelists popular in Austen's youth had of course developed metafictional relationships with the appetites of readers. Austen's pathbreaking realism combines with her occasional gestures of metafiction here to produce a strange literary ontology.

With equal self-evidence on both hands, fiction partakes in and evades reality in an untimely way. The same quality that I. A. Richards dubbed poetic "pseudo-statement," J. L. Austin allows us to think of as poetry's immodal status in *How to Do Things with Words* (10); this immodality remains literature's uncanny stake in any ontological reckoning.[12] Yet the novel's opening also bears down with ideological interpellation. Anticipating Judith Butler when she points out that "It's a girl" initiates "that long string of interpellations by which the girl is transitively girled," in *Northanger Abbey* a simple copula at once suggests the heroine's desire, an experience of her coercion, and self-identification with that inspiring constraint.[13] This bildungsroman insists "a young lady *is to be* a heroine" (*NA*, 8; italics added). We can cite the stage management of Catherine to achieve this kind of pleonastic effect for the sake of her own fulfillment: "She was come to be happy, and she felt happy already" (*NA*, 10).[14] The tautology effectively renders her projective wish-and-willfulness as the kind of promissory structure that may properly be identified with the experience it seeks. Yet however ebullient this coercively performative use of "to be," no other Austen heroine is pushed into place this way by the novel form at the start. Austen lets us sense that a heroine might be a rather bleakly necessitarian thing to be. In order for the novel to press her for service as its heroine, it shows that Catherine has to *want* to be one, to enlist. This rigged arrangement also plays on the individual character's apparently free desire so as to subject her ideologically. The gesture proves theatrical in the book, but the import for novelistic fiction is serious. It's as if there would be no "first" novel without this ontologically dizzy, entangled, fictively desiring process to get the ball going. If Austen's later development of free indirect style is such a crucial device in the history of literature due to this register's uncanny merger of "transparent minds" with opacity and limitation, this initial move in *Northanger Abbey* obtains that dual register – though not a sustained style – by a venture of prototype narrative coding.

The opening chapter of *Northanger Abbey* performatively presents Catherine's entry to language. In his foundational account of the eighteenth-century "New Realistic Novel" as the probabilistic fiction of ordinary life, published in No. 4 of *The Rambler* (1750), Samuel Johnson worried about the educational and moral impact of modern novels precisely due to the educative function these works had already begun to serve in commending young readers *to life*: "These books are written chiefly to the young, the ignorant, and the idle, to whom they serve as lectures of conduct, and introductions into life."[15] Fanny Burney's *Evelina* (1778) carries the subtitle, "The History of a Young Lady's Entrance into the World," not simply in reference to the "world" of fashionable London society. As in her friend Dr. Johnson's sense of the "new" realistic novel as an introduction to life, Burney's *Evelina* opens out to the experiential – indeed existential – scope of the "world."

Particularly because this is Austen's "first" completed novel, we rightly look to it for both prototypical and alternative principles of organization and interest. The book retains traces of different organizational interests that Austen tried out, at least part way, before the ground of her work settled on the marriage plot as a strategy for narrative that didn't need further justification. Alongside the other plots *Northanger Abbey* experiments with – the gothic, the proto-detective story – Austen investigates what I regard as an even more primary motive: making one's way in the world of language users. Austen gives us a story meant to dramatize perils of socialized communication as basic, as if Catherine Morland were making her debut *in language*. Though she is a resolutely middle subject – neither a debutante nor a foundling – Catherine seeks introduction as a young woman not simply as a commodity but as "out" in the exchange of words. The introductory roteness of this social script belies the actual complexity and vulnerability of the process. That is one reason it is so important that her temporary guardian, Mrs. Allen, tragicomically gives so little help to Catherine. She has nothing to say upon any topic but the make and cost of fabrics; repeatedly called "stupid" in what I take to be lexical free indirect speech (the word bleeds over from her mother's hardheadedness and overtasked frustration as an instructor of ten children), Catherine is a kind of ephebe to language when she arrives in Bath.

If the formal expectations of Austen's marriage plots make their terminal arcs all too intelligible for readers, *Northanger Abbey* displays the risks of isolation and incoherence in the very midst of normativity and its anxious pact with the ordinary. The novel juxtaposes even the simplest acts of communication with incoherence and risk, managed (but only in the end) to secure a marriage to Henry Tilney as the spouse with the "right" blend of play and clarity in communication. The novel executes that solution by trial-testing just the measures of difference separating the Thorpes from the Tilneys (excluding General Tilney) as a cohort for Catherine's love and friendship. Catherine's response to the General's double-talk around his expectations for dinner at Woodston suggests her own inexperience in crediting the "normal" dishonesty of what the social psychologist D. W. Harding calls civil falsehood: "why should he say one thing so positively, and mean another all the while, was most unaccountable! How were people, at that rate, to be understood?" (*NA*, 145). Austen deploys language from the credit economy that swirled throughout the era of her writing career.[16] In this scene, Henry Tilney moralizes that we always give "readymonied actual happiness for a draft on the future" (*NA*, 145).[17] Henry is talking about the prospects of planning a clergyman's dinner, but linguistic expressions and assumptions themselves make plans.

Unique among Austen's novels for engaging the possibility of nothing at all happening to its heroine,[18] *Northanger Abbey* must show how we are in fact justified to believe language promises a career of meaning, even if that's not all language must do, which we first come to understand in the incredible scene between Henry and Catherine when they meet:

"And are you altogether pleased with Bath?"

"Yes—I like it very well."

"Now I must give one smirk, and then we may be rational again."

Catherine turned away her head, not knowing whether she might venture to laugh.

"I see what you think of me," said he gravely—"I shall make but a poor figure in your journal to-morrow."

"My journal!"

"Yes, I know exactly what you will say: Friday, went to the Lower Rooms; wore my sprigged muslin robe with blue trimmings—plain black shoes—appeared to much advantage; but was strangely harassed by a queer, half-witted man, who would make me dance with him, and distressed me by his nonsense."

"Indeed I shall say no such thing."

"Shall I tell you what you ought to say?"

"If you please."

"I danced with a very agreeable young man, introduced by Mr. King; had a great deal of conversation with him—seems a most extraordinary genius—hope I may know more of him. *That*, madam, is what I *wish* you to say."

"But, perhaps I keep no journal."

"Perhaps you are not sitting in this room, and I am not sitting by you. These are points in which a doubt is equally possible. Not keep a journal!" (*NA*, 14–15)

The risks and thrills of this passage are performative through and through. From one point of view, this is a vivacious and attractive example of how a joint ruse of epistemological skepticism (met as from the other side by a front of earnestness?) is intrinsic to the grammar of flirting. Catherine and Henry manage to fulfill all the protocol of introduction with none of its tiredness. A feint in the direction of external object skepticism in fact provides the conversational opening that successfully overcomes the blight of a skepticism about shared social life.

Henry, in a passage soon to follow, meaningfully translates Catherine's refusal to say what is on her mind when pressed – her reservation of her mind as "other" to him – to the possibility of the two making their future acquaintance. "Thank you," he says, "for now we shall soon be acquainted" (*NA*, 17). Because they do *not* know each other in advance, they may become acquainted. That moment decisively marks the novel's improvised provision of sufficient interest for the sequel of their relationship as a future worthy of both: a future of *something*, an ongoing relationship like Cavellian conversation. But against this reading of the passage above as a scene of mutual rescue, one observes that Henry gets all the active lines. The exchange works like J. L. Austin's example of marriage, which puts the "I do (take this wife)" in the mouth of the man (*How to Do Things*, 5). In either case, a formally or theoretically reciprocal exchange receives unequal, unilateral, treatment in practice. In the very interpersonal liveliness that goes beyond or falls short of "communication" here, the novel also faces the problem that cooperative meaning may not always seem to prevail, especially given Henry's other recurrent qualities of chauvinism and manipulativeness. It is Henry Tilney, after all, who packages the gothic idea of Northanger that gives Catherine's fancies a structure on which to cling, confirm themselves and grow errantly ("This is just like a book!" [*NA*, 108]). There are two major scenes where Henry mystifies Catherine before he violently – and only ostensibly – clarifies the nature of the "real" world for her: the ambiguous "riots" discussed on Beechen Cliff (*NA*, 78) and the "What have you been judging from?" harangue in defense of his father, where Henry adduces *as if it were a moderating strength* to his point of view the idea that the middle of England is not part of "gothic" Europe, and is inhabitable and understandable as an "open" society, by virtue of its being covered with "voluntary spies" (*NA*, 136). In both these places Henry subjects the world of the novel to the darkest kind of surveilling oversight. Atop Beechen Cliff, he risks contemptuous treatment of his two female companions, in lording over them a miscommunication based on Catherine's use of Isabella Thorpe's language, "shocking" and "horrible" (*NA*, 77), on the difference between "violent" political acts and gothic publishing events. Whereas to mark the idea of his father's being a murderer as unthinkable, Henry invokes Britain's Enlightenment public sphere as a dispersed network of surveillance.[19]

Peter Knox-Shaw argues that Henry Tilney's reference to the British police state ought to assuage Catherine's doubt, and succeed as a gesture of reality testing for the regulating context of the "middle" of England.[20] The only qualification to the bone-chilling character of his speech is the word "voluntary," since we might understand it as opposed to hired and suborned spies – a common anti-Jacobin strategy throughout the 1790s. Knox-Shaw's assessment that the passage "bears up well" because "there *are* forces to be restrained" takes literary criticism to a weird place that echoes a Cold War military analyst's stance on the tactical meanings and uses of "intelligence."[21] At another level of representation, tonal instability regarding this "Remember we are English" passage comes into play with later illustrated editions of Austen novels. Thus, R. Brimley Johnson, writing in 1930: "The reproductions from the engravings of 1833 are interesting on account of their strained and almost violent character. Henry Tilney peacefully mounting his own stairway has the aspect of a brigand, intent on murdering the justly alarmed Catherine" (*CH* 2, 214).

For practical consequences in the politics of print, to write "philosophical" novels in Austen's day meant to be grouped with radical writers like Mary Wollstonecraft and Mary Hays – or, for a middle-class agenda, with Emma Hamilton, author of *Memoirs of Modern Philosophers*. The organization of the Romantic-era philosophical novel around the coercions of what Godwin called "things as they are" can feel exclusive. But not so, if Austen's felicity rather than subversion may offer a compelling philosophical project. This resituation of Austen's writing broadens and pluralizes the scope of Romantic-era philosophical novels by women beyond the exclusively political ("Jacobin" and "anti-Jacobin") generic labels and subcultures that either resist or subtend "things as they are." Henry nonetheless aligns the ideal transparency of a Habermasian critical public with a totalitarian police state.

Both J. L. Austin and D. W. Harding access this mentality of military foreign relations. "How do you know that IG Farben worked for war?" Austin poses the question in "Other Minds"; "'I have every reason to know: I served on the investigating commission'" (*PP*, 81). Long before he published his well-known argument on Jane Austen, "Regulated Hatred," Harding wrote a book about the group psychology of war as a social institution of "regulated combat."[22] But Austin and Harding draw from war a conclusion opposite to Knox-Shaw, that Austen does not support chauvinism but an art (for spiritual as well as potentially political reasons) that measures "standards of the unacceptable" and practices a diplomatically *regulated* hatred (*PP*, 194).[23] Replicating Henry's speech, the attitude prevalent in Knox-Shaw's overview essay on "Philosophy" in Austen both describes and campaigns for the conventionally British attributes: those that mix "liberal tradition" with more "robust" forms of oversight and control that risk shading into circumlocutions for despotism.[24] One of the last times I taught this section of *Northanger Abbey*, I paired it with a scene from the underground MI6 bunker in one of the 007 films, *Skyfall* (2012). It is not clear which cultural text would seem best to editorialize the other. Austen does not clash against, but blurs disconcertingly into, the icon of Bond and British Cold War spying.

Rather than offer a specifically historical and political judgment about this passage and where it may place Austen on the progressive to counter-revolutionary spectrum in the 1790s "war of ideas," in the allusion to a country where "every man is surrounded by a neighborhood of voluntary spies," I want to take sociolinguistic bearings.[25] Knowing and acknowledgment are at issue. This philosophical dynamic is redoubled and warped by popular culture's ritualized insistence on performing the Austen phenomenon as a game of pre-sorted knowing and unknowing affiliations. That such things as Home Office spies are *not unknown* to Jane Austen is the primary knowledge that I take away from this controversial page; hence we as readers must come to grips with the recognition that there is *nothing* proper for us to withhold as unknown to Austen. This point is made by Mary Ann O'Farrell regarding the "conjugal" interpretive act. The "conjugal" *JANE AUSTEN AND* pairings to which we compulsively make Austen submit (as I do too) are often rehearsals of our own insistence that knowing Austen, and Austen's knowing, be kept apart from the full scope of the world. O'Farrell discusses the performance of the "shocking" Austen conjugation, noting that the *Slate* headline from which she takes her title is a news digest piece on how US Intelligence, circa 2000, advised the tracking of "foreign students" by their college majors.

"Bin Laden a Huge Jane Austen Fan" is a kind of perlocutionary testament to the afterlife of the Jane Austen figure used as a means to conjure sociopolitical fantasies. O'Farrell develops this tendency as the

> contemporary habit of reimagining Austen as a punchline, always available through blunt-force juxtaposition for producing the chuckle of the knowing. The headline asks by means of its juxtaposition questions that it will not bother to answer: what could Osama bin Laden have to learn from Jane Austen, and what could Jane Austen know of a world including Bin Laden?[26]

The gesture toward "a world including Bin Laden" simultaneously fixes on one kind of attitude toward otherness (religious, ethnic, or political) in the problem of "other minds," and seizes the analogy between other minds skepticism and the structure of all knowledge of the future: a future historical world about which Jane could not have known, in an insuperable sense.

O'Farrell, developing her own ideas about Austenian conjugality from an answerable perspective, puts a lively and acute pressure on the question of what assumed realms of knowledge Austen and Bin Laden are taken metonymically to represent, and why we insist on the exclusionary ritual that they must be understood as individuals networked to wider forces by keeping them ignorant. (D. H. Lawrence's critique of Austen's "sharp knowing in apartness instead of knowing in togetherness" gives the strong version of this attitude by making it a charge and not a tacit premise [*CH* 2, 107].) O'Farrell's essay responds to the ritual insistence that a relation to Jane Austen depends on the exclusionary positioning of a "real world" of conflict elsewhere. O'Farrell evokes what is at stake in the play-acting of this boundary's violation, wherein "the introduction by force involves a fantasy of conjugality as a violent conjoining."[27] Showing how it is the conduct precisely of manners and hospitality (and tea) that promotes meaningful exchange across the most challenging rifts of hostility, fear, and otherness, O'Farrell's Austen is not a stand-in for the unknowing spheres of domestic life and female – and literary – conduct. Austen is a preeminently capable guide through these gaps of negotiation. "[T]he ignorance of manners," she sums up, "is overrated."[28] Novelist Ivy Compton-Burnett is less guarded in her bold claim about manners: "'Nothing goes deeper than manners.... They are involved with the whole of life'."[29]

An inventive approach such as O'Farrell's proves necessary in order to read *Northanger Abbey* fully as Austen's most ingenuous *and* most knowing novel. It is in this context that Catherine's forward habits of language and other instances of her non-verbal communicative behavior stand out and carry the day. We encounter these actions starting from very early on in the plot, well before the visit to Northanger. Catherine runs after the Tilneys and then fortuitously picks the right door in their townhouse in Bath (*NA*, 69). At the theater, she openly questions Henry's evident but plausibly deniable gestures of anger rather than letting him off the hook (*NA*, 64). She earnestly pursues knowledge about what the world truly is like and, in particular, about the nature of power-wielding men.

Despite his elusiveness and condescension, Henry has a foil in the novel that makes it nonetheless clear how stalwart he is in prioritizing communication – even how knightly.[30] Based on his wild and indistinct speech as a "rattle," but more, John Thorpe threatens trust. At one point he manages to suggest blithely to Catherine that her brother's life is at immediate risk in his carriage (*NA*, 43–44). He nearly ruins Catherine's prospects through miscommunications based on an idiotic level of self-interest and presumption. The villainy of Thorpe's empty speech is crucially important to the parable of *Northanger Abbey* in my reading of the novel as an entry to some form of intelligible community.

Yet Thorpe's villainy has a primitive, incomplete, or propaedeutic status to this book's argument on Jane Austen and ordinary language, simply because so many of Thorpe's statements are *clearly falsehoods*.[31] Thorpe's real threat as a figure inheres in the moments when he cannot be called simply false, but rather empty. Whereas, for D. A. Miller, Robert Ferrars, the character who "might almost be a gay man" in *Sense and Sensibility*, exists as a scandal to all that is "consistently intelligible" in Austen's economies of heteronormative social alliance, it is John Thorpe, exaggerated frat-boy, who puts intelligibility at risk in *Northanger Abbey* (*Secret of Style*, 9, 14). It is hardly an exaggeration to say the Oxford-educated Thorpe represents the banality of evil in Austen's linguistic universe. " – But you have more good-nature and all that, than any body living I believe. A monstrous deal of good nature, and it is not only good-nature, but you have so much, so much of every thing" (*NA*, 85). Such is the record of what one must call words, from an interchange reported in some way or other by Thorpe to his sister soon after the fact, words that require Catherine to contradict Isabella Thorpe's understanding that she has given definite encouragement to her brother, if not outright agreed to marry him. "Make him understand what I mean," Catherine pleads with Isabella on the heels of Thorpe's coercive non-event of a marriage proposal (*NA*, 98). Forced herself to play a sharp hand in this asymmetrical double-edged game, Isabella is willing to grant Catherine the prerogative to have encouraged John but then changed her mind: "What one means one day, you know, one may not mean the next" (*NA*, 99). Catherine insists to her friend that no change has occurred, that the report of Thorpe's proposal and of her welcoming attentions is and was in no sense true: "'But my opinion of your brother never did alter; it was always the same. You are describing what never happened'" (*NA*, 99).

As a thinker committed to accuracy, J. L. Austin nevertheless once identified "the birthright of all speakers, that of speaking unclearly and untruly" (*PP*, 97). This is the arrogation and unfortunate entitlement of John Thorpe. Explaining his turn to Jane Austen only late in life, through a kind of germinal cultivation of minor characters, Cavell adverts:

> I often found myself instead dwelling on the stupidity, the silliness, the empty-headedness, the quality of being worn-out (characteristic predicates utilized by Jane Austen) of so many of her supporting players, who reveal the character of the social conditions that the main characters, of inner aspiration, must overcome in themselves. (*P*, 126)

Though Mr. Elton comes up in a nearby context, this surprising testimonial stands as a meditation on the problem of Thorpe and "the social conditions" of characters without "inner aspiration" and self-overcoming. A list of Austen's depleted "players" must include that menacing boor and rattle – who is not only a foil "revealing the character of the social conditions" to be "overcome" in the novel, but a direct menace to *Northanger Abbey*'s protagonist. Cavell's admission of exhausted interest broaches a sociolinguistic world of hollowness, deceit, and unintelligibility: from the pathetic routine of Anne Steele with her dead-end talk of a doctor beau in *Sense and Sensibility*; to Mr. Collins and Miss De Bourgh in *Pride and Prejudice*; Lady Bertram and Mrs. Norris in *Mansfield Park*; Mrs. Elton in *Emma*; and Sir Walter and Elizabeth Elliot in *Persuasion*.[32]

Tracking exhausted fascination with the constellation of "empty" and "worn-out" minor characters might seem like an unpromising introduction, even to a restrained Romanticism. Yet as Cavell argues in *The Claim of Reason* and *In Quest of the Ordinary*, Romanticism opens with the discovery of the problem of other minds. Cavell writes in *The Claim of Reason*, " – What is the problem of the other if it is not a problem of certainty?" (353) Cavell positions his version of philosophical perfectionism in a moment, never quite amounting to a philosophy of history, understood to come after religion (because the gods are dead) and before philosophy (because we do not yet find interest in our new lives). This phrasing of the history and positionality of the long Romantic perfectionist moment of Cavell's work is often repeated, because it is important: all of Cavell's major intellectual endeavors *start out* from this admission of being at a loss and disappointed with available means of recovery. For Cavell's "creative philosopher," there are "two tasks: to oppose skepticism and to oppose false answers to skepticism."[33] The search gets under way because this sense of finding oneself and one's language stymied, or not yet (or no longer) available, is so generative for Cavell. For his explanation of why *In Quest of the Ordinary* as a book needed its final three chapters on largely American sources, the manner in which Cavell himself allows for this dissatisfaction is to say that in his dealings with Wordsworth, Coleridge, and Shakespeare's *The Winter's Tale*, "too much seemed left without clear and useful ways of going on" (*In Quest*, x); at the very head of the encounter being called a quest, we are allowed in on the lethal ambiguity of the book's title as "the discovery of false necessity," *inquest of the ordinary*: "the sense that the ordinary is subject at once to autopsy and augury, facing at once its end and its anticipation," in "our habit, or habitat" (*In Quest*, 9).

A measure of Austen's confidence in her "first" book (though it is also a revised "late" work, ultimately published along with *Persuasion*) lies in the way *Northanger Abbey* exposes the incoherence of entitled but minor characters of the Thorpe manner. In minor characters such as John and Isabella Thorpe, we have the dramatized threat that those around Catherine Morland can't successfully keep up relationships and their minimal quotients of justified trust and belief. Instead of the romantic anti-hero, it is they who carry the charge of imperiled connections in Austen's fiction.

In *Northanger Abbey*, Austen exhibits a level of primary failure with reference to anthropologist Alphonso Lingis's formulation that "[t]o address someone is not simply to address a source of information; it is to address one who will answer and answer for his or her answer."[34] Both Isabella and John Thorpe are deceitful and lacking in meaningful responsiveness. But in the latter we find a sloppy and pushy incoherence that should be judged the antitype for Austen's own program for conduct in language. And not just in terms of D. A. Miller's ideal of Style (a major parameter for judgment in *Sense and Sensibility*, where bad letter writers invariably are bad, rightly dismissed people), but for the sake of the utter and absolute, minimal conditions to have anything like grounded exchange.

Because of its similar privileging of a counterspirit to Romanticism as a project to reconceive and animate human separation, as part of an effort to establish closer discipline in the publicly shared denominator of communication, the later Cavell can have an almost Habermasian emphasis on this point of answerability. Several of the essays in *Philosophy the Day After Tomorrow* display this stress on maintaining not only our ordinary language responsiveness, but on giving final measure to a public sphere of linguistic responsibility. But both Wittgenstein and Austin, by contrast to this enhancement of responsibility found occasionally in late Cavell, consistently relieve ordinary language from the burden of delivering such certainty of connection. Never has a major philosophical text been as committed and as resourceful as *Philosophical Investigations* in allowing space for the interests of language simply "breaking off" without tragic consequence (*abbrechen*; *PI*, 84).[35] J. L. Austin's critics (apart from Cavell himself) have not prized his version of ordinary language philosophy rightly, or enough, for its refusal either to invoke language as a totalizing regime or, alternately, to blame words when the descriptions or speech acts fail to render the non-linguistic "facts" without misadventure. In one of his less-often examined essays, "The Meaning of a Word," Austin suggests that it is a kind of provision to be able to *let words fail*, and to realize that the success or appropriateness of language to convey meaning is internally linked to this unforeclosable possibility of failure as non-metaphysical and non-tragic. This openness to failure – a hospitality to an event of language and result of inquiry we cannot possibly know in advance – is thereby reframed as another form of capacity. That generosity is a sign of the methodological value now of Austin to the study of sociolinguistics and ordinary affects, but also the fruit of a temperament proper to those who come to philosophy by ordinary language. Austin opposes this attitude about language and the instrumental use of language in the definitional, variable/control-focused efforts of hard science. The definitions of physics are at once ever-tightening and dismissive: "[i]n doing physics[…] where our language is tightened up in order precisely to describe complicated and unusual cases concisely, we *prepare linguistically for the worst*. In ordinary language we do not: *words fail us*" (*PP*, 68). Thus, for Cavell, "[t]he obscurities in surveying the failures of speech and of human action are determinative of what human speech and action are" (*P*, 57). Austin's "The Meaning of a Word" heralds this capacity to *allow* words to fail (a provision that means to fail or succeed), without the tightening of a defense in advance. Such failure is a point of strength of ordinary natural language, and can rightly be called the basis of a resilient relationship to language. Here Austin could be taken to gesture at the limits beyond which words necessarily fail to reach their object – or fail to form at all. Austin is at times a kind of comic Cordelia. Mostly, the point is less portentous. He makes an ordinary if important allowance for the many specific predicaments, the scenarios, that make it difficult to provide a description in advance in sufficiently meaningful ways – just because, as Austin puns in "A Plea for Excuses," "fact is richer than diction" (*PP*, 195).

"Polite Skepticism": Romanticism, Solipsism, Gender

the polite skepticism—the little deaths—of everyday life (*P*, 128).

The mind is its own place and in his inner life each of us lives the life of a ghostly Robinson Crusoe. People can see, hear, and jolt one another's bodies, but they are irremediably blind and deaf to the workings of one another's minds and inoperative upon them.
    What sort of knowledge can be secured of the workings of a mind?

—Gilbert Ryle (*CM*, 15)

Outside, the spring sunshine poured down upon the earth, the sparrows chattered, the scent of green growing things filled the sweet air. For a moment Alex felt dizzy as she walked quickly away from the house. 'Oh, what a world! Happy! Happy! Satisfied with that? How blind we are! How hard and narrow and blind – that we cannot even get a glimpse into other people's hearts! *But she cried with happiness*, poor dear, over *that*! – it's easy to see that I shall never marry.'
    – Jane and Mary Findlater, *Crossriggs* [1908]

Cavell locates the beginnings of Romanticism with the recognition of other minds and the reception of the idea that for the subject of philosophy, the existence of other minds is a "problem." The form of this recognition,

I have argued, in J. L. Austin's writing takes the methodological shape of a refusal of defense, of his availability to the possible failures of language.

Romantic Poetry knows this failure well as an intransigent singular quest. Romantic literature that risks intelligibility in its autobiographical terms must trust the effects of a personal vision upon readers.[36] But narrative discourse and characterology by contrast are plural, and their reception largely anonymous. Is solipsism at issue in the "other minds" problem for narrative? The philosophical failure to credit the existence of others has often – indeed, paradigmatically – been read into the genre of Romantic lyric poetry with its self-and-the-world model and focus on the expressive subject. But, interestingly, Gilbert Ryle locates an older prose solipsism in the realist bourgeois figure of Robinson Crusoe: a Crusoe whose authorship is given as much to the philosophical precursor Descartes ("the life of a ghostly Robinson Crusoe") as to its fabricator, Daniel Defoe. Asked to place it in Wordsworth, concern for "other minds" would go immediately to his comment in the Fenwick notes about the "Immortality" Ode. As a boy, Wordsworth recalls, he was forced occasionally to stop and touch a wall or tree, to convince himself that more than his own inner world had existence. The egotism or silliness of this need on one register is patent. But it cannot be separated from the qualities of experience that such a fear positioned him almost uniquely as a poet to value. Wordsworth's uncanny disclosures of the mere "sentiment of being" are the result: the affective surplus of being as opposed to its merely grammatical predication. Wordsworth's poetry touches a bracingly radical philosophical substrate, a bottom before any conceptual ground, which results in "a sense of radical sufficiency in the fact that life *is*."[37] But does this ontic "sentiment" teach us about how other minds think and feel? Could we wager from its presence to any reasonable human connection?

"The sentiment of being" has also been invoked, by Lionel Trilling, to characterize the literary contribution of Austen's novels to intellectual history.[38] But even in situations where one can do so, say with the glorious banality of *Emma*, Jane Austen's admirers as a group don't wish to take their pleasure and treat Austen's discriminating fictions in this way, to pulp them down for their ontic sense of disclosing a world at all, rather than having the finely realized narratives. One of the philosophical intuitions this chapter harbors is that Austen's concern with the problem of "other minds" rather easily eschews the solipsism of a voraciously active imagination by the end of *Northanger Abbey* – so that she deploys it rather than suffering by it in the next book, *Sense and Sensibility*. Marianne Dashwood is the six novels' lone possible representation of the danger of that kind of solipsism, which she exhibits not as a mode of being but in an emotional stance. Yet, there may be other modes of solipsistic endangerment.³⁹ Against Wordsworth's fearful wish regarding the mind's creating and nullifying powers, the thought of nothing truly happening is closer and more real to Austen. Perhaps we might think of this as a solipsism not of the faculties of persons but of the means at their disposal. It is felt by those with thinking powers whose danger is not unlimited rambling, but imprisonment.

A condensation of wishes and fears represented in dream form by Wordsworth in *The Prelude*, Book 5, "On Books," relates to the apocalyptic isolation of a certain kind of visionary humanism, and to the foundational conceit of "reading nature" as a book placed before us with a purposively intentional structure of meaning.⁴⁰ Neither the powers nor the plight of this kind of solipsism occupy the novels, whose images of perilous reading instead focus outright – literally and quixotically, one can in fact say – on books. It is an alternate branch of the skeptical tradition that Austen develops, concerning the ongoing skepticisms practiced in linguistic and social life. Not, what if the mind cannot reach all the way to the world, or leave behind its own monstrous powers enough to cooperate to realize the world's presence with others; but, what if the world denies the subject's capacity to find a voice, to take action within it, until that first relationship is de-realized, and annihilated? What happens when the continual modest adult demands of practicing "polite skepticism" (Cavell), "civil falsehood" (Harding), and even the comedically skit-like "bit where you take it back" (Austin), have left nothing primary and adhesive?

This sense of the terms of a philosophical melodrama, a philosophical gothic that is not empiricist, inherits what it can in my account of *Northanger Abbey* from the critics of the novel that see genre satire and political gothic. Having gotten here, the aesthetic judgment can partake of more moderation. When there is need to invoke a philosophical line for Austen in an arc specific to the rise of eighteenth-century fiction, scholars of the novel have rightly placed her as the daughter of Samuel Johnson and of Laurence Sterne. Johnson's *Rambler* famously discusses the new realist novel and its reliance on public knowledge rather than on solitary traits. He writes in *The Rambler* 4, March 31, 1750:

> The task of our present writers…requires, together with that learning that is to be gained from books, that experience which can never be attained by solitary diligence, but must arise from general converse, and accurate observation of the living world.⁴¹

Perhaps eyeing the mad astronomer in *Rasselas* (1759), the closest thing to a novel Dr. Johnson would write, Austen likewise directs the dangers of solitude and solipsism to the practice of reading books rather than to the scene of metaphorically "reading" nature.

Although it does occur to Austen to question these kinds of foundational premises about world provisioning in a self-consciously "early" work, she is not brought to despair over them. Austen and Austin both illustrate nimbly the idea that all language users hold a violable trust. *Northanger Abbey* fulfills this demand insouciantly in Catherine Morland's relationship with Henry Tilney, and sets it outright against the perils of John Thorpe – whose relation to meaning is at once laughable and at all times dangerously unclear. Thorpe's self-interest is open-ended and bears an insidious relation to the linguistic institutions of communication and promising. At any given point in the book, he does not even pursue *definitively* a specific malign intention toward Catherine (abducting her in the carriage in Bath, forcing her into marriage, ruining her character), but presumes the ability to pursue her uncommittedly only to capitalize (or not) later. Thorpe's villainy is the opposite of a strategy; it is premised on outrageous levels of availability, opportunity, and denial, so that to himself his mishandlings bear no negative consequences. He emerges in the novel not just as the exceptional stylist's, but as the broad linguistic community's, true villain. Indeed, he "proposes" to Catherine at the end of Volume I not by making a performative offer of marriage but by making an allusion. In this way, Austin and Austen together confront the dangers we are all skirting, but that a gendered departure from the romantic self may risk constantly, of incoherence in the midst of regulative norms.

Rather than in those long "arch" conversations in which he successfully displays a knowledge of Mrs. Allen's muslins, and is "polite enough to seem interested in what she said" (*NA*, 16), I have already advertised where I find the unmistakable signal that Henry Tilney will be worthy to know Catherine Morland. The moment is present in a conversation in Vol. I, Chapter 3, when he invites her to declare her thoughts (and in quite an ordinary, not ultra-profound way) to be unknown by him:

> Mr. Tilney was polite enough to seem interested in what she said; and she kept him on the subject of muslins till the dancing recommenced. Catherine feared, as she listened to their discourse, that he indulged himself a little too much with the foibles of others. —"What are you thinking of so earnestly?" said he, as they walked back to the ball-room; —"not of your partner, I hope, for, by that shake of the head, your meditations are not satisfactory."
>
> Catherine coloured, and said, "I was not thinking of any thing."

"That is artful and deep, to be sure; but I had rather be told at once that you will not tell me."
"Well then, I will not."
"Thank you; for now we shall soon be acquainted[.]" (*NA*, 16–17)

J. L. Austin reminds us of an expressive capacity to allow language to fail. Gilbert Ryle emphasizes that the capacity for understanding depends not just on the potential, but in a way on the achievement, of grounds for misunderstanding. Wittgenstein holds that in order to make a mistake, a person must already judge in conformity with mankind. Where I have cut it off (as Henry goes on in the next line to tease again), this passage exhibits not the condescendingly knowing Henry Tilney, but the partner in interest. Here, as opposed to the knowing condescension of his lecturing to Catherine and Eleanor during the confusion over riots on Beechen Cliff, or in the chill of his position of social mastery over the surveilled world in the gallery at Northanger, Henry is capable of knowing Catherine for better reasons than simply his politeness not to insist, but for knowledge of her as separate and other: for her ingenuousness, her unthought acts of insouciance; her ability to be open the entire novel and yet still not be exhaustible.[42] Again, Henry plays at external world/object skepticism in the conversation, but he offers something more promising in this allusion to the relation of other minds. The grounds of their acquaintance depends on this acknowledgment of the standing of difference. Such improvisation unfolds the structuring conditions of an interested unknowing.[43]

In *Philosophy the Day After Tomorrow*, Cavell reflects on his delayed ability to become absorbed in the novels of Jane Austen. He understands this resistance in terms of "Austen's narrator's renowned surface of containment" (*P*, 124): the description he had before attempted as her "surface of lethal calm." The ambivalent, delayed, and apparently life-long double-take of an interest in Austen's fiction is the product of Cavell's affective relation to Austen's prose, and in particular to the nearly extinguished life of its containability. Cavell highlights a "contained" and constrained subjectivity, expressed through novelistic style. Yet the dangers of confinement are foremost literal and physical in the fiction of the Romantic Period. "Constraint, confinement, containment, distress," Eric Walker forcefully summarizes, "these are the clouded headings under which Cavell organizes his reading in Austen (and Nietzsche, Emerson, and Eliot) of the 'unrelieved routine or fixation of ordinariness'" (*P*, 122).[44] These conditions are notable in the terms of gender and genre for the way they reposition a Jacobin "gothic" predicament inside the quieter and seemingly more contented domesticity of the realist bourgeois novel, twinning skepticism with the sociable world. The late-eighteenth century novel before Austen had explored and, indeed, symptomatically expressed containment in outright historical and political terms, terms frequently associated with the imprisonment of women. Richardson's *Clarissa* had, of course, set the model of female virtue and inner fortitude in the inner world of social and spatial confinement. Burney's *Cecilia* (1782) contains an important episode of the heroine's asylum imprisonment in the final volume. With its homosocial male protagonists, Godwin's *Things As They Are: or, The Adventures of Caleb Williams* (1794) drives obsessively toward the novel's final, pulverizingly confined state. Mary Wollstonecraft's unfinished final novel, *Maria: Or, The Wrongs of Woman* (1798) and Mary Hays's *The Victim of Prejudice* (1799) pursue furthest the confinement of women.

Hays scholar Eleanor Ty describes this author's earlier and more well-known novel, *Emma Courtney* (1796), in both narrative and social registers as "an endless circle of suffocating repetition":

> The heroine's sexual and intellectual disappointments are mirrored by the novel's incessant, stifling pattern of frustrated desire and unfulfilled expectations in a style that is deliberately one-sided. Through a strong first-person narration, we hear Emma's story of exclusion, or rejection, and of self-torture. Hardly anyone else's voice is heard so that the reader's attention is focused on her affecting plight. What Hays believes to be the female experience of confinement by the "constitution of society" becomes literal in the novel as we, too, experience narrative entrapment.[45]

Mary Wollstonecraft's advertisement of her first novel, *Mary, a Fiction* (1788), addressed to "the mind of a woman, who has thinking powers," should remind us that the philosophical novel in late-eighteenth century Britain was preeminently a novel not just of ideas, but of dialogue, where dialogue does not ensure communication. The litany of confinements attests to the breakdown of dialogue. Instead of unifying and supplementing the idea of an autonomous self (as it does in Hegel's *Philosophy of Right*), marriage in Wollstonecraft's final and unfinished novel, *Maria*, breaks down the protagonist into fragments, into the form of life underwritten in law already by all women's lack of existence as legal persons. It is no help to Wollstonecraft to be a Hamlet in this world. "Was not the world a vast prison, and women born slaves?"[46]

Still, the restriction of this "ordinariness" in the organization and tone of nineteenth-century life elicits Cavell's "unconstrained fascination" (*P*, 126).[47] It is the *uncontainable* register of Austen's language, which on the return of his belated, "foreign" attention to her domestic fiction so productively arrests Cavell. Timothy Gould discusses Cavell's thinking about action, and in particular "Cavell's explorations of the genre he named the 'Melodrama of the Unknown Woman'" in film, in terms by which we may pass between the Romantic-era gothic novel and twentieth-century media. Gould's concern is with Cavell's engagement with "movies that come to ask when – and how, and with whom, and to what end – a woman can *act* in the world as it stands – a world dominated not only by male power but by the masculine definitions of action and activity." For Gould, "Cavell's accounts of the movies are haunted by the beauty of successful human action and the survivability of its failures."[48]

CHAPTER 3

Sense and Sensibility *and Suffering*

The picture of the mind revives again[.]
—William Wordsworth, "Tintern Abbey"

The word [*sense*] considers sensations not as means of knowledge, but of suffering.
—William Empson, "Sense and Sensibility";
The Structure of Complex Words

How do words refer to sensations?—There doesn't seem to be any problem here; don't we talk about sensations every day, and give them names? But how is the connexion between the name and the thing named set up? This question is the same as: how does a human being learn the meaning of the names of sensations?—of the word "pain" for example. Here is one possibility: words are connected with the primitive, the natural, expressions of the sensation and used in their place. A child has hurt himself and he cries; and then adults talk to him and teach him exclamations and, later, sentences. They teach the child new pain-behavior.

"So you are saying that the word 'pain' really means crying?" —On the contrary: the verbal expression of pain replaces crying and does not describe it.
—Ludwig Wittgenstein, *Philosophical Investigations* § 244

Nothing is closer than the inner and the outer, e.g., pain and the expression of pain. There is no *room* between.
—Wittgenstein; quoted by Stanley Cavell in *The Claim of Reason* (341)

A major tenet in the practice of ordinary language philosophy, which Stanley Cavell reinforces throughout his groundbreaking work *The Claim of Reason* (1979), is that human beings learn far more than they are systematically taught and ever could directly teach another person. What we learn and the way we learn, for Cavell in his most Wittgensteinian mood, involves reaching fluency in the gestures by which language is conducted

Sense and Sensibility *and Suffering*

along the lines of communal criteria. Most simply, this meaning is ostensive: how a word is used. But learning can also assume the burden for Cavell of a disappointment with criteria as Wittgenstein deploys them: "Since criteria and skepticism are one another's possibility, criteria cannot be meant to refute skepticism; on the contrary they show skepticism's power, even something one might call its truth. I sometimes think of this theme as our disappointment with criteria."[1] Though the discussion it hosts will become complexly intertwined soon enough, this chapter follows what I hope is a straightforward path at the start, charting a parallel between Cavell's dissatisfied, fruitfully resistant reading of Wittgenstein on rule following and criteria, and Jane Austen's *Sense and Sensibility* as a novel that is apt to leave even engaged readers dissatisfied.

So, like William Empson in one my epigraphs, and with many other scholars and theorists of the key concepts of the long-eighteenth century in recent years, we are to follow the primary "sense" not just of knowledge but also of suffering, beginning perhaps with an irritation of teaching practice and practical reading that does not seriously merit that word, and building from there. The productive frustration I have similarly felt as a teacher – that peculiar kind of public and other-oriented reader – interests me first. A groundwork question will be: How can we learn more actively to take interest in the novel's seductively binary pairing? How might we learn better ourselves in order to teach – that is, to the extent that these two sides of an extramural education can form a congruent experience – so that the inevitable character-based readings of the title's overlapping terms are at once appropriately subtle and still stick?

To start, one can mark the change from the draft title of Austen's long-held MS of the 1790s, "Elinor and Marianne," to the publication of *Sense and Sensibility* in 1811 as a kind of historically belated novel of ideas. The novel makes its appearance with this abstract, ever so slightly Jacobin choice of title (the French revolutionary resonance of Marianne came later in the nineteenth century), but after the historical moment in which such a choice would be politically laden. Titling and chronology only begin to flesh out the exploratory relation of modern philosophical controversy to "polite" Austenian Literature. Whereas Austen's own apparent source text for the novel's title evinced the need to disambiguate the semantic and cultural realms of sense and sensibility as an effect of "mistaken synonymy" (from the *Lady's Monthly Museum* of 1798–1799), the default position in a classroom can be quite far from that kind of antireductionist interpretive anxiety.[2] The general reader is very comfortable with how to read the "and." Predisposed to a certain logic of that conjunction, which conveniently stacks up according to the same geometry ruling the relationship of an older to a younger sister (like the novel's narrator, more or less, we forget the third sister Margaret), one can't help entering the novel in too much certainty.[3] Students of Austen at all levels seem to have picked up and applied a "rule following" behavior based on the single overwhelming instance of *Pride and Prejudice*. In both cases, the second polysyllabic word is read to intensify a less pejorative connotation of the first word with which it partners. We care more about and perhaps feel we know more about the exemplar of the second word, but only to disparage it: a trouser word in action. Not only is the possibility of near-synonymy and careful, layered disambiguation passed over in this reading; the gender difference and differences between sororal and spousal relationships are overlooked. The rigidity of many Janeites' rule following behavior has left a huge market to be tapped for unscrupulous others who want to have the easy fun of *Pride and Prejudice and Zombies* and *Sense and Sensibility and Sea Monsters*. The teasing is fatuous, but it works insofar as we all thought we knew what the "and" meant and did – and couldn't possibly mean or do.

That position upon opening the book remains hard to dislodge even by the novel's end, where an understandable response is to decide that Marianne ("the patroness of a village" [*S&S*, 268] married to an older man in flannel waistcoats, and deprived of the expression of her subjectivity)[4] and Elinor (an emotional marathon runner, who has just burst nearly screaming out of the room with uncontrolled tears of joy and surprise [*S&S*, 254]) have had their ruling passions telepathically switched. Supplementary critical materials only partly succeed at reimagining alternate shapes for this powerful impulse to craft a rebus for Elinor and Marianne as the symbolic pictures of Sense and Sensibility. But they help to disclose the method of reading the culturally inflected sensation words I want to press further in this chapter. Along with sharing period sources for the vogue of aesthetic and moral "sensibility" cresting in the mid-to-late eighteenth-century, Raymond Williams's entry in *Keywords* is pedagogically helpful. That entry, with an eye trained on the Marianne of the first two volumes, recounts an historical affect rooted in "a conscious openness to feelings, and also a conscious consumption of feelings."[5]

Williams's dual emphasis on Romanticism and the rise of subjectivities of consumer culture opens a range of access to Marianne's most scripted, conventional and yet surprising, behaviors: her visit to Allenham to make plans for the sitting room furniture for a future time when Willoughby's benefactress, Mrs. Smith, is dead (*S&S*, 52); her allied notion of what exact number will suffice as "competence" (£2000 a year, twice Elinor's richest fantasy; *S&S*,

67); her hoarding of sentimental pleasures and stoking up on an even greater measure of cherished pain. It can seem that Marianne's power as the expressive subject of the novel is based on *little but* this avidly transparent species of declaration. By means of her nearly constant string of avowals and disavowals in the first part of the book, she claims a role in the game of achieving Bourdieuian distinction over against the dull and duplicitous, the Middletons, Jennings, and Steeles of the world, all of whom she clumps together.

As readers we smile at Marianne's instances of predictable judgment (her views on landscape, poetry, and so forth), yet we nevertheless broadly experience the assertion of identity as Marianne does. Even if the specific positions to which she adheres are easy to condescend to (not because they are "wrong" or immature, but because Marianne does not appear to know they exist as already plotted coordinates in the sociological game of taking positions), the novel's construction grants the bigger driving truth of her character as a locus of subjective agency willed by and for herself and *as such not to be violated*. This experience of the structure of subjective freedom is so strong in Marianne that its eclipse at the end of the novel creates a problem. I return to this problem at the chapter's close. Where can a character such as Marianne be radically re-educated (re-formed, one might say), and where is her character as such to be respected as an expressive boundary? Attempts to answer necessarily place characterological representations within genre history beside questions about the emergence of the modern individual, or human subject.[6]

Working against this framework of individual choice and agency, both sense and sensibility retain operational meanings that are profoundly materialist and passive. The funny thing about a typical class devoted to this layered historical connotation from Raymond Williams is that in responding to it, even some of the strongest readers will reject its very bounty as too contextually informative to help. From there, one recourse is to an older – in some contexts medical, or pre-professionally philosophical – construction of what "sensibility" could mean at its minimal point: *The ability to receive stimuli*, to be affected *by changes in the environment*.[7] This contemporary medical description of what is called "somatosensory" sensibility, or "somatoesthetic" sensibility, connects to one *OED* definition (2.a.) that goes back to circa 1400: "readiness of an organ or tissue to respond to sensory stimuli." From the perspective of the organism susceptible to it, then, since all change rehearses a logic of trauma writ large or small, sensibility reduces to the sensation of pain, to suffering.[8]

In his brilliant essay on "Sense and Sensibility" in *The Structure of Complex Words*, William Empson starts into the topic by approaching the former as "reception-of-sensations" and the latter as "reaction-to-contexts."[9] Empson, without explicit reference to Austen's novel or to the characters of Elinor and Marianne Dashwood, goes on to write of the interrelatedness of sense and sensibility, reception and reaction, that for sensibility, "[i]n short, 'a reaction is profoundly like a reception'." Empson may seem here to anticipate later twentieth-century theory's critique of the naturalization of cultural constructions, the loadedness of the "mere" senses with "oughts." But he goes on to show multiple ways of construing the transfer of concepts in a mode of interchange. This becomes a dialogue, quickly enough, about gender: "It no longer fits the case to say a *good* reaction, except as one speaks of 'a good cry'; there is no idea of normality; but one could make it 'a reaction *ought to* be profoundly like a reception,' because this extremity of feeling is praised. I should say that *sense* retorts, 'a hardhearted man will ignore any feelings arising out of particular cases while he is carrying out his plan; he will stick to the main chance; he will use his senses only as tools or spies to help him in the great purpose of getting rich.' Here the idea is 'a reception ought to be part of a reaction, wholly subordinate to it'."[10]

If Empson may once have been read to anticipate and endorse the critique of the naturalization of culture, today his work may be taken to show the interrelatedness of cultural reactions to biological sense formation. A novel titled *Sense and Sensibility* must in great measure be about the linguistic communicability of pain in narrative and other cultural forms. From the point of view of a Wollstonecraft on education, all novels go in too heavily for an economy of physical "sensation" understood in this way. Translation in particular of the "sense" in Austen's title pairing into other languages can be instructive. Spanish offers the flexibility of *sentido*, but in French one must choose between the widely divergent *raison* and *sens*. Comparably useful in that it denatures the word to modern ears, which expect subjectivity where he gives only qualia, David Hume's understanding of "sentiment" compares to such relocation of "sensibility" in the physiological realm. "All sentiment is right," according to Hume – but it is not subject to truth claims, not a matter of cognitive investigation – in the same way as "to pretend to ascertain the real sweet or the real bitter."[11] Oren Izenberg reflects on an Emily Dickinson lyric: "These coordinates, the intrinsic, the private, the ineffable, are also applied (though not without controversy) to what in the philosophy of mind go by the name *qualia*. Qualia are (most ordinary, most difficult) the subjective or phenomenal aspects of conscious experience – what it is like to see a color or to hear a sound."[12] Too primary to call an accomplishment or any kind of personal "character" trait at all, what can an awareness of this level of response lead to as an interpretive framework for Austen? Does this collocation of issues lead us to the philosophical point where, as Wittgenstein has it in his fragmentary dialogical method in *Philosophical Investigations*, a "verbal expression of pain replaces crying and does not describe it" – such that we could call that event of replacement *learning*; what it means to "learn the meaning of the names"? Do we learn use ostensively, like the names in the title so often read as if Austen were pointing them out for the reader's benefit (*this* is Elinor; *this* is Marianne; or, why not, together, *this* is your problem)?

Intimacy is belied not only by the opacity of the one sister (Elinor), who remains the other mind par excellence, but also by the ostensible transparency of the other sister (Marianne) whose sensibility and solipsism prove continuous with the "insensible," closed-off state to which she is relegated.[13] Viewed against the cultural code of her romantic sensibility, Marianne's binary state of being either "insensible" or "rational," once she takes ill at Cleveland, suggests a bedrock at which to find Austen's relation to the older definitions of "sense."[14] In Austen's work, the opposite to sense is not sensibility, but insensibility: a caricatured want of sense – often bluntly put, or inappropriately funny.[15] *Both* Marianne and Elinor "had too much sense to be desirable companions to" Lady Middleton (*S&S*, 173) – and not only for the social reason that Lady Middleton is paralyzed by her will to pass in rich fashionable society as far as possible from her family's origins in the City and trade (she was once a Mary Jennings), but since (and in connection with this fear of displaying her striver's energy) Lady Middleton is physiologically inert and insipid. Because neither Marianne nor Elinor "flattered herself nor her children, she could not believe them good-natured; and because they were fond of reading, she fancied them satirical: perhaps without exactly knowing what it was to be satirical; but *that* did not signify" (*S&S*, 174).

As recently as 1759, "insensibility" for Adam Smith had primarily referred to the control of feeling behind the conduct of "manly fortitude" shown under extreme suffering and duress.[16] It is Smith's account of the very humanity of insensibility, and what follows from it – a social claim in the sympathetic physiological and imaginative practice of "keeping time" – that makes his deliberation on even our general dullness or "want of sensibility" of salient concern. In its discussion of "our sympathy with Sorrow" (Part 1, Section 3, Chapter 1), Smith's *Theory of Moral Sentiments* acknowledges a series of hierarchies and asymmetries. As the chapter précis outlines: "*That though our sympathy with Sorrow is generally a more lively* sensation than our sympathy with Joy, it commonly falls much more short of the violence of what is naturally felt by the person principally concerned" (55). It is hard for anyone to "sympathize entirely, and keep perfect time" with the expression of another's sorrow (57). But then, Smith argues, that very underwhelming state generates our ideas of magnanimity and greatness of spirit. There is a mismatch in the structure of subject positions and feelings in play, when pain is expressed and a measure of human sensibility is called for in response. This want of spirits actually leads to a sublimated ideal of their enlargement as a notion of heroic conduct. "It is on account of this dull sensibility to the afflictions of others, that magnanimity amidst great distress appears always so divinely graceful" (59). Smith deploys "insensibility" with reference to Roman Stoic philosophers and public figures, historical exemplars such as Cato and Seneca. He calls Seneca "that great preacher of insensibility" (60).[17]

Hard-headed and sometimes hard-hearted, Austen's fiction gives a twist to this classically derived standard of tasteful and heroic insensibility. In *Sense and Sensibility* and *Pride and Prejudice* in particular, the standard of a conduct or state of mind that "appears to be more than mortal" coincides not with stoical conduct but with comically inanimate (and inadequate, overtasked) mortality. In a reference to the Jacobin novels of Wollstonecraft and Hays, with their gothic handling of the realistic threat of female imprisonment and fragmentation, Mr. Bennet relishes inflicting the brunt of a joke on "sensibility" and his hysterical wife's nerves at the end of Volume I of *Pride and Prejudice*. This passage can be related after the manner of a vaudevillian comedy duo: [SHE] "'I cannot bear to think that they should have all this estate. If it was not for the entail I should not mind it.' [HE] 'What should you not mind?' [SHE] 'I should not mind anything at all.' [HE] 'Let us be thankful that you are preserved from a state of such insensibility'" (*P&P*, 89). One imagines Mr. Bennet lifting his head just long enough from a book of Roman comedies to deliver these lines. The dead wife joke qualifies as one of Austen's most unbecoming conjunctions.[18] From Mr. Bennet's point of view, the brutal fun (a deadened game) is that even now his living wife is not all that distinguishably preserved from forensically braindead "insensibility." Kept at a distance by the joking of a stable husband and father, the female Jacobin novel's preoccupation with social and legal power over women's bodies lingers in comic bathos at the expense of the exuberantly healthy Mrs. Bennet and her deficiency of "mind."

"Minding" that can only be felt as irritation for superactive Mrs. Bennet is present as a mentality of quick focus and attention for Austen's major characters possessing "sense," but it still can be negatived by insensibilities of distraction when profound thought must go elsewhere. Without having the word appear, one finds a kindred description of Elinor after the London ball in *Sense and Sensibility* Volume II – another instance of Austen winking at the valences of sensibility that pertain to "mere" sensory information and awareness: "Again they were both silent. Elinor was employed in walking thoughtfully from the fire to the window, from the window to the fire, without knowing that she received warmth from one, or discerning objects through the other" (*S&S*, 134). Here Elinor is non-responsive to stimuli in the room, from mental absorption. The insensibility of distraction may result alternately from too much or too little demonstrated presence of mind. Like the state of mind of an absorbed reader or an engaged writer in the act of composing – and at the opposite end of the spectrum from a certain preconception of Mrs. Bennet in *Pride and Prejudice* (who is quite mindful of one thing that reading books can obscure: the intransigent and menacing facts looming over material lives) – Elinor shows insensibility of focus. Adam Smith invokes what would become Austen's and Elinor's key term for a standard of practical and self-approving conduct in states of duress when he holds up a model based on "exertion": "In such paroxysms of distress, if I may be allowed to call them so, the wisest and firmest man, in order to preserve his equanimity, is obliged, I imagine, to make a considerable, and even a painful exertion" (170).[19]

My first point of emphasis has been to show that there are narrative contours and exemplary problems that again become appreciable or at least apparent, given this historically and aesthetically flattened point of view in which to be "insensible" means to be altogether senseless, physiologically unresponsive, playing dead, or plain dead. A second area for which I hope to frame discussion relates to *where* it is in the relationship between a philosophical approach and a literary text that the critical act might intervene on these terms. In his essay, "Perfectly Helpless," Andrew Miller identifies a similar issue by positioning the reader in a helpless relation to Austen's fictional characters:

> When the characters themselves are helpless, we discover (with something like relief, whatever our frustration) their company in our own condition, as if they have come to join us in that state in which we have languished since we first lifted the cover of the book.[20]

Miller attends to the analogy of "company" between novel and reader, arguing that Austen's readers, like her characters, are peculiarly (or, in stylistic terms, "perfectly") helpless before events recounted in a grammatical mode specific to this genre: the diegetic past tense. Absorptive reading of fiction and the fictional narrative's "perfected" past state do not contemplate each other behind walls. They share a companionship of conditions, helpless yet participatory.

My tactic here, however, will be to try to construct a new configuration of interest between two characters within the novel. This choice of location may seem naïve, yet it forces me to deal with two basic issues: the prerogative of the artist to allow or bar access to the inner thoughts of created fictional characters most generally; and the quandary presented by the opacity of other minds in the linguistic terrains of fictional life. In the context of Austen, of course, this means tackling at least some aspects of the philosophical register of her famous free indirect discourse.[21] Implicit in the philosophical choice readers face in processing free indirect style, there is a split between: (a) the idea of an omniscient narrator "playing god" but relinquishing aspects of god, wearing a mask or enacting ventriloquy while merging with limited characters; and (b) the forms of immanence, skepticism, and embodied and situated knowledges that shape the condition of our separateness as the condition and problem of knowing. Theology here is also an issue in the basic conceptualization of mental and linguistic distance, contact, and space. Poststructuralism teaches – certainly of novels and poems, but also of the textuality and iterability of experience altogether – that expressions are functions of their mediation to the point that it is no longer correct or meaningful to speak in terms of the inner "access" they provide as the corresponding "outer" sign.[22] Yet Wordsworth's "picture of the mind" must be further clarified and understood also as an expression of Wittgenstein's "forms of life" and as a practice of ordinary language. Poststructuralism and ordinary language meet in the critique of the picture of introspection.

A glaring challenge to the attempt to read fiction in terms of the philosophical problem of "other minds" results from the bracingly opposed starting coordinates of omniscient transparency and skeptical obstruction. And an account of the nineteenth-century novel requires that we formulate and model an idea of the density, the finitude, of the human other whose being and feeling are not finally reducible to mind at all: thickened features of narrative art that a book like *Sense and Sensibility* is still on the way to developing. In what ways is the free indirect style of Austen's later, "mature" phase a fuller representation of the embedded phenomenology of subjective and social life? And to what extent might that accomplishment of technique actually fulfill its task by *evasion*, offering a wish fulfillment about the fundamental situatedness of bodies, opacities and limits, which might be better kept visible by working along "flat" representational planes? These are important questions for the philosophical account of Austen's fiction. By the same measure, they ought to be questions for all readers of Austen – and for readers of the modern novel more generally. In what we used to call "experience," what can feel like the seclusion, unreliability, and impermeability of other minds is a major problem. Even Cavell reports feeling dissatisfied on his first encounters with Wittgenstein's philosophy, on account of its flatness.[23] But we can and do know things and communicate. In "Other Minds," J. L. Austin demonstrates by consulting the user's archive of what we say when that being *made to feel another's anger*, coming to *know another's taste*, are common instances of the conduct of knowing in which knowledge of the other is imparted (as much as it ever will be, as much as it is to the angry or tasteful person right then) in the manifest event (*PP*, 110). In literature, access to other minds is granted selectively through techniques and conventions of fiction – especially with the rise of focalizing techniques of character and interiority in the modern novel starting with Austen.

The rest of this chapter examines key passages from *Sense and Sensibility* about the linguistic conditions under which the protagonists share the experiences of their suffering. My account of the novel takes for its enabling premise such a deliberately blunt shift in the idea of "sensibility," in order to let reading be stimulated by (if not overly to depend on) conditions that on their face are less prone to be captivated by depth: like color-blindness, or tooth pain, or the literal understanding of the narrator's assertion in a different Austen novel, *Northanger Abbey*, that a young woman's parents never suspected she had a heart. If the "verbal expression of pain replaces crying and does not describe it," as my epigraph has relayed from Wittgenstein, the language of suffering conveys an important matter indeed: language's role appears at once learned, primitive, and already a repressive technology leveraged against what one is tempted to call the simple *fact* of pain: the unaccommodated human cry. I set the transparent Marianne's delayed recognition (usually felt to be a severe failure of her sympathetic moral imagination) and the guarded Elinor's impeded disclosure of her "true" interior state (often judged necessary and worthy of sympathy), alongside the twentieth-century philosophical concern about access to "other minds." Are other minds manifest in behavior, known by language in action? Or are minds guarded and disclosed, only ever *made* accessible, as by a narrator or a first-person subject?

This effort forms part of my venture to explore Austen's philosophical resonance beyond eighteenth-century skeptical tradition. In a passage I have already cited, at a crucial moment in "Other Minds" (1946), J. L. Austin writes:

> It is fundamental to talking (as in other matters) that we are entitled to trust others, except in so far as there is some concrete reason to distrust them. Believing persons, accepting testimony, is the, or one main, point of talking. We don't play (competitive) games except in the faith that our opponent is trying to win: if he isn't, it isn't a game, but something different. So we don't talk with people (descriptively) except in the faith that they are trying to convey information. (*PP*, 82–83)

In this important table-setting passage, Austin wants his audience to agree (he shows that, in effect, they must have already agreed) to share a basic understanding of language as grounded in an "entitle[ment] to trust others," to trust that "they are trying to convey information" unless "there is some concrete reason" for an exceptional case of mistrust. Just as importantly, Austin's fundamental claim works as a performative speech act. It seeks to create the consensus he seeks, because obliquity and withholding cannot be sequestered from language. His address in this passage of "Other Minds" precedes half as an argument and half as an aside. Of course Austin's language is not itself unambiguously just an effort to "share information"; it insinuates, it pleads, it jokes, it threatens, it presupposes. Shoshana Felman argues Austin seduces, and develops this reading at wonderful length in *The Scandal of the Speaking Body*. From this fundamentally deconstructive insight, the literary and philosophical descendants of Austin stem out in two non-exclusive lines: those committed to pursue the ethical implications and juridical contexts of "[b]elieving persons, accepting testimony" (for instance, Felman and Judith Butler); and those who follow literature as the very kind of "non-competitive game" played with language that Austin marginalizes. In this form of game, not only can we not trust the Cold-War adversarial "faith that our opponent is trying to win." Literature and critical theory comprise paradoxical endeavors where (as Barbara Johnson once wrote) "nothing fails like success."[24]

In the debates around literature and speech act theory associated with the publication of *Limited Inc*, but also in the yet more sustaining and nuanced account of Rousseau, J. L. Austin, and Paul de Man in the long essay "Typewriter Ribbon," it is Jacques Derrida, of course, who best represents the insuppressible status of "literary" language as a constitutive risk to all language.[25] For Derrida, literature is the name for the non-competitive "game" playing that Austin sidelines. And in realizing this, one also confirms the decisive role of a privileged, unargued, "aside" register of the "(competitive)" in Austin. Here it shows up not only Austin's fundamental reliance on adversarial thought (the conversation partner as combatant: an inner, constitutional enemy respected because they are always trying to "win"), but his dependence on the registers of life-and-death necessity, and implicated modes of dire reference and functionality that such "total" conflict mobilizes. All that, literature as such suspends. If we can offer a sufficient energy of critique to Austin's theory of the "opponent" as the guarantor of linguistic "trust" and "faith," perhaps new possibilities of participatory conceptual organization might emerge.

One of these potentials is brought into view by Jeremy Bentham and, later, by Derrida, when each makes definitive the question of suffering. By the time of Jane Austen – as Derrida recounts – the question of whether human and other animals could think, which was particularly marked as the inheritance of Descartes, had shifted by way of Bentham and burgeoning liberal discourses of management, to the arguably no less philosophically intractable classification of beings based on whether and how they suffer.[26] Bentham's utilitarian felicity is a measure not of intentional thoughts but of behavioral suffering. In *Sense and Sensibility*, the "tormenting problems" of knowledge are redoubled by the fact that the subject of these matters is rooted in the experience of suffering.[27] This claim, not only of reason and idea, but of feeling – in the words of Tobias Menely: "a communicativity that is passionate before it is rational, passive before it is willed" – urges that we enlarge its philosophy beyond epistemology.[28] Tempering Menely's into Cavell's sense of a claim promotes a kind of zoontological animal ethics, an ontology, moreover, based not on linguistic propriety but on dispossession.[29] The novel's method and content, combined, occasion the narrative dynamics which trouble philosophical assumptions. Twentieth-century ordinary language philosophy has recurrently taken up the quandary of a "private experience" – can it exist as such without "public" language; if so, is there cognitive access? – as the problem of "other minds." In the words of Sandra Laugier that anticipate my direction: "Here again, Cavell reverses radically the investigation of 'private language.' The problem is not being able to express what I have 'in me,' thinking or feeling something without being able to say it: it is the inverse, not being able to *mean what I say*. It is not thought that is beyond or beneath my speech; it is language that surpasses me. In this sense, I am more 'possessed' by language than I possess it" (*P*, 124).[30]

Chapter 1 argued that Jane Austen's novels respond in advance to the philosophical energies of J. L. Austin's speech act theory. There I built from the suggestion that Austen, as Cavell remarks, is more than just the "namesake" of Austin, but is kindred to him, as much in terms of their shared approach to ritual performativity and irony as in a continually devious way of presenting normative social content (*P*, 124). This chapter stresses instead a Wittgensteinian dimension shared by an Austen novel and the approach offered by ordinary language philosophers, focusing on the narrative status of "other minds" (a picture of experience that gives stress to issues involving communication, pain, and suffering) as a privileged dimension common to *Sense and Sensibility* and some of the passages frequently highlighted by readers of *Philosophical Investigations*. J. Hillis Miller instructively points out that for little apparent reason, Austin chooses anger as his privileged example of the problem of "other minds," whereas Wittgenstein's famous embodiment of the problem is pain.[31]

Jane Austen's own writings at the juncture of nineteenth-century realism and an earlier mode of representation far less concerned to provide consistency and "depth" would lead us to ask: Are her literary characters always structured to think and suffer as people, or even *like* persons?[32] Does our solidarity with these figures occur after a human pattern or on some other order? One of the subtexts of my philosophical interest in *Sense and Sensibility* is that its "early," even "immature" qualities allow readers to discern and address such questions with greater energy than would be possible for encounters within the more cohesive regime of representation at which Austen succeeds in the "later" novels.[33] In *Emma*, for example, leading characters do in fact play at eliciting the contents of other people's minds and at seeing into their hearts, even where Emma ironically has least gotten clear about her own.

> For how can I go so far as to try to use language to get between pain and its expression?
> —Wittgenstein, *Philosophical Investigations* § 245

> "... What are you thinking of? What thinking? What?
> I never know what you are thinking. Think."
> —T. S. Eliot, "A Game of Chess," *The Waste Land*, Part II

Beyond its role in describing the ostensive method of ordinary language philosophy, another reason to invoke pedagogies in this chapter is because it takes something like that dogged, step by step regression to the force and conveyance of mere "stimuli," moving back from the advanced cultural front lines of Raymond Williams's final entries on "C18" and "C19" sensibility (as *Keywords*' indexical manner puts it), to appreciate what is conceptually adventurous in some of the most morally impactful scenes in the novel. I mean the passages where Marianne finally awakens from her dream of Willoughby to see that she's not the only one in pain; or more strangely than that, to realize she's not the only person *susceptible* of having the kind of experience – with the "depth," which also always must be witnessed through vents in a "surface" – that one validates as suffering.

The drawing rooms of Austenworld provide a finely calibrated environment for testing the verbal objective correlatives of sensation that mediate between feeling and expression, experience and art. Austen's social and verbal range is, of course, less manically pleading than *The Waste Land*'s "A Game of Chess." Her sociable prose by comparison to Eliot's is at once more communal and more avowedly prescriptive.[34] "No, no, no, it cannot be […] she cannot feel," Marianne proclaims at one point of Mrs. Jennings, her kind but comfort-oriented host in London (*S&S*, 142). And her pattern of response toward other characters of more established insight and subtlety – in judging Edward Ferrars, for instance, who doesn't read the poet Cowper well aloud, or show a taste for drawing with sufficient ardor, but most of all toward her sister Elinor – is hardly more generous in its fundamentals. From her circular theory of "the business of self-command," that "with strong affections it was impossible, with calm ones it could have no merit" (*S&S*, 76), Marianne draws the following conclusion about the character of Elinor's feelings (though the entire long passage deserves quoting, it covers multiple pages, so I make excerpts):

> "Four months!"—cried Marianne again.—"So calm! so cheerful!—how have you been supported?"
>
> "By feeling that I was doing my duty.—My promise to Lucy, obliged me to be secret. I owed it to her, therefore, to avoid giving any hint of the truth, and I owed it to my family and friends not to create in them a solicitude about me, which it could not be in my power to satisfy."
>
> Marianne seemed much struck.
> [……………………………………]
> "If such is your way of thinking," said Marianne, "if the loss of what is most valued is so easily to be made up by something else, your resolution, your self-command, are, perhaps, a little less to be wondered at.—They are brought more within my comprehension."
>
> "I understand you.—You do not suppose that I have ever felt much. [……………………………] If you can think me capable of ever feeling—surely you may suppose that I have suffered *now*." (*S&S*, 185–186)

Marianne comes off badly in this interchange, though allowed to have her own thoughts in this climactic scene of dialogue, and not simply condemned for her "indulgence" by Austen's censorious narrator. From the point of view of crediting others' sensations of suffering as well as the reality of their complex emotions, her performance, however predictable, is strange.

Rather than just saying Marianne judges Elinor by her own standards of unwittingly conventional behavior (which is true), I place a philosophical weight behind Marianne's speech because of her use of a word like "comprehension." It evokes the framework of rational understanding that is marshaled under Descartes' search for "clear and distinct" ideas, as well as triggering a very different scheme from Kant's philosophy: the Kantian mathematical sublime (say, in taking in a view of the Egyptian pyramids at one glance) confounds the usual joint working of operations he calls apprehension and comprehension. Here, Marianne suggests she has gotten a better hold on Elinor's "way of thinking" by scaling out, bringing her true feelings "more within my comprehension." However, by just adopting a slightly different angle on the word, we see right away that Marianne fails to "comprehend" Elinor – in the sense of including her. The sudden coolness of this shift into a calculating rational tone, for Marianne, is striking. As hypersensitive as she is toward her own plight regarding Willoughby, right at this moment, Marianne's apprehension of reality (her keeping "touch") is distressingly thick. As readers trying not to pass over the scene having only noticed its most brutal ironies and obvious pieties of judgment against Marianne's narcissism, we need to interpret nimbly her pointed and false conclusion regarding Elinor that *she doesn't really* feel, or *couldn't* – based on her sister's way of talking.

It is the narrative tension and tone of the passage, instead of a lone word choice, that must convince us most fully of a dense philosophical texture of interest and complication. Marianne's attitude combines the tone of judging standards quite "ordinary" and habitual to her, with a taste of her permanently alien sort of moral imagination. Marianne can only credit her sister Elinor's inner feelings if she emits signs of her suffering by them. But getting to that situation would already involve, for Elinor and perhaps also from the narrator's point of view, her having not tried enough or having failed in all necessary "exertion" against their expression. The kind of allegedly communicative intimacy in which Marianne does seem to put a great deal of store, found in the meeting of minds that is the Willoughby romance in Volume I, moves in its own circle. This pattern gathers in a mordant illustration, which goes to show that if anything, conformation of exterior signs hints *nothing* may stand good for them independently on the "inside" of his character: "But Marianne abhorred all concealment where no real disgrace could attend unreserve; and to aim at the restraint of sentiments which were not in themselves illaudable, appeared to her not merely an unnecessary effort, but a disgraceful subjection of reason to common-place and mistaken notions. Willoughby thought the same" (*S&S*, 41).

Against the Wollstonecraftian candor in this proclamation of Marianne's "unreserve," free indirect style and the imbalance of the sentences take their effect. There is not much to Willoughby in the apodosis. We cannot even be sure whether he speaks up for himself in that tab onto her sentiments. Marianne, that is – just as voraciously as Descartes, who stared out his window at human beings he managed to doubt could be automata in hats – is located for most of the novel inside a sociable horizon of the solipsistic version of the problem of "other minds." Yet Austen's novelistic voice and form necessarily adopt a different perspective on this problem than Cartesian first philosophy. Especially because of her pioneering development of free indirect style as a means of characterization – a technique that blends third-person narration with the verbal signs and energy of a character (or characters, such as local rumor: what "everybody" in the village supposes, and therefore cannot be determinately traced) – the narrative vantage of an Austen novel on "other minds" begins from the mirror-opposite position from that found in the extra-fictional world.[35] If the characters each *see* the world through their limited perspectives, the definitional mode of narrators like Austen's is to get to *say*: to have the first, final, and conditioning choice of verbal presentation in any work of storytelling in writing.[36] This is the prerogative not only of fictional narrators, but of authors as creative inventors, as Brian Boyd points out in his recent argument against the idea that all fictions have a "Necessary Narrator" independent of the author.[37] While the difficulty and unavailability of knowing another person's inner life structure the skeptical approach to the problem of other minds, I agree with Boyd's contention that our practice of making and modeling inferences about other minds stands on just one plane, the behavioral footing. Whether we are reading a novel or interacting in the world, the challenge of reading other minds involves a practice based on legible but not certain indications: exchanges of cues, the mutual entrainment of thought and feeling, time, and formation of intimacy. Similarly, J. L. Austin demonstrates how many forms of available, ordinary knowing depend on manifest behavior, like being made to feel someone's anger, or know their taste, for which there is no value added by the notion of getting "behind" or "inside" the behavior observed (*PP*, 110). Indeed, Boyd's main contention regarding "the inextricability of Austen's creative decisions as conjoint inventor and narrator of the novel[s]" may be recruited to the project of reading Austen with and as ordinary language philosophy, since what it prizes most about fiction is the idea that "[w]riters want to affect audiences, and they invent the details and the order of their stories to do so."[38]

Nevertheless, within Austen's narrative art there is a premise of the sort of availability that presumes narrative as a form of privileged access, at least where the reader needs to have it toward certain key characters. Narrative theorist Dorrit Cohn has termed this novelistic construction of inner access the principle of "transparent minds."[39] As bodily cues are necessarily damped down in the interactive exchanges with works of fictional writing, we gain the sense of greater access to mind.[40] Above, I say Austen's fiction begins from a mirror-opposite grounds from the encounter with other minds in life beyond the reading of fiction. But that does not mean ontologically different. While Austen's novels *present* and model the challenge of knowing other minds, in our life beyond novel reading we *encounter* its difficulty of reality.

The plot of *Sense and Sensibility* emphasizes two modes of construing the kind of impasse that other minds philosophy poses. At the beginning of Volume II, Austen makes the reader an intensive participant in Elinor's constrained interiority, so that we are sure to judge Marianne's failure to acknowledge her sister's emotional burden. Elinor's burden is just as real, yet handled otherwise than her own.[41] Yet of the dual protagonists, it is rather surprisingly Marianne – as now we are in place to observe – who is first positioned in the questioning subject's vantage on other minds in *Sense and Sensibility*. She assumes the kind of evaluative role that is always filled by a communal "we" in the language-based philosophy of Wittgenstein. She grapples (or fails to wrestle enough) with Elinor as an object of doubt and learning; she enjoys the privilege of unknowing more typical of male figures of sensibility (though not their freedom from consequences). This is a twist on expectation insofar as the reader thinks about the novel's staging of the problem, since Elinor's perspective by contrast weaves the "subjective" nesting, and filters the tone, of almost the entire book. Later, at the start of Volume III, the axis of the novel that turns around the availability and knowledge of inner experience is made to shift forcefully, and almost toward dark comedy, as Marianne is shut off from all internal narrative representation, becoming herself an impassive object. Austen renders her an incapacitated body. This drastic measure in the plot does not simply have to occur in order to stage Willoughby's confession as a mission to Elinor, and subdue Marianne to make her later courtship by Brandon a bit more plausible; it also has a less forced effect that lets us see the unavailability of shared pain for the Dashwood sisters, but in different keys.

Muscling through the plot, and providing an essential – though again, almost raucously imbalanced – thematic parallel, Marianne's illness and "insensible" state at Cleveland should be layered into an account that goes back to Elinor's silent inward suffering from the preceding volume. The novel anticipates other minds philosophy *both* in a richly interior and in a radically, indeed stupefyingly, exterior mode, corresponding to the distinctive manner of proceeding one finds in Wittgenstein. Much as Cavell allows his response to linger on a work "flat, and arbitrary in its progress" in his first reading of *Philosophical Investigations*, Austen's own experiments with the capacities of "flat" and "deep" characterization aren't secured down as values in *Sense and Sensibility*. She is still interested in the investigations afforded by flat (at times, flattened) character: insensible, convalescent, and then precipitously married Marianne. The novel records the strain of this project as it simultaneously does the prep work, through Elinor, for the "full" psychological treatment that characterizes the novels to come. This claim accords with some of the first readers' offhanded comments on *Sense and Sensibility*, such as the one made by Lady Bessborough, that the novel ends "stupidly" because of the precipitate shift in Marianne's character.[42] That the novel seems to break its contract to provide inwardness and depth of character, for the modern reader, is one thing; to its contemporary readership, it also could be felt to violate, or "stupidly" lose interest in, the very conventions to which it has adapted its reader.[43]

"An inner process stands in need of outward criteria," maintains Wittgenstein in *Philosophical Investigations* (§ 580; qtd by Cavell in *Claim*, 6). Here I will quote from just two more, widely separated, paragraphs from the *Philosophical Investigations*. The first establishes Wittgenstein's dialogic approach to the "public" rather than "private" linguistic criterion of pain:[44]

> "'When I say "I am in pain" I am at any rate justified before myself.'—What does that mean? Does it mean: 'If someone else could know what I am calling "pain," he would admit that I was using the word correctly'? (§84)

The second entry tests the adequacy of our thought "pictures" and also plays a role in Wisdom's and Austin's discussion of other minds (see *PP*, 76):

> "Of course, if water boils in a pot, steam comes out of the pot and also pictured steam comes out of the pictured pot. But what if one insisted on saying that there must also be something boiling in the picture of the pot?" (§297).

The second entry is about inferential thinking and associative world making. Cavell responds to this passage in *The Claim of Reason*: "The philosophical task posed by Wittgenstein's parable (again, not notably unlike a literary task) is to describe what is wrong with the assertion that 'something is in the pictured pot' – i.e., to describe the emptiness of the assertion, the momentary madness in the assertion, that is, its failure to amount to an assertion within an insistent sense that it *is* one – without at the same time seeming to deny that something is in the pictured pot" (*Claim*, 338).

Any direct application of this kind of "emptiness" and "momentary madness" to the world of Austen's novels remains, I concede, just a forceful impression.[45] Only the performance of a communicable family likeness would go to "prove" its relevance. Yet this is the inherently open verification procedure, as such, of all language adduced to prove what Cavell calls the existence of the human through a literary text (*Claim*, 465–468). That Austen was capable herself of having, and interested in sharing, such an impression in the philosophical register of her art is evident from an ostentatious joke she makes about an invalid's "sensibility" and representation, through the fears of Mr. Woodhouse in *Emma*. When his judgment is elicited upon Emma's finally completing one of the many fragments of her own artistic work – the full-length portrait of Harriet Smith in Volume I, Chapter 6 – Harriet and Mr. Elton both make it clear that their great approval of the painting shoots over the art object to their interested claims on the person of Emma the artist. But Mr. Woodhouse by contrast disapproves and is utterly object-oriented. Except he is not able to properly play the game "respond aesthetically to a picture." He worries that the pictured version of Harriet is underdressed for the season and that she might catch a cold.[46]

> In what sense are my sensations private?—Well, only I can know whether I am really in pain; another person can only surmise it.—In one way this is wrong, and in another nonsense. If we are using the word "to know" as it is normally used (and how else are we to use it?), then other people very often know when I am in pain.—Yes, but all the same not with the certainty with which I know it myself!—It can't be said of me at all (Except perhaps as a joke) that I *know* I am in pain. What is it supposed to mean—except perhaps that I *am* in pain?
>
> Other people cannot be said to learn of my sensations only from my behavior,—for I cannot be said to learn of them. I *have* them.
> —Wittgenstein, *Philosophical Investigations* § 246

In her essay, "The Imagination Goes Visiting," Hina Nazar presents a conceptual account on behalf of an emotive, not arid, rationality in *Sense and Sensibility*, through Elinor Dashwood's intersubjective and social habits of judgment.[47] As opposed to Marianne's narrow and mostly self-confirming culture of enthusiasms, Elinor finds quite enough time to reflect on and know her own mind, even in the busy company of a sitting room: an argument that Nazar turns (using the writings of Hannah Arendt as a comparison) toward the idea that Austen's female-gendered domestic spaces can function as their own kind of generative public sphere. Still, it is telling that even a perspective on the novel so flexible and acute as this, for lack of all evidence on the other side, must focus entirely on what we might call Elinor's *intake* and *processing* of her environment. I use the wording of information culture reductively, for effect. It should remind us how Elinor does not let herself be found similarly accessible as an object of knowledge or source of information. The taut admission of a telling moment of free indirect speech – "she was stronger alone" – has little to do with Elinor's discipline in keeping the promise extorted from her by the reverse emotional blackmail of Lucy Steele (*S&S*, 101). It is her entire style of knowing. Later on in the plot, her effective conveyance of the offer of the Delaford living from Colonel Brandon to Edward depends, precisely, on a division between her practical mission and her emotions.

That warped version of the novel's major theme of the "promise" bond does, however, provide cover for why Elinor's soul is a locked box for much of the book. Elinor's strength derives distressingly from acts of her self-withholding. The key to our more than satisfactory knowledge of Elinor's mind as readers comes from the "transparent mind" placed before us in narrative discourse, which simply does not obtain at the level where Marianne, or anyone else in the book, lives: their level experiences the opacity, much the same as in the extra-fictional world, of "other minds" philosophical problems.[48] In Wittgenstein's terms, Elinor's and Marianne's inner feelings support a pair of analogies to judging the steam off a pictured pot and what's "beneath" or "inside" it ("something boiling in the picture"). Marianne's example presents the computational adjustment of realizing she boils at low temperatures, up there in sensibility's high altitude. Rather than constrain herself as Elinor does, she manifests her sensibility so earnestly that the inner disposition and the outer behavior are just one and the same. In place of the novel's disclosure of what the reader might wish to infer is "beneath" it all, we receive instead the extended scenes of the radical insensibility of her exposed physical body. Marianne is taken down by a cold showing "a putrid tendency" (*S&S*, 217), knocked out by a fever so as to enable the plot development to be channeled through her older sister in the climactic beginning chapters of Volume III. Marianne's illness is a "natural" recognition that her radical divide between self and other bears a structural relationship to infection. ("Marianne was of course kept in ignorance" [S&S, 218].) Whereas Elinor's case is even more of a puzzle – as if we had to infer the existence of water from a pictured pot that emits *no* steam, apart from the kind of disclosures in free indirect style that don't reach the characters but instead create intimacy in that other intimate public that moves amongst Elinor, the narrator, and the reader. "'I cannot know what is going on in him' is above all a *picture*," writes Wittgenstein in *Philosophical Investigations*: a "picture" of what we never quite adequately, and with no standard of certainty, try to clarify through language regarding our human responsiveness to others' experiences, like pain. A picture that "is the convincing expression of a conviction," but "does not give the reasons for the conviction. *They* are not readily accessible" (*PI*, 190).[49] What kind of unjustifiable and yet still perhaps convincing "picture," then, does Austen's novel have in mind for us to ruminate, if its narrative strategies both preserve this brand of inscrutability and dissolve it (almost from the beginning) into the intimate knowledge only the reader and lead character might share? The novel has a way of taking problems of social and philosophical information gathering seriously, yet not passing them on as a quandary until the very end. Elinor's intensity of feeling is at once totally opaque to every figure in her world, including those we have assumed are closest to her, and the lens we as readers see through into that world.

While she remains conscious, Marianne's challenge opens to one paradigm of canonical Romanticism discussed in my previous chapter, in solipsism: the inability to creditably acknowledge another person's, or other people's, existence as meaningful.[50] Elinor's problem, however, puts us in direct touch with the type of question that Cavell draws from his engagement with Austin and Wittgenstein – but also from *The Winter's Tale* and *King Lear*. What could it mean to be know*able*? What does it take to surrender oneself so as to be available to acknowledgment, love, by others?[51] What are the costs of insisting on one's unknowability? The prospect of failing of the measure of ultimate knowledge is not the most isolated of all imaginable human positions. Even the skeptical tradition's doubts about knowledge miss the mark as a philosophical paradigm for Austen, by presupposing a sovereign individual who does or does not arrive at secure epistemological closure. Any encouragement Austen might give to the reader to fault Marianne decisively for her belated acknowledgment of

Elinor's suffering, in this view, only volunteers skepticism or Romanticism as the novel's false versions of its worst and most interesting problem stationed in limbo in between. It might best be taken as the narrative's way of defensively getting a jump on, and redirecting the reader away from, these hints at a denser way of being stymied and unavailable to life in common. As if she wanted her narrative logic to cover the tracks of this necessarily unresolved philosophical impasse at the heart of Elinor's complex and likeable character, Austen has Marianne lodge her weakest insights against her sister later in the book, and her sharpest ones earlier: "you have made me hate myself for ever.—how barbarous have I been to you!" (*S&S*, 186); "Oh! how easy for those who have no sorrow to talk of exertion! Happy, happy Elinor, *you* cannot have an idea of what I suffer" (*S&S*, 131); "*you*— you who have confidence in no one!" (*S&S*, 120).

Elinor's lack of "confidence" in others is a burden gradually relieved from her by stages in the novel's resolution, once Lucy's extracted promise dissolves its ties: through Elinor's consultations with Brandon over the Delaford living; her open confiding in Marianne at some point (with a few unhealthy details kept back about Willoughby's speech); and ultimately with her joyous reparation of the very pattern of all broken confidence in Edward's proposal. But there remains something true to the end in the idea that Elinor's fate is to be the private sister. So Cavell writes in the "Postscript" to *Contesting Tears*, that Wittgenstein presents two bad pictures or fantasies, the "private realm as one of something like secrecy," the denial of privacy by a "public realm" that operates solely through "a set of conventions" (156).

As the novel's protagonist in terms of affective investment, Elinor is not our heroine structurally. Marianne is. Her criteria of satisfaction and intelligibility, like those of Wittgenstein, have had throughout an exposed and violable, learned, confronted – public – stake. And, similarly to the intellectual drama Cavell rehearses as the stakes of misreading the later Wittgenstein in *Must We Mean What We Say?*, Marianne's unmet challenge at the end of the novel lies in realizing the excessive rigidity in the moral that she just ought to conform to the rules, while absorbing a new, lived knowledge about what kind of social behavior "conforming to the rules" is, for a still vital adult person. What does it mean for Marianne to assume a part so seriously in that game? To learn it would offer at once a more critical and more capacious, "ordinary," form of knowledge than any hard claim to knowledge or any humbling into submission.[52] Hers is the future role as "patroness of a village"; Edward and Elinor, both of them oldest children of a family, will contentedly live under her. By the same logic through which Marianne emerges as the ultimate figure of account, as an individual she no longer makes satisfying sense to modern readers. Her tastes and desires as we have come to know them are suppressed. Marianne no longer is a possessive individual who *knows* or *has* her own character. And if it makes sense to say she *is* that character in Austen's hand, Austen provides no way for the reader to get between the reported development of Marianne's character and any separate truth about her interiority. Even the report of Marianne's inwardness – much less its direct representation – becomes too risky for Austen's narrator to handle. Every film adaptation dresses her experience of love in customary signs of a turn toward pseudo-autonomously realized feeling and choice, and repackages her second attachment to Colonel Brandon at least as symbolically coherent. The cost of this coherence is to become again cliché. In the recent BBC adaptation by Andrew Davies, through some semiludicrous wild horse references and a falconry scene, Brandon tames Marianne by giving her room, by facilitating her reading and practice time at the piano.[53]

But these things are actually more empowering if left visibly coerced, as in the text of *Sense and Sensibility*, rather than finessed plausibly. A final acknowledgment of the other minds paradigm as a sustaining and vexed measure throughout this book can be taken from the very dissolution of Marianne's "I" into a startlingly different logic constitutive instead of the reformed group. It is as if Marianne were a Moses figure who, having wandered out in exile from Norland (No Land), upon arriving safely at Delaford (an allegorical crossing) with her collective band, must relinquish subjectivity if not life itself to its Pisgah view. By analogy to my basic argument here that the most resonant, if anachronistic, philosophical contexts in which to read Austen's novels are not eighteenth-century empiricist contexts, on the last page of *Sense and Sensibility*, Marianne, perhaps as much as Wittgenstein, is not a mouthpiece for asserting bourgeois individualist culture – even though I think it's fair to say we "know" she represents such a figure nevertheless.[54] To fruitful effects, toward which I hope to have gestured, we can go on productively reading Marianne's radically shifted character in terms of its aesthetic, narrative, and social landscapes of implication, but we can appeal no further to *her* for satisfaction or grounds of justification. Here too, though not at all in the same way as Elinor may prove unavailable to others' knowledge, Marianne's situation is ordinary enough for our common experience as readers, and still it is not to be pictured. The dull, weighty domesticity of the image makes it appropriate that representation of Marianne comes to a halt with just the gnomic pot alone, her body and her estate, with all its manifestations of inner motion and expressive escape left to be conjured.

To speak as Cavell does of Wittgenstein in *The Claim of Reason*, what makes the other's experience unreachable is not the immediacy of the *sensing* of their sensations, but the fiction that redoubles and hollows this possessive immediacy. Introducing a loophole in that immanence, and productive of endless cavities into which to fold capitalist desire – is the inevitable projection we tend to make of people and characters alike, of their *having* their own life of sensations, as distinct from *being* them. "If this makes sense at all, it says rather more or rather less than I wished to say," maintains Cavell in a voice it might prove apt to hear as coming from Marianne beyond the last page of the book: "For I wanted to express my uniqueness, and this way of expressing it makes it seem so *trivial*" (*Claim*, 356) – just a grammatical distinction between possessive attributes and predication. Due to the way, analogous to the novel's, I have been arguing, in which he is able to present his writing as an opportunity for working out the dissatisfaction that is internal even to successfully negotiated criteria – to present language's grammatical limits in relation to human experience even where there is nothing else to take over from linguistic practices, or get us "inside" them – a late Wittgensteinian, antirepresentational "picture" of the mind may serve as our best critical guide on how to value the seemingly trivial and frustrating as a positive achievement of reading. It has not only helped me to construct a more rigorous narrative mapping of *Sense and Sensibility*, which does something useful with the inherited pairing that harnesses the title to the main characters, but to develop what is at stake in a timely relinquishment of Marianne within the strange form of life she occupies as a fictional human character. Just where we are apt to judge Austen's reliance on the thinness of conventions to be a sign of her "early" novelistic art losing its touch, becoming on aesthetic terms a dissociative realism, *Sense and Sensibility* shows a philosophical resiliency that may help readers now to reimagine the conditions and limitations of an account of the privacy of experience.[55] Such a critical practice is especially vital to reading Austen's fiction written before her great successes in the novels of interiority.

CHAPTER 4

Pride and Prejudice *and the Comedy of Perfectionism*

> they had wandered about, till she was beyond her own knowledge.
> —*Pride and Prejudice*

> The indulgence shown by the public to *Evelina* which, unpatronized, unaided, and unowned, past through Four Editions in one year, has encouraged its Author to risk this *second* attempt. The animation of success is too universally acknowledged to make the writer of the following sheets dread much censure of temerity; though the precariousness of any power to give pleasure suppresses all vanity of confidence, and sends *Cecilia* into the world with scarce more hope, though far more encouragement, than attended her highly honoured predecessor, *Evelina*.
> —Frances Burney, Original Preface to *Cecilia* (1782)

"Universally Acknowledged"

The topic of this chapter merges the idea of ordinary language philosophy as perfectionist conversation with a Hegelian heading of knowledge as recognition. Cavell, after Austin, recognizes an important "dimension of philosophical analysis" as the criticism of speech in action (*P*, 159). Jane Austen's novels share a set of concerns – in prose formulating and, at times, resisting an apparently compulsory responsiveness to social norms – in common with the impulse to ordinary language philosophy. Austen enjoys an understandable and yet underexplained standing amongst twentieth-century philosophers as a group. An anecdote circulates that when Gilbert Ryle – the British philosopher and author of the essay, "Jane Austen and the Moralists" – was asked if he read novels, he replied (winking at Austen): "Yes, all six, every year."[1] In a section titled "Hegel with Austen" from *The Sublime Object of Ideology* (his first book published in English), Slavoj Zizek maintains: "Aust*e*n, not Aust*i*n: it is Jane Austen who is perhaps the only counterpart to Hegel in literature: *Pride and Prejudice* is the literary

Phenomenology of Spirit; *Mansfield Park* the *Science of Logic* and *Emma* the *Encyclopedia*...No wonder, then, that we find in *Pride and Prejudice* the perfect case of this dialectic of truth arising from misrecognition."²

Conversation, Acknowledgment and the Art of the Sequel

What does the kind of recognition presented by Cavell as acknowledgment look like in the eighteenth-century print public sphere? The traditional marriage plot, which most of Austen's readers still conceive her to have happily undertaken, presses toward the fulfillment of marriage in a conventional church- and state-sponsored illocutionary rite. Yet *Pride and Prejudice* endures so vividly because of its brilliance as a perlocutionary speech act in the round – the text unfolding into an event with unfixed borders. The novel's larger-than-life stature has much to do, of course, with the lively conversation between vivid characters. If the novel was famously judged "rather too light & bright & sparkling" by Austen, that was only as a humble-brag, after she had done it.³

Others may credit the wit of *Pride and Prejudice* at the expense of the dull and silly characters, but the thinking energies of the novel, especially for Cavell, have a more complex resource in the experience of depletion. In that moment I have already brought into evidence repeatedly, Cavell confides that it was the silly, the empty-headed, the worn-out characters and routines that first held his attention and drew him to Austen's fiction (*P*, 126), signaling his own fascination with the exhausted and charged potentialities that Kathleen Stewart tracks in her book *Ordinary Affects*. Writing of such affect, Stewart rewires depletion as sort of modern-day Shelleyan intellectual beauty: "It can take off in flights of fancy or go limp, tired, done for now" (12). But in this same moment that might open up responsiveness in letting the minor characters guide the mood of meaning, Cavell re-inscribes a hierarchical pattern of meaning, one based on the novel's character system of human protagonists and merely contrastive (nearly sub-human) others. Is his perfectionist world, too, filled with just two types of people, characters and caricatures? Only "foils" designed to point out the challenges that major characters face fall, for him, within this scope of the ordinary tied to sagging potentials.

These firmly drawn characterological lines of who is designed for the reader's attention and narrative reward also bear on the social and emotional limits of other, differently mapped, boundaries. Much of my commentary here will be taken up with the force of a handful of resolute passages in *Pride and Prejudice*, moments not only of perlocutionary passion and anger, but scenes that if "disempacted" show Eve Sedgwick's "periperformative" charm of social and linguistic contest. Elizabeth Bennet exercises her affirmative strength in the act of giving her decisive *no* to outright proposals (by Mr. Collins and Mr. Darcy). In Volume III, she even stands up to assert the yet more radical *no way* in response to a threat by Lady Catherine De Bourgh. As a marriage plot, the central narrative problem of *Pride and Prejudice* is how to get the proud yet fundamentally good man Darcy *to propose twice*. This problem requires both emotional sophistication and an ingenuity of device to address. Austen's solution is a great one for this novel and its central character, because that feat is accomplished by *yet another form of no*, one which reopens the possibility of a sustained offer of engagement. The metaconversation about narrative meaning within the novel between Elizabeth and Darcy makes it clear that the puzzle is solved through the surprise event of Lady Catherine De Bourgh's showdown visit to Longbourn and the unintended consequences of her failed speech act to warn – and then threaten – Elizabeth (*P&P*, 261).

Pride and Prejudice comprises an ongoing event of uncontainable circulation and exchange, beginning with the linguistic emotional entailments that we can think of as perlocutionary exchanges in their own right, rather than merely adjuncts to the marriage plot. Since its publication in 1813, the novel has been an endless occasion of, and for, what Cavell styles "performative and passionate" utterance. As Jane Austen's second published novel, *Pride and Prejudice* represents her first and overwhelmingly successful endeavor in a sort of large-scale fictional project that is also a microdynamic of everyday conversation: the art of the "sequel."[4] Like her closest model, Fanny Burney, in the followup to publishing *Evelina*, what Austen fundamentally risks with *Pride and Prejudice* is a second attempt on the power to please an audience – to give a pleasure otherwise "unpatronized, unaided, and unowned" in the legitimation network of the largely anonymous modern print public. (Burney's own standing as a modern professional author is complicated by her accession to the role of second keeper of robes to Queen Charlotte in 1786.[5] Austen's relation to a modern, mass anonymous readership is richly counterpointed by her practice of voiced reading to her family.) Like Burney, too, Austen, in *Pride and Prejudice*, balances a good hope based on the evidence of acknowledgment of her previous work, and another, self-authorizing, source of conviction that is bold enough to formulate "universal acknowledgment" right from the start and in her own terms.[6]

Burney's Original Preface to *Cecilia* shares language of an "animation of success" too "universally acknowledged" by the public with *Evelina*, to allow for the author to express further honest fears in sending forth her second book. Surely this preface offers a model for the uber-famous opening of *Pride and Prejudice* – "It is a truth universally acknowledged…." Is the trace well enough known?⁷ This link deserves foregrounding, since its inclusion alongside the other Fanny Burney source text commonly adduced as a key paratext to *Pride and Prejudice* adds an area of resonant concern, in the confidence and "precariousness" together, of the "power to give pleasure." Darcy is at his most winning and his pride is most humbled (and most gratified) when he declares to Elizabeth (in Vol. III, Ch. 16) that she is an individual "worthy of being pleased":

> ["]What do I not owe you! You taught me a lesson, hard indeed at first, but most advantageous. By you, I was properly humbled. I came to you without a doubt of my reception. You shewed me how insufficient were all my pretensions to please a woman worthy of being pleased." (*P&P*, 252)

The mark of Darcy's adult education, making him now capable to sustain Elizabeth as partner well after he has already successfully asked, is his recognition of "doubt of [his] reception" by her, and development of an appropriately placed doubt toward the affection of any person "worthy of being pleased."⁸ Despite the fairytale ending, one imagines the success of a partnership based on carrying forward the affection and regard of this real doubt and its trial and satisfaction. If even Elizabeth Bennet and Mr. Darcy resist closure in the name of pleasure, the idea of a perfectionist form of relation based on conversation indeed has a hope.

Most of the attention to the Austen-Burney connection to date has been directed not to perlocutionary pleasures and risks of reception and exchange, but to abstractions. It is a critical commonplace to recall that Austen takes her famous published title from the recurrent use of these terms in the last chapter of Burney's *Cecilia*, after she had scuttled the draft title "First Impressions." *Cecilia* in fact numbers among the three books (*Cecilia, Camilla*, or *Belinda*) celebrated by name by the narrator in *Northanger Abbey* for their display of "the greatest powers of mind," "the most thorough knowledge of human nature, the happiest delineation of its varieties, the liveliest affusions [sic] of wit and humour," all in the "best chosen language" (*NA*, 23). Austen commentary long ago noticed the source of the novel's ultimate title in the triple, all caps, repetition of "PRIDE and PREJUDICE" in the final chapter (Vol. V, Ch. 10):

"The whole of this unfortunate business," said Dr. Lyster, "has been the result of PRIDE and PREJUDICE. Your uncle, the Dean, began it, by his arbitrary will, as if an ordinance of his own could arrest the course of nature! and as if *he* had the power to keep alive, by the loan of a name, a family in the male branch already extinct. Your father, Mr. Mortimer, continued it with the same self-partiality, preferring the wretched gratification of tickling his ear with a favourite sound, to the solid happiness of his son with a rich and deserving wife. Yet this, however, remember; if to PRIDE and PREJUDICE you owe your miseries, so wonderfully is good and evil balanced, that PRIDE and PREJUDICE you will also owe their termination; for all that I could say to Mr. Delvile either of reasoning or entreaty,—and I said all I could suggest, and I suggested all that a man need wish to hear,— was totally thrown away, till I pointed out to him his own disgrace, in having a *daughter-in-law* immured in these mean lodgings!

"Thus, my dear young lady, the terror which drove you to this house, and the sufferings which have confined you in it, will prove, in the event, the source of your future peace: for when all my best rhetoric failed to melt Mr. Delvile, I instantly brought him to terms by coupling his name with my pawnbroker's! And he could not with more disgust hear his own son called Mr. Beverley, than think of his son's wife when he hears of the *Three Blue Balls*! Thus the same passions, taking but different directions, *do* mischief and *cure* it alternately.["]⁹

Its exclusive appeal to institutions of male pride set aside, the novelistic philosophy behind this passage (boldfaced by typographical speech as the "MORAL") is that "the same passions, taking but different directions, *do* mischief and *cure* it alternately." This philosophy is on display not only in *Pride and Prejudice*, but across Austen's finished books. In several of her novels, the mixed motives of human self-interest both create problems and dissolve them for the central characters, so long as the main characters keep faith in riding them out. Think of the impacts of Lucy Steele's actions in the course of *Sense and Sensibility*.

Thus Darcy says to Elizabeth, as they alternately flirt and upbraid each other about their happy ending being sprung "from a breach of promise":

> You need not distress yourself. The moral will be perfectly fair. Lady Catherine's unjustifiable endeavors to separate us, where the means of removing all my doubts. I am not indebted for my present happiness to your eager desire of expressing your gratitude. I was not in a humour to wait for any opening of your's [sic]. My aunt's intelligence had given me hope, and I was determined at once to know every thing. (*P&P*, 261)

Mr. Darcy credits his aunt Lady Catherine's imperious meddling from her visit to Longbourn for the happy resolution of his improbable repeated courtship of Elizabeth (that second proposal of an exceedingly proud man – a real problem). Elizabeth replies with the same mix of irony: "Lady Catherine has been of infinite use, which ought to make her happy, for she loves to be of use" (*P&P*, 261). Lady Catherine's overbearing mission serves Darcy as means to gain knowledge of Elizabeth's continued, irrepressible feeling, acknowledged by her denial of Lady Catherine's bullying demands and by her non-denial of Darcy's meaningful connection to her. She gets to say "No" most adamantly as a precondition to renewing an affirmative conversation and future with Darcy.

If not a full doctrine of eighteenth-century theodicy, there is moral psychology and counsel in this moderated version of the medieval Fortune's Wheel of hydraulic plot turns based on the consistent application of character. Burney's "wise physician" Dr. Lyster accounts through one and the same motive for the main characters' "miseries" and their "termination." John Wiltshire offers astute positive remarks on Dr. Lyster's character in his discussion of "Medicine, Illness, and Disease" in Austen.[10] My approach is not homeopathic; it follows a comparison between Burney's Dr. Lyster and the character of *Mittler* (or Mediator) in Johann Wolfgang von Goethe's nearly contemporaneous experimental marriage novel, *Elective Affinities* (1809).[11] Introduced in Chapter 2 of Goethe's novel as an "eccentric guest" (32) to the estate of the Baron Eduard and his wife Charlotte – having made his fortune and bought his own farm not by means of his profession of law, but because he had "won a big prize in a lottery" (33) – thereafter Mittler quixotically devotes himself from "fixed habit and inclination, never to enter any house where there was not a dispute to settle or difficulties to put right. People superstitious about the significance of names say it was the name Mittler, which means mediator, which compelled him to adopt this oddest of vocations" (33–34). The many delicious ironies of Mittler's allegorical name and random calling – his comically absent force of character, and his superfluous, inept, and ultimately lethal functions throughout the novel – include the fact that Mittler talks a parson to death standing up with the length of his peroration at the birth of Charlotte's child (222).

Two passages nicely exhibit the "philosophy" Mittler has to purvey. The first comes from just after his introduction and the passage on his name and vocation I have quoted:

> "Either you don't know me," he cried, "or don't understand me, or this is some malicious joke. Is there any contention here? Is assistance needed here? Do you think I exist to hand out advice? That's the most preposterous trade a man can ply. Let each advise himself and do what he can't help doing. If it turns out well, let him congratulate himself on his wisdom and good

fortune; if it goes ill, he can always turn to me. He who wants to rid himself of an evil always knows what he wants, but he who wants something better than he already has is night-blind—yes, you can laugh!— he's playing blind man's buff. He will catch something, perhaps—but what? Do what you wish: it's all one! Invite your friends, don't invite them: it's all one! I've seen the most judicious plans miscarry, the absurdist succeed. Don't go racking your brains over it, and if it goes ill, in one way or another, still don't go racking 'em. Just send for me and I'll come to your assistance. Till then, your servant!" (34)

And this one from Goethe's narrator at the start of Chapter 18:

> We have already got to know Mittler and something of the curious way in which that gentleman occupied his time, so it will come as no surprise to learn that, as soon as he had heard of the misfortune which had struck these friends of his, he felt a strong inclination to prove his friendship and demonstrate his dexterity in this instance too, notwithstanding none of the parties involved has as yet called upon him for assistance. Yet he felt it would be advisable to delay a while first; he knew only too well that when cultured people get themselves into a moral muddle they are more difficult to assist out of it than are uncultured people in a like predicament. For that reason he left them for a time on their own resources. But at last he could endure it no longer and, since he had already got on to Eduard's track during his period of inactivity, he now hurried to seek him out. (143)

The last pronouncement of this "obstinate gentleman" (290) offers a recalibration of the Ten Commandments, and in particular "Thou shalt not commit adultery," over which Mittler pronounces (of the commandment if not the act) "'How coarse, how improper!'," just as Ottilie enters. Her "face and aspect transformed" upon hearing Mittler's speech urging the positive reverence for the marriage bond ("rejoice thereat and be glad as at the happiness of a bright day" [291]), Ottilie begins dying straight off and is dead within three pages. In his early essay on *Elective Affinities*, Walter Benjamin in effect offers a darker Cavellian reading by arguing that Goethe "did not want, like Mittler, to justify marriage, but rather to show the forces released by its disintegration." On these terms marriage is not justified by law, but solely by "continuance in love."[12]

As the means to keep the lovers apart for five volumes and then at last conveniently die, *Camilla*'s Dr. Marchmont served as an aversive and comedic model for Austen of the kind of narrative not to follow in her art.[13] Yet, in line with Burney's use as well as the long-established Classic theory of comedy, Austen's six finished novels do repeatedly employ figures of ordinary selfishness as blocking and relieving agents.[14] Her theory and practice of marriage comedy persistently straddle the line between

(Classic) external oppositions and the new (Hegelian or Cavellian) logics of internal transformation. (Both, I will argue in this chapter, submit to the understanding of capitalism's relations to social life and desire that fundamentally inform and might derange comedic plotting.) Throughout Austen's six finished novels, bad characters and their exploitative acts systematically make trouble and persist, to the point of springing a final twist to enable the protagonists' marriage. General Tilney's and John Thorpe's greed in miscommunications over Catherine Morland's prospects for inherited wealth exemplify the hydraulics of "good and evil balanced" by an acquisitive plot in *Northanger Abbey*. Lucy Steele's tactics suddenly enable not only the marriage, but also the long-suppressed open communications regarding the past, between Edward Ferrars and Elinor Dashwood in *Sense and Sensibility*. (The latter is as ever a problematically pivotal book: Is Edward's sincere but inwardly meaningless engagement to Lucy an external or internal problem?) In *Pride and Prejudice*, not only Lady Catherine, but Lydia and Wickham, facilitate learning and the ultimate disclosure between Darcy and Elizabeth. The imbroglios of the Crawfords remove the enticements and obstacles alike from *Mansfield Park*'s crowded marriage field. There is the relationship of Frank Churchill and Jane Fairfax in *Emma*. In *Persuasion*, Louisa Musgrove and Captain Benwick are more forgivingly positioned, perhaps, but their relation is the most brusque of all these pairings, since it is the result of the new emotional tendrils that grow from a purely physical accident (Louisa's fall from the high, hard steps of the Cobb).

The hardheaded "philosophy" that waits for deliverance from the dual, and thereby unwittingly helpful, application of interfering characters' ruling traits is not short on validating examples in Austen's fiction. But rather than fail by the standard of mechanical plotting, the failure of this moral to provide richness of outlook away from the theater is measured internally within the conduct of *Pride and Prejudice*. Leaving Dr. Lyster's plotworks as a gratuitous bonus of relief and satisfaction, Austen commits to internal transformation in the terms of what Cavell calls "an improvisation of meaning, out of the present."[15] What Austen brings first, and most visibly from the perspective of the history of the novel, to Cavell's moral perfectionism and comedy of remarriage, is a stylistic rejection of all prior "philosophical" novels' rigid political and rhetorical address. She recognizes style as language in action.[16]

Lacking the philosophical improvisation Austen develops, Burney's rigid Johnsonian sentence style informs a hydraulic moral psychology of "good and evil balanced." In his study *The Prose Style of Samuel Johnson*, a book about style as meaning, W. K. Wimsatt notices at the forefront of Johnson's "logic" of style "its settled pattern and answering of part to part." Wimsatt excoriates its effects on Burney, writing in his final chapter on the "Effects of Johnson's Style": "And all the world knows that by far the most deplorable effect of Johnson's style was upon that young member of the Streatham set, Fanny Burney. The change from the maiden graces of *Evelina* to the mature pretensions of *Cecilia, Camilla, The Wanderer*, and the *Memoirs of Dr. Burney* has become through Macaulay a notorious event in the history of the English language."[17] The rigid, teetering and sawing, motion in which Dr. Lyster sees the occasion for moral meaning lacks the power to please, however much it might lend stability and timely relief to plot. It lacks, on both ends, the precarity and confidence in pleasing, out of which Burney and Austen as authors, and Darcy and Elizabeth as characters, make livable openings. Even before the Cavellian theme of knowing versus acknowledgment has gotten traction in a reading of *Pride and Prejudice*, the multiple frame allusions to Burney pose the idea of acknowledgment in the mass public reception of domestic fiction. The "unpatronized" status of *Evelina* marks the modern character of the literary marketplace. In its acknowledgment, "the precariousness of any power to give pleasure" makes vulnerability over into an improvisation of confidence.

Comedy and "Vulnerable Conformity"

Beyond the passivity and patience required of the heroine in the Dr. Lyster/Dr. Marchmont morality of fiction, this theory also is unacceptable because it depends on a settled identification with a virtuous character in preformulated possession of concurred-upon virtuous traits. Such pictures of long-suffering perfection make Austen feel sick and wicked.[18] Instead, an exuberant if acerbic comic style distributes authority across the many variegated and moving surfaces of the writing. To accept this reminder from one of Austen's most famous letters is to ask again the question – long under investigation with regard to free indirect style – of whether Austen's comedic style performs a socially regulative function. Most strikingly, William Hazlitt makes just this argument concerning all comedy in the expanded print-public sphere. His 1813 essay "On Modern Comedy" decries the public taste's "insipid sameness" and laments the decline of wit to "wisdom at second hand" recirculated in a "nation of authors and readers." Hazlitt, by contrast, affirms the vital role served by the peculiarity of prejudice over the "common stock," the "general form."

With restive acumen, his outburst against formal generality and equivalency uses Locke's famous metaphor both to target the idea of a cultural blank slate, and to receive disruptive embodiment: "We all follow the same profession, which is criticism, each individual is every thing but himself, not one but all mankind's epitome, and the gradations of vice and virtue, of sense and folly, of refinement and grossness of character, seem lost in a kind of intellectual *hermaphroditism*. But on this *tabula rasa*, according to your Correspondent, the most lively and sparkling hues of comedy may be laid."[19] Hazlitt decries the generic standardization of comedy together with the *sensus communis* of judgments of taste (that judgments not be partisan and individual "but all mankind's epitome"). He renders this modernizing homogeneity as the image of sexual being. An implicitly anti-capitalist theory of comedy, Hazlitt's "intellectual" hermaphrodite image means, I think, to suggest androgyny, but instead is explicitly and "excessively" sexed; it marks the "insipid sameness" of modern comedic subjectivities with a kind of intersex excess.

It is hard to say exactly why Hazlitt chooses the archaic *hermaphroditism* as a figure for modern homogeneity and leveling. But whatever response one might offer, on similar terms, the gendered markings of stylistic identity and the most radical scenarios of disembodied narrative voice witness each other in the case of Austen. "What we took for Style," writes D. A. Miller in *Jane Austen, or The Secret of Style*, "everyone else took for Woman" (2). Miller's stylish account of style as a "fantasy of unconditioned being," the impersonal mode of style itself, registers the writerly rejection of the Comte de Buffon's well-known personification of style as the man himself. This rendition of style may also be linked to the psychoanalytic discourse on comedy. What aligns Austen's irony with that particularly English, decorously sangfroid brand of stoic comedy? On this matter, Freud (preceding pun intended) shares insight. His paper on "Humour" (1927) distinguishes from jokes the "grandeur and elevation" of humor, which Freud classes the "triumph of narcissism." Through humor, Freud claims, the ego is able to assert its invulnerability, its refusal to be impacted by traumatic distress. Through the successful display of humor, "the ego refuses to be distressed by the provocations of reality, to let itself be compelled to suffer."[20] If Freud finds links to psychopathology in this positive achievement to refuse compulsory distress, there are also ties to the practice of fiction, in "the rejection of the claims of reality and the putting through of the pleasure principle."[21]

Freudian humor erects a masterful defensive structure in advance of experience. It blocks the affiliation of comedy with the shaping linguistic, psychic, and societal forces of vulnerability and wounding – and from possible forms of repair. *Pride and Prejudice*, however, moves from that masterful opening stance of "omnipotent" defensive humor to comedic forms of mutuality, vulnerability, and participation. The opening passage of *Pride and Prejudice* does indeed seek and supply the counterfactual well-being that Freud ascribes to humor at the end of his essay in paraphrasing its effect – "Look! Here is the world, which seems so dangerous!"[22] One can see why Austen assumes this position just here. Especially on the heels of the perilous exile of the Dashwood sisters in Austen's only preceding published book, *Sense and Sensibility*, Freud's exclamation of the ego's refusal to admit suffering seems an apt rendering of the magical function of *Pride and Prejudice*'s famous beginning, the "truth universally acknowledged" that a rich, single man *must* "be in want of a wife" (*P&P*, 3). Miller's reading of this moment as the pinnacle of impersonal Austen Style shows attunement to the triumph of an unperturbed comic irony over the social forces that determine the many vulnerabilities of (especially female and queer) bodies. His reading aligns with yet also queerly neutralizes Freud's with a move of exemption, since Austen "enact[s] a fantasy of divine authority" according to Miller: "Of that godlike authority which we think of as the default mode of narration in the traditional novel, Jane Austen may well be the *only* English example" (*Secret of Style*, 31; original emphasis). The registers of "fantasy" and empirical "example" abut in Miller's reading of Austen's stylistic performance of authority. Yet nevertheless they are celebrated as impossible and non-reproductive; they cannot be broadened. If Austen's writing "may well be the *only*" example of "divine authority" in English (we note the theological language and its queer overlay), readers abound who deny that the very passages Miller cites are impersonal at all, thus leaving the divine realm empty of its god figure (but not of its queer style).[23] It should not surprise us that the analysis of Austen's prose involves such theological language. The ironies of Miller's impervious, impersonal vantage refuse the demand of exigent social desires but approach the stylothete in a whirl of scholastic turns as a theological enigma: "We last left the secret of Style at this: that the stylothete harbors a hidden wish—of whose impossible fulfillment she has made an absolute refusal—to renounce the renunciation that makes her one" (*Secret of Style*, 59).

Terms of knowledge and autonomy assume an ironic stress in the novel right from the start. Austen's most famous sentence is charismatically counterfactual. Its triumphant economy is distilled from a psychology of need and the social doxa of gossip. This social voice is represented in the humor of the following sentence of "ironic or comic addendum."[24] Austen's maxim-maker narrator turns screwball in the novel's second sentence, informing the reader of the genre of enjoyment she has fortuitously entered: "However little known the feelings or view of such a man may be on his first entering into a neighborhood, this truth is fixed in the minds of the surrounding families, that he is considered as the rightful property of some one or other of their daughters" (P&P, 3). The cadence of this sentence certainly resembles a joke. Still, a serious philosophy of the communal subject is in play and at stake in this purportedly godlike instance of impersonal narration. Miller's dazzlingly intricate, dense, and quick reading of the stylist's "hidden wish ... to renounce the renunciation *that makes her one*" (one: that is, embodied, human, and finite; one of us, one of them; but with more than a hint of the One God), through its virtuosic action as prose, may help to revisit how other dynamics assume partly revisable forms within the novel's structured political and gender fields that claim pleasure by renouncing renunciation.

The breathtaking implications of Miller's sharp turns in such small space help mark, for instance, the precarity and exchangeability of "*some one or other* of their daughters" (as an individual disempowerment that also conveys vibrancy and health in the collective) in terms of the false autonomy and illusory free choice of the "*single*" young man of means (an empowerment that may at the same time suggest he is outnumbered). The joke Austen delivers stems not from the notion that the neighborhood hasn't yet had a chance to get to know the newly arrived single man's "feelings or views" (though that is true). It moots the notion that the initial feelings or views of the powerful young man carry weight, even to himself and his intentions. With the density of a neighborhood, it mitigates the assumption that it is the prerogative of the single man – if he is like Bingley – not yet to know his mind in all the "ductility of his temper" (P&P, 12), or that – like Darcy – he knows his mind as quite firmly composed of a different brand of truth. Then so brilliantly, with a success prefigured here due to the compressed, light, energy of this prose if by nothing else, neither of these kinds of resistance based on the privilege of male cluelessness is allowed to matter. Comfortably established young men like Bingley and even Darcy – in whom is concentrated the material wealth and lawful power of Austen's world – nonetheless are not consulted regarding their views on the universally acknowledged truth, at least in the domain of this fiction. They instead become the unknowing subjects of the novel's program of knowledge, naïve players in a field tilted toward Mrs. Bennet's zany, but relentlessly serious, version of social placement as acknowledgment. The gendered power dynamics of male "possession" in persons and property are compelled to serve in a plot in which marriage both attests to a remaining, fundamental lack or "want" in the man of wealth and taste on the make, and also completes the entitled logic of male acquisition. But in the same concentrated gesture, the young man himself is reconfigured as "the rightful property" of the neighborhood he enters so unwittingly, the ultimate property himself of what he would presume to possess (not even to possess Netherfield, so much as Bingley). And with indefinitely loose specification of who gets control over him: "some one or other" of the local daughters.[25] In this regard, the opening of the novel presents more radical opportunities and energies for thinking through an alternative theory of collective subjectivity and its risks, the chorus of a plural life whose plots and energies are not explored but recaptured within bourgeois individuality by the big-ticket Elizabeth-Darcy pairing.

Those invulnerable high spirits would be adjusted downward in the less famous, contraveningly dour, statement in the expository opening chapter of *Mansfield Park*: "But there certainly are not so many men of large fortune in the world, as there are pretty women to deserve them" (*MP*, 3). It is as if the ebulliently counterfactual comedian had read nothing but Malthus for research in the interval between these two novels. As an expression of prose style, the scarcity of the marriage economy in the opening of *Mansfield Park* anticipates Thomas Carlyle's notorious characterization of political economy as "the dismal science."[26] In hindsight, the stylistic economy and energy of *Pride and Prejudice* might be seen as blithely pre-Malthusian in tenor: a world where "want" is an accelerant not a check, and is governed by the sanguinity of Mrs. Bennet, if not guided by Godwinian "benevolence." Within Austen's lifetime we see a shift from moral philosophy to political economy as the dominant framework of social understanding.[27] This shift places philosophical pressure on expenditures of stylistic energy.[28] The ebullient style of *Pride and Prejudice* may be analyzed, too, in terms of the stylistic energies demanded and expressed by the affective structure of capital. Hardly "dismal" in worldview, this capitalist nexus above all values energy, confidence, and the expansive cultural metabolism of speculative elation. Yet as opposed to the idealizing capitalist function of Mr. Parker in Austen's *Sanditon*, it is the gendered location of *Pride and Prejudice*'s overriding libidinal investment that finds bourgeois ebullience in the substance of women's embodied risk. Even if we don't identify with her, we are all in on a bet for Mrs. Bennet, and the chorus of interests she represents.

The "universal" truth posited in the novel's famous opening sentence – both proposed and taken for given – quickly relocates from a plane of abstract truth to the consensus projection of the urgent material desires from the local women such as Mrs. Long and (of course) Mrs. Bennet.[29] As we enter the novel through the perspective of their desires and occupations, our sense of the opening of *Pride and Prejudice* has to depart from D. A. Miller's association of Austen's narrator with a "fantasy of unconditioned being." "[S]he always writes like a real god, without anthropomorphism" (*Secret of Style*, 32). In this context it is interesting to note that Miller does not explicitly analyze the opening sentence of *Pride and Prejudice* anywhere in *Jane Austen, or the Secret of Style*. He instead refers to it in passing during a striking discussion of the "almost infantile desire" for closeness in interpretive close reading – a state of near but impossible identification he links to the practice of free indirect style as a form of "close writing" (60): "(In an essay once, citing the first sentence of *Pride and Prejudice*, I left out the quotation marks)" (62).

The lively, vast body of critical commentary on *Pride and Prejudice* has not yet taken measure of the Cavellian philosophical dialogue sustained from the novel's famous opening sentence onward. To be sure, this linguistic environment of desperation, insistence, and rumor is not that of "acknowledgment" as it is intensively developed and contested in *The Claim of Reason* and *Must We Mean What We Say?* The "must" is socially dense and normative in its pressure. Shoshana Felman, in a different context, remarks on "what Hegel hailed in womanhood and woman: 'the eternal irony of the community.'"[30] Chapter 1 commented on the identifiably English comic style that jointly characterizes Jane Austen and J. L. Austin. With the opening of *Pride and Prejudice* – a relief from the preoccupation with suffering that guided the reading of *Sense and Sensibility* in Chapter 3 – I venture further to analyze the workings of comedic styling. As counterfactual as this narrative logic about gender, desire, and possessive power may be in historical terms for the turn of the nineteenth century, the opening paragraphs of *Pride and Prejudice* announce transformation.[31] Cavell's one sustained comment on Jane Austen in *Cities of Words* (2004) makes this point in terms of an "element of change or interruption breaking into th[e] world" on which the narrative opens:

> A familiar form of narrative opens by laying out a time and place in which a character or characters in whom we are to take an interest are described as carrying on a way of life, and then the plot proper, as it were, begins with an element of change or interruption breaking into this world. An obvious instance is Jane Austen's *Pride and Prejudice*, where the interruption of the

ordinary days of this little world is the unheralded appearance in it of a pair of rich and handsome bachelors. Sometimes the narrative opens precisely with the element of change, noted as such, hence implying the ordinary state of affairs that has been interrupted. Austen's *Emma* is an example (Emma's lifelong companion and mother figure has married and left Emma and her father to shift, with their servants, for themselves.)[32]

Acknowledgment provides not only the boisterous main theme of the novel's marriage-obsessed female chorus, but is the bass note of the book's comedic transformation of a mutual acknowledgment through education.

Quiet moments in the novel attest to Cavell's perfectionist disposition. As in Vol. III, Ch. 17, when Elizabeth and Mr. Darcy have just returned from their walk to Oakmount:

> "My dear Lizzy, where can you have been walking to?" was a question which Elizabeth received from Jane as soon as she entered their room, and from all the others when they sat down to table. She had only to say in reply, that they had wandered about, till she was beyond her own knowledge. She coloured as she spoke; but neither that, nor anything else, awakened a suspicion of truth.
>
> The evening passed quietly; unmarked by any thing extraordinary. The acknowledged lovers talked and laughed, the unacknowledged were silent. Darcy was not of a disposition in which happiness overflows in mirth; and Elizabeth, agitated and confused, rather *knew* that she was happy, than *felt* herself to be so[.] (*P&P*, 254)

The new couple's meandering walk beyond pre-established bounds (in a landscape around Longbourn more familiar to Elizabeth than to Darcy, they nonetheless mutually "had wandered about…"), leads on to Elizabeth's singular expression of discovery beyond her knowing ("till she was beyond her own knowledge"). More than the length added to the usual walk is encompassed here. "[W]here can you have been walking to?," Jane asks on their return, as if naively requesting information about the mise en scène from which Cavell reads the coordinates of remarriage comedy – famously in the final scene of the Frank Capra film *It Happened One Night* (1934). More is at stake in the reply Elizabeth offers to Jane than an accounting of time spent and ground covered.[33] Knowledge and certainty are not enough to provide the philosophical space for the recognition of Elizabeth and Darcy as a couple. This walk beyond the regular boundaries of place and emotional topography, alike, importantly counters the final spatial centering of the novel and the couple at Pemberley.

Cavell develops his approach to the comedy of remarriage in the Introduction to *Pursuits of Happiness*, "Words for a Conversation," by placing it in contrast to Northrop Frye's understanding of classical "Old" and "New" Comedy. Here the shape taken by the theory of comedy, again, turns on different notions of causes of opposition to the comedic pair. Is the opposition to be formalized as "external" (generational, social), or is the challenge fundamentally at issue to the couple in marriage one of internal recognitions and transformations? Cavell understands his moral perfectionist approach to comedy in terms of literary forms that go back to the history of Ancient Greek "Old Comedy" and its highly scripted performative roles:

> What I am calling the comedy of remarriage is, because of its emphasis on the heroine, more intimately related to Old Comedy than to New, but it is significantly different from either, indeed it seems to transgress an important feature of both, in casting as its heroine a married woman; and the drive of its plot is not to get the central pair together, but to get them *back* together, together *again*. (*Pursuits*, 1–2)

Philosophy the Day After Tomorrow enlarges upon the meaning of these conditions: "comedy works out a festive abatement of skepticism, call it an affirmation of existence" (*P*, 26). "The genre it projected, on my interpretation, can be said to require the creation of a new woman, or the new creation of a woman, something I describe as a new creation of the human" (*P*, 16). Cavell's longtime interlocutor William Rothman summarizes this philosophical genre theory of comedy: "In comedies of remarriage a woman and a man pursue happiness not by overcoming societal obstacles to their marriage, as in classical comedies, but by overcoming obstacles that are between and within themselves, obstacles they cannot overcome without achieving a radically changed perspective."[34]

Along with this Emersonian perfectionist narrative, though, I find in Cavell's interpretation of "the creation of a new woman, or the new creation of a woman, … a new creation of the human" an unspoken adjustment by means of gender to the displaced identities of twentieth- and twenty-first century capitalist labor. As topics of emergent interest in what we may loosely call the later works of Cavell, in books from *Contesting Tears* (1996) to *Philosophy the Day after Tomorrow* (2005), the gendered dynamics of affective labor (economics) and damaged consent (politics and ethics) reconstitute the field of a perfectionism jolted from post-war boom to post-industrial – even "post-work" – vulnerability.

The very phrase "day after tomorrow" carries a different overtone when gender is made central to the perspective. Nietzsche thinks of the philosopher, pointedly, as "the man of tomorrow and the day after tomorrow" (*P*, 4). *Übermorgen* extends the will and promise of the (definitively male) *Übermensch* in time – beyond the mere optimism or wistfulness of tomorrow to the more robust, but unmasterable, "day after tomorrow" that inspires Cavell in his improvisational dimension of a perfectionism without end. For a woman relegated to the inherited idiom and social representation of her sexuality, at once desired and feared by men, tomorrow and "the day after tomorrow" can mean something quite different. The difference is especially heard with the word for tomorrow in Nietzsche's German, *Morgen*, or morning. Michael Wood writes the following about consequences for actress Rita Hayworth of her career-defining bombshell role in *Gilda* (1946) in *America in the Movies* (1975) – a study that bears comparison to Cavell's *The World Viewed*: "Hayworth herself, a few years later, worrying about her impending marriage to Aly Khan, put the blame on Mame, or at least on Virginia Van Upp, who wrote *Gilda*. 'It's your fault ... because you wrote Gilda. And every man I've known has fallen in love with Gilda and wakened with me.' Gilda was glamour that couldn't be sustained in the morning light—not morning after morning in any case."[35]

The "Little Deaths" of Everyday Life

With the decision to write on Jane Austen's novels in his 2005 book *Philosophy the Day after Tomorrow*, Cavell revisits a remarkably fruitful and provocative engagement with British Romantic Literature that had begun in his work decades before in a different key. As he sets forth in his Preface to the Beckman Lectures of 1983, assembled as roughly the first half of *In Quest of the Ordinary* (1988), the most well-known, powerful trajectory Cavell offered to British Romantic studies up to that date can be outlined as "the theme of a romantic call for the unity of philosophy and poetry precipitated in the aftermath of Kant's revolution in philosophy" (*In Quest*, xi).[36] It is this formulation of the topic of Cavell and Romanticism with which readers are most likely familiar.[37] In two chapters from *In Quest of the Ordinary* (framed as a chiasmus in titling, "Emerson, Coleridge, Kant (Terms as Conditions)" and "Texts of Recovery (Coleridge, Wordsworth, Heidegger...)" [*In Quest*, 27–75]), Cavell presents astonishing variations on the post-Kantian situation he finds in reading the most famous products of Wordsworth's and Coleridge's poetry and poetic theory. Cavell charts "the Kantian bargain with skepticism (buying back knowledge of objects by giving up things in themselves) and Romanticism's bargain with the Kantian project (buying back the thing in itself by taking on animism)" (*In Quest*, 65). In this account, British Romanticism represents both a schematic and an encounter with the words of texts and their specific weights. As I note recurrently in this book, Romanticism serves pivotally for Cavell as the name for an indefinite, ongoing moment in the history of philosophical life. It marks the moment "too late for religion, because nothing is any longer common to our gods, and too soon for philosophy, because human beings are not interested in their new lives" (*In Quest*, 63).

In the place where the novel typically intervenes in the historical scheme of modernity as its dominant representational form, Cavell's account articulates instead a lacuna opening to the untimeliness of moral perfectionism. Generically, this opening and its moment refer to no dominant genre such as the novel, but to the everyday-life genre, if it is anything so formalized, of conversation. *Philosophy the Day After Tomorrow* turns from poetic election toward a contrasting starting place in sociality, communication and inclusion. Yet this sociable change brings with it the tension that these are not only generic conventions in "polite" Austenian literature, but forms of life held at risk of merely compulsory participation, coercive and endangering to those who must find their place and voice within them. Convention is the bane of the Emersonian tradition and of Cavell's writing going back to *The Senses of Walden*. In his later works, such as *Contesting Tears* and *A Pitch of Philosophy*, Cavell associates the female subject with the constraints of a philosophical dilemma in which all consensual possibilities are structured by compromise and damage, and "perfectionist" aspirations are felt primarily through a condition – after trauma, before conviction – he names "convalescence." "[T]he necessity for meaning something (for, I suppose, saying anything) is encountered as the reason for mournfulness" (*P*, 116). This condition reflects what Miranda Fricker has called epistemic injustice, the violence done specifically to someone as a knower.[38]

If the Wordsworth-Coleridge frame of Romanticism from *In Quest of the Ordinary* asks after the costs that animism poses to respectable shared knowledge, at stake in his reading of Austen is a philosophical melodrama just under the novels' "renowned surface of containment" (*P*, 124). How should one respond to Cavell's paradoxical elaboration of an "unconstrained" interest in Austen's characteristic style and social world, if that interest is determined by "containment" (*P*, 126)? Cavell in his comments on Austen follows out a different economy of utterance than in his hyperbolic investment in Romantic poetry. In discussing her novelistic treatment of a dynamic of "vulnerable conformity," Cavell sees the pedagogical lesson in Austen as "to exemplify instances in which the soul can learn not to be crushed by compromise." Cavell's romantic reading of Jane Austen contributes to an account of global modernity in which structural crisis is understood as the elicitation of damaged consent to an intolerable world. This account highlights the "vulnerable conformity" and "damaged consent" experienced by subordinated middle-class women in a privileged society. In scholarly responses to Cavell and Romanticism, this framework makes a new contribution to the existing arguments on Romantic poetry's figurations of world-making or -losing. The drama of Austen's heroines and readers is that "one senses one's consent to be elicited" by the intolerable existing world (*P*, 123).[39]

Cavell's prompting to take up Jane Austen's fiction – ostensibly in order to introduce a more "sensible" temper into the reckoning of Romanticism (and to encounters between literature and philosophy) than his prior engagement with poets had done – can make him sound unexpectedly Habermasian at times, as if he held a firm allegiance to the public values of responsibility, sharing, and communication. A further comparison may be drawn on these terms between aspects of Cavell's Emersonian moral perfectionism and the more common and widely distributed social phenomena of eighteenth- and nineteenth-century discourses of self-improvement. Yet in the global chronology encompassing his own historical life, these material and ethical dimensions also, pervasively and implicitly, reflect the shifting affective terrain of American perfectionism's economic landscape from post-war boom to the precarity of what recent commentators have taken to calling the "vulnerability" economy. The element of what Cavell elsewhere calls the female voice in philosophy functions as a means to process a drastic alteration that has occurred in the material base of the American dream in the late twentieth and twenty-first centuries. Here the biggest name for the antithesis of renewal – the name for endlessly compulsory, illusory renewal – is capitalism. To the extent that "America" has served Cavell as the name of a project of (aversive, self-critical) hope and renewal, the recognition of the "cruel optimism" that structures this liberatory narrative registers in his later books through a shifted gender modeling of the philosophical subject. Distress, damaged and coercive consent, and a mood of crepuscular dawning-or-setting hope he calls "convalescence" are the structural coordinates of "late" Cavellian affect. This shift of coordinates in gender, mood, and the material and affective determinants of Cavell's philosophical project carries a specific dimension of risk.

Cavell's sensitivity to the dynamics of "vulnerable conformity" in Austen's novels registers how allegiance to be comprehensible to the group runs the risk of turning out infelicitously at every turn. In contrast to the inspiration or madness of much romantic poetic discourse, Austen's novels for Cavell in fact instance the conditions of human separation. His readings of Austen show conditions of "intellectual solitude" as much as they celebrate and rehearse modes of social inclusion and remarriage. Their purchase on a novelistic ordinary world makes no simple counter to the romantic extraordinary, if "at any moment the extraordinary might invade the commonplace and either wreck it or clothe it with some surprising glory."[40] Cavell understands the everyday as both the site of estranged powers and the legacy of extraordinary rupture and change. This understanding authorizes a strategy for interpreting the Austenian novel alongside the philosophical occasions (such as solipsism and the "animist" nature lyric) in Romantic poetry. Developed from J. L. Austin's formal taxonomies and dictionary word lists, and then escaping these methods, Cavell's important chapter "Performative and Passionate Utterance" in *Philosophy the Day after Tomorrow* strikingly argues how Jane Austen's novels emerge so as to voice "the rights of desire" and the "imperative of expression" (*P*, 185, 188), in opposition to the institutional realm of social "responsibilities of implication" (*P*, 185). *Cavell's Jane Austen is unlawful.*

As fundamentally different a philosopher and film theorist as Gilles Deleuze converges with Cavell in stressing the relation of expressive conditions and media history within the territory of speech acts. The confluence is seen especially in the media transition from silent to talking cinema in the period just before that of the films Cavell associates with remarriage. The end of the silent film era meant the collapse of its division between "visible image" and "readable speech," according to Deleuze. "But when speech makes itself heard, it is as if it makes something new visible."[41] The modern medium of film thus lets us "see" something that is not only visual, but relational.[42] Deleuze then moves closer yet to Cavell's range of interests: "An actress like Katharine Hepburn reveals her mastery in the sociability stakes through the speed of her retorts, the way that she disorients her partner and ties him in a knot, the indifference to contents, the variety of reversal of perspectives through which she passes. Cukor, McCarey and Hawks make conversation, the craziness of conversation, the essence of American comedy" (*Cinema 2*, 232). Unsurprisingly (because this is Deleuze), and yet forcefully (because it shatters the continuity of conversational marriage), the Deleuzian version of screwball comedy advances a theory of conversation as determining of social relations and even of "feeling" and "love." But the relations are schizophrenic and dissociative; they enact non-communication:

> The less of a pre-existing social structure there is, the better is revealed, not a silent natural life, but pure forms of sociability necessarily passing through *conversation*. And conversation is undoubtedly inseparable from structures, places, and functions, from interests and motives, from actions

and reactions which are external to it. But it also possesses the power of artificially subordinating all these determinations, of making them a stake, or rather of making them the variables of an interaction which corresponds to it. Interests, feeling or love no longer determine conversation, they themselves depend on the division of stimulation in conversation, the latter determining relations of force and structurations which are particular to it. This is why there is always something mad, schizophrenic, in a conversation taken for itself (with bar conversations, lovers' conversations, money conversations, or small talk as its essence). Psychiatrists have studied the conversation of schizophrenics, with its mannerisms, its interactional bringing closer and putting at a distance, but all conversation is schizophrenic, conversation is a model of schizophrenia, not the other way around. Berthet rightly says: "Seeing conversation as the whole of what comes to be said, what polycephalic, and almost half-mad, subject is to be imagined to utter it?" It would be wrong to consider conversation in terms of partners who are already joined or linked. Even in this case, the specificity of conversation lies in its redistributing the stakes, and its initiation of interactions between supposedly dispersed and independent people who pass through the scene by chance: so that conversation is a contracted rumour, and rumour an expanded conversation, both of which reveal the autonomy of communication or circulation. (*Cinema 2*, 230)

Conversation is imagined here as the "autonomy" of "circulation" prior to relationship, even prior to the intimacy with oneself. Not solitude and solipsism, but a "polycephalic," riotous multiplicity images madness here. In Deleuze's equation ("conversation is a contracted rumour, and rumour an expanded conversation"), the autonomy of capitalist commodity form circulates across scales to fulfill its own logic, rather than for the individual expressive subject, or the "partners who are already joined or linked." Deleuze brings this "half-mad" model of conversation into critical media representation.[43]

The comparison to Deleuze's schizophrenic theory of early film conversation is crucial for me because conversation serves as the genre of the novelistic ordinary – perhaps the only means by which the conscripted ordinary is made livable for late capitalist subjects. For Cavell in the eponymous essay of *Philosophy the Day After Tomorrow*, conversations represent "moral encounter," "one soul's examination of another, and of itself," as embodied by the film couples played by "Katharine Hepburn with Cary Grant, of Hepburn with Spencer Tracy, of Clark Gable with Claudette Colbert, or Barbara Stanwyck with Henry Fonda." The conversational routines between these characters develop the possibilities of remarriage as a privileged form of relationship, though they touch upon such interpersonal dynamics as "contemptuousness, inattentiveness, brutality, coldness, cowardice, vanity, thoughtlessness, unimaginativeness, heartlessness, deviousness, vengefulness" (*P*, 121). "The education of the pair by each other" is a process not so much structured by the novel, for Cavell, as transversed by the philosophical genre of conversation (*P*, 122). Indeed, Austen's philosophical couples lead perfectionist moral and erotic lives, not through plots and in the novels' strictly narrative dynamics, but in conversing. How are we to understand these improvised, everyday conversations as sustaining of mutual education, if they in fact express not sincere voices seeking and improvising terms of equality, but the generically equalizing conditions of capital, half-mindlessly ever-renewed?

Perfectionism/Perfectibility

By contrast to Deleuzian schizophrenic theory, restorative readings of conversation in comedy show how the multiplicities of knowledge are not dissociative but intelligent conduct. The felicities of Jane Austen's comedy offer a compelling illustration of Gilbert Ryle's distinction between knowing *how* and knowing *that* in *The Concept of Mind*. According to Ryle's argument, the inability to recognize "[t]he clown's trippings and tumblings" as "the workings of his mind" – to account for the mental interwrought with the physical, the body in cognition – should be traced back to "Descartes' Myth."[44] For Ryle, that myth locates the foundations of philosophy solely in introspection and an "occulted" scene of cognition.[45] This category mistake, for Ryle, lays much of the foundation of modern skepticism and is the key philosophical instantiation of the problem of other minds. In the most rigid and perplexed of "other minds" philosophizing, a metaphysical quest launches from Adam Smith's essentially physiological concession on the first page of *A Theory of Moral Sentiments* that we cannot directly experience what another is feeling, sense another's sensation, suffer another's pain – a prior and enabling condition being the limitation of our own bodies.[46] Nevertheless, Adam Smith's paradoxically enabling concession serves an epistemological and ontological point of fixation for philosophers. In Ryle's account, the move attributed to Descartes leads to more than the notorious picture of the thinking part as the ghost in the machine. It yields a theory of mind in which "minds are not merely ghosts harnessed to machines, they are themselves just spectral machines" (*CM*, 21). Against this, in a fruitful reading of Ryle's essay "Jane Austen and the Moralists" (1966), Alice Crary points to the unfolding of Austen's vocabularies of cognition through the novelist's multilevel rendering of human emotional capacities, showing "that Austen's moral vocabulary reflects a conception of human cognitive capacities and capacities for feeling as essentially tied together."[47]

Responsiveness is a key term for this imbrication of thought and feeling. How far can a human response go? Crary describes a "central motif of Cavellian moral perfectionism" as an attuned and adaptive process in which "the idea that particular modes of affective response are necessary for moral understanding and that it is inevitably possible that new modes of response will bring fresh moral insights within reach – and will in this sense further 'perfect' us." Crary claims that this perfectionist idea of response-ability "becomes available to us when we develop our conception of language to make room for Cavell's passionate utterances."[48] Ryle's argument in "Jane Austen and the Moralists," according to Crary, is "that Jane Austen's conception of human understanding leaves room for the possibility of forms of instruction that persuade in that they engage our feelings and that contribute directly to understanding in so far as they do so. Further, he attempts to show that the moral thought her novels contain is tied to various elements of their narrative form—to ways in which they elicit emotional responses from us specifically as novels."[49] Such language of response-ability and conversation on the one hand travels with the radical projects of Romantic-era utopian perfectibility; on the other, it attests to the modest claim that dimensions of emotional and affective response are fundamental to the engaged unfolding of cognitive capacities.

Cavell's "Emersonian" perfectionism thus carries on dialogue with traditions of *both* top-to-bottom transformational radical thought, and with New Critical pedagogical convictions (some might say bromides) about the irreducibility of literature to information. Moral perfectionism converses with the works of Erasmus Darwin, Godwin, Wollstonecraft, and Percy Shelley – and with *The Well-Wrought Urn*. In Ryle's day, and again in ours, philosophy is still finding ways to say for itself what Cleanth Brooks said for verbal art (specifically the lyric poem) in 1949: that literary form does not exclude ideas, but does include attitudes. Was it news to J. L. Austin that "the 'tone' of an utterance gets stuck to the utterance," Cavell wonders (*P*, 163)? (No. Austin is "calling attention to the obviousness of the fact" as he refreshes it [*P*, 163].) As we see in his discussion of Derrida's very partial critique of Austin in *Limited Inc*, Cavell knows very well that both the style and the tonal conduct of intellectual exchange matter a great deal to Austin's sense of what counts as philosophical interest – even if, with regard to the illocution-perlocution distinction, *How to*

Do Things with Words spares little time for perlocutionary passion within its organizational framework.[50]

How far, again, can the activity of human response go? On what arc of intelligibility, or idea of philosophical history? Cavell's version of Emersonian "moral perfectionism" has never explicitly laid out or paid homage to the trajectory, tensions, and implications of perfectibility as a concept found in European philosophy and literature of the late Enlightenment. The entry in the wonderful recent English edition of the *Dictionary of Untranslatables* charts "multiple refractions" of perfectibility (*perfectibilité*, in French; *Perfektibilität*, or *Vervollkommenheit*, in German) after the point when Jean-Jacques Rousseau first introduced the term in 1755. "Initially, perfectibility appears as a 'faculty of self-improvement'." The term is a neologism in Rousseau's *Discourse on the Origin of Inequality*. It describes the very idea of educability both as an inner horizon and as a social or species-level process. Perfectibility represents "a kind of metafaculty on which the development of all other faculties depends."[51] The key passage, with my own insertions from the Pléiade in French, reads as follows:

> Nature commands every animal, and the beast obeys. Man feels the same impetus, but he realizes that he is free to acquiesce or resist; and it is above all in the consciousness of this freedom that the spirituality of his own soul is shown. For physics explains in some way the mechanism of the senses and the formation of ideas; but in the power of willing, or rather of choosing, and in the sentiment of this power are found only purely spiritual acts about which the laws of mechanics explain nothing.
>
> But if the difficulties surrounding all these questions should leave some room for dispute on this difference between man and animal, there is another very specific quality that distinguishes them and about which there can be no dispute [*il ne peut y avoir de contestation*; Pléiade III 142]: the faculty of self-perfection [*c'est la faculté de se perfectionner*],[52] a faculty which, with the aid of circumstances, successively develops [*développe successivement*] all the others, and resides among us as much in the species as in the individual. By contrast an animal is at the end of a few months what it will be all its life; and its species is at the end of a thousand years what it was the first year of that thousand. Why is man alone subject to becoming imbecile? Is it not that he thereby returns to his primitive state; and that— while the beast, which has acquired nothing and which has, moreover, nothing to lose, always retains its instinct—man, losing again by old age or other accidents all that his *perfectibility* had made him acquire [*tout ce que sa perfectibilité lui avoit fait acquerir*], thus falls back lower than the beast itself? It would be sad for us to be forced to agree that this distinctive and almost unlimited faculty is the

source of all man's misfortunes; that it is this faculty which, by dint of time, draws him out of that original condition in which he would pass tranquil and innocent days; that it is this faculty which, bringing to flower over the centuries his enlightenment and his errors, his vices and his virtues, in the long run makes him the tyrant of himself and of nature."[53]

French allows closer ties between "self-perfection" and development or progress than does English. Yet *The Dictionary of Untranslatables* entry makes clear that we should understand perfectibility as opposed to progress and improvement (French *perfectionnement*). Drawing us from "tranquil and innocent days," the condition of perfectibility is not a vector but a bifold susceptibility. In Rousseauian thinking, perfectibility is inseparable from degradation. And perfectibility "in the long run" produces a tyrant of humanity. Rousseau posits the historical logic in which, through the faculty of self-development, the human animal becomes "tyrant of himself and of nature." Through this absolute break, from its origin perfectibility is beyond nature, in opposition to the nineteenth-century proto-and post-Darwinian understanding of perfectibility and degradation in languages drawn from the evolutionary natural sciences.

The human capacity for perfectibility is "almost unlimited," according to Rousseau. Yet limits to the concept register internally to its grammar, not merely as an ultimate verge. For the materialist Helvétius, writing *De l'homme* in 1758, "the reactive faculty of self-improvement becomes basically the passive faculty of 'being improved'," resulting in the conception of the human mind as "*susceptible* of perfectibility." The German translation by Moses Mendelssohn does not choose *Perfektibilität* but rather *Vermögen* (ability). In a letter Mendelssohn stresses the even more theological terms *Bemühung, Bestreben* (effort and aspiration). "[I]f perfectibility thus becomes the mute impulse that leads humans to perfection, it is still a task, a vocation (*Beruf*)" – as Bertrand Binoche summarizes the German tradition. German idealist and religious thought was uncomfortable with French materialism in the latter half of the eighteenth century. Hence there is European dispute, contestation, about whether perfectibility is a passive and reactive, is actively willed, or a spontaneous tendency. (Here the *Dictionary* cites Isaac Iselin's effort at resolution: *der Trieb zur Vollkomenheit*: impulse, drive to perfection). Anxiety over this issue in the philosophy of history leads to an insidious German stadial history that tells a story of the movement from Oriental sensibility to Mediterranean imagination to Nordic reason (770). Hegel finally challenged the concept of perfectibility on the grounds of its indeterminacy, as "something just as deprived of determination as change in general," change without purpose or goal (*ohne Zweck und Ziel*).

An English translation of *perfectibilité* came in 1767. The *Dictionary of Untranslatables* entry states that "Scottish thinkers clearly avoided it" due to their empiricist commitment to "inductive superimposition." By contrast to Scottish intellectuals, however, the "English Protestant dissidents" (Price, Priestley, and Godwin are named) affirm that "human progress is the immanent work of society as opposed to government" (771). The endpoint of this view is the ultimate withering away of government. As in the German tradition, the self-realizing faculty involves "a duty of which one must become aware" (771). At stake is the status of the human as both rational animal and autonomous moral being. For Godwin at least, the horizon was not "collective resurrection" but "absolutely secular perfectibility." Godwin's rational anarchism expects of all individual subjects of the human community that "when they are fully grown-up, they have to govern themselves, without any coercion being required." Yet the Scottish Enlightenment aversion to perfectibility and avoidance of its use did not result in contesting traditions in Britain, but the entire absorption and loss of philosophical perfectionism/-ability in the consuming idea of progress. There is a constant tendency for perfectionism to be "supplanted by progress" (771). As readers can trace through the polemic in various editions of Malthus's *Essay on the Principle of Population*, perfectibility is "set aside in the name of Progress" very rapidly in the early nineteenth century, "as a kind of useless and even embarrassing scaffolding. Thus perfectibility was not a preliminary version of progress, but on the contrary what had to be concealed in order to be able to conceive progress in its entirely diverse modalities depending on the context" (771). "Perfectibility" is pushed aside and concealed on two flanks: by the action of its opponents (such as Hegel) in Europe who find its terms too indeterminate to serve philosophy ("something just as deprived of determination as change in general"), and by a Scottish Enlightenment historiography which reacts to the germ of perfectibility-thought as extravagant in its base claims – an embarrassment and scandal to the homogeneous and reputable conditions of progress.

On the basis of the "sentiment of being" adduced in her work, Lionel Trilling makes the argument in *Sincerity and Authenticity* that Jane Austen shows an affinity with the thought of Rousseau. The key value they share promotes honor as a mode of life, although, Trilling argues, Austen's critique of the modern consciousness is dialectical and not categorical everywhere but in *Mansfield Park* – and therefore critically distinct from Rousseau's.[54] Austen signals a topical awareness of Rousseau in *Pride and Prejudice* through Mr. Darcy's sneering comment to Sir William Lucas about the savagery of dancing, in Vol. I, Ch. 6: "What a charming amusement for the young people this is, Mr. Darcy!— There is nothing like dancing after all.— I consider it as one of the first refinements of polished societies." "Certainly, Sir,— and it has the advantage also of being in vogue amongst the less polished societies of the world.— Every savage can dance" (*P&P*, 18). Does such a social rhythm of participation express of the impulse to art and culture, or is it "savage," as Darcy thinks? For Rousseau it is neither alone. Dancing provides the occasion for the display distinctions of beauty that at once formalize the social contract and shape social hierarchy by modeling structures of inequality and vice. Dancing enacts a primal scene of individuation-in-publicity. This dancing scene appears in his *Second Discourse*: "As they gather [...] they dance and sing around a tree. At first the dancer and the dance are indistinguishable, but there comes a moment when the dancers glimpse themselves as individuals among other individuals. 'Each began to look at the others and to want to be looked at himself, and public esteem had a value. The one who sang or danced the best, the most beautiful, the strongest, the most clever, or the most eloquent became the most highly considered—and this, then, was the first step toward inequality and vice'."[55] The passage in Rousseau bears a conclusion particularly engaging to read against Jane Austen: "As soon as men began to appreciate one another, and the idea of consideration was formed in their minds, each one claimed a right to it, and it was no longer possible to be disrespectful toward anyone with impunity. From this came the first duties of civility, even among savage; and from this any voluntary wrong became an outrage, because along with the harm that resulted from the injury, the offended man saw in it contempt for his person which was often more unbearable than the harm itself."[56]

Rousseau's source text and its intertext with Austen show why D. W. Harding's thesis on regulated hatred is so appropriate: "Thus, everyone punishing the contempt shown him by another in a manner proportionate to the importance he accorded himself, vengeances become terrible, and men bloodthirsty and cruel."[57]

Moral Perfectionism & Godwinian Perfectibility

A virtue of the new formalist criticisms of all stripes is not to separate concerns of style from social location. In a recent interview, the poet-critic Jeff Dolven speaks of a "[p]art of stylistic knowledge—and knowledge is barely the word for it—[a]s the sense that, when you encounter a text, you recognize where it comes from, when it comes from, where you are. [...] Styles of grief, or styles in nature, or styles of madness. God's style.

Each limit is different, but all make us hesitant to use the word. Of course, everything has a style, doesn't it? That's just to say that it has a place and a time and gives itself away."[58] What impresses me about this comment is the style with which it recognizes history, whether social or psychic. The resistance of style to the transportability and transparency of forthright statement – and what Dolven suggestively casts "stylistic knowledge" – bears at the same time the writing's conditioned signature of marked time and place. One must first have this vulner*ability*, have allowed oneself to be impressed by a time and place, to have a style. What style formalizes and expresses is not even so much choice, as that prior receptivity. (Cavell: "I must let it make an impression upon me.") It is style, too, rather than a more official dimension of knowledge production and distribution, which imparts a peculiarly Freudian-Cavellian insight about what the act of utterance in an expressive community truly means: to "give itself," and give oneself, "away." In a 1950 *TLS* article reviewing *The Concept of Mind*, Austin activates a similar insight, in praising Ryle not only for his intellectual shrewdness at identifying worthwhile philosophical problems and offering good ideas, but for a "manner of writing" that is "racy, untechnical and idiosyncratic." Austin concludes that piece by evincing flair of his own and by honoring Ryle's tripping clown as a figure of his colleague's style: "The jokes of a clown, says the professor, *are* the workings of his mind; and certainly his own wisecracks and epigrams (though far from clowning) go to bear out his theory in his own case. *Le style, c'est Ryle.*"[59]

If Fanny Burney's allegedly rigid prose and teeter-tottering moral plotlines are a close model from which Austen distinguishes her fiction in what I think of as Cavellian terms, Cavell's own relation to the rigid rationality of Godwinian utopian perfectibility offers a parallel, a mode of distance that is also an intimacy. With *Philosophy the Day after Tomorrow*, Cavell's list of perfectionist writers includes Jane Austen but does not include Wollstonecraft or Godwin. How should British Romanticists feel about this: puzzled, defensive, even aggrieved? Are we already complicit in knowing why? For all *Pride and Prejudice*'s apparent ideological conservatism, its wish-fulfilling success, Austen makes a Wollstonecraftian point about the deformation of proper ladies – the deformation of women *into* ladies – by the attentions of men, through the unlikely means of Caroline Bingley and Louisa Hurst: "Their powers of conversation were considerable. They could describe an entertainment with accuracy, relate an anecdote with humour, and laugh at their acquaintance with spirit. But when the gentlemen entered,…" (*P&P*, 39). But is it only Cavell's mid-century sense of the High Romantic canon, drawn from Abrams and Frye, that leads to the omission of Godwin's political philosophy and novels? Or does the lack of interest speak to Cavell's broader lack of interest in expanding his reach into British Romantic-era philosophy? Here the signal move Cavell makes, like that of Lacoue-Labarthe and Nancy in *The Literary Absolute*, is to "examine the inauguration of the *theoretical* project in literature. As the inauguration, in other words, of a project whose place we know only too well, almost [and now over] two hundred years later": a configuration of literature formed in response to the triple threat of "social and moral crisis of a bourgeoisie, with new-found access to culture," "the political crisis of the French Revolution," and to "Kantian Critique."[60] The German Romantic "literary absolute," as a powerful heuristic model emerging in scholarship at nearly the same time as Cavell's concern with British and European Romanticism, merges critical philosophy, aesthetic criticism, and poetics. The book was published in French in 1978 and translated into English in 1988, dates which track with *The Claim of Reason* and *In Quest of the Ordinary*.

Cavell in his vocation as a teacher and lifelong learner tests out philosophical meanings autobiographically through the responsive body. The intellectual arc of enlightenment "perfectibility" theory fuses French atheist materialist thought (Condorcet, Helvétius, d'Holbach, La Mettrie), and an English Dissenting tradition from which Godwin adapts "secularising Dissenting arguments for the sanctity of private judgment [while] generalising their application to every mode of human activity."[61] Scientific theories in which meliorism is an adaptive feature of human bodies sit excitingly but awkwardly alongside Godwin's commitment to "rational anarchism." For Godwin, the embrace of "anarchy" signals not a decentralized overthrow of the institutions of state power, but inner harmonizing or attunement with the compulsion of truth – a conviction in the path of egalitarian justice that will make law needless. The reach of reason will expand, once known. But the mechanisms of change never *perform* this conviction convincingly in Godwin's writing.

Nor – certainly from the point of view of style or ordinary language – does the prose of Godwin's treatises and novels. If it indeed mattered to Cavell, Godwin's brand of rigid rational utopianism that makes "libels against the body" finally weighs decisively against Godwin's perfectionist philosophical thought as it is understood in *The Claim of Reason* (471).[62] Even Godwin's own biographer and editor admits: "While his style is clear and eloquent, it can be a little ponderous at times and he did not always know when to stop."[63] Godwin comes across as a prim builder of systems as opposed to the "ruggedness" and "zaniness" of Emerson and the film characters Cavell explores (*Conditions*, 101). Where Godwin *is* zany, his fanaticism voices an excess of rationalist optimism that denies human finitude.[64] A "stiffening of moral" without the tonic of "social satire" sets Godwin apart from the continental philosophes he might overwise resemble.[65] Underlying Godwin's political philosophy is a fantasy of rational discourse endowed with benign powers of monstrous omnipotence. When he turns to writing a more affectively saturated, psychological kind of domestic novel in the wake of the sudden death of Mary Wollstonecraft, Godwin's later novels including *St Leon* and *Fleetwood* confirm this relation – now played out in sentimental registers – between phantasmatic knowledge and a "soul-blind" drive toward destructive control.[66] Tellingly, Wordsworth narrates his rejection of Godwinism in *The Prelude* as an abstractedly self-blinded and unconversant space "Where passions had the privilege to work, / And never hear the sound of their own names—" (1805 *Prelude*, 10.812–813). In an appendix to the 1798 edition of *Political Justice*, Godwin presents a teleology by which even the motions of the blood eventually submit to willful control. He audaciously holds that human "perfectibility" (not Cavell's moral perfectionism) involves a movement from the domain of autonomous body systems into voluntary domains, leading individuals not only to regulate but to "despise the mere animal function."[67]

The same appendix ("Of Health, and the Prolongation of Human Life") begins by citing Ben Franklin on the conjecture that "mind one day will become omnipotent over matter." Godwin presses Franklin's sanguine conjecture on "human invention," "machines," and "labor" to lay speculative claim to "the power of intellect…over all other matter…[hence] why not over the matter of our own bodies?" The body, to Godwin, is simply matter "we seem always to carry about with us."[68] In the face of a Blakean celebration of vital embodiment that Cavell calls a "brave acceptance of the sufficiency of human finitude," few of the philosophical productions of British Romanticism sustain commensurate conviction of situated interest.[69] Even Cavell's proposed and unwritten "proper dissertation" on the "concept of human action" references a Romantic-era topic (William Hazlitt wrote his first book on *The Principle of Human Action*) only to swerve away (*Claim*, xv). That dissertation was jolted from of its course with Austin's visit to Harvard in 1955 and to Berkeley in 1958–1959.

By comparison to the punctual, immediate, and institutional character of speech acts in Austinian performatives, Cavell's decision not to write the dissertation on the concept of human action can be understood as a recognition that as it stands, the act as such is an inadequate category through which to articulate the range of human participation in meaning. One strand of Romanticism – for instance, Coleridge's assertion that the positings of imagination and faith themselves are primal acts – is liable to seek in forms of action decisive and absolute redress for the predicaments of skepticism.[70] Cavell's dimension of the ordinary, by contrast, argues that "the act" must always be re-inaugurated, improvised over and over, and is never concluded. Similarly, Cavell's commitment to the undervalued Austinian category of perlocution (rather than Austin's officially privileged illocution), attends to the "endless passionate exchanges" that unfold in speech acts.

In contrast to Blake's resolute vision of embodied spirit and spiritual embodiment, no philosophical productions of the British Romantic era bear up to Cavell's admiration of Emerson for the ability to shake and chagrin official discourse, to rouse philosophical thinking by means of the very force of linguistic responsiveness the latter has disowned. Still it is helpful – it could prove important – to be explicit about why Godwin's writing in particular does not figure in Cavell's recounting of the relationship between philosophy and literature. If Lacoue-Labarthe and Nancy's "literary absolute" and Cavell's approach both convey the mutual exposure of philosophy and literature in interrelations at once limitless, fraught, and fragmentary, Godwin's professional writing career enacts a kind of bad seriality in its transition from rational political philosophy to affective prose fiction (in the wake of Wollstonecraft's death, as well as the domestic crackdown on the British public sphere in the 1790s). Whether understood as a biographical, historical, generic, or political process of transfer, the chronology attests to a simplified version of what it means for philosophy to place its project into literature's hands. To put this another way: How does Godwin's thinking inherit and know itself?

Yet Godwin's is a painfully comic exclusion from the discursive community of Emersonian moral perfectionism, because as a novelist, Godwin's plots *do* often take up the very problems of domestic knowing and acknowledgment that so interest Cavell. The historical novel *St. Leon* (1799) takes as its main theme the tensions between vulnerable human finitude and a fantasy of omnipotence. *Fleetwood* (1805), even more plausibly a "Cavellian" work, contains a plot line of unmotivated sexual jealousy, denial, and (ultimately) penance that anticipates Cavell's celebrated reading in *Disowning Knowledge* (1987) of Shakespeare's *The Winter's Tale*. Godwin's controversial attempt to represent the co-existence of rationality and precarious dispossession by passion, in his *Memoirs* of Mary Wollstonecraft, shade into his fictions. The character of Mary (Macneil)

Fleetwood is typically seen as a displaced version of Mary Wollstonecraft and of her tragic female protagonists. The editors of the Broadview edition of *Fleetwood* write that in the novel "Godwin extends [the critique mounted in his *Memoirs*] to the general place of women in society. Indeed *Fleetwood* is in many ways a continuation of Wollstonecraft's goal of exposing the exploitation of women in her unfinished novel *The Wrongs of Woman; Or, Maria* (1798). In effect, Fleetwood rewrites "that novel from the unsettling perspective of the male perpetrator's mind rather than that of the female victim."[71]

The contact between Romantic studies and Cavell deepens what it means to restrict the course of even progressive literary sympathy to its reality in a "male perpetrator's mind." Similarly, one of the most important scenes of Cavell's "performative and passionate utterance" in the novel takes place not between Mary Macneil and Fleetwood, but between Fleetwood and the Macneil father in a context of homosocial male bonds and transactional conversation (no less, "on the banks of Windermere").[72] In negotiating his daughter, Macneil considers marriage something in between "a logical experiment" and "the deepest game that can be played in this sublunary scene," a risk especially fraught in light of Fleetwood's angry temper.[73] Fleetwood, like Godwin, has established himself as an outspoken critic of marriage. Macneil has been repeatedly trying the argument in the abstract that Fleetwood should marry, but is brought up short at the question, "Will you give me one of your daughters?," at which point the conversation becomes a muddle of both illocutionary and perlocutionary unhappinesses. The two men confirm a marriage contract in a tone at once mincingly respectful and destructive to common humanity:

> My friend [Macneil] paused. "A question like this compels one to be serious indeed.—But——you have no grave meaning in proposing the interrogatory?"
>
> "I cannot tell. Your arguments have made me think: I do not say they have converted me. Macneil, I do not wish to trifle with you: if my question touches you too nearly, I dispense you from a reply."
>
> "No; the question has been asked, and it shall be answered. Only, as I by no means wish to restrain you, by treating your question as a proposal, so I must request you in return to consider my answer, as belonging merely to an abstract illustration, a logical experiment to try to the soundness of my recommendation. I should be as much to blame in violating the modesty and maiden dignity of my children, as in imposing fetters of any sort on the freedom of your deliberations."
>
> "Agreed! Nothing can be more reasonable." (*Fleetwood*, 257)

A transactional conversation thus framed imparts a foreboding yet comic rigidity to the novel's ultimate mood of tragic self-recrimination. Godwin's psychological point of view (as the subtitle of *Fleetwood: The New Man of Feeling* shows at a glance) remains circumscribed by the fictionalized psyches of men, going back to the icons of sensibility in Henry Mackenzie and Rousseau. Much as in *The Winter's Tale* (with *Othello* the other comparison looming), the reality of female subjectivity is acknowledged as actual only in the event of a metaphysical male violation, of correspondingly violent denial, and an aftermath of commemorative penance. Restaging the theatrical miracle enacted at the end of *The Winter's Tale*, Fleetwood, at his lowest depth of sexual jealousy, has wax figures made of Mary and her supposed lover, Kenrick, which he theatrically places at a dinner setting before smashing them to pieces (*Fleetwood*, 386–388).[74] Shakespeare's post-tragic theater brings this difficult performance back to life and a future. In Godwin's novel, the female subject only ceases being an exchangeable piece in "the deepest game" by being cast into a traumatic ordeal. To quote from the last scene of *King Lear*, it is as if the reality of gender difference – the existence and separateness of a female subject position – were in *Fleetwood* the "Great thing of us forgot!" *Fleetwood* plays out the volatility and menace of a form of perfectionism that makes libels against the body – as, indeed, the goal of Godwin's perfectibility is to eliminate the body.

Cavell's philosophical theme in the *King Lear* chapter of *Disowning Knowledge* is the avoidance of love. There he presents love as the repressed and disavowed term, one masked to great cost by the obsessive pursuit of epistemological issues of doubt, where the price is measured in the tragedy with vengeance. The last pages of *The Claim of Reason* conclude in a discussion of *Othello* and with William Blake's Romanticism, emphasizing the related costs of the denial of the body and of imaginative energies. These will become again vengeful if they are not, as in Blake's incarnate poetics, dynamically engaged as energies of primary knowledge. The conditioning fact that our bodies, as Cavell says elsewhere, are "endlessly" separate from one another may unfold into comic or tragic variations of human interconnection. If gender and the voice of the female subject emerge finally and violently into view as the Shakespearean "Great thing of us forgot!" in the Wollstonecraft-haunted fiction of Godwin, and the body's elision is at the occluded center of vision of Godwinian rational anarchist philosophy, this unlivable condition is not his disaster individually. It expresses the fate of the body in the discourses of European perfectibility.

Cavell's self-narration of the lineage of moral perfectionism through Emerson from the start provides one way – not the only way – to think the life of perfectibility by means of embodied energies – capacities and susceptibilities. It is a serious and surprising feature of its intellectual history that Cavellian perfectionism itself does not speak of its European precursors' double elision of the body and comedy. (His early indebtedness to Ingmar Bergman's 1955 film of arch-bourgeois Europe, *Smiles of a Summer Night*, a perfectionist's marriage farce, attests to both realms spiritedly together.[75]) Yet Cavell increasingly finds his own preoccupations and work in this rich space left in disarray by European philosophical Enlightenment: the gaps opened by the enmeshing of German Idealisms, English utopian radical traditions, and the critique of both from the prevailing views and demands of Scottish Empiricism and liberal thought. These marked forgettings show not just why Cavell would have conceived of his career path first through a disused topic of Romantic-era philosophy, the problem of human action, but why and where having left that project aside, he later finds Jane Austen's prose fiction so belatedly compelling.

In this European history of ideas, "Austen Style" stands out not for the remove established in its godlike impersonality of narrative voice, but for its multiform embodied intelligence as language in action: as both instance and model of the philosophical value of conversation. Elizabeth Bennet displays perlocutionary conversational deftness and courage in that tour de force chapter in which she is threatened by Lady Catherine De Bourgh (Volume III, Ch. 14). Lady Catherine has come to deliver a command and a warning, and expects obeisance from a Bennet as a person of inferior status. But Elizabeth does not assume the inferior social position. She refuses to give Lady Catherine the informative statements requested (and thus exposes the veneer of polite informational exchange as in fact what it is, a threat and command).[76] Elizabeth also renders the performative aim of the visit ridiculous, screwballing it by playing off Lady Catherine's attempt to enforce her meaning without, as was her first aim, ever having to utter the actual threatening words. (Elizabeth makes her do it though: "What could your Ladyship propose?" [*P&P*, 241]). By recognizing that some questions themselves may be invalid, out of order, in their situation and address, Elizabeth refuses to offer any information at all to Lady Catherine: "I do not pretend to possess equal frankness with your Ladyship. *You* may ask questions, which *I* may choose not to answer" (*P&P*, 242). She gives

Lady Catherine crackling yet formal replies, nulling and "non-playing" the way in which Lady Catherine presumes to hide her sheer commands as formalities. Marked "out of order" socially for the extreme rudeness of her demand as well as in her arrogation to speak for the other's feelings, Lady Catherine is also discomposed in her plain assertions of fact.[77] The statement "Mr. Darcy is engaged to *my daughter*" (*P&P*, 242) is not only a false statement referentially; it is a performative, a wish, a promise, a threat, and in the event, a statement that no longer has supporting context, in the very testing of which the novel crosses an historical threshold around the social construction of elective companionate marriage. To complete the scene of Elizabeth's outmaneuvering her in satisfyingly comic Austinian terms, upon her leaving, Lady Catherine is all but forced to utter the textbook example of the illocution/perlocution distinction from Austin's "Performative Utterances" address, the comically futile "I insult you" (*PP*, 245). "'I take no leave of you, Miss Bennet. I send no compliments to your mother. You deserve no such attention. I am most seriously displeased'" (*P&P*, 245). Like Godwin's mincing and violent male perpetrators if only in this respect, Lady Catherine's rhetorical floundering marks her as incapable of improvising a future from passionate utterance. Out of the deliciously upturned order of this scene, framed by pro forma hierarchies and the shadow of a chaise and four, not only the novel's plot solution but a new sociolinguistic dispensation emerges into view. Not simply the plot, but the footing has shifted.[78]

CHAPTER 5

Perlocutionary Entailments

An adult consents where a child obeys.
— Hannah Arendt, *Responsibility and Judgment*

[O]ne feels one's consent to be elicited.
— Stanley Cavell, *Philosophy the Day after Tomorrow*

The anxiety in teaching, in serious communication, is that I myself require education. And for grownups this is not natural growth, but *change*.
— Stanley Cavell, *The Claim of Reason*

A Metropolitan Conversation

In the crowded field of Jane Austen film adaptions, Whit Stillman's *Metropolitan* (1990) is not a much-known entry.[1] In separate but linked scenes from the film, two privileged young Manhattanites discuss Lionel Trilling's essay on *Mansfield Park* in the context of their social anxieties. A character named Audrey Rouget puts Austen's *Persuasion* and *Mansfield Park* (along with *War and Peace*) atop the list of great novels she has read, and later says that she finds Fanny Price likable in spite of the reported widespread dislike of her for being a virtuous heroine: "What's wrong with a novel having a virtuous heroine?" In reply, another character, Tom Townsend, cites Trilling's argument that for the modern reader, the novel's moral position against theater is absurd. In fact, Tom finds the essay a better alternative to reading the book, and voices his preference for reading literary criticism to reading novels. Tom thus unwittingly reproduces a long history of male non-readers (fictional and non-fictional alike: John Thorpe) who pronounce upon the status of novels without engaging them. He replies to Audrey's inclusion of *Mansfield Park* on her shortlist: "But it's a notoriously bad book; even Lionel Trilling, one of her greatest admirers, thought that."

Tom infelicitously inverts Gilbert Ryle's well-known remark on Austen, discussed in previous chapters. In a later dialogue, he opines in response to Audrey's question, "What Jane Austen novels have you read?": "None. I don't read novels. I prefer good literary criticism. That way I get both the novelist's ideas as well as the critic's thinking. With fiction, I can never really forget that none of it really happened, that it's all made up by the author." Tom is allowed to imagine he *can* get to the "novelist's ideas" without immersion in their fictions. But the scene in the film is contextually qualified to suggest that discursive ideas and narrative environments comment upon – if not implicate and entail – one another. For instance, a quasi-legendary sleazy character who forms a central reference point in the film, Rick Von Sloneker, has just a moment before been introduced by the hearsay of a character named Nick. Von Sloneker may be a sort of distorted echo of Austen's Henry Crawford. Both are "highly attractive to women" they also degrade. Looking out the window with Audrey at the view of his father's apartment, Tom says he has an unusually good relationship with his father but doesn't see him much beyond "lunch when I am in town." His presence at his father's home, Tom says, makes his stepmother, a writer, nervous. In his callow and defensive support of criticism as a substitute for actual novel reading, Tom Townsend nonetheless crosses paths with a startling insight regarding the ontological relation of literary fiction to literary criticism. The endeavor of critical commentary does provide a non-fictional testimony and extension of fictional representations that themselves are not "real." In this regard, criticism must *realize* even the nineteenth-century "realist" novel. Is this fundamental to the idea of criticism itself? That it realizes or tests the actuality of literature's potentiality?

In the milieu of their wider cultural afterlife, Jane Austen's novels thus serve, alike, as a witty stand-in for a philosopher's reading of all novels (Gilbert Ryle) and as a knowing stand-in for a prep school boy who says he does not need to read novels at all (Tom Townsend). In view, too, of Cavell's well-known turn of phrasemaking that sees philosophy as education for grownups, the main characters in *Metropolitan*, along with those in Austen's novels, straddle the transition between the terms that seek to but cannot lock this rhetoric in, as definitional of either childhood or adulthood, obedience or consent, the education of early tuition or of later intuitions. The line is seemingly drawable somewhere by ethical institutions and enlightened judges, but it is one which – to develop the three points in my epigraph – the social forces of *elicitation* may intimately re-draw and blur. An economic frame nests within this political and philosophical-critical discourse. "As a movie about debutantes and their dates," set during the Christmas holiday social season during what is deemed "a bit of an escort shortage," there is a burgeoning romance plot – or at least a crush – between Audrey and Tom, and a focus in particular on the negotiation of the aspirations of Tom (a self-declared Fourierist) as a middle-class newcomer to the Upper East Side group.[2]

Stillman would continue with Austen as a subject in his 2016 film *Love and Friendship*: a rendition of Jane Austen which I am tempted to call more direct in its treatment than *Metropolitan*, were it not that *Love and Friendship* adapts not *that* novella from the corpus of Austen's juvenilia, but another novella entirely, *Lady Susan*. Stillman's two Austen movies are films almost entirely composed of conversation. They are comedies of dialogue. They catch a quality in Austen's fiction and implicitly themselves make an argument that the Austenian sociolinguistic field is one to be dramatized rather than narrated. For all its emphasis on callow and entitled characters, *Metropolitan* depicts the kind of conversations that actually make up (or once made for?) literary criticism. The screenplays for both films are cheeky, equivocal, and arch in their literariness and deliberate writtenness. But, as important to their tone of novel-of-ideas wit and sincerity, stylistically the films of Stillman are also redundant, literal, flat. *Metropolitan* and *Love and Friendship* show an Austen that might be placed on a literary arc spanning not from Samuel Richardson to Virginia Woolf, but from Fanny Burney through Thomas Love Peacock to Henry Green and Ivy Compton-Burnett. The Wikipedia page for Whit Stillman links to the information that his grandfather, one E. Digby Baltzell, was a Professor of Sociology at the University of Pennsylvania who achieved notoriety by popularizing the term WASP. One of Stillman's characters in *Metropolitan* unironically tries to establish "UHB" (*urbaine haute bourgeoisie*) as a more accurate substitute for WASP to describe the social existence of this group of representative characters from the film's downwardly socially mobile "preppy class." At the end of *Metropolitan*, one morning after New Year's Day, the likable and virtuous Audre, along with Tom and Charlie (the last of whom is the most earnestly conservative and blighted of the "rat pack" of supporting characters), are walking along a street in Southampton, Long Island. An odd squad UHB remnant, they are out of cash and in search of a ride back to Manhattan. It is the morning of short days, the close of the professed "last real deb season." The mood at the film's end is one in which finality and morning align.

Austen and the Terror

Like *Metropolitan*, this chapter does not attempt a full-scale reading of *Mansfield Park*. Instead it provides a formal space to converse around the concerns the novel houses and occasions. If the philosophical idea of entailment involves the notion of a necessary part or consequence of using a word or defining an entity – a logical element of the use of criteria – the chapter's materials provoke discussion of historically and politically informing and consequent features of Jane Austen's legacy (empire, gender, and ideologies of liberal consent) that nonetheless might seem tangential to her Janeite fellowship. The legal construction of the entail involves restriction of property within a family, usually to bypass direct female descendants in order to keep property "in the family" through distantly related men. Yet the ties of kinship pursued and revealed here will be a strange kind, and not so constrained.[3] The entail as a region of consequent but unpredictable involvement describes the region through which this chapter moves: *Mansfield Park* less as a textual object of close reading than as an unconstrained provocation to the idea of cosmopolitanism – and modernity itself – refigured under a sign of damaged consent. It also considers the circulation of Austen's image and name. Where nearly any historical moment after her death in 1817 might serve this purpose, I situate this legacy in the depressed global economic atmosphere after 2008, and in passionate publics of 2016 Britain and America. Cavell still very much remains in focus. But affect studies, alongside ordinary language philosophy, will supply my critical method.

The open-ended, improvised, and uncontrollable nature of feelingly impactful speech links conversation as such – both as a concept and as a sequence of acts, which I choose to think of as the everyday life genre of the "sequel" – to what J. L. Austin calls the perlocutionary realm of performative language (*How to Do Things*, 120). The chapter pursues the idea of literary criticism by way of a close analogy to aspects of perlocutionary exchange. It does so despite at least two readily apparent obstacles, by definition: criticism is not usually face-to-face speech; and its interests are electively taken up, not (at least not widely) experienced outside the structure of an intention to participate. Speech acts in their perlocutionary register characteristically occur near at hand, and often – especially for the impacted person – are involuntary. When Austin opens the conversation to perlocution as "yet a third kind of act," in Lecture VIII of *How to Do Things with Words*, he presents the perlocutionary aspect of speech acts as by definition a transitive form of linguistic entailment, one in which "[s]aying something will often, or even normally, produce certain consequential effects upon the feelings, thoughts, or actions of the audience, or of the speaker, or of other persons" (101). This concern with the effects of language (doing things *by* our words as well as *in* them) recognizes the force of language within reciprocal, or indeed unendingly multisided, emotional and social life. But I believe it also evokes a central feature of the enterprise of literary criticism. Critical encounters are unbounded flow-on events. Like perlocutions in relation to illocutions in another sense, their affective and passional realms mobilize a formal position in the shifting present, a protean shaping of futurity in relation to the ontologically unchangeable pastness of the established literary text (if you like, its Austenian "perfection.")

Yet allusions and associations do work (if they do, here in *Metropolitan*'s extended allusion to Trilling, and behind it *Mansfield Park*'s eponymous allusion to the 1772 Mansfield Decision in the chattel slavery case, Somerset versus Stewart) not just by direct consequential effect, but through regions both potentially more intimate and larger than a theory of immediate consequence allows. In this way, literary criticism takes the perlocutionary setting of near encounters into what David Kurnick calls a "massified," anonymous and impersonal, scene.[4] These effects carry on collaterally with unexpended cultural and intellectual forces. Seldom entirely conscious, they are sticky, intertwining, and often ugly. The 2013 film *Belle* (dir. Amma Asante) tells the story of Somerset versus Stewart as well as of the later Zong case from Dido Belle's point of view as moral triumph. Yet even its reductive narrative shows a level of current popular interest in the Mansfield Decision. As does Patricia Rozema's 1999 adaptation of *Mansfield Park*, a film which takes every opportunity to foreground the presence of transatlantic slavery in Britain, the Bertram household's direct involvement in slavery, and plantation culture's racialized sexual violence – while making Fanny an open drawing-room opponent of Sir Thomas's involvement in the slave trade in Antigua. Ironically and brutally, one of the aspects of the limited Mansfield Decision that judged the condition of slavery in Britain (but *not* the colonies) to be unjustified by natural law (though still open to being upheld under specific applications of positive commercial law) was to reinforce the status of women as not subject to even such qualified claims to freedom. Explicitly under Mansfield, women are the property of men and themselves have no rights. Women exist under a domain separate from that of either natural rights or chattel slavery, that of "municipal" law.[5]

Perlocution is an illimitable dimension of language and signals organizational breakdown to J. L. Austin in his official capacity. Austin encounters perlocution as a bogging down in the progress (out of prejudice, no less) of his illocutionary speech-act theory built on consensus producing group research. Perlocution is typically approached through the ordinary-life genres of conversational exchange between two people. In this chapter, it is also the sociolinguistic dimension or feature of language through which historical consequences – allusions, conversations, revisions, and eventful readings – persist as cultural forms of entailment. In this way, allusions are cooperative artifacts that challenge the default to a first-person prerogative to meaning. "Secondary" criticism is often infused with such non-intentional, contingent, overly and inconsequential entailments, from the point of view of a possessive "primary" authorship.[6] But this contingent, adhesive texture is true not only of criticism, of course. The political life of texts is embedded in the same potentiality for ever-new and yet irregularly maintained and broken relations. Lionel Trilling's *Mansfield Park* chapter in *The Opposing Self* (1955) begins not with an interpretation of Austen's novel, but with a discussion of the recurrently provocative status of Austen's textual personhood. This means especially the effort to square Austen's convincing display in *Pride and Prejudice* of "physical energy" as a moral force, with the "preference for rest over motion" in *Mansfield Park* as a novel where her "characteristic irony seems not to be at work."[7] "The great charm, the charming greatness, of *Pride and Prejudice* is that it permits us to conceive of morality as style."[8] That escort shortage from Stillman's *Metropolitan* carries over from *Mansfield Park*, the novel in whose marriage economy "there certainly are not so many men of large fortune in the world, as there are pretty women to deserve them" (*MP*, 3). In this novel, diagnostically, the indolent Lady Bertram thinks of her cheap sister Mrs. Norris as an "economist" (*MP*, 24).

Austen herself becomes a "physical" and "moral" target when no longer conceived as a figure of movement. Her status as the target of ritualized violence is evident in Ralph Waldo Emerson's notorious 1861 journal entry (a sort of informal addendum to his 1857 book *English Traits*), which judges Austen's novels "sterile in artistic invention, imprisoned in the wretched conventions of English society." Austen furnishes a "life so pinched and narrow" that Emerson issues the appalling directive to the dead author to consider killing herself: "Suicide is more respectable" (*CH* I, 28). Jane Austen's novels have an iconic status as exemplars of the central role of marriage in "illocutionary" speech-act theory. Austen's public image incites so much passion that by itself it may be taken to demonstrate, by contrast, the uncontainable scope of Austin's perlocutionary dimension of language. "About this antagonism a word must be said," declares Trilling. "Few writers have been the object of an admiration so fervent as that which is given to Jane Austen. At the same time, she has been the object of great dislike."[9] Whether she is being adored (by Janeites) or reviled (often dismissively by male non-readers) – and paradoxically even for those who find her fiction and imagined life "safe" – Austen acts as a sounding board for more-than-literary responsiveness. For all her "pinched and narrow" constraint, amplification is a fundamental characteristic of the ongoing life her writing entails and elicits. Yet "responsiveness," the language I have just chosen for a ubiquitous register of linguistic exchange, is perhaps too unmarked as it suggests a universalism that proves false. In citing Mark Twain's feeling of "animal repugnance" toward Austen, Trilling straightaway offers an analysis much more located than a blanket opinion on the passionate antagonisms of taste. Where Emerson bullies the ghost of Austen to suicide over his claim that her novels reduce the mind's concerns to the one idea of "marriageableness" (*CH* I, 28), and hence might be heard not simply as hate but as Socratic or Stoic advice, the Austen who features in Twain's response is hated in the flesh.

"[T]he *animality* of Mark Twain's repugnance," comments Trilling, "is probably to be taken as the male's revulsion from a society in which women seem to be at the center of interest and power"; this response concerns "a man's panic fear at a fictional world in which the masculine principle, although represented as admirable and necessary, is prescribed and controlled by a female mind."[10] Among other factors that single out the novel for this approach, *Mansfield Park* provides a striking object lesson by representing two major and seemingly divergent forces: the first is Trilling's claim that *Mansfield Park* is among the earliest major works of literary fiction to represent "society, the general culture, as playing a part in the moral life";[11] and the second – hardly limited to Twain – is this very pointed, particularized and toxic male response to women's public embodiment, voice and power. Beyond Twain's misogyny, that discomfort with power can be seen as distributed to Austen's common reader, who senses how voice and power are at once seated in the social and artistic function of the whole novel, and denied to the identificatory relationship with its "unlikable" heroine.

As a dimension of the speech act, perlocution is at once a transverse movement of all language and a classifiable, though peculiar, mode of the performative. To say that the force of perlocution is uncontainable is not to class this dimension of language with Promethean aspirations, but in the light of what Carol Jacobs in *Uncontainable Romanticism* deems a "Romanticism beyond fixed temporal boundaries, Romanticism (then as now) as a discipline-challenging field constituted as an unbinding resistance to forces of control – representation, authority (artistic, political, theological, legal), and criticism."[12] Countering "forces of control" based on social distribution, a critical fascination with the irreducible "force" of literary language as distinct from its historical context, meaning, or persuasive function can be found in the deconstructive tradition of Romantic studies at least as far back as *Deconstruction and Criticism*, the obliquely consolidating document of the Yale School (published 1979). By contrast to the radically destabilizing skepticism in Paul de Man's split between what language *says* and what language *does*, the perlocutionary realm of Austinian ordinary language is constituted by a middling world found in the intersubjective and social. Yet the positing of meaning and the career of meaning, performed, do not often or safely align. Domains of publicity and intimacy are highly personal yet also im- and trans-personal, conditioned by "language's power to produce effects that exceed a single act or an individual intention." Intelligible convention and individuated expression exert divergent, but ceaselessly interrelated, demands. Perlocutionary speech acts "persist through time and entangle people and things, self and others," as Andrew Warren observes in his coinage of the helpful term, *speech actant*.[13]

The gerund-noun *actant* – used to describe a person, creature, or object with agency in narrative – conveys disruption to the traditional paradigm of intentional *active* agency. In the non-statist realms of the perlocutionary effects of language, things often get real on terms not of our own choosing. So in the summer of 2013, Austen's capacity to trigger passionate response as a subject beyond cognitive determination came again to the foreground – and still very much in the terms of the "sexual objection" that Trilling saw in 1955. With the decision to replace Romantic-era prison reformer Elizabeth Fry (1780–1845) with Winston Churchill on the British ten-pound banknote, women's advocacy groups in Britain brought suit under the Equality Rights Acts of 2010, drawing attention to the lack of representation of women on British paper money (leaving aside the image of Queen Elizabeth). Jane Austen's name soon emerged as a substitute. But as the daily newspaper *The Guardian* reported, the status of Austen herself quickly came under fire.[14] Was Jane Austen an unduly safe choice? (It is not inspiring to be told, via the then-Governor of the Bank of England, that she is dutifully "waiting in the wings" for promotion.) Jane Austen is not a radical author, like Mary Wollstonecraft, or the creator of disturbingly gripping fiction, like Mary Shelley. In a follow-up article for an American audience published in *Slate*, the controversy took on further inflections from the objection to Austen's over-represented and privileged status as a white woman, her perceived and supposedly disqualifying standing as "a bitchy marriage broker who never married," and her physical appearance.[15]

A *New York Times* piece, by contrast, highlighted comments from literary scholars who pointed out the unintentional irony of the bank bill's choice of quotation from Austen's fiction: "I declare after all there is no enjoyment like reading." Taken from *Pride and Prejudice*, this anodyne reflection is spoken in the drawing room at Netherfield by the scheming and superficial Caroline Bingley, for whom an open book is no more than a strategic prop to try to lure the attention of Mr. Darcy. Is it still a suitable bit of nation blurbing if Caroline Bingley doesn't mean it? Are Austen scholars and Janeites just nitpicking, as is suggested by the *London Times* concerning the intervention of John Mullan?[16] A *New Yorker* piece suggested that Austen's ironies are actually far from (keeping us) safe, and not so containable for those in British politics and the bank administration who wish to use her image risk-free.[17] In the same summer of 2013, Caroline Criado-Perez, the journalist and women's rights advocate who led the initial effort to have gender balance on representations of bank notes, was threatened with rape on Twitter. Tragically, the summer of 2016 saw, under intensified political circumstances, the murder of Labor Party MP Jo Cox, in West Yorkshire in the days before voting on the "Brexit" referendum. Whatever role the specific animus of the Leave campaign played in this Neo-Nazi political murder, hatred toward Cox's status as a woman speaking effectively in the public domain at all stands at a prior level. The Brexit-associated violence shows the constant and periodically visible structural violence behind such "ugly couplings."[18]

The range of dysphoric affects found in *Mansfield Park* (envy and anxiety being just the most prevalent) suggests the fruitfulness of reading the novel in light of Sianne Ngai's bestiary of "ugly feelings." I think particularly of moments where the powers of otherwise sympathetic inference are used to test self-interest and division. For instance, in Julia Bertram's assessment of Henry Crawford's "treacherous play" in the rehearsal of private theatricals, the look on her sister Maria's "countenance was to decide it" – but inversely; "if she were vexed and alarmed—but Maria looked all serenity and satisfaction, and Julia well knew that on this ground Maria could not be happy but at her expense" (*MP*, 96). Other minds thinking in the Bertram family often takes this form of closely inimical observation and strategy. There are multiple situations in the novel where two characters are suffering, similarly but alone, in shifting dyads – Fanny-Rushworth; Fanny-Julia; Maria-Julia; Maria-Mrs. Norris – with an ugly non-cathartic feeling such as envy in common between them. Immediately following the passage above, Fanny pities Julia's jealousy of Maria's intimacy with Crawford in the acting scene: "And so saying, [Julia] walked hastily out of the room, leaving awkward feelings to more than one, but exciting small compassion in any except Fanny, who had been a quiet auditor of the whole, and who could not think of her as under the agitations of *jealousy*, without great pity" (*MP*, 96). Fanny is of course jealous not of Maria, but of Mary Crawford. She desires not Henry, but Edmund. This strange but quite ordinary moment of what we might call a blocked negative solidarity – here negated further, as it is unvoiced – at the same time trains the reader in the relations and psychology of Austen's character system. A different kind of repertoire and rehearsal goes on between the text and its reader in the midst of the line readings of *Lovers' Vows*. It suggests nothing so much as a modern soap opera and indicates the kinds of both inferred and manifest "other minds" thinking that predominate in *Mansfield Park*.

Characters in the novel and the readers of the book, alike, share a bind in what Eve Sedgwick calls "the inability to look away" from compulsory marriage. The triadic relationships amongst Edmund Bertram, Mary (and Henry) Crawford, and Fanny Price instance the argument that Sedgwick makes regarding the presence of compulsory social witness to the couple in heterosexual marriage. After Sedgwick, one tracks the displacement that occurs "when the fact of a marriage's unhappiness ceases to be a pseudo-secret or an open secret and becomes a bond of mutuality with someone outside the marriage."[19] The reader of *Mansfield Park* is forced to witness such conditions in the couplings of Sir Thomas and Lady Bertram, Maria and Rushworth, and (arguably) Fanny and Edmund in advance of their coupling; but also and perhaps most importantly in the enforced condition (insofar as the reader is a member of this society and lives under its conditions) of being witness to the historical complicities of the Mansfield estate itself. Austen's plotting of the transition from Volume II to III – always a telling critical juncture in her fictions – further estranges the tone of a compulsory and celebratory marriage plot as it prolongs the interstitial action, over which we vicariously feel the tortured extension of Henry Crawford's proposal to Fanny. Over a volume break, Henry seeks to persuade, press advantage, and extract consent by patronage and social force, with the concerted help of both Sir Thomas and Edmund.

J. L. Austin gives "I convince you that" as a prime example of the kind of perlocutionary action that cannot do what it says (*How to Do Things*, 104);

"I seduce you" comes to anyone's mind soon after. Does Henry attempt to persuade, win, or seduce Fanny – or simply to surround her and wear her down? The creepy quality in his prosecution of Fanny's consent to marry reflects that multiple, yet still curiously undermotivated, combination of conjoined patriarchal forces. Ordinary life in this section of *Mansfield Park* may feel especially distressing because the trial narrative in the novel, the conjoined siege of Fanny's consent not only by Henry Crawford but piled on by character and place, besieges and infiltrates choice.[20] The pursuit involves Crawford's real and increasing feelings of attraction toward Fanny and his increasingly meaningful potential for change; but it also includes an instigating element of his character that is accountable only to chance – the gaming spirit of a man who prefers female company to games at table but thinks of them in the same way. Fanny wishes to consider Henry Crawford's proposals and Mary's urging to accept him as "nonsense": a further Austinian resonance (*MP*, 205). Crawford's seductive charms are most felt by Fanny when he performs as a reader of Shakespeare (*MP*, 228–229). Crawford's elocutionary reading is especially noteworthy in light of Austin's meticulous ordering of the types of performative language as divided into *lo*cutionary, *ill*ocutionary, and *per*locutionary speech acts. The last of these registers curiously applies not just to others' caring or wounding effects upon Fanny, but to Fanny's embeddedness in a Wordsworthian poetics of the life of things. Her relationships to memory, to the everyday things of her world, and to places themselves form part of the medium of her impressed, responsive, and dependent sociality: "Every thing was a friend, or bore her thoughts to a friend" (*MP*, 106). Yet it is *Mansfield Park* that justifies Cavell's account of Austen's "novels of economy" in the terms of an "economy of horror" (*P*, 123, 127). On Cavell's view, Mansfield Park is not just a landed estate but a world that registers the global impress of heteronomy as degradation.[21]

Along with these "ugly feelings" and non-conversations, national character, understood through the prisms of British empire and the professions, is a major preoccupation of *Mansfield Park*. A secondary allusion made by the novel's title and estate – beyond the Mansfield Decision – might well gesture to the role (status, duties) of the "MP."[22] The hostility and aggression witnessed in Jo Cox's murder indicate a register of what we must call unregulated hatred, in reference to the position regarding Austen's "regulated hatred" that D. W. Harding imputed to her novels in the early years of World War II. Writing in the pages of *Scrutiny* in 1940, Harding meant that Austen's satire and ironically restrained treatment of conflicts in everyday life offered a means, a technique and style, to deal with potentially suicidal and murderous differences. In such an environment, the function of Austen's writing is spiritual as well as artistic. Harding's emphasis on regulation develops Austen's strategic need to practice diplomacy in a domestic theater, while working from a situation that – unlike a conventional war – obtains without relief. In his social research of the same period, Harding sought to theorize not only the unexceptional social psychology of coercion and war, but to arrive at a radical theory of peace.[23] The place of Austen's writings in such a setting represents the difficult achievement of culture in opposition to brutalities of aggression.

Trilling's *Mansfield Park* essay identifies Austen as "an agent of the Terror." By this provocative term Trilling means neither the partisan use of "terrorist" in the romantic era to vilify Jacobin authors, nor (of course) the mode of terror enacted in Jo Cox's murder. Trilling's Austen brings terror in the form of the modern artist's ruthless standard of truth-seeking: "She herself is an agent of the Terror – we learn from her what our lives should be and by what subtle and fierce criteria they will be judged, and how to pass upon the lives of our friends and fellows."[24] Unintentionally, Trilling echoes Harding's thesis regarding Austen's individual stylistic manifestation of an art of survival, to broaden and refine the field of her hate of a hateful culture into the spiritual economy of modern art. Having disavowed Trilling's mandarin moralism and the weight and mystique of the Leavisite "great tradition," we are now seeing effects of populist hatred deregulated. The online trolling threats to Criado-Perez show that it was not Austen's ironic multivalence that precipitated hate crime, but what Trilling terms "panic fear" and aggression at the agency of the "female mind." Katie Roiphe writes at the conclusion of her *Slate* piece: "It is ironic that Austen, the elegant, precise satirist that she was, should provoke this crude and unsophisticated and wild meanness. She was no stranger to anger, to simmering resentments and harsh judgments, to taking people down a notch, but her sentences were if anything the opposite of 'a bomb was placed in front of your house.'"[25]

Again, by deed if not intentionally, the Trilling of *The Opposing Self* and *Sincerity and Authenticity* (1971) may be Cavell's unspoken lead example in showing the force still inherent to this connection of Austen's world to an "economy of horrors," even as Trilling practices a very un-Cavellian gesture to intentionally wound Austen's common readers, who seek a different kind of love and trust in her care. Trilling's Austen as "an agent of Terror" challenges the reader to "comprehend her mode of judgment," after which, "the moral and spiritual lessons of contemporary literature are easy."[26] Adam Kirsch summarizes the main Austenian headings of the

"Terror" of such modernist authenticity: "If modern literature, as Trilling says, 'asks us if we are content with our marriages, with our family lives, with our professional lives, with our friends,' then Austen is absolutely modern, even though her questions are asked with more reserve, and admit of happier answers, than Nietzsche's or Freud's."[27] Trilling uses Austen to form the generalized paradigm of the modern artist who is cultured but far from content.

Mansfield Park destabilizes the notion and function of liberal progress, and insists on the close tie between notions of improvement and histories of degradation.[28] In this it breaks and reassigns the threat of Rousseau's bond between human perfectibility and degradation. The novel offers a well-known, multi-level critique of self-regarding "innovation" both as an eighteenth-century fad in the aesthetics of landscape design, and as an overarching conceptual narrative in what would become the practice of liberal social history. Austen's early plotting mocks the school of Humphrey Repton's confected landscape "improvements" and innovations (the theme begins in Volume I as the diversion of a day trip to the laughable Mr. Rushworth's Sotherton Court [*MP*, 38–76]); and it does so exactingly and unsparingly later, at murkier depths. The devotional "improvements" (liberalization of customs) of religious worship feature in the inset visit to Sotherton Chapel. The uncomfortably sexualized mention of improvement extends into the later return of Sir Thomas Bertram and the objectification of Fanny Price (*MP*, 123). It resurfaces in the cultural idiom of landscape in the persistently deranged yet plausible vision of Crawford, who wants to reverse the very foundations and orientation of Thornton Lacey, Edmund's vicarage house (*MP*, 166–167). Finally, the narrator intervenes in the plot of *Mansfield Park* to make clear at the end of the novel that if Crawford had only returned to his own estate at Everingham to continue the good stewardship practice in which he lately had taken sudden interest (with impressing Fanny in mind [*MP*, 267, 275]), he would have avoided entrapment in the London affair with Maria, with the result that Fanny herself would have "no doubt" ultimately fallen to him (*MP*, 317). In these instances the novel depicts censoriously, at an increasing depth, the various captivations of improvement: in the landscape at Sotherton Court and Thornton Lacey as Crawford plays with them; in Mansfield's structurally informing framework of British empire and its economic interests; and in terms of Fanny Price's sexuality and the attention to her "person" (*MP*, 123).

The novel's critique of faddish and secular improvements is easy to spot, but to focus attention only at this level omits Austen's preoccupation with the "dismal science" of the everyday, statistics and probability. These have not at all been checked, but have metastasized, becoming the fabric of modern theories of knowledge and indeed of social being. *Mansfield Park*'s narrator emphasizes probability in the marriage tie-ups of its final chapter, with the jarringly actuarial statement regarding Fanny and Crawford that "there would have been every probability of success and felicity for him" (*MP*, 317). *Mansfield Park* is not simply the conservative anti-innovation novel that many readers have judged it to be. It reflects a new and distinct Malthusian demographic calculus – particularly in the telling front and back schematic bookends, which show the new philosophy of "reading tables."[29] Austen's alternately stagy or godlike narrator is invoked at the conclusion of *Mansfield Park* to disruptive effect so as to do no more than state probabilities, or state where a set of probabilities is summed, where realized life and the actuarial tables very nearly coalesce. As with the products of present-day logarithmic digital services, the horizon of "every probability" may condition an ultimate or ontological reality out of which not just contingencies of plot, but moral acts of choice as events, are seen to precipitate.

"Lethal Calm"

Cavell's relationship to Austen's novels is framed by the meaning and pursuit of what he calls Emersonian moral perfectionism. He nowhere states the view recorded in Emerson's journals that these novels are sterile, imprisoned, pinched and narrow. Instead Cavell's engagement with Austen begins from a powerfully formalized expression of that threat of inertia. In the UC-Berkeley lecture where he gave a version of the chapter "Philosophy the Day After Tomorrow," Cavell refers to Austen's narrator's "celebrated surface of lethal calm" in the place where the published book has "Jane Austen's narrator's renowned surface of containment" (*P*, 124). Cavell's "lethal calm" may invoke the "dead silence" that befalls the Bertram family over discussion of Antigua and the slave trade (*MP*, 136). If we hear an allusion to Emerson's Austen, it reverts to that judgment of Austen's novels by making them not suicidal but murderous.

Calm or contained, the two phrases share a description of the polished surface of Austen's writing. But the revision of strategic "containment" for the earlier, identifying style of a "lethal calm" is arresting. This substitution plays against the idea that there are free ranges of Romantic prose style, emotionality, and narrative economy. It leaves as a question whether it is Austen's narrator being described, or if Austen herself is characterized as contained and constrained by her participation. Cavell already has planned an only apparent contrast of Austen to Nietzsche, with a deeper ("not inaccurate") litotes of affinity underneath the contrasting surfaces of their conduct in prose. Cavell's joining of the expressive predicaments of Austen and Nietzsche in *Philosophy the Day After Tomorrow* is a striking and unexpected move not only as a philosophical connection, but as a venture in critical affiliation – in trusting a disruptive alliance of projects and tones. From its title forward, *Philosophy the Day after Tomorrow* understands moral perfectionism in terms of a Nietzschean "convalescence," to which Cavell is attuned in the eponymous chapter as he discusses Jane Austen heroines.[30]

Cavell views Austen's "stress upon propriety and promise-keeping" and Nietzsche's "spiritual distress" as alike "expression[s] of distress in everyday existence." "Nietzsche's garish emotionality" provides a conspicuous – Cavell says "somewhat shocking" – point of connection to the distress of the ordinary found in Austen's and George Eliot's realist "novels of economy." By the end of this important paragraph, Cavell has aligned Austen with Nietzsche as names for two polar strategies for managing pervasive distress in the everyday. The succinct account of Kant in *Cities of Words* canvasses "his achievement as the philosophy of limitation."[31] It is as if Cavell were laying out a post-Kantian critical project for handling distress in nineteenth-century prose: "You might say that her prose seeks incessantly to minimize (hence maintain) the expression of distress in everyday existence no less drastically than Nietzsche's seeks to maximize it" (*P*, 124). If all this is at stake in the published paragraph, the Berkeley lecture of "Philosophy the Day After Tomorrow" compounds the interest and challenge radically, by adding the lethal perfection of Austen Style to the forces she manages. Anti-economical, a style of "lethal calm" would demonstrate its aloofness and separation from the distressing economy wherein women's bodies are moved about and valued, but their lives are not, in the society that would extract their damaged consent.

When Cavell lands on "constraint" in the printed version of "Philosophy the Day After Tomorrow," he preserves a tension found in the domestic spaces of the novel in the Romantic and Victorian eras between managed domesticity and unrestrained expressions of patriarchal control, and of women's suffering and dissidence. The announcement a page or two later that Cavell came "somewhat late to an unconstrained fascination with Jane Austen" suggests the main heading of his engagement with Austen is also structured on autobiographical terms. How can Cavell's concern with the belated flourishing of his own interest bear on the issue of women's distressed and damaged consent? The reading act is conceived in terms of the spatio-affective logic of constraint and unconstraint. While the association of Austen with Nietzsche remarkably overturns at least one aspect of their prescribed genders (it is Nietzsche's "emotionality" that is marked excessive and "garish"), the later phrase "unconstrained fascination" is ambiguous both psychologically and formally. What could it mean to release the idea of limits from an "unconstrained" focus, stimulation, or fixation? What does it entail to come under an endless or unconstrained spell? What sort of domestic bewilderment is that? We experience Austen's domestic spatiality internalized as a mode (rhythm, temporality) of intensive reading attention. In his reading method Cavell works back, though both auto-affective and institutional modes of recall, from the Yale School of the 1980s. He belatedly marks his full participation in a rich autobiographical mode of what Carol Jacobs terms *Uncontainable Romanticism*.

The primary topic in the eponymous chapter of *Philosophy the Day after Tomorrow* is the crisis ordinary of a novelistic version of Cavell's abiding interest in "Emerson's moral perfectionism" (*P*, 111). In choosing *constraint* as the word for a set of affective, social, and formal modes that he describes as outward features of nineteenth-century "novels of economy" by women, Cavell raises tensions that point outward to the career of "passionate utterance" in the world. The move singles out perlocution as the linguistic register of illimitable, unmasterable feeling in action. Cavell's treatment of perlocution isolates the very dimension of speech most characterized by its uncontainable multiplicity. In *Sense and Sensibilia*, Austin charges against the perpetrators of the "descriptive fallacy" that language everywhere does not do one thing but many things. He insists there is no single class or kind of verbal action in "A Plea for Excuses," one of the most resonant and still underutilized essays in *Philosophical Papers*. In *How to Do Things with Words* Austin comically laments the condition that there is no end to the complications that may befall the systematizing effort of organizing an ordinary language philosophy. But he never grants the career of perlocutionary actions with similar acknowledgment.

Pride and Prejudice links to the cinematic model of Cavell's comedy of remarriage in *Pursuits of Happiness*. *Mansfield Park* travels with the cinematic and philosophical genre Cavell calls the "melodrama of the unknown woman." In *Pride and Prejudice*, a tonal, stylistic counterforce to capitalism and patriarchy sustains a narrative environment where collective women's desires and interests prevail contrary to sociohistorical force. But an alternate idiom, one Cavell calls an "economy of horror," poses unsettling questions within the increasingly global and contemporary bounds of *Mansfield Park* and its dismal economies. If consent must be extracted, and celebrated even for that – are there really choices? Media presentation of Austen positions her authorship in two ubiquitously ordinary and disturbing roles: (1) the favorite aunt or friend through the strong implicit insistence that we *know* her; and (2) through never-tiring juxtapositions of Austen with contemporary life, out of the endlessly exploitable premise that she is a ubiquitous reference for the restricted and *un*knowing. Often a rehearsal of sexualized violence, this dynamic exhibits what Miranda Fricker calls epistemic injustice: the violence done specifically to someone to their position as a knower. Cavell's reading of the 1944 film *Gaslight* in *Contesting Tears* (1996) demonstrates not only the silencing of women's voices, but just such a form of violence done specifically to the female subject in her capacity as a knower.

In the Postscript to the Bette Davis chapter to *Contesting Tears* – a chapter about "the capacity to find astonishments and intimacies in a world with little play in it"; and "the second-rateness of the world – anyway of the choice of men in it" (*CT*, 127, 146) – Cavell explicitly engages with Eve Sedgwick's trope of queer closeting in terms of the classic scene of the philosophical closet. Such a location is found recurrently in first-person accounts of the skeptic's introspective position and "orientation" to the world in first philosophy. By contrast, Cavell follows Wittgenstein in the critique of "private language" as he engages fantasies behind this foundational act of skepticism and its narration. He addresses a set of mutually supporting fantasies as "the inside and the outside of philosophical thinking," "the inside and outside of the closet" (*CT*, 156–157). In taking up the conditions of secrecy and fixed idiomatic conventionality that are typically forced upon discussions of the possibility of private language in Wittgenstein, it is "as if the ordinary is the perfectly open secret" (*CT*, 157). In his readings of films revolving around the melodramatic "figure of the unknown woman" in *Contesting Tears*, and in his remarks on nineteenth-century novels by Austen and Eliot in *Philosophy the Day After Tomorrow*, Cavell particularizes his earlier critical account of the Rawlsian drama of consent in terms of gender.

In "Philosophy the Day After Tomorrow," Cavell writes about Austen's novels as exemplifying "instances in which the soul can learn not to be crushed by the force of compromise with injustice that modern society assumes and exacts" (*P*, 123). Here Cavell maintains that an "economy of horror invisibly sustain[s] the main house of *Mansfield Park*" (*P*, 127). But Fanny Price gets what and whom she wants at the end of the novel. How do we respond to the character of Fanny, in view of this environment of enforced consent and damaging compromise? The fulfillment of Fanny's desire for her cousin Edmund, and her final status as the true inheritor of Mansfield Park, rather confirm than allay the damaging expression of consent to an order shaped by ugly forces of compromise. Sandra Laugier writes helpfully on this topic, though not speaking of gender:

> For Cavell, the question of the social contract underlies or defines the question of language agreements, as his analysis of Rousseau at the beginning of *The Claim of Reason* shows. If I am representative, I must have my voice in the common conversation. If my society is my expression, it must also allow me to find my voice. But is this really the case? As Cavell subsequently showed in *Conditions Handsome and Unhandsome*, it is not at all obvious. This is the illusion or mark that he denounces in Rawls and his *Theory of Justice*. What makes it possible to say that in the "original position" I consented to society and, to thus summarize Rawls's stance, that I consent to it at present? If others stifle my voice or speak for me, I will always seem to consent.[32]

Cavell's re-founding of voice in the inheritance of Emersonian perfectionism moves forward into his late interest in Austen and Eliot under the terms of constraint and consent, and the need to acknowledge female voice in philosophy, against the male arrogation of voice – including the risk to Cavell's own and of Cavell imposing his own: "as if to say: no one can perform the *cogito* for you" (*CT*, 146).

A passage in *Contesting Tears* shows the interlocking predicament of Bette Davis's character in the film *Now, Voyager* (1942), the position of the skeptic in Cartesian meditation, and the foundational terms of Lockean social consent:

> Now the significance I draw from the way the grown daughter contests the authority over her—a woman who has everything money can buy and that position can secure—is that the legitimacy of the social order in which she is to participate is determined (to the extent to which it can be determined) by her consent, by whether she, in her state of freedom, finds that she wants the balance of renunciation and security the present constitution of society affords her. The price is madly high: the life of desire (outside the price of marriage) is one of irony, of enforced transcendence, and of romance as creating "cads," a name Charlotte and Jerry [the names of the romantic couple in *Now, Voyager*] each claim for themselves. It turns out in Locke's *Second Treatise* that the existence of consent, hence of the social order, may be no easier to be clear about and establish than, as in Descartes's *Meditations*, the existence of a finite other proved to be. (*CT*, 147)

So far this chapter has layered and contrasted the legal institution of gender-based property entailments and the uncontainable registers of what I am calling perlocutionary entailment. In Cavell's account of the "figure of the unknown woman" in *Contesting Tears*, the melodrama as a genre places the "order of law" in insurmountable tension with the "order of desire." This impasse and its intensities break the surface tension of the novel to become readable. Yet they are not taken as heard by Sir Thomas Bertram, in Fanny Price's (dis)avowal of her forbidden desire for Edmund, "mouthed" in interview with Sir Thomas, in an almost King Lear-like "*no*" (*MP*, 214).

The clearest social function of *Mansfield Park* is not to liberate desire; neither to reconcile its force to the structure of law nor to show their tragic opposition. It is rather to validate the "legitimacy of the social order" through a narrative development of terms for the unlikely heroine's besieged participation: Fanny's price in a liberal, ostensibly free, moral universe. Going back at least to the private theatricals about which Lionel Trilling and his fictional student Tom Townsend are so uncomprehending, the pervasive allegory of *Mansfield Park* (an allegory and critique of the infrastructures and material drives of modern Atlantic history) is the "private" theater of getting Fanny to participate. The novel elaborates and insists upon the terms of Fanny's participation in a world that is "second rate" (at best), a world of damage and compromise – on terms historical, patriarchal, public, and intimate; ultimately, to degrade as it elevates her – as a theater of consent. In an important recent account of the novel, from his study of liberalism beyond the units of the individual person and action, Daniel Stout sees *Mansfield Park* as a feudal novel of the early corporation, which "put[s] the claims of circumstance over and above the claims of persons," subjugating the individual character to the corporate estate.[33] After Cavell, I see *Mansfield Park* as a distressingly paradigmatic and modern novel about liberal consent, participation, and compromise. *Mansfield Park* is neither a remarriage comedy nor an instance of the melodrama of the unknown woman in the Cavellian scheme. The performative institution to which the novel most refers is not the promise, or marriage, but the contract of a world order with its members, the damages to the conversation of justice.

The Problem of Praise

The Introduction to *Philosophy the Day after Tomorrow* outlines the book's project overall in terms of Cavell's interest in perlocution, the topic of his chapter on "Performative and Passionate Utterance." In raising this interest, Cavell shares words that suggest his own attraction to a project of praise while delimiting many of the examples of abusive perlocutionary speech acts: "Passionate utterance is just one form in which perlocutionary effect structures itself: moralistic abusiveness is another; hate speech another; political oratory still another. Praising as well as cursing or denouncing, must fit somewhere here" (*P*, 5). As it introduces an important undertaking for Cavell, this comment makes strikingly minimal provision for the topic of praise – especially in view of his outsider relation to literary criticism and cultural studies throughout the decades in which skeptical methodologies of suspicion prevailed in the humanities. Here praise represents just one of many examples of "passionate utterance," the majority of the others tending to the abuse of power and the vulnerabilities of exposure to language. Still praise "must fit somewhere"; it deserves a place of welcome at this table full of abuses. The tone of this provision lies between a desultory aside and a normative insistence.

Later, though, Cavell, with more colorfully epigrammatic language, affirms, "humankind would rather praise the void than be void of praise" (*P*, 65). Following a maneuver possible to identify as Kantian, this turn of melodrama-with-wit asserts a threshold bare minimum claim it will dramatize, and enlarge to an end in itself. In fact, *Philosophy the Day After Tomorrow* takes up the project of praise (the project's values and risks) as its primary subject. Individual chapters are multiply framed by occasions of praise as well, at different levels of organization. The book as a whole comes to us as a collection of "celebratory addresses" assembled from a set of lectures and readings that represent acts of homage *by* Cavell to his mainstay philosophical writers, including J. L. Austin, Wittgenstein, Thoreau, and Nietzsche; but also to less anticipated others, writers of fiction including Jane Austen, George Eliot, and Henry James, in reference to newly activated relationships of reading conducted after Cavell's retirement from regular teaching (*P*, 6). In particular, Cavell reads Austen's work under the exigent heading of *Philosophy the Day After Tomorrow* as a whole, in the urgent, sobering project appropriate to his life after retirement from teaching – and with candor to the remaining scope of his life. It is, Cavell writes, "the experience of the remains of my day that concerns me—the facts of hunger and stalking and aggression and cunning and cooking aroma and resting and companionship and conversing"; all stand in need of assertion because that life is "vulnerable" to skepticism (*P*, 2). Many of the occasions of these lectures and essays stem from the invitations of organizational hosts in celebrations of Cavell's lifelong achievement (*P*, 1).[34] Placed in such context it is easy to see how "[c]riticism accordingly," as Cavell explains of the heading he takes from the Kantian critical project, "becomes a work of determining, as it were after the fact, the grounds of (the concepts shaping) pleasure and value in the working of the object. In this light criticism becomes a conduct of gratitude, one could say, a specification and test of tribute, a test in which I am inherently exposed to rebuke" (*P*, 67).

Gathering up: we have criticism defined as "a conduct of gratitude," the perlocutionary speech act affirmed, despite the acknowledgment of a crowded field of what seem to be more ethically and politically urgent negations, as an occasion of praise. Cavell's way of receiving these invitations of praise pays forward the idea that tribute ought to and can constitute a methodological field. Provocatively, *Philosophy the Day After Tomorrow* may be construed as a self-authored *Festschrift*. There are few scholars as self-referential and auto-affective as Cavell. Pursuing this idea seriously – and Cavell's inability to leave the "latitudes" of celebration wholly to others suggests we should: the gracious inviting, the encomiastic planning – we may realize alongside that irreverent move the stake of a first-person recapture of the third-person character of praise and blame; to test what could not have been testified so fully by friendly neighbors, students, admiring colleagues, and organizations. It all attests to a dogged subject in itself hard to give praise in the progressive and cumulative manner: the "interest in the pervasiveness of the threat of skepticism" (*P*, 1). This condition of vulnerability precisely cannot be met or evaluated in its full measure by acts of homage that consolidate third-person meaning (*P*, 2). "Philosophy the Day After Tomorrow," book and essay, are about the concepts of instruction and education as well as about praise; and Cavell opens the eponymous essay with a meditation through the example of Wittgenstein on what it means for the idea of education that "at some point in teaching the pupil must go on—and want to go on—alone" (*P*, 114). Here we find a paradoxical challenge central to the importance of Cavell's entire way of thinking and writing, and one not very compatible with the genre of *Festschrift*. That form of challenge takes its orientation and discovers energies in the recognition of possible groundlessness, in the rifts and rough terrain opened by obsessive worry at failing to reach or to sustain interest. Can there be a *Festschrift* that questions not just the legacy of accumulated meanings, but the interest of the subject in sustaining itself – the subject's adhesion, or availability?

As Cavell hints by referring to skepticism as wearing the devil's many guises (*P*, 2), the primary expression of the human threat of skepticism lies in the multiform ways one sustainably denies it, cannot actually "believe it," or take an interest in facing its predicaments, to care, for oneself. Cavell refuses to retire in that sense, to leave off risk-taking in the first person.

Celebration of that work cannot be ceded to others. He phrases this insistence in disciplinary terms that are also intimate personal terms: "Can I, must I, leave it to, say, literature, or history, or anthropology, to articulate and preserve the richness of my experience for me? Are their authorities in positions to word their impressions that are essentially different from my capacities as a participant of a human culture? To cede the understanding of my experience, trivial and crucial, to them would require, from my point of view, a massive effort of discounting" (*P*, 2–3).

Receiving praise on such terms is indeed a vulnerable (and quite possibly a contextually offensive) act. Cavell melodramatically and insightfully fears such "discounting" as defined by the articulation of his experience by others, preserved through other authorities and expressed by another's terms. On Kant's terms this indeed would be a loss of enlightenment, even though human warmth and reciprocity require letting others think with him – if not for him, at this late moment. Cavell attests to the "right to praise" (*P*, 68) and is attracted to the exercise of this "right" (which can hardly be said of a classical Rawlsian, contractual right). Yet the act of praise does not presume consensus of interest. To conceive of criticism as praise puts group and self to test in the claim to judgment. Here and in many places elsewhere in his work, Cavell worries about the "arrogation of the right to speak for others" (*P*, 9). Under that legitimate threat, he conscientiously *raises* the right of praise (*P*, 68). "Criticism accordingly," again, "becomes a conduct of gratitude, one could say, a specification and test of tribute, a test in which I am inherently exposed to rebuke." Critical activity for Cavell involves the "trial of pleasure" in passionate utterance, aesthetic judgment, the claim that it does matter that you agree with me (*P*, 67), and that such attunement ultimately if unpredictably makes a path to "homage" (*P*, 69).

In what is undoubtedly the most difficult chapter to process sociopolitically in *Philosophy the Day After Tomorrow*, "Fred Astaire Asserts the Right to Praise," Cavell transitions from the topic of the bardolatry of Shakespeare to the philosophical "pertinence" of praising Fred Astaire, "a Hollywood song-and-dance man" from the Golden Age (*P*, 62). He asserts that "false praise kills what it is we have to be grateful for" (*P*, 66). About the chapter's example of Astaire's performance of an historically African American dance in the musical film *The Bandwagon* (1953), Cavell says the risk is that the effort of criticism as praise be "not so much false as vain" (*P*, 66). Accompanying his song, "I Have A Shine," Astaire's dancing in *The Bandwagon* is an important, recurrent interest to Cavell in *Philosophy the Day After Tomorrow*. In "Something Out of the Ordinary" he discusses a sequence of the film around the song, "By Myself," in terms of a missable dimension of the ordinary (*P*, 11), located in physical movement around an equivocal border between Astaire's acts of walking and dancing (*P*, 21–25). There Cavell anticipates the materials of "Fred Astaire Asserts the Right to Praise" and its song, "I Have a Shine," as "an occasion for acknowledging his indebtedness for his existence as a dancer—his deepest identity—to the genius of black dancing" (*P*, 24). If the first instance of the Astaire film seeks to win back for philosophy "the understanding of my experience, trivial and crucial," from "a massive effort of discounting," this is because the ordinary is typically discounted "as what is missable" (*P*, 11). This devaluation registers not only as what is "perceptually missable but as what is intellectually dismissable" (*P*, 12). The second and longer discussion of Astaire and the practice of criticism as praise encounters the problem of praise as a trial of "consent to America's partial democracy happier or more heartened than it might otherwise be" (*P*, 62). Here the danger in making the idea of praise the integral act and sponsoring mood of the project of critical judgment comes with the danger of racialized white appropriation of Black American cultural productivity.[35] In the idiom of the book, this praise economy accompanies the dual form of a Shakespearean language economy: praise in the form of exorbitant "promissory notes" (*P*, 37; in the context of Cavell discussing perlocution in the Roman plays); and a destructively endless hunger for the need for praise (*P*, 52; in discussing *King Lear*).

The critical undertaking must specify and test, as Cavell says, "the grounds of (the concepts shaping) pleasure and value in the working of the object." But in doing so, exposure to "rebuke" is equally an "inherent" part or entailment of such a project of affirmative criticism. Cavell, in his engagement with skepticism, has his own way of rejecting the hermeneutics of suspicion by showing greater concern for false accusation than for false praise (*P*, 82). He addresses the skeptical pressures on that affirmative project: the "logic of my claim is that it is open to rebuke, perhaps even from myself, from whom I must fear and bear rebuke" (*P*, 82). "Must we withhold the praise because the glimpse contains its terrible rebuke?" (*P*, 79)

Cavell's difficult critical performance shows how a "right" to praise exists only in its being risked and questioned. Its justifications are only to be determined through the complex acts of judgment and interchange, not secured in advance. For critical judgments as for philosophical dialogues, these are "arguments that must not be won" (*Pitch*, 22). The specified grounds of pleasure in judgment are shaped by concepts whose elaboration still does not exempt praise from dissatisfaction and dissent. Cavell marks the awareness of historical conditions and stipulates the role of participation here under the terms of dance, in which "conditions of the dance are part of the dance" (*P*, 79). The way this claim ends, on further unforeseen openings to criticism, proves as important as the initiating stake of criticism as "a conduct of gratitude" and "tribute." Evolving grounds have been shaped through the act of an aesthetic specification. In turn they are left available and vulnerable to unknown regions of human responsiveness. The "specification and test of tribute" offers a test in which I am exposed to rebuke, "inherently exposed to rebuke" (*P*, 67). A self-critical responsiveness that broadens illimitably in this way constitutes the grammar of Cavellian praise. The project of praise for Cavell is always charged in both senses (in its ethical mission and in its vibratory affect) by a vulnerable and motivating proximity to exposure. We can be impressed only because we are impressible, liable to impression.

Philosophy the Day after Tomorrow places such claims on historical footing. The passage from the book's Introduction continues (overlapping with the quotation regarding the forms of perlocution above):

> Praising, as well as cursing or denouncing, must fit somewhere here. It obviously is placed in question in one of the sublime, not to say sacred, moments in American history, when Abraham Lincoln questions whether he or "we" are in a position to dedicate, consecrate, and hallow the ground which holds honored dead—which, in the context of the Gettysburg funeral oration, implies precisely the act of praising them. (*P*, 5)

The historical occasion to memorialize the Union dead at Gettysburg requires praise, as does the classical political genre Cavell specifies, the funeral oration. Lincoln himself "questions whether he or 'we' are in a position to dedicate, consecrate and hallow the ground"; and within this quotation of Lincoln, Cavell puts in questioning suspension that status of the "we" who are thus addressed as assembled: "we" (they) the assembled? "we" (some of) "the people"? The speech brings a ponderous and doubtful attitude to the project of re-consecration. It thus participates in the philosophical movement I track back through Cavell's creative inheritance of Kantian aesthetics – a critical philosophy transmuted in its very skepticism, minimalism, and risk-taking to the project of praise (the "conduct of gratitude," "test of tribute"). In this mode and its tradition, the objects of philosophical analysis are not predefined concepts, but matters and ventures of concern sustained by acts of critique in praise. The Gettysburg battlefield requires an act of witness in that place, despite language's inadequacy to address loss, or provide any redress in kind. The declared failure of the address to ground the identity of the subject and task undertaken is actually necessary to provide for the constitution (or the chance?) of a collectively promising future. How much might it might matter to Cavell – as the philosopher of pursuits of happiness in a plot he calls remarriage – that the Gettysburg Address concerns the burial of Union soldiers, with its words spoken to consecrate Union dead only? There were still remains of slain northern and southern soldiers alike on the battlefield.

The Gettysburg Address resolves the more perfect union which Lincoln's Army was fighting to preserve and to create. In its resolve at once to describe and transform the meaning of suffering, Lincoln's performative address sustains the gravity of honorable description that associates (*elicits*: description too is perlocutionary) mass intimacy with tragic public events. For the national task of mourning and making, the overt inadequacy of the Gettysburg Address comprises the sole adequacy and decency. But also, its recognition of the performative career of the democratic "experiment" of government of, by, and for, the people says something important about the role of constation and descriptive speech acts in history's performative, self-confrontational unfolding. What could it mean to denote or describe the position of commitment in a re-committed national experiment? Cavell's inclusion of Lincoln and comments on The Gettysburg Address are admittedly brief. They occupy the second half of just one paragraph on "passionate utterance" and involve the structuring effects of acts of denunciation and abuse, as well as of praise (*P*, 5). But even at this scale, Cavell's investment in a performative (perlocutionary, "passionate") reading of Lincoln's re-inaugural moment compares forcefully with Derrida's deconstructive reading in "Declarations of Independence."[36] No longer an impossible instation at once from God and the voice of natural right into the representative structure of the not-yet-existing "good people" – as the "American" linguistic event serves in Derrida – for Cavell the traumatic constituting act, the "sublime, not to say sacred, moment[]," is an event of re-inauguration: remarriage (*P*, 5). Lincoln's unfinished America is a project of care within violently transformational process.

Not simply the facts of American history but the status of its event is at stake. "A strange business this in America," says a character, to kill time, in *Mansfield Park* (*MP*, 85). For Derrida, the crux of the speech act lies in how the not-yet-existing nation can sign in the name of its own representation, how the colonial outlaws (through discursive political fictions of the "good people" and with God's co-signature) instate American authority so outrageously as to become legitimate "founding fathers." The linguistic and political coup for which "Declarations of Independence" accounts is the rhetorical act of delivering this "impossible" aporetic event by means of descriptive grammar; getting this done by what Derrida punningly nominates the act of a state-ment. For Lincoln's America, though, the constituting event is not orig-ination (to match Derrida's pun with my own), but reinauguration, not a liberatory fiat but a trueing of purpose mid-voyage.[37] (Antietam and Gettysburg are the shorthand battleground names for the moment when Lincoln finally resolved that the end of slavery *is* the meaning of the war, though before, for him, it had not been.) However foreshortened in scope, Cavell's words on Lincoln at Gettysburg offer an occasion to think about America's damaging continuity, its perfectibility without progress, its radical transformations within the continuum of a crisis ordinary.

There is a further compelling tie that I can't prove determinately between Cavell's and Eve Sedgwick's writings on perlocutionary "passionate utterances" with reference to Lincoln. Sedgwick's collection *Touching Feeling* was published in 2003, two years before *Philosophy the Day After Tomorrow*.[38] This is how Sedgwick begins her essay, "Around the Performative: Periperformative Vicinities in Nineteenth-Century Narrative" (the essay takes its epigraph, the words with which it also begins by separately quoting, from Lincoln):

> "But, in a larger sense, we cannot dedicate—we cannot consecrate—we cannot hallow this ground." I begin with this sentence as one of the best-known examples of a kind of utterance, actually very common, that seems worth thinking about. The utterances I explore in this chapter do not fulfill the conditions that the British philosopher J. L. Austin articulated in his classic description of explicit performative utterances properly so-called. *In How to Do Things with Words*, the explicit performative is exemplified in a cluster of sentences in the first-person singular present indicative active, about which, Austin says, "it seems clear that to utter the sentence (in, of course, the appropriate circumstances) is not to describe my doing [a thing]... or to state that I am doing it: it is to do it" (6). Examples of the Austinian performative include, "I promise," "I bet...," "I bequeath...," "I christen...," "I apologize," "I dare you," and "I sentence you...."[39]

This passage and the essay as a whole anticipate, respond to, and tactically instruct Cavell's moral perfectionism from the vantage of anti-homophobic queer theory. In seeking a "spatialized and local performativity" (68), Sedgwick tacks between deploying forthright curses and eliciting non-dualistic possibilities through the (pre-)position of the *beside* (8). In the weak theory nonce concept of the "periperformative," Sedgwick affords her reader a framework with "more tensile and nuanced ways than we've had so far of pushing further with the Althusserian concept of interpellation" (69).

The exemplary passages brought to bear alike curse, deny, and declare the failure and inopportunity of performative powers ("we cannot dedicate"); they allude to explicit performative utterances and cite the spatial constructions presumed to be in place by institutional speech acts (70). These "feats" of disinterpellation – sometimes as simple as "Don't do it on my account," or "Not playing" – allow for a critical "disempaction of the scene" of the speech act. Such everyday tactics may force a "crisis in the ground or space of authority" (69–70).[40] Sedgwick's literary and narrative examples include not only the Gettysburg Address, but the malediction of Charlotte Stant over the marriage vow in Henry James's novel *The Golden Bowl*; Lydia Glasher's curse and gift of diamonds to Gwendolyn Harleth in George Eliot's *Daniel Deronda*; the example of triangular blackmail and forced witness to a hateful marriage in Charles Dickens's *Dombey and Son* (one that "successfully deroutinizes" the common topos of the "marriage as slavery" plot in Victorian novels [79]); the non-literary examples of "performative acts that structured the month-to-month culture of New World slavery—buying, selling, willing, inheriting, claiming, advertising for, manumitting" (80); and the complex "braid" of performative acts and citations of acts throughout Harriet Jacobs's *Incidents in the Life of a Slave Girl* (87).

Sedgwick's selection of texts makes more visible and usable a similar compilation of nineteenth-century texts in Cavell – a relay that for the most part stands aside from his Emersonian syllabus that would engage the complex field of the American promissory act, from Lincoln through blackface performance and Jim Crow. These encounters confront racist history while affirming the status of American popular entertainment, music and dance, as philosophical and artistic expression. The information that a recording of Cavell's own piano performances of 1930s era popular standards was played at his June, 2018 funeral service deepens my conviction that there is unfinished work to do in this area.

In an inaugural *J19* "Pleasure Reading" essay that implicitly shows the influence of Sedgwick's post-critical moodwork, Priscilla Wald begins with Lincoln's Address and the alloy of its prose pleasure. For her pleasure text Wald shares Allen Grossman's "The Poetics of Union in Whitman and Lincoln: An Inquiry Toward the Relationship of Art and Policy." As cited by Wald, Grossman proclaims a Cavellian project for America, in process (not progress) between the intelligible forms of religion and philosophy: "Proclaiming his America 'a society waiting … unformed … between things ended and things begun.'"[41]

Mansfield Park and its heroine Fanny Price are also concerned deeply with the conduct of gratitude and the possibility of its rebuke.[42] "'I must be a brute indeed, if I can be really ungrateful!' said she in soliloquy; 'Heaven defend me from being ungrateful!'" (*MP*, 219). "She must be courteous, and she must be compassionate. She must have a sensation of being honored, and whether thinking of herself or her brother, she must have a strong feeling of gratitude" (*MP*, 222). In *Philosophy the Day After Tomorrow*, gender, genre, and a shift of cultural locus to British and transatlantic texts serve Cavell as a means to consider how forms of exhaustion are a challenge and resource to the project of philosophical perfectionism. These aesthetic and philosophical considerations signal further encounters with a world that is not shaped anew but experienced under a chartered continuity of modernity's horrors. *Philosophy the Day After Tomorrow* implicitly responds to the longstanding charge of American exceptionalism made against Cavell's and Emerson's thought. Rather than withdrawing in modesty or shame, the book enlarges the rebuke to exceptionalism. Its "economy of horrors" refers an Atlantic modernity that bears and inflicts the costs of its idea of limitlessness, to exhaustion.

In this way the challenge Cavell identifies in the Preface of *Conditions Handsome and Unhandsome* – the challenge of "shaking [our] memories and starting again," at which "Europeans" are said to fail – carries in its hunger for limitless new beginnings a heavy account.[43] Of Cavell's idea of America, Simon Critchley asks in *Very Little … Almost Nothing*: "What is the relation of Cavell's Emersonian perfectionism to the hybrid ensemble of traditions and inheritances which make up the great rhizome of American cultural identity?"[44] The reader with a book bearing the intriguingly similar title of *Little Did I Know* in hand is positioned to reply through Cavell's autobiography: not only with his Jewish family heritage from the days in Sacramento and Atlanta, but with Cavell's teaching (for instance) at Tougaloo College in Jackson, Mississippi at an HBC during the Freedom Summer; or in terms of his involvement with student protests of Vietnam (*Little*, 4; 505–508). Even before the autobiography was published, anyone must have acknowledged Cavell's many full, honest, and difficult acts of attention directed to America's repressive historical legacies – so much so that these interventions could be observed a constitutive task: "As if the subjection to history *is* human nature." Yet Critchley insists there is a more than nationalism, a "continual *continentalism* in

The Problem of Praise

Cavell's writing that typifies a whole genre of philosophical and political discourse, a continental drift" to which a character in Jean-Luc Godard's film *Éloge de l'amour* (2001) also fiercely objects, in the way "we" tend to say "America" either in place of North America – as when we evoke myths of discovery and limitless futurity – or, alternately, in place of The United States – as when aggressions are disowned by reference to their supposed innocence or idealism. This vein of Critchley's discussion gets quite devastating. "America, Cavell insists, needs to be loved." Critchley even offers the compelling metaphysical speculation that "[t]he union of love is what America has always wanted"; historically, this "is what it tore itself apart in the Civil War trying to achieve. America has never been able to bear its separateness."[45] Is America altogether a perpetrator of the monstrous denial of skepticism? This fear is implied in Cavell's repeated judgment that the originality of America's most distinctive productions has been overpraised yet undervalued.

But Critchley's ear for the internal restiveness and resistance in Cavell's writing is not very sharp. If his question rings true, his attitude about the role the American idea serves specifically for Cavell cannot help being provocatively obtuse. One can respond anyway to Critchley's aim to follow Cavell's thought stripped or de-natured of what goes by "America." The theme of self-reliance, the tone of optimism, are hardly all (or for Cavell the great part) of the creative entailment of Emerson. What there is of that sort seems the least convincing inheritance. Why is it that Sarah Beckwith's book about medieval and early modern religious rites in England can be so exhilaratingly and troublingly "Cavellian" through and through?[46] Or – to reposition this dynamic in terms of gender instead of nation – how can the female leads who anchor Cavell's accounts of "remarriage" and "the melodrama of the unknown woman" invite us to acknowledge the reality of human feelings in their "passive" aspect more fully than Emerson does? It is partly on account of Cavell's work that America has not yet completed its processing into one of those "poisonous names" that Percy Shelley called on in "Hymn to Intellectual Beauty," as toxic manifestations of power, religion, and state.

Oddly for a deconstructive theorist, Critchley rushes through the gap between the Cavellian "uncanniness of the ordinary" and a naturalized domain of the ordinary. Branka Arsic dismisses the allegation through a reminder of Cavell's dispossessive and receptive language: "'undone by pain,' affirming its passivity, receptiveness, and incapacity to possess. Such a self does not appropriate but acknowledges its existence."[47] The passage from which Arsic draws in *On Leaving* begins by remarking on the

Heideggerian "idea of thinking as reception," which Cavell understands as posing a problem whose "answer does not consist in denying the conclusion of skepticism but reconceiving its truth" (*Senses*, 133). At issue in Emerson is "his power of affirmation, or of his weakness for it" (*Senses*, 132).[48] These words do support ressentiment – Emerson's indulging in a robust disposition toward false or facile affirmations. The mood of philosophy's undertaking as Cavell knows it makes clear its derivation from the nineteenth-century American narrative of "Europe" – an association that is increasingly untenable and costly to hold, in a global climate of exhaustion and overproduction. Thus it is not Cavell's idea of Europe as a zone of depletion, but his allegorical restriction of that idea to Anglo-European cultural expression, that critics of his Emersonian perfectionism should justly reject. Cavell identifies the challenge of "shaking [our] memories and starting again," at which "Europeans" (on the example of Kleist) are said to fail: "It is as if Kleist will neither accept nor refuse the Emersonian vision, an excruciating one for those who can call for it but who cannot imagine themselves shaking their memories and starting again; call them Europeans."[49]

To take these words of re-inauguration as exceptionalist misses their strain to express a weakness in the very "power of affirmation," showing it to be received only by those who know "incapacity to possess." Incapacity to possess and dispossession meet in Cavell's work regarding the unforeseeable, unforeseen registers of historical linguistic responsiveness. For Cavell, an "Emersonian judgment" obtains over the entire period in which Jane Austen wrote – "around the middle third of the nineteenth century": the period between the abolition of slavery in principle and in practice – "as a scene of incessant heteronomy, looking solely to borrow or steal."[50] Perlocutionary acts and effects may assist in the work of reparation and justice as they often bear critically "beside" this possessive historical theft. Historical and spiritual attributes of Cavell's America open out via analogy the registers of perlocutionary responsiveness, in a manner we may revise to turn capitalist structures toward passionate utterance and its improvisation, by saying that no one is entitled in advance to them; they are for the taking.[51]

CHAPTER 6

Emma *and Other Minds*

69. I should like to say: "If I am wrong about *this*, I have no guarantee that anything I say is true." But others won't say that about me, nor will I say it about other people.

116. Instead of "I know ...," couldn't Moore have said: "It stands fast for me that ...?" And further: 'It stands fast for me and many others ...."

—Ludwig Wittgenstein, *On Certainty*

Prophecy and the Normal Processes of Living

Among the most important passages in J. L. Austin's formidable paper, "Other Minds" (1946), is this one – a plea against the philosophical obsession with certainty and making predictions:

> We all *feel* the very great difference between saying even "I'm *absolutely* sure" and saying "I know": it is like the difference between saying "I firmly and irrevocably intend" and "I promise." If someone has promised me to do A, then I am entitled to rely on it, and can myself make promises on the strength of it: and so, where someone has said to me "I know," I am entitled to say *I* know too, at second hand. The right to say "I know" is transmissible, in the sort of way that other authority is transmissible. Hence, if I say it lightly, I may be *responsible* for getting *you* into trouble.
>
> If you say you *know* something, the most immediate challenge takes the form of asking "Are you in a position to know?": that is, you must undertake to show, not merely that you are sure of it, but that it is within your cognizance. There is a similar form of challenge in the case of promising: fully intending is not enough— you must also undertake to show that "you are in a position to promise," that is, that it is within your power. Over these points in the two cases a parallel series of doubts are apt to infect philosophers, on the ground that I cannot foresee the future. Some begin to hold that I should never, or practically never, say I know anything—perhaps only what I am sensing at this moment: others, that I should never, or

> practically never, say I promise—perhaps only what is actually within my power at this moment. In both cases there is an obsession: if *I know I can't be wrong*, so I can't have the right to say I know, and if I promise *I can't fail*, so I can't have the right to say I promise. And in both cases this obsession fastens on my inability to make *predictions* as the root of the matter, meaning by predictions claims to know the future. But this is doubly mistaken in both cases. As has been seen, we may be perfectly justified in saying we know or we promise, in spite of the fact that things "may" turn out badly, and it's a more or less serious matter if they do. (*PP*, 101)

Austin shows that cognitive and performative claims share the character of transmissibility – and hence of responsibility and trouble. The plea he makes is that we forgo the philosophical obsession over the avoidance of predicative mistakes, and hence with the impounding of "I know" through an "inability to make predictions." Such a doubt is an "infect[ion]" without cure. On this issue Austin views his philosophical opponents as "doubly mistaken." Opponents here include not only his contemporaries' positivist thought on certainty, but the skeptical critique of the linguistic and social institution of the promise, found alike in Hume and Godwin. Yet instead of triumphing in his dry satire, the passage anticipates a Cavellian way of treating the "infect[ions]" and "obsession[s]" about knowledge to which a positivist turned skeptic (or the positivist assuming skepticism for argument) is prone. Austin is concerned with the price of certainty.

My Introduction has already shared Austin's critique of "incorrigible" knowledge. If to be incorrigible in philosophical terms means to enjoy immunity from error, in human and narrative terms, it means to be *ineducable*. Austin's rejection of the exclusive dimension of certainty in much modern theory of knowledge goes hand in hand with his recognition of the epistemological character of social responsibility. On these terms I find a therapeutic critical direction in the above passage. It relates to Austin's sense of the pervasiveness of the obsession, and to the kind of deceptively fatuous linguistic expressions that voice it: "if *I know I can't be wrong*, so I can't have the right to say I know, and if I promise *I can't fail*, so I can't have the right to say I promise."[1] Austin gives permission back to the promising animal. For Austin, these are the assumptions that the positivist-turned-skeptic holds to obsessively but will not feel it necessary to say. Drawing these patterns of thought out into the open is a large part of Austin's aim and argument in "Other Minds." Do the criteria involved in claiming to know demand (demand first, or at last, or ever?) that one establish the impossibility of being mistaken?[2] Does the ability to make a promise require in advance the elimination of possible failure, as an unhappy outcome and "more or less serious" event?

Austin parallels the claim to say "I know" and the right to say "I promise" more often than one might expect of a thinker who precedes deconstruction. In "Other Minds" and *How to Do Things with Words*, he rebukes the common notion that knowledge claims are purely constative statements, calling this assumption the "descriptive fallacy." Knowledge claims are at least in part performative speech acts because making them puts the speaker's authority and trust to test. They do not merely state and convey information. Whereas to make a promise is a full-fledged leap for Austin – not only a leap for the speaker to stake her worth in words, but a "plunge" of commitment, a pledge that is actionable for the person to whom the promise is made; also to the audience, the community, in witness (*PP*, 99).[3]

Despite their situational negativity, the words liability and responsibility retain an ethical flavor of the notion of capacity, found in these words' suffix. The positivist's way of approaching the meaning of knowing and promising puts impossible demands on a decisive future dimension, where "in both cases this obsession fastens on my inability to make *predictions* as the root of the matter, meaning by predictions claims to know the future." Austin might equally have said *prophecies, foretellings*, if he were less critical of assuming a profound voice. Like John Dewey, he might have spoken of the active role played by imagination and, indeed, of something like a down-to-earth prophecy – pragmatic prophecy – in the "normal processes of living."[4] From a position that unfolds within the capacities that elicit us, "we have to a considerable extent, given up thinking of this *life* as merely a preparation."[5] Elizabeth Bennet and Fanny Price are two very different novelistic heroines of tomorrow, and of the day after tomorrow. Emma Woodhouse in this chapter will be a philosophical heroine whose contribution – normalizing prophecy to everyday dimensions of knowledge – aids us in refusing the idea of life as only a preparation. Even *Emma*'s level-headed Mr. Knightley is credited with the office of everyday prophecy for speaking "prophetically, when he once said, 'Emma, you have been no friend to Harriet Smith'" (*E*, 277).

Austin of course doesn't use these words, *prophecy, foretelling*. (He does use the word "foresee.") The sense that a future – the very condition of futurity, and the inevitability of a future that is uncontrollable and open to events – puts all knowledge at risk is insistent in the skeptic. Philosophers concerned with the problem of other minds, John Wisdom notes, tend "to say similar things about other sorts of knowledge: knowledge of the future, knowledge of the past, knowledge of the material world as opposed to knowledge of what at the moment appears to be so."[6] Skepticism over the reach of knowledge into the future exposes its ground in difference, a structural and internal issue. Cavell throughout his career identifies this as the *avoidance* of knowledge. The root problem is not uncertainty. The solution isn't a better method of forming predictions, as if the central matter were how best to anticipate and control that future. Such a view just makes philosophy a chapter of the history of science, and an actuarial science at that (*P*, 2, 13). The grammar of knowing does not depend on a predictive mindset to secure the claim to know.[7] Efforts to restrict the meaning of "I know" so that its claim to knowledge depends on a predictive future reach are risk averse to the common life of ordinary language commitments.

Supporting the argument of "Other Minds," Austin in *Sense and Sensibilia* concludes that the goal of the sense data theory of knowledge is not truth as such but – his caps – "THE PURSUIT OF THE INCORRIGIBLE" (*SS*, 104). He makes it clear that he means by this not Plato's search for "something that will be *always true*," but "the idea that there is or could be a kind of sentence in the utterance of which I take no chances *at all*, my commitment is absolutely minimal; so that in principle *nothing* could show that I had made a mistake, and my remark would be 'incorrigible'" (*SS*, 104, 112).[8] Indeed, rather than deciding on the truth or falsity of the skeptical sense data doctrine (*SS*, 1), *Sense and Sensibilia* concludes here with the *critique of commitment*. The lectures' ultimate target is the professional philosopher's cautiously reduced idea of a philosophical claim. *Sense and Sensibilia* in this way offers not only a counter to skeptical epistemology; it advances a moral critique of a philosophical project that is unlivable and unattractive, even perhaps ignoble: the philosopher's hedge on the performative and eventful power of what it means to write or utter any sentence at all (*SS*, 134). Austin's arguments in these lectures, then, possess not only cognitive and epistemological dimensions. They are rich investigations of moral thought and sociality, of the dimensions of life in which our very interdependencies, mixed with our desires, produce endless opportunities for "mistake."

Price's, Ayer's, and Warnock's philosophical behaviors show they want the indirect-perception approach to knowledge to *retreat* from the participation of ordinary statements (*SS*, 141). Austin compellingly calls out the impacts of this philosophical "blunder" in narrative and moral terms (*SS*, 55). He characterizes the aim of (his later editor) Warnock's study of Berkeley as trying "to produce, not a maximally certain, but a *minimally adventurous* form of words, by the use of which we can always stick our necks out as little as possible" (*SS*, 139). Austin anticipates Cavellian dimensions – and seems to authorize Cavellian prose – in this argument against the minimally adventurous form of a statement that could never be shown to be false: "But in fact this ideal [of incorrigibility] is completely unattainable. There isn't, there couldn't be, any kind of sentence which as such is incapable, once uttered, of being subsequently amended or retracted" (*SS*, 112). Among other things, what the challenging title of Cavell's *Must We Mean What We Say?* conveys is that we are exceedingly staked in what we say. Words often commit us to greater meaning than we may want, or own, or know. A moral version of Freud's "overdetermination," and analog to the richness of ambiguity in literary close reading, words overcommit us. Reciprocally, the meaning of the full life or career of our words is correspondingly alive (or not) in us. Austin's approach goes without this aspect of existential self-definition; he shows the grounds of the endless revisability of conduct in language, how any sentence may be "subsequently amended." Just so, *undoing* things with words takes place not in some kind of metaphysical space of negation. It is another effort, a pragmatics, a conduct.

This situation is philosophical and literary, but also social and behavioral. The "most fundamental thing about knowledge of other minds," argues Toril Moi – repressed by the skeptic and the positivist alike – is that expressions, actions, and behavior place claims on us as they "*place a claim on others.*"[9] The passage I've been discussing in "Other Minds" is not a breezy defense of the latitudes of saying "I know." If his main effort in "Other Minds" lies in the justification of our claiming to know certain things with appropriateness and intelligibility even if they sometimes prove mistaken, wrong, or false, Austin locates responsibility as a key dimension of human knowledge.

In Jane Austen's *Emma*, the impacts of Emma's opposition to Harriet Smith's proposal from Robert Martin and the snowballing, screwball implications over the misunderstanding regarding Harriet's later crush on Mr. Knightley – when Emma thinks Harriet's sights are on Frank Churchill, the other male character to "save" her, and advises Harriet accordingly (*E*, 235–236) – instance Austin's claim that by lightly saying "I know," I "may be *responsible* for getting *you* into trouble." Emma's mistaken presumptions about her knowledge expose Harriet to damage to her marital and social prospects, and to potential shame. As Volume III moves toward its close, and even after she has reconfigured her relationship to Harriet on cooler, more distant, and more mindful – if also classist – terms, Emma must summon an extraordinary effort to prevent the disclosure of Harriet's hopes for Mr. Knightley, given the gratuitous pain and humiliation that this knowledge would bring. (Despite the hardcore snobbery involved, somehow Austen persuasively represents the mislocated desire of Harriet for Mr. Knightley as different in kind from Harriet's earlier feelings for Mr. Elton. Such a match warns a monstrous breech. Harriet is Emma's fostered and abandoned Frankenstein Creature. "Oh God! that I had never seen her!" [*E*, 284]).[10]

This aspect of "Other Minds" looks a decade ahead in J. L. Austin's work and already seems to realize and appreciate the complications of the boggiest parts of *How to Do Things with Words*. Knowledge claims are performative in their relationship to transmissive authority, as promises are in relation to social and linguistic trust. Austin's standards for invoking authority prove iterable in their structure, transmissible in their form from person to person, and relational in their implications. The strength of ties based on promises as well as the openness of such networks to infection depend on these internal characteristics. In *The Claim of Reason*, Cavell similarly underlines the difference between what the human subject may be responsive *to* and what she may find herself responsible *for*. "We are endlessly separate, for *no* reason. But then we are answerable for everything that comes between us; if not for causing it then for continuing it; if not for denying it then for affirming it; if not *for* it then *to* it" (*Claim*, 369).[11] The preposition shifts index the character of a responsibility that may be taken on either side of the "event" of realizing our separation. They mark the transition from the classic speech act, illocution (with *by* and *in* the key prepositions characteristic of the executive act of speech), to perlocution, and what Cavell in *Philosophy the Day after Tomorrow* calls "passionate" utterance (where key prepositions of relationships and forces of speech are *by*, *through*, *to*). "There is no restriction to the minimum physical act at all. That we can import an arbitrarily long stretch of what might also be called the 'consequences' of our act into the nomenclature of the act itself is, or should be, a fundamental commonplace of the theory of our language about all 'action' in general" (*How to Do Things*, 107). Cavell, after Austin, thus recognizes an important "dimension of philosophical analysis" as the criticism of speech as illimitable action (*P*, 159).

By recommencing with a "positive fresh start" in "the philosophical study of conduct," Austin's paper "A Plea for Excuses" (1956–1957) offers bracing terms for how to relate ordinary language philosophy to the concerns of Austen's fiction (*PP*, 180).[12] In the genres of the educational treatise and the early novel, "conduct" of course names the gendered discourse of socialized behavior that Austen inherits, mimics, and creatively revises from her precursors. For *Emma* in particular, the excuse becomes

Austen's focus of narratological literary invention par excellence. "A Plea for Excuses" follows the philosophical method of testing "what we should say when" by naming its "way of doing philosophy" a "linguistic phenomenology" – a "mouthful" that Austin takes back as a term, but not as his method (*PP*, 182).[13] We see an *Emma* in miniature throughout the opening paragraph of "A Plea for Excuses": with its focus on constraint ("within such limits"); its tone ranging from the "regrettably lofty" to the "congenial"; its discovery of "unexpected results" from "expected lessons"; in Austin's lesson of "amusement and discovery" from a hounding of "the coverts of the microglot"; and in his celebration of the pleasures of cooperation and agreement (agreement and pleasure over real and severe grounds of dissensus) (*PP*, 175).

Before I dig into this chapter's series of topics – Austen's own dismissal of certainty as a standard of "perfect" knowledge; Frank Churchill's elaborate framing of a linguistic phenomenology of excuses; and the novel as play on the problem of other minds – I wish to point out simply that *Emma* ends with the touchstone word, *prediction*. In Austin's "Other Minds" it is the sticking point in the future that halts the skeptic's claim to know, yet in Austen's *Emma* the word is included conspicuously in a list of features to which the novel is finally and fully, and satisfyingly, answerable: "But, in spite of these deficiencies, the wishes, the hopes, the confidence, the predictions of the small band of true friends who witnessed the ceremony, were fully answered in the perfect happiness of the union" (*E*, 333).

"Predictions" is perhaps a word that Austen could only have used in the novel's last sentence. It would be understandable to ask: doesn't *Emma*'s concluding emphasis on the role of predictions imply disagreement with Austin's claim that a predictive model is wrongheaded?[14] Doesn't *Emma* rework, retell, this model of knowing so as to legitimate it? *Mansfield Park* ends with probabilities. Can the predictive enterprise really be criticized away? Why otherwise should Austen's narrator suggest this predictive account of knowing comes out alright? These questions put pressure on the status of "predictions" in the thematic context of the final sentence. They would have us inquire, as well, into the rhythm and tone of the list of attributes: deficiencies, wishes, hopes, and confidence, with predictions launching into the predicate. In this last sentence of the novel, Austen rings several of the book's many bells, not only to echo back, but positively to call out for the kind of intensively linguistic approach of ordinary language criticism.

Austen's narrator rounds up the "deficiencies" of the small "band" of main characters. She plays upon "confidence" in the multiple senses of this word: self-assurance, disclosures of intimacy and the keeping of secrets, and lastly – the state of feeling solid or certain. So Austen unrepentantly *mocks while preserving* her main character's addiction to forming "predictions." (It is worth pointing out that Mr. Knightley last plays the role of matchmaker.) As opposed to the skeptic holding out for the impossible achievement of certainty in and about the future, the deficiencies of this core band of characters ultimately comprise a dimension of experience "fully answered" by events in the "perfect happiness of the union."[15] It is the ongoing deficiencies that bring "perfect happiness," that satisfy. Though the judgment that the novel's culminating event proves deficient in fact comes from Mrs. Elton – who finds the bride deficient in "finery or parade," in "white satin" and "lace veils" (*E*, 333) – her dismissal is not allowed to stay in her perspective. The narrator asserts that "union" itself makes good on the confidence, hopes, predictions, and wishes of the novel's two main couples. In contrast to a reading that finds deep and undercutting ironies, hopes and confidence *are* answered – though neither in the ritual conduct of the marriage ceremony itself (by rites of words, by yards of lace), nor by projections of omniscient future knowledge. The very ongoingness of this terminus devotes the last phrase of *Emma* to the everyday. The novel's last word unites the main characters as a "small band of true friends," not caring to separate them beyond the British, and Cavellian, idea of their "union."

At the close of *Emma*, Austen's narrator shows how her characters' well-established "deficiencies" are richly comprehensible as relational expressions of human limits. By the same measure, the full answer (or answerable fullness) that *Emma* across its registers provides is never available to any or all at once. Acts of knowing and sharing seldom exactly match up. Even in the fullness of recognition and disclosure, not simply of possible, but actual, union between Knightley and Emma starting in Vol. III, Chapter 13, Austen's narrator describe the limits, obliquities, and opacities of communicated knowing via the litotes of the "little" gaps that keep the couple (though not very materially) apart:

> Seldom, very seldom, does complete truth belong to any human disclosure; seldom can it happen that something is not a little disguised, or a little mistaken; but where, as in this case, though the conduct is mistaken, the feelings are not, it may not be very material.—Mr. Knightley could not impute to Emma a more relenting heart than she possessed, or a heart more disposed to accept of his. (*E*, 297)

Reconceived as situatedness, acknowledged limitation underwrites the conditioning possibility of the claim to say "I know." But in *Emma*, no one character can possess, receive, and confer all their knowledge fully in free exchange. This holds true all the way down to the idiomatic and microstylistic level: not accept his heart, the entirety of it, but the partitive and oddly more generous, "accept *of* his," as if Austen were revising Marvell's "sit and eat" in "Love III." (The idiom "accept of" was available and interchangeable with "accept" in Austen's time, but still I see implications in her choice.) That remainder, after we have taken the score of what a full possession knowledge involves, is neither evasive nor unforthcoming. The deficiency is not metaphysical lack. In the realized ordinary at the close of *Emma*, characters are released to their enjoyment.

"But, in spite of these deficiencies …": *Emma* represents an unusual moment for Jane Austen, in which irony is constrained by another mode of social facility, one compatible with the ability to acknowledge weakness and forgive. Emma is thus a comedy of Cavell's "abatement of skepticism" (*P*, 26). There are despicable characters but no comedic scapegoats in *Emma*. In this final sentence, Austen's irony merges into her capacity for the communitarian ethos, from which not even the Eltons are excluded.[16] Subject nevertheless to endless and ongoing irritations, *Emma*'s final grace note falls on a festive abatement in marriage comedy. The novel's very absence of a space of exclusion helps us to understand why *Emma* is also a novel of (mostly) "regulated hatred," "civil falsehood," and moral injury.[17] The three or four families *remain* in the country village.

Taking an Interest in *Emma*

[A] little world of our own, close-packed and insulated like ants in an ant-hill, or bees in a hive, or sheep in a fold, or nuns in a convent, or sailors in a ship; where we know every one, are known to every one, and authorised to hope that everyone takes an interest in us.[18]
— Mary Russell Mitford, *Our Village* (1824)

[T]he wavering between the boring and the interesting seems internal to the interesting.[19]
— Sianne Ngai, *Our Aesthetic Categories*

Discussions of *Emma* always get around to the nature itself of novelistic interest – whether routed through Walter Scott's (anonymous) review noting *Emma*'s original, close relation to depictions of common life in "The Flemish School," or to Maria Edgeworth's complaint that "there is no story to it" beyond Mr. Woodhouse's gruel, or to the concession (or brag?) by Austen herself that "I am going to take a heroine whom no one but myself will much like."[20] *Emma*'s complex interest holds up irrespective of whether we "like" the heroine right away or whether we find the plot engrossing – or can even identify much of a plotline on first reading. Seldom has such a truly great novel so fully relied on, and taken the risks of, an art of the "merely" interesting.[21] Emma herself foregrounds the novel's paucity of events in a discussion with her brother-in-law John Knightley at the close of Volume II. Whereas at the same structural moment, *Pride and Prejudice* turns toward the climactic visit to Pemberley, and *Mansfield Park* at its comparable juncture dramatizes Henry Crawford's insistent proposal of marriage to Fanny Price, here is Emma summing up the season of events since the Mr. and Mrs. Elton's return from Bath, in effect two-thirds of "her" novel: "These amazing engagements of mine—what have they been? Dining once with the Coles—and having a ball talked of, which never took place" (*E*, 216).[22]

Writing for *Blackwood's Edinburgh Magazine* in 1859, G. H. Lewes agrees: "Her subjects have little intrinsic interest" (*CH* I, 160). Lewes reiterates this judgment even as he promotes Austen to the pantheon of literary fame, in a review that editor B. C. Southam calls "The great appraisal." For Lewes, Austen's focus on "treatment and art" as opposed to eventful plotting will only captivate the attention of readers with "critical and refined tastes," and will give (such "homely comedies" as they are) "little pleasure" to those "whose passionate and insurgent activities demand in art a reflection of their own emotions and struggles" (*CH* I, 160). One such "insurgent" reader was Charlotte Brontë, who upon Lewes's own recommendation had read *Pride and Prejudice* and famously was left cold by its art of an "accurate daguerreotyped portrait of a common face" and its "carefully fenced, highly cultivated garden, with neat borders" (*CH* I, 126). In another 1850 letter to a publisher's reader for *Jane Eyre*, Brontë reports reading *Emma* on the threshold of "interest" – her word – by which she meant, experiencing "just the degree of admiration which Miss Austen herself would have thought suitable" (*CH* I, 127). (The phrasing mimics Cavell's lethal calm, indeed.) In the 1859 "great appraisal," Lewes melds a vision of aesthetic structure with the broadly Kantian sense of aesthetics as a fundamental if peculiar form of merely purposive attention. This approach emphasizes the formalization, over the incitement, of interest:

> If, as probably few will dispute, the art of the novelist be the representation of human life by means of a story; and if the *truest* representation, effected by the *least expenditure* of means, constitutes the highest claim of art, then we say that Miss Austen has carried the art to a point of excellence surpassing that reached by any of her rivals. Observe we say "the art;" we do not say that she equals many of them in the *interest* excited by the art; that is a

separate question. It is probable, nay certain, that the interest excited by the *Antigone* is very inferior to that excited by *Black-eyed Susan*. It is probable that *Uncle Tom* and *Dred* surpassed in interest the *Antiquary* or *Ivanhoe*. It is probable that *Jane Eyre* produced a far greater excitement than the *Vicar of Wakefield*. But the critic justly disregards these fervid elements of immediate success, and fixes his attention mainly on the art which is of eternal substance. Miss Austen has nothing fervid in her works. She is not capable of producing a profound agitation in the mind. (*CH* I, 152)

This account leaves unstated whether the opposite of "interest" is disinterest or boredom; and an "art … of eternal substance" does not disclose much detail. Perhaps it is something like the aesthetics of "keeping" I discuss in the book's final chapter, a care perfect in its mundane kind like the stewardship of Knightley's apples.

Taking an interest in *Emma* invokes aesthetic registers of experience and philosophical criticism. Can plot-based novels be Kantian aesthetic experiences? This criterion, however roughed in, would involve judgment that a novel is beautifully formed, rewards attention, but need not plug into the reader's interestedness in order to give pleasure. Yet this kind of "interest," as opposed to that of Kant's *Critique of Judgment*, does imply aesthetic receptivity to social networks and pressures. Sianne Ngai's work going back to *Ugly Feelings* (2005) has established "the basic affect of 'interest' underwriting all acts of intellectual inquiry."[23] In the Afterword of *Our Aesthetic Categories*, Ngai assembles her reflections from an earlier chapter on the *interessante* and the "merely interesting" from German Romanticism through 1960s art criticism and contemporary conceptual art. Ngai notices a particular temporality of the interesting that Cavell values under the sign of "conversation." Ngai writes: "While interesting art is serial or ongoing and comparative and dialogic, […] to performatively call something 'interesting' (often with an implicit ellipsis, 'interesting …') is to highlight and extend the period of an ongoing conversation. The judgment of the object as 'interesting,' with all its glaring conceptual indeterminacy, almost seems designed to facilitate the subject's formation of ties with another subject."[24]

The aesthetic category of the interesting prompts intersubjective ties. Again, with Cavell, Ngai follows a shift from verdictive terms to those of latent and unfolding conversational effects, though the "interesting" mutes the transitive aspect of the perlocutionary: "The work of such criticism is to reveal its object as having yet to achieve its due effect."[25] Even prior to the conversations of aesthetic judgment, though, the act of taking an interest defines the emergence of what we call empirical "objects," as such. For

William James, there must be "selective interest" to deliver experience and the details of empirical inspection from "utter chaos": "Interest alone gives accent and emphasis, light and shade, background and foreground—intelligible perspective, in a word."[26]

Though there is little of that kind of "excitation which depends on a narrative of uncommon events" (*E*, 365), on these terms so very much is made interesting in *Emma*: the "interesting, and certainly [...] very kind undertaking" of Harriet Smith (*E*, 18), which as Mrs. Weston argues against Knightley will supply Emma "with a new object of interest" (*E*, 27); the "objects of interest, objects for the affections," that as Emma maintains to Harriet will always distinguish her from the downwardly-mobile spinster Miss Bates (*E*, 63, also 66); the "local information" and farming interests of George and John Knightley (*E*, 72); the "interesting silence" that Mr. Elton reads as a confession of understanding in his impulsive proposal to Emma (*E*, 93); and the long-delayed, then sudden, arrival of Frank Churchill, "so high in interest" (*E*, 132). In a passage that halts the novel with its somber tone, we learn of the marriage of Lieutenant Fairfax and Miss Jane Bates, which "had had its day of fame and pleasure, hope and interest; but nothing now remained of it, save the melancholy remembrance of him dying in action abroad—of his widow sinking under consumption and grief soon afterwards—and this girl": little Jane Fairfax (*E*, 113). Jumping far ahead, here is Emma in the moment of full discovery of her feelings toward Knightley: "Till now that she was threatened with its loss, Emma had never known how much of her happiness depended on being *first* with Mr. Knightley, first in interest and affection" (*E*, 286). And Jane to Emma, now relieved of the burden of concealing her engagement with Frank: "You could not have gratified me more than by taking an interest—. Indeed, Miss Woodhouse, (speaking more collectedly,) with the consciousness which I have of misconduct, very great misconduct, it is particularly consoling to me to know that those of my friends, whose good opinion is most worth preserving, are not disgusted to such a degree as to—I have not time for half that I could wish to say" (*E*, 316). And Mr. Knightley to Emma, regarding the surprise engagement of Harriet to Robert Martin, with mock self-importance: "Your friend Harriet will make a much longer history when you see her.—She will give you all the minute particulars, which only woman's language can make interesting.— In our communications we deal only in the great" (*E*, 325). Placed next to the reviews that attest to *Emma*'s blandness as a work of the gruel-like substance of the everyday, these plot reminders of the novel's continual sense of small-town communal interestedness might re-ground the high-flying promise of reading *Emma* with Kant. They remind us that *Emma* is about tactics and gossip. Yet the stake of human interest in these plot points also conveys the intensiveness of Austen's feat to combine the play of aesthetic and social modalities.

Cavell's *In Quest of the Ordinary* dramatizes the post-Kantian situation he finds in Wordsworth's poetry and Coleridge's poetic theory. Cavell weighs "the Kantian bargain with skepticism (buying back knowledge of objects by giving up things in themselves) and romanticism's bargain with the Kantian (buying back the thing in itself by taking on animism)" (*In Quest*, 65). As a roaming horizon, rather than a set of texts with national boundaries and dates, Romanticism names the moment "too late for religion, because nothing is any longer common to our gods, and too soon for philosophy, because human beings are not interested in their new lives" (*In Quest*, 63). Though he had not yet begun reading Austen as part of his expression of interest in Romanticism, *Emma* soon enters the field of Cavell's idea that the time of philosophy (and the "too soon for philosophy") is measured by a challenge to take interest in painfully new lives. It is worth stressing here the core social implication of Kant's prohibition on knowing the *Ding-an-sich* in terms of other minds. Sealed off from things "in themselves," we may seek this impossible knowledge as a displacement of negotiating the available criteria of human knowledge.

Cavell's later encounter with the novels of Jane Austen also takes Kantian philosophical critique for its orientation: this time, *The Critique of Judgment* rather than the *Critique of Pure Reason*. If the impact of the First Critique for Cavell returns again and again to the romantic dissatisfaction with Kant as the philosopher of limits, with Kant's enabling precondition that we cannot know the thing-in-itself, a Cavellian reading of the Third Critique emphasizes the communicative and public stake of making "merely" subjective judgments. Kant's model of critical reflecting judgment is not limited to experiences of art, as "questions of aesthetic form and subjectivity in the *Critique of Judgment* cannot be separated."[27] To formulate an aesthetic judgment is already to be committed to making it known, to sharing the aesthetic emotion and vying for its communication, and to stand by public communities of implication. In Kant's *Critique of Judgment*, reflective judgments are opposed to determining judgments in that they follow no preset rule, and are not justified by conceptual content.[28] Reflecting judgments are at once decided and indeterminate. To earn their name as judgments of taste, they must involve more than a "liking." Judgments of taste are inherently robust – indeed, Kant argues they embed a subjectively universal validity in their structure. At the same time, they are conceptually weak and "unfit for knowledge."[29] Judgments of taste in their medial role find a novelistic correlate in the mediality of free indirect style, defined as a narrative mode sustained in the oscillation between narrator and character. Aligned with the Kantian genre of Critique, Austen's novels develop free indirect style – and its judgment without set rule or concept[30] – with a pervasive though unique *mode of human intelligibility*.

The arena in which such judgments are articulated, shared, and tested models a sensible critical community in its exchanges. Ngai comments in *Our Aesthetic Categories* on this social aspect of Cavell's aesthetic thinking, which she links unexpectedly to the "Frankfurt school tradition of Marxist aesthetics" in their "conceptually mixed efforts at evidentiary justification" in "cultural criticism." For Ngai, Cavell "defines 'criticism' not as the sharing of pleasure per se, but as the concept-based justification of a pleasure-based claim for a particular object's cultural worth" (117). "Cavell also speaks of his 'deriving the task of criticism from Kant's portrayal of the universality and necessity of aesthetic judgment, namely as grounded in its demand of agreement with its response to its object as one of pleasure without a concept. Criticism accordingly becomes a work of determining, as it were after the fact, the grounds of (the concepts shaping) pleasure and value in the working of the object'" (*P*, 67).[31] Yet Kant's focus on the beautiful as the nearly-exclusive category of aesthetic experience has been varied and challenged by the main figures in *Jane Austen and Other Minds*: by J. L. Austin in "A Plea for Excuses" (as Austin commends fieldwork on the dainty and dumpy as relief from the overworking of the beautiful); and by Ngai in *Our Aesthetic Categories* (which tracks the cute, the zany, and the merely interesting as crucial aesthetic categories for affective labor in the era from Romanticism to the contemporary moment). By comparing the quotidian social pastimes of matchmaking and judging in Austen's *Emma* to the complexity, sobriety, and schematic architectures found in Kant, this segment of my argument participates in that sociolinguistic and aesthetic fieldwork.

Kant's hinging grammar of "purposiveness without purpose" appears in recognizable form in Mr. Knightley's conclusion (via the narrator and free indirect speech) that Emma is "faultless in spite of all her faults" (*E*, 298). This paradoxical judgment plays off elements given from the novel's opening chapter: Governess Miss Taylor's affection for Emma, such as she "could never find fault" (*E*, 6); the narrator's projection from Emma's own and her father's point of view, that she is thought "perfect by every body," having "such an affection for her as could never find fault" (*E*, 6);

and in Knightley's role for Emma, in her own words: "Mr. Knightley loves to find fault with me you know—in a joke—it is all a joke. We always say what we like to one another" (*E*, 9). For the reader arriving at the end of the novel, who has now seen all into Emma's motives and doings, what could this claim to perfection even pretend to mean? By Volume III, with Highbury's two principal landholders about to merge assets under the blessing of joint epistemological and romantic recognitions, Knightley's epithet for his beloved risks obnoxiousness. The moment is truly Hegelian in its simultaneous preservation, elevation, and erasure (*Aufhebung*) of all Emma's mistakes, as her many mistaken concrete acts are absorbed into this perfectly negative universal judgment. Even if class interest did not make this paean to "perfection" troublesome (the word Mr. Weston has just used to evoke Emma at her worst in the Box Hill scene), the cooing paternalism is a toxic performance. Nevertheless, Emma could be called "faultless, in spite of all her faults," that is, not liable for them. Under that aspect, the phrase is not outright paradox but instead turns on a kind of embedded syllepsis, in which fault is not one thing that blankets a subject (like sin and its justification), but multiple more or less social forms of life, and their assessment. One way to find the syllepsis here would register how "faults" throughout the novel are products of uncertainty, and *certainty* itself is not referable to a single type or plane. To say "faultless" isn't quite to say (the yet more intolerable) "perfect."[32] For Cavell, these unacceptable conditions show "Moral Perfectionism to be the rescue from false perfectionism."[33] Knightley's doting redemption of Emma's faults in lover's discourse balances on the difference between making a category mistake and rendering a fine distinction.

A handful of perspicacious commentators already have seen how *Emma* captures philosopher Bernard Williams's idea of "moral luck."[34] *Emma* too is a book about the subjectively "universal" dimension of making reflecting judgments (singular judgments without a set prior framework of rules to govern them at a conceptual level) and the mental state Kant calls "free play." Without supporting Kant's disinterested judgment, *Emma* provocatively aligns with Cavell's sense that disavowing the strength of judgment is a mistake. On this view, *Emma* is not ultimately a novel about the subject getting clear of illusion, or absorbing a disciplinary "lesson" en route to adult leadership – that is, about her hard corrigibility or correctableness – but a test of the difference between trivial and full claims to judging in regions of the ordinary. Critical judgment is a Deweyan normal process of living that elicits and further develops human capacities, including responsibility. The register of ordinary language by which we lay hold of its discounted possibility abides in a striking and very Cavellian idea, one that emerges (again) from the opening chapter of *Emma*: in Austen, a conversing pair who quarrel over word usage are suited for life together.

Knightley and Emma debate the application of the words "endeavor" and "luck." For philosophers, developing Williams's coinage of the term and his important account, "Moral luck occurs when an agent can be correctly treated as an object of moral judgment despite the fact that a significant aspect of what she is assessed for depends on factors beyond her control."[35] According to the *Stanford Encyclopedia of Philosophy*, there are three ways of treating moral luck: by accepting it as a feature of human events and their moral experience; by its denial as a concept; or through the assertion of its incoherence. Is moral luck in fact what Emma and Knightley debate in Vol. I, Chapter 1? The *Stanford Encyclopedia* offers that "[t]he idea that morality is immune from luck finds inspiration in Kant," and proceeds to cite an aspect of his famous construction of the categorical imperative from the *Groundwork for a Metaphysics of Morals* (1784): "A good will is not good because of what it effects or accomplishes, because of its fitness to attain some proposed end, but only because of its volition, that is, it is good in itself." Emma and Knightley's debate relates to the idea of moral luck because their disagreement forms over whether Emma deserves credit for the marriage between Mr. Weston and Miss Taylor. Knightley's argument fits the view that takes moral agency to be causational and understands causal form as linear: "'I do not understand what you mean by "success,"' said Mr. Knightley. 'Success supposes endeavor'" (*E*, 10). Whereas Emma by contrast has only passively planned the match in her head and thought to herself about it "one idle day" (*E*, 11). The gender implications are clear and stereotypical in this contrast between consequential action and the guesswork of intuitive feeling. "This is the method of changing the world through action, as the other is the method of changing the self in emotion and idea."[36]

Yet Emma adopts and playfully affirms the dubious logical ground that Knightley allows her moral agency. "'What are you proud of?—you made a lucky guess; and *that* is all that can be said'" (*E*, 11). To a mode of inquiry that prizes conversation as a means of growth, knowledge, and exchange, the prime force we feel is not Knightley's consequentialist moral theory; it is rather his perlocutionary way of rounding off their exchange to discredit Emma: "*that* is all that can be said." Ongoing conversation is the negotiation not only between persons, but also between the relative forces of language Cavell calls "rational transformation" and the "invitation to improvisation in the disorders of desire" (*P*, 189, 185). Emma may concede Knightley's characterization of moral agency as "endeavor" in fixed terms, while keeping alive and in play the stylistics of a moral conversation that continues between them. But by no means can he put an end to all there is to say.[37] Her immediate riposte to Knightley enacts the more-to-say, before placing her argument behind a different distinction between luck and talent:

> And have you never known the pleasure and triumph of a lucky guess?—I pity you.—I thought you cleverer—for depend upon it, a lucky guess is never merely luck. There is always some talent in it. And to my poor word "success," which you quarrel with, I do not know that I am so entirely without any claim to it. You have drawn two pretty pictures—but I think there may be a third—a something between the do-nothing and the do-all. If I had not promoted Mr. Weston's visits here, and given many little encouragements, and smoothed many little matters, it might not have come to any thing after all. I think you must know Hartfield enough to comprehend that. (*E*, 11)

So J. L. Austin turns around the language of Polonius: *Neither a be-all nor an end-all be* (*PP*, 271). Austin's linguistic phenomenology tends toward the side of Emma's contextualized triumph of luck, rather than Knightley's theory of punctual action. Those who argue for a Control Principle with regard to concepts of moral judgment, or who deny the existence of moral luck, seek to protect moral knowledge from its environments: from contingency, vulnerability, and preoccupation; to preserve moral knowledge "intact," and prescribe a model of "all that can be said" of discrete consequence, in advance of and after the endless and manifold consequences, sequels, of language and action. The opposition might stress how Knightley's "all that can be said" functions not only as a conceptual bookend, but bristles performatively as a warning or threat. In his impatience and righteousness, Knightley exposes the role of the limit, the distribution of sense and nonsense, in its ideological form in this speech situation, not of critical reason but of gender and social authority. *Emma* is a Deweyan novel in another sense, too, in rejecting certainty for security.[38]

Emma's Taking an Interest

I've argued so far that J. L. Austin's redescription and critique of the epistemological goal of predictive certainty offers a compelling template for renewed readings of *Emma* that diversify the novel's philosophical play of interests. Pausing over a singular area in the novel's texture (and returning from the collective "answer" of "union" provided in *Emma*'s last chapter to the individual predicament laid down in the first), another point to stress is that the protagonist's taking an interest in her own life is non-trivially important. Indeed, it is foundational. In addition to the novel's relation to aesthetic and moral judgment, the "interesting" in *Emma* bears on the formation of primary investments to sustain subjectivity. This concern, expressed in the novel in Cavellian language of conversation and interest, upends the framing story about Emma's transgressions and misperceptions as a matchmaker. Similarly, *Emma* in my reading gives rather more weight and pause to retrojective psychologies, in place of the usual emphasis on fashioning predictions. Simply said, Emma overcomes a challenge to *invest* in her life and the conditions available to her. As readers, we tend to focus so much on Emma's ongoing schemes, that we downplay, or fail to register at all, the psychological shading of Emma's claim to have instrumentally encouraged her governess Miss Taylor's marriage to Mr. Weston in the novel's first instance of lucky guessing.

After the four well-known opening paragraphs on Emma's disposition, here is how the "event" of Miss Taylor's marriage, shaped by the protagonist's anticipation and response to that event, enters the novel:

> Sorrow came— a gentle sorrow—but not at all in the shape of any disagreeable consciousness.—Miss Taylor married. It was Miss Taylor's loss which first brought grief. It was on the wedding-day of this beloved friend that Emma first sat in mournful thought of any continuance. The wedding over and the bride-people gone, her father and herself were left to dine together, with no prospect of a third to cheer a long evening. Her father composed himself to sleep after dinner, as usual, and she had then only to sit and think of what she had lost.
>
> The event had every promise of happiness for her friend. Mr. Weston was a man of unexceptionable character, easy fortune, suitable age and pleasant manners; and there was some satisfaction in considering with what self-denying, generous friendship she had always wished for and promoted the match; but it was a black morning's work for her. The want of Miss Taylor would be felt every hour of every day. She recalled her past kindness—the kindness, the affection of sixteen years—how she had taught and how she had played with her from five years old—how she had devoted all her powers to attach and amuse her in health—and how nursed her through the various illnesses of childhood. A large debt of gratitude was owing here; but the intercourse of the last seven years, the equal footing and perfect unreserve which had soon followed Isabella's marriage on their being left to each other, was yet a dearer, tenderer recollection. It had been a friend and companion such as few possessed, intelligent, well-informed, useful, gentle, knowing all the ways of the family, interested in all its concerns, and peculiarly interested in herself, in every pleasure, every scheme of her's;—one to whom she could speak every thought as it arose, and who had such an affection for her as could never find fault.
>
> How was she to bear the change? (*E*, 5–6)

The summary question at the end of this passage (the start of a new paragraph about Emma's isolation, which I want to discuss in its course) carries a double meaning. Considered as free indirect style, it ironically underlines the loss of a mentor especially valued for a pettish reason – for never finding fault with Emma. A "change" away from this condition is non-tragic, the loss of this aspect of her relationship to Miss Taylor a necessary "change." On the next page we also read of "Matrimony, as the origin of change" (*E*, 7). The transition of marriage too is not a departure from the established course of life, but is a given precisely *as* change.

But there is another sense of "*the* change" in play, registering seismic shift. The definite article especially invites us to realize one referent governing change. That is the death which has long ago taken place. The loss is reopened and recognized now as potentially decisive with the departure of Miss Taylor, whose continual "interest" in Emma had preserved her from feeling the full effects of such a crisis, for sixteen years. Attending Miss Taylor's wedding had proved "a black morning's work," because it ensnares a longer work of mourning. Emma's prospect for the days and years ahead looks bleak. In the opening sentence of the novel, Emma is introduced as a kind of modern figura of a regal person who seems to unite "blessings of existence" – but of course she echoes queenly bearing for the Regency middle sphere (keeping close, as Scott says, to "common incidents" and "ordinary walks"). Emma's predicament is now revealed in its acutest dimension: she lives neither in sovereign loneliness nor as a suburban teenager, but in a *middling society of no equals*.[39]

Emma is not only able to witness and celebrate Miss Taylor's marriage on the day the novel begins – but to *over*invest in it enthusiastically, to the extent that Mr. Knightley charges her with magical thinking about the positive scope of her agency.[40] The very sentence in which we are told Emma enjoys the "satisfaction" of considering herself "self-denying, generous" in her act of "friendship" to Miss Taylor/Mrs. Weston also contains a tell: she believes herself to have "*always* wished and promoted the match" (*E*, 6; emphasis added). How could this be true? The "always" signals retrojective psychology and wishful transference. This description of Emma's involvement cannot be empirical. The slight elision, "wished *for*" rendered simply as "wished," may also suggest non-localized and indeterminate "wish" – moving away from a wish that takes a direct object to one that is intransitive, reflecting the subject herself, her being. Whether Emma *did* materially forward this relationship as she maintains, her positive claim to have done so actively assents to the change. Her participation in change embraces a strategy for living and counteracts the prospect of her life as a quietly desperate predicament. In saying this, I know I am in danger of forgetting the opening characterization of Emma Woodhouse as "handsome, clever, and rich, with a comfortable home and happy disposition": the merger of personal disposition and social standing that seems "to unite some of the best blessings of existence" (*E*, 5).[41] Miss Taylor's marriage and departure from Hartfield carry an impact somewhere between "a gentle sorrow" (*E*, 5) from the narrator's point of view, and the death seen by Mr. Woodhouse (based on his inability to regard Miss Taylor and Mrs. Weston as the same person [*E*, 6]). The overextended investment in Miss Taylor's change of name and address as a death displays how transferable a woman's identity becomes in marriage. It also underlines the death that has shaped the Woodhouses, the death of Emma's mother "too long ago" for "more than an indistinct remembrance" (*E*, 5). (Though Emma's illiberal forms of agency may border on expressing that "indistinct remembrance," if she knows "triumph" as a thinker of moral luck because there is devastation.)

If most readers come away from the first chapter with a sense of Emma's entitlement, it is to something like the character's credit that Emma promotes this overwhelming impression of her undistressed privilege. Austen gives almost no space to demonstrate what Emma has "done" to be resilient beyond her "happy disposition," and devotes the novel instead to her presumptuous matchmaking. But how should we weigh this initially generous donation of her character? A novel based on these initial "facts" (the early death of the protagonist's mother; the terrorized meekness of her invalid father, for whom she performs the role of a caretaker; the marriage and departure of her teacher and only friend) positions the reader to expect the heroine's breakdown. Instead, Emma's abounding attachment to life can bear the reproof of her schemes and distractions; these are both signs and strategies of her investment.

Insofar as the novel's generic effect is comic and critical, not tragic and empathizing, in Vol. I, Chapter 1, it is not due to the fact that the worst hasn't happened, but through Emma's creaturely talent for participation. When Emma is despondent in Vol. III, Chapter 12, and she must face the loss of hope by realizing the loss of the person of Knightley ("She had no hope, nothing to deserve the name of hope" [*E*, 286]), the text returns to this aspect of the opening chapter as if fully to round on its psychological mood of "deserted" atmosphere:

> The prospect before her now, was threatening to a degree that could not be entirely dispelled – that might not be even partially brightened. If all took place that might take place among the circle of her friends, Hartfield must be comparatively deserted; and she left to cheer her father with the spirits only of ruined happiness. (*E*, 291)

In opposition to Volume I when only Mr. Woodhouse's imbecility and Emma's imagination register loss, something offered as the worst threatens here. Though it is July on the calendar, Emma tries stoically to process perennial winter:

> The evening of this day was very long, and melancholy, at Hartfield. The weather added what it could of gloom. A cold stormy rain set in, and nothing of July appeared but in the trees and shrubs, which the wind was despoiling, and the length of the day, which only made such cruel sights the longer visible. [...] When it came to such a pitch as this, she was not able to refrain from a start, or a heavy sigh, or from walking about the room for a few seconds—and the only source whence any thing like consolation or composure could be drawn, was in the resolution of her own better conduct, and the hope, that however inferior in spirit and gaiety might be the following and every future winter of her life to the past, it would yet find her more rational, more acquainted with herself, and leave her less to regret when it were gone. (*E*, 290–291)

There is irony on the part of Austen's narrator in these passages; but it belongs to the juxtaposition of Emma's moral resolve as out of character – and volunteering more than will be demanded of her – with the imminent resolution of the marriage plot in the next chapter. With a turn of the page, the weather turns "tranquil, warm, and brilliant after a storm," and Knightley, whom Emma "had been thinking" of just a moment before as "unquestionably sixteen miles distant in London," stands there before her (*E*, 292).

The disclosure scene of the novel's romance plot works only because Knightley and Emma alike accept hopelessness in the proceeding moment. Here it is not Emma, but Austen, who runs the risk to merge hard-won fulfillment and glibness, uniting her two main characters in a complex of interest that involves entitlement, exposure to loss, and judgment, as well as a potentially insufferable both-and-ism that gives excess of love and security. Austen cannot guarantee by mandate that her reader should have the intuition that Emma and Knightley's compound interests in Volume III relate meaningfully back to the vulnerability in Volume I. But she signals the investment. Sixteen miles, Knightley's imagined distance from Emma at the climactic point in the plot – London to Highbury – measures the years between Emma and the death of her mother.

"Intellectual Solitude"

To the extent that Austen succeeds in constructing these forms of interest without indulging in triumph to the point of obnoxiousness, she does so on the back of the "blessed" Emma's surprising relationship to distress.[42] As Eric Walker observes, Cavell's writings on Austen take us far from the fairy tale marriage plot, and focus instead on the distress of unlivable social and spiritual conditions. Following Cavell, Walker compares Austen to Nietzsche in terms of a dimension of philosophical perfectionism that responds to living a co-opted and stifled existence. Walker emphasizes that "[t]he proposition that Austen's novels strike many as offering images of human lives that can appear 'too confined' lines up with Cavell's subsequent observation that one of the features of Austen's fiction that long kept him at arm's length was 'Austen's narrator's renowned surface of containment'" (*P*, 124).[43] Walker forcefully summarizes: "Constraint, confinement, containment, distress, these are the clouded headings under which Cavell organizes his reading in Austen (and Nietzsche, Emerson, and Eliot) of the 'unrelieved routine or fixation of ordinariness' (*P* 122), which yields a 'state of vulnerable conformity,' a human condition that suffers, in Cavell's most extreme formulation, 'brutalities'" (*P*, 123).[44]

Philosophy the Day after Tomorrow characterizes the vulnerability Cavell later attributes to Austen's heroines to the position of philosophy altogether – particularly the philosophy of the ordinary – as threatened by skepticism (*P*, 1–2). Cavell points back toward himself and to the "remains of my day" as he puts it, quoting from another famous example of the fiction of mannered restraint. This remark points to the same blankness of philosophical interest that intercepts Emma's life at the start of the novel. More developed remarks upon *Emma* occur in two separate chapters from *Philosophy the Day after Tomorrow*. In the eponymous chapter he explores "a philosophical dimension" in the "state of vulnerable conformity" that characterizes the novels of Austen and George Eliot (*P*, 123). Cavell draws out the full depth of a predicament embedded in a phrase from the start of *Emma*, "intellectual solitude," to evoke the threat of the protagonist's isolation, her unshareable consciousness (*E*, 6). What kind of philosophical claim on Austen's work does this constitute? Chiara Alfano has observed that "[w]hat sets Cavell apart from other proponents of ordinary language philosophy is that in his reading neither Austin nor Wittgenstein denies the reality of separateness."[45] Respecting this state of human separateness, Cavell reads Austen's fiction so as "to exemplify instances in which the soul can learn not to be crushed by the force of compromise" (*P*, 122).[46]

The idea of writing against "quiet desperation" returns in a different modality, as we move from the early stages of Cavell's career to this late encounter, from a voice that would maximize protest to one that must "minimize (hence maintain) the expression of distress in everyday existence." The compromised, even degrading terms of a conventional, intelligible, and shared world seem in conflict with the minimal conditions of individual voice, never mind moral perfectionism. *The Senses of Walden* (1972) lays everything on the conviction that an errant, extravagant writerliness alone engages us to mean (and truly to read) every word. *Walden* insists with a tone of path-breaking hostility that "[i]t is a ridiculous demand which England and America make, that you shall speak so that they can understand you. [...] As if that were important, and there were not enough to understand you without them. [...] As if there were safety in stupidity alone."[47] Cavell's writings on Romanticism in the 1980s render this aversive ethos melodramatically. The animating life of the world depends on the possibility of a successful negotiation between acts of individual expression in philosophical poetics, and the recognition of the place these acts hold in democracy, for inaugurating a new communicative public. Twenty years onward, Cavell's motivation and apparent aim in turning to Austen's contemporaneous-but-not-self-evidently romantic novels in *Philosophy the Day After Tomorrow* takes another step in the direction of shared pleasure in responsive rational inquiry. Has Cavell given up Thoreauvian extravagance?[48]

How exhaustive is public communication to the project Cavell calls "rational transformation" (*P*, 189)? Alternately, how much like a tragic sign of election does the fate of an "unshareable" consciousness remain (*P*, 128)? And then, Cavell pointedly wonders, could "women, of Eliot's, let alone Jane Austen's time, [...] have afforded" such a "cost of a great separation" (*P*, 129)? Thus, in a penetrating note concerning a cinematic theme – the melodrama of the unknown woman – which in several books precedes Cavell's interest in Austen's novels and anticipates that subject thematically, Michael Fischer has observed: "Cavell links Wittgenstein's concentration on pain in the *Philosophical Investigations* to the fascination of psychoanalysis and cinema with the sufferings of women. By the turn of the [twentieth] century, [according to Cavell] 'psychic reality, the fact of the existence of mind, has become believable primarily in its feminine (you may say passive) aspect'."[49] Cavell's reading of Austen figures this gendered instantiation of "the existence of mind" and registers the conviction in (or problem of) "other minds," as he treats different, character-specific versions of the passion and suffering incident to the intellectual tragedy of separation. Risks of nullification emerge for Elizabeth Bennet, Fanny Price, and Emma Woodhouse, along the extremes of a criterial dimension Cavell has repeatedly discussed in the philosophy of Wittgenstein, sourced to a fantasized rift between total privacy and transparent, rule-following convention. Under these terms Cavell tracks the "vulnerable conformity" and "damaged consent" experienced by subordinated women in a privileged society.

In one of the key textual object lessons of his essay, "Austen and Cavell," Eric Walker admires the way Cavell "zooms in on a sentence—indeed, a phrase—from the opening chapter" of *Emma*. Walker observes that it strikes "as no accident that this is a scene in which Austen herself upends convention by pitching a wedding as a funeral, as an occasion of distress, of vulnerability. As Emma and her father grieve the passing of Miss Taylor into Mrs. Weston, the narrator remarks that this is a moment when 'Emma first sat in mournful thought of any continuance.'" Walker presents Cavell's gloss on the passage:

> I find that I am unsure whether this meditation means that she is vexed not to have her friend to continue their happy mode of existence; or whether it suggests that she is so grief-stricken that she cannot imagine wanting her own existence to continue; or whether, as mostly seems to me the case, that Emma herself cannot tell the difference. (*P*, 124)

Walker remarks that "[i]f I ever paused previously at the phrase 'mournful thought of any continuance,' I understood it as a jab at the unlikely prospect that Emma's thoughts of any kind (even grief) might exhibit duration. But I had certainly never before understood this moment as Emma entirely halted in her tracks, where 'continuance' itself is substantively at stake. [...] [T]he fine tuning of Cavell's ear catches (indeed, brings to our attention) the radical vulnerability of Emma's new form of confinement and distress."[50]

This sensitive and alarming description allows Cavell's interpretation of *Emma* to develop its multiple directions. The startling consequences of that reading include not only the disruption and doubt over Emma's continuance, but also the disorientation registered – another kind of distress – between this response and the inherited reading. There is a distressing gap between the idea that Emma has never suffered for very long before, and the intimation that her means of continuing her life is at risk. Ambiguously positioned in relation to his earlier forceful readings of writers such as Thoreau, Shakespeare, and the Romantic poets, in his engagement with Austen's fiction Cavell appears at once to start out from

"Intellectual Solitude" 185

a standard of communicative sociability, and to press an aversive limit case meant to show that idiosyncrasy and solitude persist especially in Austen.

From the perspective of the larger context on offer, methodically developed from Austin's formal taxonomies and dictionary word lists in Cavell's "Performative and Passionate Utterance," it is particularly striking that Jane Austen's novels are taken to voice "the rights of desire" and the "imperative of expression" (*P*, 185, 188), in opposition to the institutional realm of social "responsibilities of implication" (*P*, 185). The affirmation of imperatives of passionate utterance is striking in this chapter on Austen and Austin, writers typically understood to ritualize normative sociality within established limits.

In the later chapter in *Philosophy the Day after Tomorrow* on passionate utterance, Cavell comes back to *Emma*. This chapter offers Cavell's most careful discussion of Austin's initially under-emphasized theory of perlocution (the realm of intersubjective contact registered *through* and *by* speech acts, from hate speech to seduction). Cavell delivers this region from the institutional formalism in the famous account of illocution in *How to Do Things with Words*. "Performative and Passionate Utterance" concludes with a long quotation from the awkward "proposal" that Mr. Elton forces upon Emma at the end of Volume I (*P*, 190). On the previous page, Cavell has framed his interest in the "rational transformation" of the female subject and protagonist (*P*, 189). "[R]ecasting" Austin's nearly exclusive focus on the explicit speech act, he understands the field of transformation "as an interaction of two developed and contrasting fields of force," illocution and perlocution. In the next paragraph he recommends the extended classificatory program of counting up perlocutionary verbs, as Austin had started to do with verbs of illocution (*P*, 189). Cavell, however, suggests that methodology only as prospective advice. The itemized list never appears.

Cavell has already performed this temporally foreclosed, elliptical gesture with reference to Austin's *Sense and Sensibilia* lectures, as discussed in my Introduction: "Because it is not to my hand here, or perhaps ever, to lay out a fuller geography of the courses that 'endless' passionate exchanges can take in satisfying the conditions of perlocutionary utterance" (*P*, 188). The annulled, extenuating act of never taking something fully to hand weighs on the discussion of Jane Austen within the realm of the ready-to-hand and the ordinary. Is the failure to reach the material he might have "br[ought] to hand" not a major concession of loss? The "endlessness" of the improvised performances and unforeseen consequences of passionate exchange gives a conceptual rationale for why Cavell cannot map the field of performative speech acts fully (as a "geography" of illocution), or place them in a curriculum (his language moves from landscape to pedagogy, with an eye to the irregular "courses" such speech acts may take). As an act of homage and prompt to others' future work, the roadmap to Austin's neglected terrain of perlocution asked to be received itself as perlocutionary encouragement in this gesture to continue with its terms.

The passage quoted from the end of Vol. I of *Emma* (Vol. I, Chapter 15) stops short on the program Cavell has set out, to provide a "comparable weighing" of many other passages (*P*, 189). The close reading of a single text interrupts this programmatic agenda of lists. Cavell admits he is only a "partial, indebted Austinian," not a "faithful" student. He does not follow with an exhaustive list but with intensive meditation. Cavell notes the "proportionality" in his *Emma* passage between J. L. Austin's "paradigmatic" illocutionary verbs and perlocutionary verbs "as an interaction of two developed and contrasting fields of force in which speech may be said to perform, to do what it implies" (*P*, 189). But to detail these interacting linguistic forces would require, he continues, "a continual weighing of passages from other of Austen's novels, as well as from analogous exchanges in [...] the works of her contemporary novelists, as well as in those of, say, Scott, Madame de Staël, George Eliot, Thackeray, and Dickens" (*P*, 189). The passage he then shares from *Emma* compacts illocutionary speech acts with perlocutionary invitations, pressures, responses, and conditions. Mr. Elton's attempted illocution (his semi-drunken proposal in the carriage) is not the star. That role goes to Emma, who "blocks" and "non-plays" Elton's behavior as a formal speech act she would otherwise be expected to treat seriously.[51] Though the carriage door is "lawfully shut on them" (*E*, 84) and Emma is at great discomfort and disadvantage of situation – with the scene suggesting capture and shaded by threat of assault – like most readers, Cavell does not respond to Emma as a victim of aggression or even of verbal wounding. She is not subject to a rape attempt, or the victim of hate speech. She is, however, the rational and feeling subject who is cornered by Elton's "nonsense."

The passage furnishes a phrase about love's "little zigzags of embarrassment" that Cavell adopts and turns over into an important allusion to the plot of Volume III, applying it insightfully to the idea that Emma and Mr. Knightley never completely find each other's minds in "perfect communication" regarding Harriet Smith and Robert Martin.[52] This slightest of evasions – the lone point of reserve before an otherwise transparently shared happiness? – involves Emma's looking away to get control of her too-significant expression of joy, when Knightley shares the news of Robert

Martin's accepted proposal.[53] (There seems to be an offsetting "secret" not dramatized: Knightley himself has sent Robert Martin to London on business, since he knows that Harriet is staying there in Brunswick Street with his brother John's family.) Soon afterward, the narrator suggests that this "confidence" held *from* Knightley may be appropriately converted to a confidence shared *with* him, under the privilege of full communication granted to both as a right of the Hegelian fulfillment of marriage, and compensation for its confines. In *Emma*, it is the Eltons alone who share full disclosures as a married couple, and they only make it a show. (Another novel has the equally cringeworthy Mr. Collins: "My dear Charlotte and I have one mind and one way of thinking [*P&P*, 149]). Until the last sitting room conversation with Jane Fairfax at the Bates's rooms, the Eltons appear to communicate information completely, from their malicious joint treatment of Harriet at the dance at the Crown, where Harriet's past hopes are treated as a sacrifice to marital unreserve; to Elton's code-switching gossip, as he moves unreflectively from the role of church officiant to critical onlooker, in detailing to his wife the allegedly 'shabby' particulars of Emma and Knightley's wedding on the novel's final page."

Cavell maintains that even for Austin at his most programmatic, it is "exceptions and refinements that give him his characteristic pleasure in philosophizing" (*P*, 166). The pleasure of improvisation and the philosophical importance of mistakes matter a great deal to Cavell, as the philosopher of "passionate utterance," in homage and modification of Austin's official and "lawful" institutions of speech.[54] In *On Certainty*, Wittgenstein gives pause to just the kind of philosophical program of enumeration toward which Cavell gestures: "Now, can one enumerate what one knows (like Moore)? Straight off like that, I believe not.—For otherwise the expression 'I know' gets misused. And through this misuse a queer and extremely important mental state seems to be revealed" (§6). Wittgenstein's sections represent near-continual (and continental) shifts in perspective rather than stacking exemplifications. Setting his thought against the whetstone of G. E. Moore, Wittgenstein explores what it would mean to recognize conviction in a language of "holding" and "standing fast" when he wonders: "Instead of 'I know …', couldn't Moore have said: 'It stands fast for me that …'? And further: 'It stands fast for me and many others….'" (§116). For Wittgenstein, contingency is not a suspect measure of knowledge: "144. What stands fast does so, not because it is intrinsically obvious or convincing; it is rather held fast by what lies around it." As the language of "standing fast" serves in place of that of truth and certainty, the bound relationality of secure knowing displaces the thought-picture of truth as a decontextualized single entity.

Wittgenstein rejects the premise that truth is a form of extension. His move can rehabilitate knowledge. A meaningful claim to know does not refer to an isolated challenge subject to line-item doubt or verification, but draws on the co-implications of linguistic and social conduct, persons and things. It is a reminder for us that in *Emma*, the loss of relationships spurs the protagonist to her relation to truth, and to her entering (if not by choice) a more philosophical mode of existence. Cavell, in various passages of *The Claim of Reason*, underscores the relational sanity of *On Certainty*, which offers a series of agile rebuffs to the skeptical derangement made all too easy by locating value only in the philosophical subject, a knowing subject willing to stake it all and pretend to be left with nothing in the event of coming up short: "69. I should like to say: 'If I am wrong about *this*, I have no guarantee that anything I say is true.' But others won't say that about me, nor will I say it about other people."

In his commentary on Emma's intellectual solitude and doubt of continuance, Cavell has no direct recourse to Wittgenstein's anti-epistemological standard of knowledge "held fast by what lies around it." Instead he pursues a traditional literary-critical technique of identifying doubles and foils that register the heroines' plights. This reading gives depth to the sense that Emma's commonality with other characters registers a threat of debasement. An aspect of Cavell's film criticism is helpful to draw upon, as there he acknowledges snobbery as a spiritual and political risk of his embrace of perfectionist characters. Countervailing this, he is fascinated by depletion. Mr. Elton (along with John Thorpe from *Northanger Abbey*) is a prime instance of not only a worn-out character but one who threatens depletion to others.

D. W. Harding, an influential critic of Austen, and contemporary of Austin, makes compelling sense of the novel's caricatured minor characters as representatives of the "perfectly comfortable … detestable people" one must continue to live with on unbroken terms. Harding extends this portrayal to Austen's characters to her contemporary world and readership. His argument puts the "supporting players" in an essential relation with the serious work done by Austenian style and manners (*P*, 126). Despite the ungenerous appearance of his intervention in Austen Studies with "Regulated Hatred," Harding is a sensitive commentator on the novels, and his Austen is no simple misanthrope.[55] Harding thinks in something like Cavellian terms regarding Austen's commitment to her own "spiritual survival," to be fought for and preserved merely by "finding some mode of existence for her critical attitudes."⁵⁶ Restoring deserved prominence to Harding's scholarship on war and group psychology, Wendy Lee presents his sociopolitically shrewd Austen as a writer who understands the psychological landscape of global *realpolitik*. Austen's fiction provides a resource to understand the meaning of hatred for Europe at total war. Harding, in making a repertoire of Austen's well-mannered tactics, looks for the meaningful possibility of a concept of peace in Europe's post-war order.⁵⁷ This version of Austen practices skills required to live on unbroken terms with enemies in a small, closed-in, yet still close-knit, world.

The linkage from Harding to Cavell's investment in Austen is apparent and substantial. Austen maintains the ironic double register of her style so that her attitudes may find expression, and she herself may have a social space to exist. She understood her own voice and consent to be solicited by society, as the consent of her heroines is solicited by the confining promises of marriage. She is at once intensely critical of others and strongly attached to the people among whom she lives – people whose affection she needs – who are often the same people. *Emma* is the novel closest to the model of three or four families in a country village, but there is little of snugness in the fact. Notice the difference between Harding's and Cavell's accounts of Austen's regulation of "lethal" style and Mitford's prefatory comment on the sketches in *Our Village*: "She has painted, as they appeared to her, their ['her villagers'] little frailties and their many virtues, under an intense and thankful conviction, that in every condition of life goodness and happiness may be found by those who seek them."⁵⁸

Austin and Other Minds at Box Hill

Harding highlights Mr. Collins in *Pride and Prejudice* and Mrs. Elton from *Emma* as examples of those with values inimical to Austen and her surrogates. Yet it may be the social atmosphere of Highbury itself, as the paradigm of three or four families in a country village, that evinces Cavell's fascination with the confined and "worn out" in Austen (*P*, 126). Highbury, with its invalid patriarch in the family of first consequence (*E*, 7), its venally social-climbing vicar, and its down-at-the-mouth Crown Inn (*E*, 175). Even in the most lively parties, the usual flow of dinner conversation in Highbury is described as "a few clever things said, a few downright silly, but by much the larger proportion neither the one nor the other – nothing worse than every day remarks, dull repetitions, old news, and heavy jokes" (*E*, 151–152). Nothing worse here than the everyday; but everyday Highbury is dull, old, repetitious, heavy. Harding's "regulated hatred" thesis is driven home by an ironic (yet importantly, unavoidable) nicety of cleanup detail, as the village clergyman Elton officiates and blesses the "union" of Emma and Knightley, after serving in the same awkward role a month earlier for Harriet and Robert Martin.

The blend of sharp criticism with attachment brings to mind a major scene in *Emma* that I turn to now: the Box Hill excursion. This famous chapter ends with Emma's act of open ridicule of Miss Bates, followed by Mr. Knightley's rebuke. While the reader is distracted by games, Emma's public transgression and intimate recognition of wrongdoing each register in short space, and similarly reorient her reader.[59] Box Hill is not the climax of the novel in terms of plot, but it is here that the moral center of gravity alters. Here the words wound. No one will argue with the idea that the excursion to Box Hill represents a key turning point in *Emma*. The scene contains perhaps the novel's only major incident. At the same time, the Box Hill episode can be thought of as an event built around distractions and narrative "fillers."[60] The yield in this section for *Austen and Other Minds* is simple, but I think it carries pervasive implications. The Box Hill episode as a whole, and Frank Churchill's enforced game within it, ostentatiously poses the question of access to the content of "other minds." My contribution finds its place one step further. For all occasions I can think of besides formal philosophical discussion, the way we conduct questions of other minds is fundamentally perlocutionary. When we engage in this form of affective exchange – and no differently, when authors engage in it too – the primary thing we are doing, the cultural competency in practice, and its effect, is perlocutionary. Verification and epistemological questions about the content and intent of others' minds all of course do matter; but the route even to these issues is perlocutionary. Issues are aired. Questions aren't asked in an airtight proof. We are threatened, we are offended; we are flirting, we are seducing; or teasing, or alienating (and of course both giving and receiving these impressions). We intertwine many of these effects. So does Austen.

The Box Hill scene takes place as a discretionary leisure outing, a picnic. Its verbal interest derives from characters making shift in the confined space of their uninterested conversations, filling up the "stupid" time with games, pretenses, and excuses (*E*, 242). The presiding tone – hinting of national allegory – is the disunion of the party ("a want of spirits, a want of union" [*E*, 253]). Frank's command acts in the name of Emma as the "presid[ing]" figure over the outing, thus presenting Emma both as judge (a role Mrs. Elton would affectedly claim for herself as "*Chaperon*" [*E*, 255]), and as figure of sovereign. He commands the party to deliver over not only the content of their minds, but spark conversation in the first place. Knightley's response to this command makes him the honest servant who is willing to risk his sovereign's rebuke (*Lear*'s Kent): "Is Miss Woodhouse sure that she would like to hear what we are all thinking of?" (*E*, 255)

The climactic wounding of Miss Bates because she is silly, inconsequential and talks too much is thus especially perverse in light of Frank's first command to the party simply to talk and say anything ("Any nonsense will serve" [*E*, 255]). Frank's behavior in this scene particularly requires his excuse later in the resolution chapters of the novel. Conducting himself throughout the outing at "a pitch almost unpleasant" (*E*, 258), Frank shouts over the group to the neighboring hills of Surrey in a mock rhetorical address to the middling landscape: "'I say nothing of which I am ashamed,' replied he, with lively impudence. 'I saw you first in February. Let every body in the Hill hear me if they can. Let my accents swell to Mickleham on one side, and Dorking on the other. I saw you first in February'" (*E*, 255). His loud-talking oscillates with asides to Emma in undertone: "And then whispering—'Our companions are excessively stupid. What shall we do to rouse them? Any nonsense will serve'" (*E*, 255). Part of what we hear in this antic display of ill-keyed charm – a display at once intimate and public, as the mock assumption of lyric and diaristic address suggests – is the tension of Frank's growing conflict with Jane Fairfax, which has just played out on the previous day of strawberry picking at Donwell. In this regard it is interesting that no one pays much attention to the picturesque prospect that ostensibly draws them all there. A similar lacuna of expected interest in the previous chapter is Donwell's ruined abbey. Knightley and Harriet overlook it to discuss functional Abbey Mill Farm.

In Jane's first act of meaningful reliance upon Emma, Jane departs in haste at the end of the preceding day at Donwell, asking Emma to make her excuses. Just after this moment and seemingly with no connection, Frank complains about the heat and declares himself "sick of England" (*E*, 252). More, though, is going on at Box Hill than the carryover of Frank's heated state from the day before (*E*, 238). The intent of Frank's actions cannot be attributed entirely to his aim to be seen as flirting with Emma (*E*, 241). His drive to extract conversation from the party betrays a joyless hilarity that is surplus to his intention. It reveals a deep slip from his usual ease to a grimace of mock sociability. Harding's "civil falsehood" is a phrase in fact used, ironically and disingenuously, by Frank back in Volume II (*E*, 162). Just these few seconds betray Frank's unregulated contempt for Highbury folk. His address makes for painfully sad sport: "Our companions are excessively stupid. What shall we do to rouse them? Any nonsense will serve. They *shall* talk. Ladies and Gentleman, I am ordered by Miss

Woodhouse (who, wherever she is, presides,) to say, that she desires to know what you are all thinking of" (*E*, 255). Pretending to act on Emma's lawful order, he euphemistically calls Emma's sovereign command to the group her own "desire." Frank establishes the relationship between Emma and other minds as a command performance that makes them both offensive. Similarly, Knightley's rebuke to Emma later is based especially on the inequality in Emma's social and economic relation to Miss Bates. He does not just enforce the seriousness of behaving ethically in a world of continuous interdependencies. He deputizes Emma.

"Is Miss Woodhouse sure that she would like to hear what we are all thinking of?," Mr. Knightley replies to Emma rather than Frank (*E*, 255). Knightley responds bluntly, as usual. But his remark is salty and carries a hinted threat. It exhibits a reflex to disaffiliate from the self-deputized Frank. Knightley's comment both warns Emma and affords her the chance to distance herself from Frank. She vaguely welcomes that chance in returning, "Oh no, no, no!" Yet even Mrs. Elton's response wins a touch of sympathy at Emma's expense: "'It is a sort of thing,' cried Mrs. Elton emphatically, 'which *I* should not have thought myself privileged to inquire into'" (*E*, 255). As if it were really Emma pushing – and not Mrs. Elton who is presumptuous and meddlesome: we know Mrs. Elton's role is that of an upstart rival to Emma's taste and social position, and an alternate convener of the event. The irony of her protest recoils on Mrs. Elton and her dearth of thinking, though for once she shares an accurate observation, contrasting her official standing as "*Chaperon* of the party" to Frank's fanciful insinuation that Emma is the sovereign and judge, specifically, of its conversation. Getting no uptake on his initial request, then, Frank tries the strategy again at a different angle and "attack[s] … with more address." His second forced invitation shifts from Austin's illocutionary performative to soliciting response. It asks for entertainment instead of the description of an inner state (and occurs after another change of pitch, from a private whisper to public announcement). It is this second request that Miss Bates answers and in her answer – already self-deprecating – offers the gratuitous temptation to wound that "Emma could not resist" (*E*, 256).

In an essay from her book about how readers form social and emotional investments in fictional literary characters, Blakey Vermeule concedes an "almost overwhelming" impulse to criticize Emma, based in part on the observation that she thinks of herself more like an author than as a heroine.[61] Mary Poovey has pointed out that Emma's "sharp jibe at Miss Bates expresses exactly what she thinks about the unfortunate old maid," thus fulfilling, with wincing irony, Frank's command to the group to tell Emma just what they are thinking in the previous instant.[62] Poovey also notices that Emma's comment arrives a question late. It is very much to the point of Austen's treatment of this pervasive novelistic and philosophical concern, that attention to Box Hill will not deliver *as direct access to cognition* an answer to the "other minds" problem. Nor will any reply resolve the status of the other in relation to knowledge. Austen's, and Frank's, and Emma's preoccupations with what the others are thinking hold interest not at the thematic level alone, but transversely across the topic as performative human comedy. This episode, perhaps more than any other chapter in Austen, shows that the terrain of "other minds" philosophy is an intensive stylistic and behavioral resource for her writerly project, one to be played upon *in*, and *by*, and *through* the novel's social and aesthetic effects. Even Frank's first arrival in Highbury signals "other minds" as a topic of sympathetic preoccupation: "Think of me tomorrow," Mrs. Weston says to Emma in Volume II, "at four o'clock" (*E*, 131). And of course a "problem" prone to mistake: the next day, there is Frank peremptorily before them in the parlor at Hartfield, "a day before his time" (*E*, 132).

Theory of Mind theory on the "other minds" problem is often oriented *not* toward a final shared referential knowledge with and about the other, but to rehearse a model of reflexive knowledge concerning *what the other cannot know*, based on the information they possess, their particularized knowledge and situated experience.[63] A canvassing irony of these behavioral parameters in the context of the Box Hill scene is how Miss Bates, as William Galperin points out, actually holds a uniquely privileged position on knowledge in the larger context of the novel's "mystery" plot.[64]

It is not in perfected omniscience, but in the trans-, between-, and beside-places of these linguistic and social forms of life that Austen and *Emma* so intelligently work. Austen's movement across, around, and athwart the other minds problematic (after Eve Sedgwick we might call this a *peri-* rather than metacritical theory), demonstrates her indifference to penetrative epistemological thinking. Neither is Austen approaching knowledge as better and better approximations of omniscient vantage.[65] Like the ordinary language philosophers, Austen moves from thinking about knowledge in terms of the deliverable of content (dry goods, boxed!), to the performance and assessment of how language acts in the contextualized event (concerned not with the summative prospect, but with picnicking upon the hill). Adela Pinch argues that "viewing the forms of nineteenth-century literature from the point of view of theories of thinking as action, rather than from the point of view of the problem of representing other minds, can illuminate crucial aspects of these forms. A focus on thinking as action will allow us … to question whether omniscience is the most salient term for understanding representations of thinking in the Victorian novel."[66]

A Plea for Excuses

Something more, and less, and otherwise than omniscient knowing is at stake at Box Hill. J. L. Austin's most resonant paper for thinking through Frank Churchill's behavior is possibly neither "A Plea for Excuses" (as wonderful as that paper is as a deconstruction of the punctual account of the boundary of an "action"), nor "Other Minds" (which shares a philosophical scheme for issues creatively fictionalized in *Emma*). It is his essay on "Pretending," where Austin opposes the metaphysical contrast between the "pretend" and the "real" by undertaking a key aspect of his "long-term project of classifying and clarifying all possible ways and varieties of *not exactly doing things.*" Here Austin strives to expose the preoccupations, and supply alternative models, for the mistaken insistence upon the question, "Pretended or real?" (*PP*, 254).

The contrast between "pretense" and "reality" as a metaphysical issue tends to force observation-numbing equations upon behavioral situations of pretense and dissimulation. Though "of course there is *something*" in the nature of an opposition in play in such circumstances, "Pretending" loosens up and allows us to specify better the relations preset into the following formulae:

(1) not really being = pretending
(2) pretending = not really being
(3) not pretending = really being
(4) really being = not pretending (*PP*, 257)

Exhibiting the non-equivalency of these formulae, Austin gives the examples of magicians pretending to saw girls, of a high-end thief doing reconnaissance by pretending to be a window cleaner, and of "[t]wo miscreants surprised in the act" by police – that is, men having public sex, fairly explicitly as I read it – who, "hastily agree, the wherewithal being handy, to pretend to be sawing a tree" (*PP*, 259). These are examples not of metaphysical doubt regarding the nature of experience as real or fake (and the last instance of criminalized sex doubles down on the social and not metaphysical import), but of specific, intelligible, micro-events in which some real behavior dissembled "goes on during the course of" the pretense, "which facilitates and distracts attention from it" (*PP*, 262).

"Pretending" thus can point readers of *Emma* away from an ingenuously obsessed reading (an improperly virginal reading too) of certainty and doubt, and toward sociolinguistically detailed and adult (uninnocently experienced) investigations of the dynamics of "concealing or expressing" behavior (*PP*, 260). "Pretending" can also help us better see the de Manian performative aspect of Frank's quasi-exculpatory letter, a confession of an excuse. Austin ends "Pretending" in earnest:

> What, finally, is the importance of all this about pretending? I will answer this shortly, although I am not sure importance is important: truth is. In the first place, it does seem that philosophers, who are fond of invoking pretending, have exaggerated its scope and distorted its meaning. In the second place, in the long-term project of classifying and clarifying all possible ways and varieties of *not exactly doing things*, which has to be carried through if we are ever to understand properly what doing things is, the clarification of pretending, and the assignment to it of its proper place within the family of related concepts, must find some place, if only a humble one. (*PP*, 271)

Look back to notice the contour of the Box Hill chapter in *Emma*. It starts with the awkward ruse of Frank's command to each group member to say "what you are thinking of" – a performative announcement ("Ladies and Gentlemen") that begs the terms of its reply in constative statement; but the chapter climaxes with Emma's wounding joke at Miss Bates's expense (a perlocutionary speech act that induces a "slight blush" and causes her "pain" [*E*, 243]); the chapter ends with Mr. Knightley's cutting rebuke for this act ("Her situation should secure your compassion. It was badly done indeed!—[....] Never had she felt so agitated, mortified, grieved, at any circumstance in her life. She was most forcibly struck" [*E*, 259]). Then, think of Frank's conduct. As much as his first request puts pressure on the partygoers to deliver the content of their "inner" thoughts, we remember that Frank's larger objective and project in this scene is to generate something for the Highbury gossips to talk about – to ensure a screen or "blind" (as a noun), in the novel's repeated later wording – between himself and Emma. The scene's emotionally high-strung tensions and Frank and Jane's recriminations, pique, and regret all agitate, but do not cancel, this mission. Frank knows what he is holding forth as a screen, or pre-tending, and never allows himself to forget that all the people he deceives are making a "wrong" inference about his love object (though not about the state he is in). Frank implicitly relies on the voluble capacity of the community to group-process and share knowledge. He depends on getting an effect from the intelligent uptake of companions he calls under his breath, "excessively stupid."

In its remarks on the difference between pretending "that you are in love" and pretending "to be in love," Austin's "Pretending" offers instruction both on Frank Churchill's behavioral screening strategy of pretending to be in love (with Emma), and also regarding Emma's own questioning and modeling practice to discern whether she herself is in love with Frank (*PP*, 269). Her process is not a pretense, though it is a form of fictional modeling, and serves almost as a means for Emma to convince herself at the start of Volume III that she does love Frank. Hence the importance of her ability to respond sincerely later to Mrs. Weston's concern, that she is unwounded.

In addition to the discrepancy between what Frank says and what Frank does (and what he says to Emma he is doing), Frank also introduces an allegorically political space into conversations around other minds. He forces the framework of sovereignty not only on Emma but over the audience itself of a command conversation, coercing knowledge into its extraction or delivery, mapping it according to a spatial logic of imbalanced power that even Mrs. Elton is able to discern and decry. After the day at Box Hill, Austen marks Emma's relationship to the other minds problem with heavy underlining in the chapters to come, beyond simply demonstrating yet again that Emma's matchmaking is based on self-motivated misperceptions and that as a judge she is a fallible subject of knowledge. Frank forces Emma into a multiply ironic stance toward knowledge and her own cluelessness at Box Hill, where she is unknowing and serves as his "blind" (*E*, 294). But back in the village, Harriet Smith does not relate to Emma's knowledge at all ironically. Harriet still thinks of her mentor's relation to knowledge as a privileged all-knowingness in a world of mind-blindness. This attitude is nicely captured by Harriet's flat, allegorical identification with the "heart" over the head: "'Had you any idea,' cried Harriet, 'of his being in love with her? —You, perhaps, might. —You (blushing as she spoke) who can see into everybody's heart; but nobody else—'" (*E*, 279). And the later exclamation that suggests Harriet's name is an allegorical pun for this sole feature, the harried heart and the feeling heart's metaphorical location in the body: "Such a heart—such a Harriet!" (*E*, 327).

Because Emma had *not* reached this insight on her own about Frank and Jane's secret, and in fact *only right now* comes to discover Harriet's indifference to Frank, and along with it her monstrous if plausible love of Mr. Knightley, Harriet's admiration finally produces something like a reversal of Emma's conscious relation to knowledge. It is from this reckoning that the epistemological side of moral revaluation springs: "With insufferable vanity she had believed herself in the secret of everybody's feelings; with unpardonable arrogance proposed to arrange everybody's destiny. She was proved to have been universally mistaken; and she had not quite done nothing—for she had done mischief" (*E*, 283–284). At almost the same moment, that negative revelation concerning her knowledge and judgment of character enables her realization (experienced by Emma with both heart and mind) that she loves Knightley: "A few minutes were sufficient for making her acquainted with her own heart. A mind like hers, once opening to suspicion, made rapid progress. She touched—she admitted—she acknowledged the whole truth" (*E*, 281). The arrow image at the end of this paragraph positions Emma not as the agent of Cupid's matchmaking, but as an object whose susceptible feelings afford her the knowledge she is a love-struck person. The cliché is won with such surprise that it represents not the bathos of emotive first-person love, but is satisfying emotional representation of love's discovery in the third-person. Such depth releases out of this flat image. It's one of several passages at the end of *Emma* that fit into place with a click.

For Emma the "whole truth," the awful truth in the sense born by her sudden and fixed antagonism with Harriet from this moment onward, is a matter not of recognition but of acknowledgment. Her person had been used as Frank's excuse. The "first" young lady of Highbury in terms of social status, she was to Frank pragmatically the first suitable object to excuse himself upon in the search to throw attention away from himself and Jane. (To borrow from Rousseau, via de Man, on the famous story concerning Marion and the ribbon in *The Confessions*: "*Je m'excusai sur le premier objet qui s'offrit.*") Frank writes the letter to Mrs. Weston attempting to convey a proper excuse in Volume III, Chapter 14. But in this other overriding deployment of the excuse, the availing object is a feeling person. In the same manner for the reader, the traditional epistemological question of Emma's fallible judgment and lack of omniscience serves as diversion to the serious unending work of linguistic phenomenology, the investigation of language relations in social conduct. Here even in Emma's recognition of her "insufferable" presumption and flawed knowledge of character, the profound shift from cognitive penetration to social and linguistic action has already taken place.[67] "With insufferable vanity she had believed herself in the secret of everybody's feelings": Emma's jolt out of metaphysics into linguistic sociality is visible with that "*in* the secret," a phrase that suggests intimacy and conspiracy as a "positive" knowledge term; and implies not just mistakenness, but exclusion, as its negation. Emma is blind to the true feelings of others in the prevailing reading of the book, but all too understandably on this Austinian reading, because to

Frank Churchill, Emma has been used as *a* blind (a cover, a beard). That is the piece of information required to make sense of the mystery, not a correct interpretation of the moral and philosophical value of skepticism and Emma's special mind "blindness."

There is no impasse for Emma to face regarding the uncertainty of finally knowing the content of another mind, from the vantage of my phenomenological reading. Instead there is a very rich and entangled kind of ordinary misconduct. The obsession with choosing between "blindness" and omniscience in the sovereign and knowing subject thus is led back from metaphysics, to the ordinary yet startling recognition that the active subject of thoughts can and must be from one aspect an object to others, and is subject to being used. To be mortified into a major correction by this indefensible form of relationship is to confess about oneself that the ego had wished to be an author in all spaces, an Emma in *Emma*. To experience this defenselessness as a source of moral surprise, the condition of living with others must be structured and felt as the betrayal that Emma could be expected to feel – though she admirably doesn't – through her interactions with Frank and Jane.

Frank's elaborate subterfuge in *Emma* isn't best seen as a rare exception or even a hyper-enrichment of the mainstream approach to understanding the knowledge and motivations of "other minds," or the inferential role-playing (a precondition of empathy) of Theory of Mind theory. Frank's performance is not an anomaly. Cognitive readings of *Emma* treat reading the novel as a correctible experiment. But here again is Austin from "The Meaning of a Word": "[i]n doing physics[…] where our language is tightened up in order precisely to describe complicated and unusual cases concisely, we *prepare linguistically for the worst*. In ordinary language we do not: *words fail us*" (*PP*, 68). For Cavell, "[t]he obscurities in surveying the failures of speech and of human action are, in Austin, determinative of what human speech and action are" (*P*, 57). "The Meaning of a Word" heralds this capacity to allow words to fail (to fail as to succeed) without the preparation of a whole new language for the purpose of defense. As opposed to the controlled operations of scientific experiment, in literary and philosophical studies this skeptical operation does not precede but may often follow the event of reading. Emma's disabuse of her false pretense to know everyone's inner life does not zero out in demystification, but opens her to the experience of being struck from without by her own prior committedness to her world, to acknowledge the place another holds in her heart and thinking and to her continued form of life.

A Plea for Excuses

We should not come to expect demystification from the excuse as a speech-act genre.[68] Getting to know Frank Churchill provides the lesson on that. In *Emma*, excuses tend to be either explicitly, or mischievously and surreptitiously, inseparable from undisavowed pleasure. The subject of excuses affords J. L. Austin amusement, instruction, and pleasure. In fact, the essay "A Plea for Excuses" starts off – before Austin has even fully defined his subject – with a great deal of admitted pleasure. This is both pleasure of the covert sort, and a satisfaction communicative and public:

> Much, of course, of the amusement, and of the instruction, comes in drawing the coverts of the microglot, in hounding down minutiae, and to this I can do no more here than incite you. But I owe it to the subject to say, that it has long afforded me what philosophy is so often thought, and made, barren of —the fun of discovery, the pleasures of co-operation, and the satisfaction of reaching agreement.
> What, then, is the subject? (*PP*, 175)[69]

The reader not in his lecture audience already knows the subject is excuses, so in the written paper Austin revels in the community of "amusement" and "instruction," extending the interest of a subject matter whose typically ascribed function as a speech act is to demarcate liability. The paper opposes a mode of inquiry that presents metaphysical dichotomies as philosophical "dummies," through bizarrely leveled "actions" that are made to stand in for verbs with a personal subject (*PP*, 178–179). For Austin, the subject of excuses in ordinary language philosophy offers a rare chance to experience "the pleasures of co-operation, and the satisfaction of reaching agreement." This is just the kind of "microglot," tonally ironic, answerable and happy "union" which *Emma* conducts as a performance of our unending exposure to and through language.

CHAPTER 7

Persuasion, *Conviction,* and *Care*
Jane Austen's Keeping

> That she should have died before "Persuasion" was given to the world would be starkly tragic were it not that it failed to hurt her as it would have hurt Charlotte Brontë.
> —R. Brimley Johnson (1930); *CH* 2, 213

> Beside, she hath prosperous art
> When she will play with reason and discourse,
> And well she can persuade.
> —William Shakespeare, *Measure for Measure* (I. 3. 68–70)

It is worth keeping in mind as we embark on an end in *Persuasion*, the tone of professional ingenuousness found in the "second stage" of the "verification movement," according to J. L. Austin's summary:

> It is not the case, I think, that all kinds of nonsense have been adequately classified yet, and perhaps some things have been dismissed as nonsense which really are not; but still this movement, the verification movement, was, in its way, excellent.
> However, we then come to the second stage. After all, we set some limits to the amount of nonsense that we talk, or at least the amount of nonsense that we are prepared to admit we talk; and so people began to ask whether after all some of those things which, treated as statements, were in danger of being dismissed as nonsense did after all really set out to be statements at all. Mightn't they perhaps be intended not to report facts but to influence people in this way or that, or to let off steam in this way or that? (*PP*, 234)

The passage is one of several in which Austin's basic purpose is to broach the "descriptive fallacy," the clear inadequacy of thinking that to describe things by making statements is the only function of language. The banal, belated self-congratulation of discovering – or allowing, at long last – that language might set out not just to *state* things but to *do* things (things like the true-enough, but unsubtle, "influence people," or the dismissive "let off steam in this way or that," which rejoins the mock pragmatism of

How to Do Things with Words as a play on the degraded pragmatism of business guides or self-help literature) is not to be attributed sincerely to Austin. He ironizes the positivist's very modest conversion.[1] To use the Elizabethan term for irony, this is dry mock, an instance of the critical free indirect style that we frequently drop into when we take stock of our academic field, summarizing with a tone. Persuasion and symbolic expression (poetry and fiction; but also blessing, cursing, wounding etc.) count among those "different uses of language" (*PP*, 234). But they also contribute everywhere to the informing environments of language and social life. "Persuasion" looked at in this way is not a rhetorical tool or goal so much as the logical-affective word for the mediality of language. It justly figures in the Foucauldian critical analysis of distributed powers and networks, as well as in the Benjaminian fields of "– abilities."[2]

Persuasiveness and persuadability are not attributes of the subject alone, but capacities and susceptibilities where the individual meets their culture in social exchange. Cavell quotes from Foucault to this effect in an epigraph to the chapter "Performative and Passionate Utterance" in *Philosophy the Day after Tomorrow*: "It is in so far as discourse is common that is can become at once a place and an instrument of confrontation" (*P*, 155). As both the place – drawing room or forum – and the instrument of confrontation, common discourse holds and transmits moral action. Cavell strikingly takes up perlocution "in service of something I want from moral theory, namely, a systematic recognition of speech as confrontation, as demanding, as owed [...], each instance of which directs, and risks, if not costs, blood" (*P*, 186–187).[3] The epigraph gives strong evidence that Cavell sees Foucault as a fellow traveler in the project of "confronting everyday life with itself" (*P*, 123).

Jane Austen's *Persuasion* engages with this idea of the distributed and impersonal agency of its title concept in terms of a field of abilities (and "—abilities"), potentialities, and vulnerabilities, while unfolding what would become its Cavellian narrative line more evidently than perhaps any other Austen work. Alongside the problem of skepticism and the dynamics of acknowledgment and avoidance, the philosophical narrative of remarriage ranks atop Cavell's lifelong themes. The bearings of Cavell's thought on Jane Austen's fiction in *Persuasion* require no further appeal than the Cavellian theme of remarriage. *Persuasion*, Eric Walker has said, is a book about the "foundational Cavellian trope of remarriage," which "everywhere recasts the question of marriage as the question of remarriage."[4] For Walker and many other critics going back to Virginia Woolf, the novel represents a new kind of venture for

Austen, in which a future for conjugal marriage is only conceivable outside of the symbolic space and institutional setting of the landed estate.[5] At the point of her marriage, this observation occurs self-comfortingly but not wrongly to Anne's envious (and first-to-be married) sister, Mary Musgrove: "Anne had no Uppercross-hall before her, no landed estate, no headship of a family" (*Per*, 176). As Cavell's couple in the genre he calls the comedy of remarriage keep on walking, Anne and Frederick Wentworth will keep on sailing, resettling and disembarking.

Yet Anne Elliot and Frederick Wentworth's landless partnership broaches a further and especially Cavellian problem in the narrative economies of perfectionism: how to conduct a mutual life of unsettled, perhaps unsettling, interest and movement.[6] Austen's novel anchors external coordinates to account for this tension, in the historical concerns of geopolitics and the demands of professional life of a naval family.[7] But the continual uprooting, the rhythms of wear and renewals of interest, the persistence of anxiety, and patterns of continual physical movement are inwardly circulating human characteristics (abilities, susceptibilities) that supplement and complicate the clearly mapped geopolitical and professional duties incumbent upon the male navy professionals and their families in Jane Austen's time. So Austen gives the very last sentence of *Persuasion* to the national importance of the profession of sailor's wife (*Per*, 178). But Waterloo, which wasn't a naval battle anyway, and the looming inevitability of post-war redeployments in the global empire aren't the only factors to unsettle the future of the couple and their (re)marriage. Austen's lack of interest in the marital lives of her main couples combines with other long-shadowing narrative patterns. Michael Wood cites Cavell from *The World Viewed*: "'When the man (in the movies) goes home to his wife,... his life is over. In a thousand other instances, the marriage must not be seen, and the walk into the sunset is into a dying star: they live happily ever after—as long as they keep walking.'"[8]

Persuasion furnishes too this chapter's concern with the period-based aesthetic terminology that is a curational historical technique, of "keeping" (in) Jane Austen. It may be understood as a novel in which Cavell's *they keep walking* is open to being elaborated multiply and differently: neither in sexist and destructively individualist terms as a man (at the bar or his club, as is Cary Grant's character in the opening scene of *The Awful Truth*) who puts off the return home to his wife; nor as a fadeout to prevent withering conjugal representations; but as a description of life shared in the motives and motions of sustained and renewed mutual interest. Though this isn't, in my view, what the relationship of the main couple in

Persuasion exactly achieves. One of the chapter's critical problems will be to spell out and address this difference between the perfectionist endeavor and the representation of conjugal object choice. The alternate unsettling of Anne and Wentworth's marriage suggests eventually a means by which this book concludes: on a gesture that itself keeps the double thought going of Austen-with-Cavell in unsettled movement.

Wentworth stands in a mitigated relationship to Shakespeare's Leontes (and Cavell's powerful account of Leontes) in *The Winter's Tale*. And though Wentworth's role as the male protagonist of a restorative romance sets decided limits to a comparison between his expression of skepticism and those of Othello regarding the passion of jealousy as an unassuageable demand to be certain, his jealousy of the relationship he misperceives between Anne and William Walter Elliot comes disturbingly late in the text of *Persuasion*. On its own terms it is never fully addressed.[9] The emotional and physiological nuances of this triangle are rendered with a fidelity to the density of responsiveness in moral reality. Something like the following occurs: Anne infers from Wentworth's behavior in their last conversation in Bath that Wentworth must still love her (*Per*, 131); she is suffused by this realization while attending to her next, perfunctory social engagement with William Walter Elliot and her family; the conviction of her knowledge of Wentworth's feeling shows through her person, while William Walter Elliot presses his attention upon her (and even offers Anne a disregarded, unheard proposal of marriage – Jane Austen's second of such moments) (*Per*, 132); when Wentworth sees Anne at the concert with William Walter Elliot, he breaks from her in the hall, misrecognizing the signs of Anne's manifest love, and radiant self-worth, as the expression of her acceptance of Elliot (*Per*, 133).

Wentworth expresses jealousy of himself. He rejects his own long-withheld love's very effects, distrusting and disowning them. He evinces, at a level prior to any of these plot events, his jealousy and envy of the otherness of Anne's embodiment of love for him. "Their last meeting had been most important in opening his feelings; she had derived from it a delightful conviction; but she feared from his looks, that the same unfortunate persuasion, which had hastened him away from the concert room, still governed. He did not seem to want to be near enough for conversation" (*Per*, 156). Is Wentworth finally persuaded by Anne's ardor, in overhearing her redundant confession of "constancy," despite already having all the evidence he needs of her constancy (*Per*, 165–166)? In his letter, written simultaneous to Anne's speech in defense of women's constancy, Wentworth finds himself moved by Anne to relent. But he is not changed. Here we remember a further small point on the role of the jealousy of the ordinary as it functions for Wentworth: news in hindsight of Anne's rejection of Charles Musgrove first draws Wentworth's attentions back to her. He is both drawn by her perceived flirtation with William Walter Elliot and angered – yet again after eight years – by its expression of a vitality only understood to be intelligible as a betrayal of him (a public, gloating, triumphant rejection). Wentworth rises and leaves, despite Anne's superb line from a golden-age Hollywood script:

> "Is not this song worth staying for?" said Anne, suddenly struck by an idea which made her yet more anxious to be encouraging.
> "No!" he replied impressively, "there is nothing worth my staying for;" and he was gone directly.
> Jealousy of Mr. Elliot! It was the only intelligible motive. Captain Wentworth jealous of her affection! Could she have believed it a week ago—three hours ago! For a moment the gratification was exquisite. But alas! there were very different thoughts to succeed. How was such jealousy to be quieted? How was the truth to reach him? How, in all the peculiar disadvantages of their respective situations, would he ever learn her real sentiments? It was misery to think of Mr. Elliot's attentions.—Their evil was incalculable. (*Per*, 134–135)

This chapter proceeds in light of the distinction Cavell draws between conviction and persuasion – or rather, the grammatically passive criteria for being "convinced" and for being "persuaded" – found in Part Two of *The Claim of Reason*. Cavell's magnum opus was published in 1979, a signal year for philosophical theory. A second goal of this chapter will be to consider Cavell's relationship to the cluster of projects – on care of the self, government of the living, and *parrhesia* or truth-telling – conducted in the last several years of Michel Foucault's lectures at the Collège de France (1979–1984).

Persuasion offers a model instance of the account of remarriage in the larger frame of Cavell's perfectionist endeavor. I treat that basic argument as undebatable and pressing in application to the text – but it also falls short as a description of the novel's social nuances and psychological details. I want to explore a more oblique relationship to the Cavellian dimension of *Persuasion* that is open to doubt, if signaled already by Eric Walker's reference to recovery and cure in his recognition of Anne

Elliot as a Cavellian heroine.[10] This is the novel's participation – further attached to the meaningful way in which it links to Cavell's thought – in a Foucauldian discourse of "care of the self." Here I hope to find a less apparent and prescribed connection.

Cavell shares with Foucault the aspiration to return philosophy to the project of how to improvise and conduct (a) meaningful life. More than a restoration of possibilities from her lost past, this too is the philosophical valence of the conduct of Anne Elliot, as seen in the company of Wentworth's navy friends (*Per*, 71), or in her decisive break with the numbing everyday engagements of rank and family (*Per*, 110–111). Cavell in his autobiography *Little Did I Know* marks his engagement with Foucault's concept of *parrhesia*, developing from a seminar he co-taught with Arnold Davidson at The University of Chicago in 1999.[11] Beyond the American Transcendentalist dimension of perfectionism, the dossier of ordinary language criticism in *Jane Austen and Other Minds* thus includes not only English Oxford and Cambridge School thinkers of ordinary language (Austin, Wittgenstein, Ryle, Harding), but instances of more recent continental philosophical commentary (Foucault, Shoshana Felman, Leo Bersani, Sandra Laugier, and Barbara Cassin). Usefully, Daniele Lorenzini categorizes five techniques of the ordinary, throughout Part 2 of his recent French-language study investigating the shared terrain of the thought of Foucault, Cavell, and Pierre Hadot, the historian of Ancient Greek philosophy as a way of life: 1) techniques of attention; 2) techniques of thought; 3) techniques of speech [*parole*]; 4) techniques of the body; 5) techniques of resistance and otherness [*refus et de l'altérité*].[12] I cross these five categories in my discussion of Austen's *Persuasion* as a narrative field of techniques.

Persuasion and Conviction

A discussion tucked away in Part 2 of *The Claim of Reason* titles this chapter. There, near the conclusion of an extended critical response to the philosopher Charles Stevenson's 1944 study, *Ethics and Language*, Cavell becomes troubled by an "apparent indifference" in this philosopher's usage of the words "persuade" and "convince" (*Claim*, 276–277). Cavell's training to recognize the importance of conviction reflects his orientation in the late work of Wittgenstein. The sensitivity he shows to an overlooked difference in ordinary language reflects Austin. However, from there Cavell turns – with notable facility in the novelistic tradition – to George Eliot's novel *The Mill on the Floss* for an example to elaborate his case. Cavell offers this example of the difference between "persuade" and "convince" from Nineteenth Century British Literature:

> I am not sure what it would be to persuade Maggie Tulliver that she ought to stay and marry the man; but I know what it might be to convince her that she ought to. Contrariwise, I am not clear what, if anything, should be meant by "convincing her to marry him," but I might undertake to persuade her to, even if I could not convince her, and even if I were not myself convinced that she ought to. If, then, as is suggested by these quick examples, you can (grammatically) persuade someone to take a course of action but must convince them of the truth or soundness of a judgment, one theoretical benefit of interchanging the terms will be that you lend to the idea of persuading someone the respectability of the idea of convincing someone, and you make convincing someone seem directly a matter of getting them to do something, and thereby remove it from a direct connection with the validity of support you offer. (*Claim*, 277–278)

Worrying Stevenson's "apparent indifference" to these distinctions, the passage works through a textured difference between what it means to persuade someone by "getting them to do something," and the effort of convincing so as to provide "validity of support."[13] This further articulates the difference between the "establishing of a judgment" and the "taking of an action," the de-ontological (convince) and the practical (persuade) (*Claim*, 278). But having drawn this theoretically structuring distinction, Cavell, interestingly, proceeds with a judgment of what is to be gained by carelessly or strategically "interchanging the terms."

The course the discussion takes is consistent with Cavell's approach to thinking about aesthetics, criteria, and moral judgments in his publications from the early *Must We Mean What We Say* (1969) to *Philosophy the Day After Tomorrow* (2005). He proceeds throughout from the critical rather than transcendental legacy of Kant.[14] The passage equally is grounded in humanistic theory of the nineteenth century. John Stuart Mill defines eloquence in opposition to poetry in his influential essay "What is Poetry?": "Eloquence is feeling pouring itself out to other minds, courting their sympathy, or endeavouring to influence their belief, or move them to passion or action."[15] Mill's famous essay is most-often cited as a foundational text in the practice of reading lyric poetry by means of the figure of overhearing.[16] By contrast, Mill defines eloquence in terms of a persuasive influential effect, one exercised not so much over the executive function of reason as over belief – sympathy, passion, and feeling. (Mill's vision, in *The Subjection of Women*, of marriage "as it may be," is the subject of his "profoundest conviction.")[17] Cavell writes again about the "further acts" of convincing and persuading in "Performative and Passionate Utterance" so as to suggest that these verbal registers – "consequential effects upon [...] feelings, thoughts, or actions" according to Austin – are "salient" in "that they are not illocutionary" (*P*, 169). Persuading (persuasion) and convincing (conviction) are perlocutionary modalities that engage domains of reason in the action of truth-telling. Yet they are also the outcomes or outlets of perlocutionary feelings and responses – or even, to play upon Foucault's famous essay on Kant, their rational "exits." As a realm of displacement and consequence in the following quoted passage, persuasion-conviction figures both as an underlining of the "further" event of the uptake of perlocutionary feeling, and as what one might call a yet further "further": "To say 'I warn you' (locutionary) is to warn you (illocutionary), and it may, further (as perlocutionary) alarm you or exasperate you or intimidate you, which are surely not illocutions; as it may further convince you (that I am serious in my concern) and persuade you (to take action), which are also not illocutions" (*P*, 169). Such terms provide the grounds of an action or its resolve. The working persuasion-conviction difference thereby digs further into the seductions and irritations of the perlocutionary, even as its work may reach and announce executive decision.

Austen uses the persuasion / conviction distinction in *Pride and Prejudice* in a dialogue between Elizabeth and Darcy that suggests the latter is being rigid, ungenerous, to insist on a criterion higher than a friendly urging: [Elizabeth] "To yield readily—easily—to the persuasion of a friend is no merit with you." [Darcy] "To yield without conviction is no compliment to the understanding of either" (*P&P*, 36). If the reader is guided by Elizabeth's warmth (manifesting in her quick trust of Bingley) in this scene, later in the novel it is Darcy whose constant habits of scrutiny show their merit (Bingley is his close friend, but he is flighty and manipulable as well as good-natured). Mill's model of eloquence is persuasive to the end of taking action upon belief, but the effect of the title concept tends to passive suffering in the gendered environment of Austen's *Persuasion*. Take the passage: "Anne could just acknowledge within herself such a possibility of having been induced to marry him, as made her shudder at the idea of the misery which must have followed. It was just possible that she might have been persuaded by Lady Russell! And under such a supposition, which would have been the most miserable, when time had disclosed all, too late?" (*Per*, 149). The barely escaped possibility of a wrongful "over-" persuasion by Anne's mentor and only confidant in the first half of the novel, Lady Russell, here takes the term. The logical word "induced" reads with an undertone of sibilant creep. It combines discourses of persuasion, logic, and physics. It all leads Anne to a "shudder." Anne Elliot had been persuaded at age nineteen by her mentor and family not to go through with the engagement to then "nobody" Frederick Wentworth (*Per*, 20). Despite the consequentiality of this influence she was never convinced (those acting to influence her never required her to be convinced) of the grounds of her act. If she comes again perilously close to a second optative-hypothetical persuasion by Lady Russell to accept the stomach-turning William Walter Elliot, conviction there too is not only unmet as a criterion but unnecessary, diminished to the word *induced* – a word that tautologically just means *successfully persuaded* (and might convey dragging, or drugging). The grounds, rather, of Anne's conviction are to be seen broadly as a way of life, not narrowly as a protocol of support through reason-giving. The array of reasons for supporting a choice of life may never be brought fully to mind. In this sense, by contrast to the voluble edge of persuasion, conviction is the true and almost silent subject of *Persuasion*.

Beyond establishing *Persuasion* as a Cavellian work of fiction on the theme of remarriage, the reading of the novel I wish to provide extends from that common territory in two directions. These paths intertwine to conclude *Jane Austen and Other Minds*. I take up the moral commentary on resolve and action, in which Captain Wentworth erotically commends a hazelnut as a model for human health and resiliency, before his presumed fiancée Louisa Musgrove almost immediately leaps and falls on the Cobb at Lyme Regis – cracking her head! While, reading back from this tactless and uncomfortably allegorical moment of violent levity, I glimpse anew Austen's touted relation to Shakespeare. Here first I locate in the character of Anne Elliot a narrative reference for Cavell's striking and compellingly voiced interest in Michel Foucault's final works on the "care of the self" (*Le souci de soi*), as an alternate contemporary version of moral perfectionism. As a novelistic investigation and working out of the conviction-persuasion concept in the course of this borderline novel of ideas, *Persuasion* suggests the value of rethinking the idea of being convinced through a practice of reason giving whose grounds are to provide advance rational procedures for their validity of support. Standard Foucauldian critical practice instead would assess persuasion through the analysis of disciplinary techniques: in the context of the early works, this means the "repressive hypothesis" of a modern disciplinary self, while the later headings include governmentality, truth-speaking, and care. It is in this double (if you like, passive and active) sense of Foucauldian common practice that Cavell finds "a place and an instrument of confrontation" (*P*, 155).

Can the persuasion-conviction difference bear upon Foucauldian discursive practice as an intellectual event? Under such scrutiny the procedure of reason-giving broadens to the "grammar of responsiveness" and even to "democratic responsiveness."[18] Foucault writes of governmentality and truth-telling with reference to Ancient Greek philosophy and political practices, a context in which the act of persuasion takes effect – whether proximately or ultimately – with one man and one man only: the figure of the sovereign. In contrast, Cavell's engagement with moral perfectionism as an analogous interest to "care of the self" poses the democratic field of persuasion insistently as both a condition to celebrate and as a problem. Yet in *The Government of Self and Others*, Foucault does speak of democracy in the ancient city:

> Which is better? For the life of the city to be indexed properly to the truth, is it better than all those who can, or want to, or think they are able to speak, be permitted to do so in a democracy? Or is it better to rely on the wisdom of a Prince enlightened by a good advisor? I think that there is a crucial feature here on which we should focus, namely that the great political debate in ancient thought between democracy and monarchy is not just a debate between democracy and autocratic power. It is a confrontation between two couples: the couple of a democracy and certain people who stand up to tell the truth (consequently, if you like: democracy and orator, democracy and the citizen who exercises his right to speak), and the other couple of the Prince and his advisor. (*The Government of Self and Others*, 195–196)

Foucault's discussion of democracy is concerned intriguingly with the notion of confrontation in the form of couples. It rejects the righteous split between "democracy and autocratic power" and instead understands the meaningful confrontation as one between two sets of non-conjugal couples: "the couple of a democracy and certain people who stand up to tell the truth ... and the other couple of the Prince and his advisor."

Foucault's posing of these two relationally and internally asymmetrical couples offers a critique not only of heteronormative coupling, but of what otherwise might be seen as the self-congratulatory, or justified, element of modern liberal conceptions of democracy as a practice of mass self-persuasion. As the protagonist of *Persuasion*, Anne Elliot undertakes the turn from an obedient subject of persuasion to a linguistic and social agent defined by her conviction. It is the domestic version of the public arena of Foucault's courage of truth. But in what further sense does Anne's emergence into conviction invoke Foucault's account of parrhesiastic utterance – as well as "care of the self," government of self and others? Recognizing truth again in Austinian terms as a function of the critique of what we say, Anne Elliot emerges in (and from?) *Persuasion* with conviction grounded not so much in the right object-choice of her spouse (Captain Frederick Wentworth) as in a mode of life (*manière de vivre*). Philosophy as a way or a mode of life for Anne expresses "care of the self" in the action of alignment with oneself, and intelligibility to herself. This example of a late-Foucauldian reading of Austen in rapport of with the ordinary, everyday, and *quotidienne* departs markedly from earlier influential Foucauldian readings of Austen which understand sociolinguistic and formal narrative features such as rumor and free indirect speech in terms of the dispersed power/ knowledge framework of subjectivation.[19] This shift marks the last instance of Cavell's Austen under the aegis of "vulnerable conformity" – and does so by underlining a new emergence in the meaning of conformity as such. Drawing from creaturely habit rather the political authority, the parrhesiast's truth is that of a visible, lived self that *conforms* to a manner of life. In making true the debased parodic form of Polonius's statement in *Hamlet* to be true to the temperament of oneself, Foucault's courage to truth thus performs a revolution in *conformity*, through "a set of everyday practices intended more to form than to inform."[20]

Against the maneuvers of accommodation and adjustment, there are standout instances in Jane Austen's life and works of frank truth-speaking and risk, as well as of comic truth-telling. One of Austen's pair of 1809 letters to the publisher Richard Crosby, who saw fit in 1803 to purchase the manuscript of what would become *Northanger Abbey*, but still had not published it at the end of the decade, was signed Mrs. Ashton Dennis or "MAD" (*NA*, 215). (It's a pseudonym that interestingly is meant rather to raise than deflect aggression, more like a Swiftian satirical author scoring a wound deeper than a "ladylike" cover.) Austen wrote the MAD letter as an unpublished writer, but she can be seen to maintain the comic strategy of blunt truth-telling in self-alignment in her humorous sequence of letters of resistance to the Prince Regent's librarian, James Stanier Clarke: "I am sure I should be hung," Austen writes to this emissary of the Prince, rather than be forced (or be able) to write the requested historical novel about the history of the royal house of Saxe Cobourg (*E*, 355). Though nonetheless Austen did allow the dedication of *Emma* to the Prince Regent to go to print on a posh title page with John Murray, the letters to Stanier Clarke, who was the intermediary of royal command, indicate an author who does more than demur in the ironic protest that she is "the most unlearned and uninformed female who ever dared to be an authoress" (*E*, 354). She knows who she is and she deploys these gestures as effective survival tactics.

In *Persuasion* Anne Elliot stands up to her father and to her older sister Elizabeth, in the oppositional choice to visit her old school friend Mrs. Smith at Westgate Buildings, and to cut the Dowager Viscountess Dalrymple of Laura Place (*Per*, 111). Anne later confronts the schemes of William Walter Elliot and Mrs. Clay. Her debate with Captain Harville over the nature of constancy and gender – a famous climactic scene in *Persuasion* that rivals the act of proposal as the novel's culmination of interest (*Per*, 165–166) – is a broadside announcement, however tactful and among friends, that shoots across literary history all the way back to the Wife of Bath's "Who painted the lion, tell me who?" She insists to Wentworth even after their engagement that she was right in her past conduct (*Per*, 174). And she readmits her advisor Lady Russell to intimacy (arguably, not to her confidence) only after it is clear that the latter has absorbed not so much her own fault and misplaced judgment, as Anne's independence.

D. A. Miller presents *Persuasion* and its heroine as self-mortifying and self-shaming, primarily on the evidence of the novel's tone. But the book's moral action runs in quite the opposite direction, toward Anne Elliot's inward validation and strengthened habits of self-support. This complicates the view in which it is only Anne's passive or self-regulative comportment that earns Austen's comment about her in a letter, "You may perhaps like the Heroine, as she is almost too good for me" (*Per*, 201). In *Persuasion*, as in the last lectures of Foucault, it is internal conformation of the self as much as the act of outward confrontation that matters philosophically. *Persuasion* develops the figure of Anne Elliot in the direction of a courageous if never exactly "freely" spoken truthfulness. The voice of *Persuasion*'s paradoxically compelling heroine – the female "nobody" Anne Elliot – compares with Cavell's discerning self-summary of his work on skepticism (the version he calls the "melodrama of the unknown woman") in *Contesting Tears*: as demonstrated by "[t]his withdrawal of the world (a formulation that recurs in my various reformulations or replacements of skepticism), or this withholding of a voice before it" (*CT*, 191). Withholding of voice from the world has long been a gendered dimension of truth attestation, rather than courage to truth in outspokenness. Fanny Price at a critical moment in *Mansfield Park* even feels that she would rather die than speak her truth aloud.

The issue of gender – and what Cavell calls the feminine voice of philosophy in *Contesting Tears*, including the distress of muting and the stakes of non-compliance to an unacceptable world – inflects the meaning of this relay from (1) persuasion and persuading, (2) to convincing and being convinced, finally (3) to conviction and parrhesiastic truth-telling, alike in domestic and political spaces. Insofar as late Austen is a useful textual object for the further examination of Foucault's truth-telling critique, gender and violence are the joined signal concerns that make such a critical move productively conjunctural. Violence in some form appears to be implacable as the bedrock of truth-telling.[21] Foucault's scene of veridiction involves risk, "costly consequences" (*Government of Self and Others*, 56). For risk-taking parrhesiastic utterance, "the price is death" (56). "Or more precisely, parrhesiasts are those who undertake to tell the truth at an unspecified price, which may be as high as their own death" (56).[22] For this "irruptive truth telling," the demonstration of which does not take place in "neutral" conditions (63), it is not constative truth but "veridicity" that matters (66), the binding of oneself to the truth by truth-telling.

Foucault considers ordinary language philosophy – the theory of the performative in particular – a "pragmatics" of veridiction rather than systemic historical critique of truth.[23] He sets up an ancient opposition of philosophy to rhetoric in *The Government of Self* (380). But the dismissal of rhetoric to pragmatics and non-theoretical pursuits is itself unpersuasive and unwarranted. Arnold Davidson revaluates Foucault's debt to Anglo-American philosophy in order to disclose and assess the performative dimension of truth.[24] Foucault shows limited interest in Austinian illocution specifically as a "pragmatics of discourse." He instead opens the history of Ancient Greek philosophical practice through the speech act of veridiction. But he fails to address the perlocutionary heading of Austin's project, the part which unsettles and resists the institutional character of classic speech acts. Foucault takes no account of the multi-positionality of Austin's theory as well as his tonal-tactical deployments. Perlocution is ambivalently and doubly entangling and entangled: it entails a whole range of variously vulnerable, desiring, and dis-identifying experiences; as a conceptual tool it is caught between a dimension of all language and "a notoriously tricky species of speech act."[25] "Persist[ing] through time and entangl[ing] people and things, self and others," what Andrew Warren calls the *speech actant* of perlocution bears an uncontainable, restive Romanticism.[26] The figure of binding, entangled and intertextured networks replaces that of a liberational escape. "Austin repeatedly tries to contrast this diffusion with what he takes to be a more stable target, illocutionary acts' specific force to get something done. If in an illocutionary act the effect must be contained in what is said, in a perlocutionary act the effect *cannot* be contained in it."[27]

Barbara Cassin contends in *Sophistical Practice* that "rhetoric is the affair of philosophy"; "[g]ood rhetoric is thus philosophy itself."[28] The idea of philosophy as veridiction must keep terms with the uncomfortable proximities of a sophistical practice. In a brilliant discussion of the performative that involves Austin and Cavell, Cassin puts forward the argumentative reversal that "when the performative is happy, the constative that it becomes is true" (207).[29] We have seen this perspective, instantiated, in Elizabeth Bennet's powerfully satisfying outmaneuvering of Lady Catherine De Bourgh in the famous scene of Vol. III of *Pride and Prejudice*. A narrative encounter which really does unfold as a felicitous performative in the broadest possible, and not conventional, sense, Elizabeth's refusal and gamely expert blocking of Lady Catherine *makes* the conditions of opening for the novel's final constative truth. Yet despite how much what exactly is said matters, official philosophy has delegitimated the role of rhetoric in the production of truth. The perlocutionary functions as Austin's name for rhetoric, "presented only after the evidence of the locutionary and the finding of the illocutionary" (197). Rhetoric so-named is otherwise excluded from *How to Do Things with Words*. "All the characteristics are there, but not the name" (203). "In a certain manner," Cassin argues, Austin treats rhetoric and the perlocutionary in the same way that philosophy at large has done: "he confers on it the vocation of vanishing" (204). Cassin's account of the place of rhetoric in philosophy stipulates the role felicity plays in the constitutive work of performative happiness, to "true" knowledge as a verb – to open the session, to make true, and keep truth. "Austin wakes philosophy up from its apophantic sleep," she declares, echoing Kant's famous statement about David Hume's skepticism as awakening him from dogmatic slumber. "Let us begin from this awakening, which—if Austin is to be believed—is in the process of 'producing a revolution in philosophy': 'if anyone wishes to call it the greatest and most salutary in its history, this is not, if you come to think of it, a large claim.'" (208; citing *How to Do Things*, 4).

Arnold Davidson has observed Foucault's first inflection by Anglo-American linguistic philosophy as early as 1967.[30] After the terms of the 1958 Royaumont Conference, Foucault called it "Anglo-Saxon analytical philosophy" (*Government of Self and Others*, 20). A 1978 lecture Foucault delivered in Japan, "*La Philosophie analytique de la politique*," merges reference to analytic philosophy with a Wittgenstein-inflected (as Davidson shows) interest in the critique of power in terms that stress the aim "to make visible precisely what is visible, [...] to let us see what we see."[31] In the lecture "Foucault calls for a descriptive analytic of our *jeux de pouvoir*."[32] Foucault's pages on "Writing the Self," included in Davidson's volume, consider the "arts of the self" as a practice of writing a book or account of the self in "complementary relation to anchoritism" and private stoicism in ancient practice.[33] Foucault stresses that such books of account are not "intimate journals" or "narratives of personal experience (temptations, struggles, failures, and victories)" – and not yet the "book of spiritual combat" – but rather are collections based on records of conversation and the reading of others.[34] This essay and the collection from which it comes are in dialogue with the writings of Pierre Hadot and the concept of "spiritual exercise." Hadot is a formative influence on Foucault's late work on the care of the self, government of self and others, and courage of truth. Hadot's project concenters in "philosophy and the conduct of everyday life" (211).[35]

Cavell's remarks comprise a last addition to this dossier on ordinary language and Foucault. Cavell reflects at length on Foucault and the hermeneutics of the self, in an entry of *Little Did I Know* (July 21, 2004):

> I noted that there were various causes for my awareness, and wariness, of the rush and reception of literary-philosophical publications from France. A rather different cause has occurred in my conversations over the years with Arnold Davidson and his insistence on the decisive importance of Michel Foucault in this reception and eventually, with specific pertinence for me, in stressing the relation of Foucault's late work on the care of the self to what I was calling moral perfectionism. This culminated in Davidson's and my offering a joint seminar on Foucault and Freud at the University of Chicago in 1999, for which Davidson assigned us some of this work of Foucault's. It did indeed fascinate me, but I found it hard to use, mostly I thought because of its attention to Hellenistic philosophy, which was—is—perhaps the most painful blank in my philosophical education; it nevertheless confirmed my interest in texts across Western civilization (and beyond, so far as I could glimpse beyond) contributing to and participating in aspects of moral perfectionism. When it came time for my opening considerations I outlined a project in comparing Freud and Austin and Foucault on the subject of accidents and slips and lapses in human existence. Freud is moved to interpret moments of asynchrony between motivation and behavior as specifically revelatory slips contrasted with an aptly functioning body and mind, whereas Austin and Foucault wish to see the need for excuses and the preparation for the accidental as essential to what possessing a human body and mind makes perpetual and inevitable. But it was not until just this past year that I read Foucault's published lectures at the

Collège de France on the hermeneutics of the self to discover for myself a sense that Foucault's program there, whatever the professional success of his scholarship, is to respond to a reading of ancient philosophy as the inspiration of current philosophizing. Its pertinence to what I have described as perfectionism, however different in motivation (for example, I begin from a counterreading of Rawls and from a sense that Emersonian and Thoreauvian perfectionisms take on preoccupations evident throughout Western philosophical and literary culture), crosses paths at alarmingly many points with what Foucault translates and perceives as the care of the self. I am not at an age at which to make promises to follow out desires of learning and of new acquaintance, but I can attest here sharply to the desire inspired by these connections. (*Little Did I Know*, 479–480)

Foucault's lectures on the hermeneutics of the subject analyze the "techniques" of a care of the self, versus self-renunciation and the obligation to obey (*The Courage of Truth*, 353). This set of practices is not a solitary exercise but a social praxis (354), and a function of the relationship between reader and writer. Yet the implications of a Classical Greek political sphere for the parrhesiast exclusively assume male positions, and often militarist overtones. Daniele Lorenzini exemplifies this tendency in his essay on Foucauldian parrhesia and perlocution: "Foucault's study of parrhesia can provide us with a class of ethical utterances that are neither true nor false but whose truthfulness plays an essential role for the speaker in the act of uttering them. We must not consider this truthfulness from a logical or epistemological point of view but rather from a strategic point of view because the truth manifested in parrhesia is clearly a force in a field of battle."[36] This underlines the contrast between a view of truth as the product of a logical procedure and as a manifestation of strategic force. But, however much it proves an exercise in self-conformity and resistance, Anne Elliot's writing of the self in *Persuasion* is not of the nature of a spiritual combat or field of battle. Those fields press their anxieties upon the protagonist of *Persuasion* from elsewhere in the text: in "the tax of quick alarm" of its geopolitics (*Per*, 178).

The novel's recent commentators agree that *Persuasion*'s Anne Elliot is a subject of intensive narratological care. Readers disagree widely over how to assess this immersive experience in terms of conceptual strategies and historical values of representation.[37] D. A. Miller, among the nineteenth-century novel's ablest Foucauldian and queer critics, argues with vehemence against what he considers Austen's narrative "fall" from the art of an impersonal, perfect style to the immersive experience of a finite human sensibility. Miller locates Jane Austen's fall from style in Anne Elliot's practice of self-mortification: "mortification is more than the daily bread of Anne's spinsterly social existence; for this Spartan diet she has developed so decided a taste that she has made it the basis of what Foucault would call 'a practice of the self'" (*Secret of Style*, 70). So Miller contends for *Persuasion*'s style as a definitive "false step" (68). Miller continues to deepen and nuance the comparative reading of Anne Elliot, not just in relation to Austen's other protagonists, but with regard to "Austen Style" through triangulation with a series of styles of narration in Austen's novels. In none of the other novels, he argues, does the character's growth impugn the separate idea of narrative style as already perfect. Or indeed, I would say, as incorrigible:

> In the previous novels, the judgment pronounced against style in the sphere of character had in no way deterred the performance of Style embarked on by the narration. It was Elizabeth or Emma who came to renounce her presumption to style, and redeem herself personally in the process; for itself, the narration never ceased to uphold that presumption, affirming with each and every sentence its inhuman mastery of, as Gide put it, "everything that *can* be mastered." In *Mansfield Park*, for instance, where its thematic condemnation of style was harshest, the narration may have had the goodness to choose a heroine devoid of style, and the kindliness to shelter her under the cloak of its own eloquence and authority, but never did it dream of taking charity to the point of partaking in her self-mistrust, much less her linguistic indigence. Let Fanny enjoy the honor of always being what Elizabeth or Emma enjoys the honor of eventually becoming: her own person; the figure of Austen Style—the figure I've been calling the stylothete—remained No One. However deeply it peered down from its divine pinnacle to observe the somebodies below, it suffered no vertigo, struggled with no panic temptation to take the plunge into their midst. Yet in *Persuasion*, as if this resolutely melancholy figure had all of a sudden turned suicidal, it lets itself—and us too—contemplate the possibility of its falling into personification. (*Secret of Style*, 69)

Miller tasks the "plunge" in the narrator-protagonist relationship of *Persuasion* with a new humbling of personification.

The close narrative atmosphere of Anne's sensibility, to be sure, is immersive. But the buffeting of "somebodies below" might instead be appropriately taken as a description of all the narrator-character relations in *Persuasion*. A wild general applicability disrupts Miller's central claim regarding Anne Elliot. Where Miller rightly finds a quality of emotional and affective immanence at the heart of this novel, the insight he treats so aversively in the form of the style's conformation to the situation of Anne Elliot points to the fragility of all Austen's characters. This regards the violence of their care at the hands of the narrator; as well as to time's passage and to the human limits of aging. *Persuasion*'s fall into finitude applies not just to the dual personhood of the narrator-heroine.

The condition of personhood throughout *Persuasion* figures of course in the intensive and privileged relation to Anne. But it is also distributed across the cast of the novel's characters, whether treated roundly as people or rough-cast as dramatic "persons." *Persuasion* takes a raucous and arguably incoherent variety of tones toward the condition of that "fall" into finite human sensibility as the breakable and time-born situation of bodies.[38] The themes of damage and repair in the Anne-Wentworth main plot are dignified by the new vulnerability of Austen's restrained yet also emotionally intensive, "sentimental" mood in the book, and by the pressures of love and war. Yet Miller omits the novel's exuberant guilt-free violence from his account of the career of the stylothete. Alongside the immersively dense and delicate treatment of Anne, *Persuasion* pulls from a stylistically contrary world, and calls on an incongruously opposite strategy of measuring personification in broken heads. Rather than inwardly mortified, as Miller argues of Anne, these characters are extrovertedly punctured and dashed. Such treatment applies especially to "poor" dead Dick Musgrove and Louisa Musgrove, his sister: members of the Musgrove family whose crest, Janine Barchas has shown, was *Never Change*.[39] The godlike distance and irony of Austen the "stylothete" is transversely present in *Persuasion*. It may be found in the disruptive comic violence of the text, in its morally tasteless jokes and remorseless accumulations of broken bones.

Persuasion's new narratological immersion in the experience of embodiment is partnered in an unsettling way with the book's deployment of a cruder prerogative to aggressively exploit the vulnerabilities and affordances of the body. In *Disowning Knowledge* and *The Claim of Reason* Cavell announces a turn from aesthetic perfectionism to ethics under the terms of an affirmation of joyful finitude. Cavell writes in "Othello and the Stake of the Other" (the text also appears as the conclusion to *The Claim of Reason*):

> Is the cover of skepticism—the conversion of metaphysical finitude to intellectual lack—a denial of the human or an expression of it? For of course there are those for whom the denial of the human *is* the human. Call this the Christian view. It would be why Nietzsche undertook to identify the task of overcoming the human with the task of overcoming the denial of the human; which implies overcoming the human not through mortification but through joy, say ecstasy. If the former can be thought of as the denial of the body then the latter may be thought of as the affirmation of the body."[40]

218   *Persuasion*, Conviction, and Care: Jane Austen's Keeping

In identifying his task as "overcoming the denial of the human," Nietzsche writes against the morality of self-mortification. The essays of Leo Bersani collected in *Thoughts and Things* recurrently draw from Foucault's historical analysis of "the elevation of knowledge over what he calls 'care of the self,' or spirituality, in post-Cartesian constructs of subjectivity." Bersani reinforces, in what he considers to be the collection's "most fully elaborated" and impactful essay, that "Foucault goes so far as to identify the beginning of the modern age in the history of Western configurations of subjectivity with what he calls 'the Cartesian moment,' the moment of prioritizing of knowledge to the detriment of what Foucault designates as 'care of the self,' or spirituality."[41] This summary of Foucault on "the Cartesian moment," when Descartes overturns the care of the self in favor of an exclusively rational and cognitive knowledge, is a repeated topic of emphasis throughout *Thoughts and Things*. In addition to the appearances cited above – from the Introduction and chapter on "Ardent Masturbation (Descartes, Freud, Proust, et. al.)" – the idea that a Cartesian first philosophy of knowledge eclipses self-relation as a *souci de soi* appears for a third time in the essay, "I Can Dream, Can't I" (62). Bersani's collection articulates a philosophical framework with affinity to Cavell's major project to understand violence in the ground-clearing first maneuvers of skepticism. A lineage based on care of the self and others, philosophy as a way of life, has been expunged by Cartesian first philosophy and its skeptical ground-clearings. It takes but slight adjustment to understand Bersani's distinctive and challenging work in psychoanalytical queer theory in the idiom of Cavellian acknowledgment. Thus, for Bersani, "[p]sychoanalysis shifts the investigative emphasis from the nature and conditions of knowledge, or from the desire to know, to the desire to know desire" (4). This project affirms the need "to elaborate a concept of impersonal intimacy" (5) in which the practices of "care" do not elaborate defensive reaction. For Cavell, this project describes "philosophy's aspiration to exchange intimacy without taking it personally" (*CT*, 158).

Jane Austen's Keeping

> In the dark blue sky you keep.
> —Jane Taylor, "The Star" (1806)

I have been discussing care and violence in terms of the dynamics of an arguably post-ironic "late" Austen style that plays with perspectives of narrative immersion and distance. I want to look now at a dimension of *Persuasion* and its legacy in the repertoire of aesthetics that would revisit care and violence as elements in the course of the historical handling of personified (and so differently non-human) textual features. This section examines an idiomatic rather than conceptual practice, "keeping" in Austen – here especially the keeping of Austen's last work – as an allied alternative to Foucauldian care. Because Austen herself did not complete and see into print a single authoritative final version – or keeping copy – of what we know as *Persuasion*, both a little of this necessary editorial care and, arguably, a larger culture and aesthetics of caretaking attaches with special meaning(s) to this novel. Coming out of an idiom of dons and belles lettres, drawing from landscapes and portrait painting, the topic of "keeping" has a very English pedigree. Reviewing Jane Austen's oeuvre in 1894, George Saintsbury wrote that "*Persuasion*, relatively faint in tone, and not enthralling in interest, has devotees who exalt above all the others its exquisite delicacy and keeping" (*CH* 2, 215). Writing for *Blackwood's Edinburgh Magazine* in 1859, G. H. Lewes agreed in advance with this judgment of Austen's "faint" tone and unenthralling "interest" – and in fact broadened the generalization: "Her subjects have little intrinsic interest" beyond how well they are kept (*CH* I, 160).

Saintsbury's account was published as the introduction for the Hugh Thomson illustrated edition of Austen. A testament to the visual idiom of a Janeite world of homey gestures and common culture, it opens linguistically to ordinary language criticism. I doubt whether the language of "keeping" applies much to the Thomson illustrations, cultural benchmarks as they are of the familiarization of Austen's customs and characters from the vantage of the demands of her later nineteenth-century mass readership. Keeping, if anything, here, may be understood as a visual culture around the mourning of Austen and her idealized lost country world. Saintsbury's critical idiom instead takes its visual metaphor not from the illustrations, but from a sense sufficient to Austen's language. His idiom of appreciation is, in effect, a countering judgment of what should constitute a proper keeping. His language of the exquisite "keeping" of *Persuasion* exhibits the difference between Anglophile literary stewardship in a spirit of belles lettres, and continental philosophy and theoretical critique. At issue between Janeite personal loving care and Foucauldian critique is the question: What does "keeping" denote or imply as a critical term of art? Is it just recasting D. A. Miller's dismissal of *Persuasion* as "the great sentimental favorite" (*Secret of Style*, 68)? Present-day usages that still reflect "keeping" as a social and aesthetic affect might include the practices of promise keeping, housekeeping, timekeeping, record keeping, keeping in touch, and effort of keeping up appearances.

The "keeping" apples of Knightley's Donwell figure in the *Oxford English Dictionary* definition.[42] In the opinions recorded of *Emma*, Austen noted that one reader (loaned the book by Austen's niece Fanny) delighted in the story "better than any," expressing the judgment that "[e]very character is thoroughly kept up" (*E*, 364). Examples of "keeping" in British fiction of the Romantic Period invoke an aesthetics of harmony in proportions and depth of perspective. As here, from Walton's self-narrative in one of the letters to his sister that begin *Frankenstein*:

> But it is a still greater evil to me that I am self-educated: for the first fourteen years of my life I ran wild on a common, and read nothing but our uncle Thomas's books of voyages. At that age I became acquainted with the celebrated poets of our own country; but it was only when it had ceased to be in my power to derive its most important benefits from such a conviction, that I perceived the necessity of becoming acquainted with more languages than that of my native country. Now I am twenty-eight, and am in reality more illiterate than many schoolboys of fifteen. It is true that I have thought more, and that my day dreams are more extended and magnificent but they want (as the painters call it), *keeping*; and I greatly need a friend who would have sense enough not to despise me as romantic, and affection enough for me to endeavor to regulate my mind.[43]

"Keeping" in this letter refers to a proportion and scale of management. Walton says his wild daydreams want keeping, harmony of perspective between the foreground and distance.[44] The *OED* stresses the period meanings of "keeping" as a term for the aesthetic evaluation of landscape painting (found in Gilpin and elsewhere) which stresses proper, harmonious relation and subservience of parts ("Keeping in the Whole"). So Virginia Woolf writes: "[t]here is a peculiar beauty and a peculiar dullness in *Persuasion*."[45] The "keeping" would mean getting these peculiarities mutually composed right. There can be *fine* keeping or *perfect* keeping. For Adam Smith, the musical metaphor of "keeping time" figures as a means to think with the coordinating rhythms and proportions of human sympathy. And in the phrases of *in* or *out of keeping with*, what is being stressed by its presence or absence is not just propriety but agreement, congruity, and attunement. From his use of the term, Saintsbury's evaluation suggests an aesthetic category from the eighteenth and nineteenth centuries, now lost to aesthetic criticism. Saintsbury's review presents the argument that loving literature by "allowance" or general repute leads to uniformity in judgments of the best single work in a body of works; whereas "loving with personal love," as in the case of Austen, leads to many forms of affectionate difference that are tended in judgment.

Jane Austen's Keeping

"Keeping" as an aesthetic idiom for appreciating *Persuasion* suggests an intimacy that does without the personal identification that governs the "loving" reading of Austen's other novels. The "keeping" of *Persuasion* is most directly juxtaposed to what Saintsbury calls the "entrain" – or "drawing" joy and vivacity, captivating high spirits – of *Northanger Abbey*, the other short two-volume novel that was published along with *Persuasion*:

> Walt Whitman has somewhere a fine and just distinction between "loving by allowance" and "loving with personal love." This distinction applies to books as well as to men and women; and in the case of the not very numerous authors who are the objects of personal affection, it brings a curious consequence with it. There is much more difference as to their best work than in the case of those others who are loved "by allowance," by convention, and because it is felt to be the right and proper thing to love them. And in the sect—fairly large and yet unusually choice—of Austenians or Janeites, there would probably be found partisans of the claim to primacy of almost every one of the novels. To some the delightful freshness and humour of *Northanger Abbey*, its completeness, finish, and *entrain*, obscure the undoubted critical facts that its scale is small, and its scheme, after all, that of a burlesque or parody, a kind in which the first rank is reached with difficulty. *Persuasion*, relatively faint in tone, and not enthralling in interest, has devotees who exalt above all the others its exquisite delicacy and keeping. The catastrophe of *Mansfield Park* is admittedly theatrical, the hero and heroine are insipid, and the author has almost wickedly destroyed all romantic interest by expressly admitting that Edmund only took Fanny because Mary shocked him, and that Fanny might very likely have taken Crawford if he had been a little more assiduous; yet the matchless rehearsal-scenes and the characters of Mrs Norris and others have secured, I believe, a considerable party for it. *Sense and Sensibility* has perhaps the fewest out-and-out admirers; but it does not want them. (*CH* 2, 215)

The review not only shares the idiom of keeping from pictures, but promotes an attentive and durational "keeping" practice over the insurgent excitements of art. The "sect" of "Austenians or Janeites" presides over her creation with specific acts of devotional care. As opposed in particular to the joyous immediate appeal or "entrain" – in which the lead character draws the enthusiastic reader after her – of Catherine Morland in *Northanger Abbey*, the "exquisite delicacy and keeping" of *Persuasion* and its heroine Anne Elliot invoke artistic investment in and over time. "Delicacy and keeping" connote temporal care, living with and continuously looking on, rather than excitement, and as an alternative to the tradition of hermeneutically productive models of critical reading.

Though Austen died before the literary phenomenon of the gift annual rose to prominence, the title of the most successful and prestigious of these efforts, *The Keepsake* (1828–1857), conveys the socialized and commemorative nature of "keeping" as such a practice of book culture. Keepsake gift-annual volumes promoted forms of caregiving and curacy that exist within and beyond reading. In *OED* citations of literature from 1790 on, a keeping room is a sitting room or parlor. "Keep" also has roots in an Old English word, the original sense of which was to lay hold with the hands, before its meaning got tangled up in the visual sense of the Latin *observare* (keep an eye on, to watch). "To keep" is to observe custom with due formality in the prescribed manner; also to provide for the sustenance of; or carry on; to offer care, attention, heed, notice. And of course the most ubiquitous cultural messaging around the globalized English brand now is to *keep calm* – not simply to *be* calm. Yet "keeping" also governs the actions to hide, conceal, not to divulge. Mistresses are "kept," as in Wycherly's play *The Country Wife* (1675). As an alternate to the visual, the haptic poetics of "keeping" promotes Sedgwick's textured criticism. But it also may suggest enclosure, the castle keep or bulwark of Lionel Trilling's Mansfield Park. Hence keeping involves a sense of "pay attention to" that is vigilant (French, *garder*). A popular and sensitively addressed modern-day book series for adolescent girls is titled *The Care and Keeping of You: The Body Book for Younger Girls/ ... Older Girls*. These titles foster "keeping" as care or heed in tending, watching, or preserving. Our bodies are a keeping in trust, a self-charge.

As a regulative aesthetic notion that governs subservience and harmony in the establishment of both human social values and aesthetic perspective, "keeping" would seem to be a Foucauldian term in the production of cultural docility. Does the practice of "keeping" have bearing on a Foucauldian dimension of care of the self? Can care of the self be a literary curacy, a care in terms of characters, or even of texts and books as material objects? If wrested from Saintsbury and the dons, could *keeping* replace the notion of *canon*? Or be used to re-describe art technique or practice? If so, "keeping" may yet furnish a practice of literary criticism and history. The immethodical concept of "keeping" provides an example of fruitful ordinary language critical practice and may guide us to other, similarly lapsed and yet still-to-be registered historical aesthetic practices.

"No Injury but to the Head"

To identify "keeping" solely as an objective property in *Persuasion* is to miss the dimension of this term as a cumulative subjective practice of its treatment, and to fail to provide a reason why this narrative among all

Austen's works requires communal efforts to be kept (as Woolf likes to say of Austen) whole and entire. Why does this novel in particular elicit that often-neglected office of literary study, of preservation? Saintsbury's aesthetic and affective characterization of *Persuasion* for its balanced "keeping" is telling as a compensation for disruptive forces that require handling with care. Especially for a novel often characterized as "autumnal," somber, and romantic, *Persuasion* contains a persistent strain of knockabout near-comedy that focuses an oddly philosophical sort of aggression upon attacks on the head.[46] Both Miller and Saintsbury omit this violent aspect of the concern with finitude, the novel's violence of care. The caretaking, co-habiting, and even nurturing activities that are involved in the "keeping" found by Saintsbury in *Persuasion* attest to their obverse: spillage, breakage, and gratuitous loss. In the case of Austen, the idea of a more broadly distributed attentive care must sit uncomfortably alongside the author's own disposition to slice off heads, to laugh without crying (both comments made by Woolf), and to judge coolly and conclusively without any seeming awareness of an ongoing capacity to wound. Austen is not especially sensitive to issues of precarity in her novelistic office. As a fictional disposer of worlds and persons, Austen often harms, mocks, dismisses, and otherwise roughly treats bodies in characterological space. Her narrator is repeatedly called godlike by scholars of the novel. This attribution raises more than just the ideas of impersonality and omniscience. It entangles with impossible ethical and cognitive demands that we place on a fantasy of human relationship where (as Cavell argues) human beings are asked to play god for each other. But it also evokes the squashing foot of a Monty Python skit.

The imperturbable aspect of Austen's human comedy has seen her linked to Shakespeare almost since her death. By the 1840s, Macauley and Lewes both associate Austen's name and liken her art to that of a "prose Shakespeare" (*CH* I, 22; also see 125, 130, 140). In fact, an earlier critic, Richard Whately, Archbishop of Dublin, writing on Austen in 1821 had already compared Austen's ability "to give a faithful representation of real life" to the way Shakespeare individuates even the rudes and clowns in his comedies: "Slender and Shallow, and Aguecheek, as Shakespeare has painted them, though equally fools, resemble one another no more than Richard, and Macbeth, and Julius Caesar; and Miss Austin's [sic] Mrs. Bennet, Mr. Rushworth, and Miss Bates, are no more alike than Darcy, Knightley, and Edmund Bertram" (*CH* I, 98). Macauley retraces this path by allusion to eighteenth-century comedies and their characterological rendering of human difference: "Harpagon is not more unlike to Jourdain,

Joseph Surface is not more unlike to Sir Lucius O' Trigger, than every one of Miss Austen's young divines to all his reverend brethren" (*CH* I, 122–123). Richard Simpson, a Victorian scholar of Shakespeare, persuasively contends that Austen must have held *Twelfth Night* in mind during the composition of the climactic debate between *Persuasion*'s Anne Elliot and Captain Harville, on constancy and gender (*CH* I, 256). Jane Austen's keeping provides an alternate record of her survival and canonicity as "prose Shakespeare," Woolf's female novelist in the guise of Shakespeare's Sister. Woolf presents Jane Austen again as a figure who does not suffer artistically from her own drive to expression, placing Austen in contrast to the figure of precariously unsupported aspiration in the Elizabethan age, and to the genius and anger of Charlotte Brontë. For Woolf, Austen is the fifteen-year-old girl found always laughing from the corner at the world. Even more, she is the girl who never mixes cries and laughter. For Woolf, Austen is the necessary artistic precursor of the female writer who got her artistic vision out whole and entire.[47]

The judgment of Austen's likeness to Shakespeare is made on canonical grounds by linking their dynamic individuation of characters. On this reading Austen is Shakespeare's (happy) sister by way of family likeness in the Bloomian invention of the human. But in an alternate selection of passages what less grandiose versions of Austen and Shakespeare might share is the comic berating and violent beating of characters. In both, the unsublimated social and physical violence of comedy finds something like naïve expression.[48] *Twelfth Night* exemplifies this commonality in the beatings of its side scenes, as much as in patient Viola. I also think of the two servant-slaves (Dromio of Ephesus and Dromio of Syracuse) who are repeatedly beaten by each other's masters (Antipholus of Syracuse and Antipholus of Ephesus) in *The Comedy of Errors*. The link can be glimpsed as a flash in advance of the bad Emersonian pun on perfectionist *understanding* as standing under the blows of knowledge: "Nay, he struck so plainly I could too well feel his blows, and withal so doubtfully that I could scarce under-stand them" (II.i. 52–53). Quasi-jocose beatings are also often administered for sexual misdeeds. In *Love's Labours Lost*, Costard – whose names references a kind of cooking apple the size of a person's head, also a simile for the head when it is bruised and busted ("a costard was broken in a shin" [*Love's Labours*, II.i. 102]) – is apprehended for breaking the King of Navarre's three-year sex ban. In the following passage the infraction follows the form of a philosophical parody, crosscutting our own contemporary theories of affordances with Aristotle and Costard the Clown:

COSTARD: The manner is to me, sir, as concerning Jaquenetta. The manner of it is, I was taken with the manner.
BIRON: In what manner?
COSTARD: In manner and in form following, sir – all those three. I was seen with her in the manor house, sitting with her upon the form, and taken following her into the park; which put together is "in manner and form following." Now, sir, for the manner: it is the manner of a man to speak to a woman. For the form: in some form. (I. ii.198–208)

Part of the comedy here, in a speech that mixes confession with a Dogberryesque report, involves the scholastic flavor of Costard's malapropisms and euphemisms regarding the nature of the sex acts under penalty. Pursued with an evident discursive interest, the forms of legal penalty and forms, positions, of the offending acts are related with spurious precision.

I go there to Shakespeare's bawdy in order to pursue the observation that *Persuasion*'s knockabout, unregulated or inhumane expressions of physical violence exist together in unsteady combination with rich art, feeling, and philosophy. In this regard, they function similarly to the speeches of Costard and Shakespeare's metaphysical dialogue comedy of love. Wentworth's exemplificatory speech about the hazelnut (*Per*, 62–63) is offered in the moment as general praise for the attributes that appear in Louisa Musgrove's personal resolution. Yet in the context of the novel as a whole – and for this study of ordinary language and the problem of other minds in literary fiction – the hazelnut scene provides uproarious metacommentary.

The moment is not just temptingly but irresistibly allegorical. *Mansfield Park*'s long set-piece scene in the wilderness at Sotherton is perhaps its only parallel in the clear amplitude of allegorical signaling. Both scenes are borderline campy. "Anne, really tired herself, was glad to sit down; and she very soon heard Captain Wentworth and Louisa in the hedge-row, behind her, as if making their way back, along the rough, wild sort of channel, down the centre" (*Per*, 62). Meanwhile "Louisa drew Captain Wentworth away, to try for a gleaning of nuts in an adjoining hedge-row" (*Per*, 62). To glean is to collect leftover crop after the regular harvest, bit by bit, amidst the decayed and broken members. Wentworth's and Louisa's "centre" channel path suggests a conjugal course, one that is normative while advocating headstrong obstinacy and resistance to impression. At this point in the novel, one of *Persuasion*'s subplots underlines the theme of resolution and wavering with the stalled relationship between Henrietta Musgrove and Charles Hayter, into which Louisa has stepped to restore direction (*Per*, 62). Wentworth's speech to Louisa bridles with his resentment and anger with the memory of Anne Elliot eight years before:

> "It is the worst evil of too yielding and indecisive a character, that no influence over it can be depended on.—You are never sure of a good impression being durable. Every body may sway it; let those who would be happy be firm.—Here is a nut," said he, catching one down from an upper bough. "To exemplify,—a beautiful glossy nut, which, blessed with original strength, has outlived all the storms of autumn. Not a puncture, not a weak spot any where.—This nut," he continued, with playful solemnity,—"while so many of its brethren have fallen and been trodden under foot, is still in possession of all the happiness that a hazel-nut can be supposed capable of." Then, returning to his former earnest tone: "My first wish for all, whom I am interested in, is that they should be firm. If Louisa Musgrove would be beautiful and happy in her November of life, she will cherish all her present powers of mind." (*Per*, 63)

As his tone modulates between "earnest" and "playful," the ostensible meaning of Wentworth's exemplum of the hazelnut is inconsistent and self-refuting. He praises the good "firm" nut (Louisa) for its evident strength, endurance (amid the gleaning of fallen and broken peers) and physical integrity. But, as critics before me have pointed out, the point of the tenor of this quick critical lecture on the evils of "too yielding and indecisive a character" (as if addressed to the actually overhearing Anne, not merely to her bitter memory) is *not* that such a figure isn't self-assured and autonomous, but that her form cannot be relied upon to hold particularly *his* "influence." Wentworth values not so much the firmness of self-reliance as the "durable" receptivity to his "good impression." A jokey if morphologically clear-enough figure of the skull and brain that cases the problem of other minds, Wentworth's hazelnut also carries secondary qualities of the philosophical prop-object going back to Descartes's ball of wax.

The "beautiful glossy nut" is an overtly sexualized object as an allegory of other minds. A male genital image, it nonetheless conveys the patriarchal norm and fetish of female sexual intactness – casting all sexual knowledge in shapes of brokenness. A nut's components include the shell and flesh; but there are also formal elements with sexual implications: break, integrity, intactness and structure; especially feminized sexual aspects of this otherwise aggressively male symbol and object-lesson. Indeed, in taking up the nut as an exemplum of the qualities he seeks in moral personhood (resolve), the military Wentworth might have been (but he is apparently not) sharply aware of the wider and tragicomic field of battle here: the associations between the nuts already fallen, to be broken underfoot and exposed to weather, and the bodies of fallen soldiers on a battlefield of Napoleon's Europe. Adding to this irony is the very individual nut he picks up to praise and, presumably, conspicuously or inconspicuously, later will drop.[49]

All these aspects of the hazelnut passage recur in the disruptively traumatic and yet comic events two chapters later at Lyme Regis. To the example of the hazelnut, this key plot event adds willful individual consciousness:

> In all their walks, he had had to jump her from the stiles; the sensation was delightful to her. The hardness of the pavement for her feet, made him less willing upon the present occasion; he did it, however; she was safely down, and instantly, to shew her enjoyment, ran up the steps to be jumped down again. He advised her against it, thought the jar too great; but no, he reasoned and talked in vain; she smiled and said, "I am determined I will": he put out his hands; she was too precipitate by half a second, she fell on the pavement on the Lower Cobb, and was taken up lifeless!
>
> There was no wound, no blood, no visible bruise; but her eyes were closed; she breathed not, her face was like death.—The horror of that moment to all who stood around! (*Per*, 79)

After the shock of the initial response – an interval of time when it is Anne's thinking hands as much as her head that succeed in giving crucial direction – Louisa's injury is summarized later in its own one sentence paragraph: "Louisa's limbs had escaped. There was no injury but to the head" (*Per*, 81).

Austen's novels provide a dynamic and useful extended object-lesson for our methodological and ethical conversations about violence and care in the interdisciplinary humanities.[50] In recent years, these occasions have often yielded expositions in which the proposed historical analysis of the role of the literary humanities instead offers up cartoonish models of our analytical investments, and of how critical thinking gets done and sounds – in effect, a characterology of personifications at the level not of the fictions studied but through a voice of professional self-description.[51] To notice this is to begin to unfold a general question about literary theory and disciplinary self-critique and justification. What do we expect from the surface and reparative reading practices that in the context of both ubiquitous and specific, embedded precarity have taken increasing hold of our field and our world? Directed to my own aims: How to incorporate the fact that Austen's works as a field for these questions, however rich and destabilizing, offer perhaps the least outwardly disruptive – least traumatic – lesson to think through and feel with? A condition at risk of violence seems particularly insistent in this account of the joint agency and vulnerability of human action at the interface with Foucault's idea of the emergent courage of truth.

Austen herself as a comic writer, a godlike disposer (and dispenser) of fictional worlds, often treats her own characters in a guilt-free manner as non-persons. This focus on minor characters draws out threats and foils for Austen's heroines, but it also highlights the undeniable situation in which the standing and attributes of humanity are distributed unevenly to figures we might otherwise model as persons. In her extended "Critical Theory of Jane Austen's Writings" (1941–1944), Q. D. Leavis called this the "habit of not taking too seriously the puppet's feelings."[52] Writing about Austen's Juvenilia as well as the just-published "last work," *Sanditon*, Virginia Woolf had observed in 1925 that "[s]ometimes it seems as if her creatures were born merely to give Jane Austen the supreme delight of slicing their heads off."[53] These are justified and enabling aesthetic judgments – and they are fun. How shall we square them with the use of Austen's texts as an interface for doing collective work on intimacy and public feeling?

Persuasion documents the injured body across a spectrum ranging from domestic life to the Napoleonic Wars; nephew Walter Elliot's broken collarbone; Captain Harville's lameness from battle injury; Poor Louisa Musgrove's broken head! But can the "keeping" of a specifically textual body, Saintsbury's "exquisite" rather than ill body of the late Austen – relate to Foucault's hermeneutics of the subject, or care of the self, in a way that is not sheltering? What are we to do, too, with R. Brimley Johnson's assertion that Austen's own inability to unequivocally finish *Persuasion* and oversee the novel's publication as a posthumous text "failed to hurt her as it would have hurt Charlotte Brontë"? Johnson speaks to the very relation between Austen's writing and her death, as though he were saying that it is not alone the lost chance to see the afterlife of her work, or the fracturing of art's formal expression, but mortality itself that failed to injure her. The "romantic" *Persuasion*'s immersive, affective sense of finitude and embodiment vies almost to the point of dissociation with the irruptive aspects of the book's aggressively playful mockery of human forms and limits. That people hurt, age, and die is just as obviously available a fact to the Austen of *Persuasion* (and in her unfinished "last work," *Sanditon*, too) as the fact that writers of fiction and their narrative stand-ins can always do whatever they like with characters' paper minds, and to their bodies. In part, this aspect of *Persuasion* can be so unnerving to us because we sense Austen values these two facts not just as logically and trivially equal. She appears to value them interconnectedly, in the same way.

"I Am Not Asking for More Stream-of-Consciousness"

This book has argued for an understanding of Jane Austen's relation to philosophy in opposition to eighteenth-century empiricist epistemology, and against the names invoked to secure her broad allegiance to Scottish Enlightenment thought in its epistemological (rather than essayistic) tradition.[54] Still, it ends with Adam Smith. For Cavell, the communicable claim and the intersubjective dimension of the aesthetic reflecting judgment at times face hard limits of experience as a shareable domain: "I am thrown back upon myself; I as it were turn my palms outward, as if to exhibit the kind of creature I am, and declare my ground occupied, only mine, ceding yours" (*Claim*, 155). Nevertheless, many historically significant thinkers don't care to the same degree over differences of attunement in our aesthetic responses. Adam Smith's admission of the situation when words fail in the sociable relation of sympathy offers a telling point of contrast to Cavell's arresting discussion, in *The Claim of Reason* and elsewhere, of such sudden and incontrovertible limits. For Cavell, the dispensation of modernity writ large names an era in which an intensified, interested version of the Kantian aesthetic response – felt as our "mutual attunements in judgments" – sponsors or fails to conduct claims to community (*Claim*, 115).[55] The moment recurs often in Cavell's writing, as when, in concluding the important early essay "Aesthetic Problems in Moral Philosophy," he writes: "the implication is that philosophy, like art, is, and should be, powerless to prove its relevance; and that says something about the kind of relevance it wishes to have" (*Must*, 96). Toward the end of the fourth chapter of Part 1 of *The Theory of Moral Sentiments*, Smith allows for the difficulty of preserving "harmony and correspondence," but volunteers that such a break at the extremity of dissensus does not really apply to our commitments to literature, art, and philosophy. For Smith, disagreements are always tolerable in these areas:

> Though you despise that picture, or that poem, or even that system of philosophy, which I admire, there is little danger of our quarrelling upon that account. Neither of us can reasonably be much interested about them. They ought all of them to be matters of great indifference to us both; so that, though our opinions may be opposite, our affections may still be very nearly the same. But it is quite otherwise with regard to those objects by which either you or I are particularly affected. Though your judgments in matters of speculation, though your sentiments in matters of taste, are quite opposite to mine, I can easily overlook this opposition; and if I have any degree of temper, I may still find some entertainment in your conversation, even upon those very subjects. But if you have either no fellow-feeling for

> the misfortunes I have met with, or none that bears any proportion to the grief which distracts me; or if you have either no indignation at the injuries I have suffered, or none that bears any proportion to the resentment which transports me, we can no longer converse upon these subjects. We become intolerable to one another. I can neither support your company, nor you mine.[56]

Differing judgments and sentiments of taste can be overlooked and may even provide entertainment. Even incompatible systems of philosophy present no real danger of quarrel. Unshared communications of misfortune, grief, injury, and resentment, however, can lead to a break in which mutual company becomes unsupportable.

Smith's *Theory of Moral Sentiments* begins with a postulation of the essential limit of all embodied knowledges – an acknowledgment in less rigid form of the problem of other minds: "As we have no immediate experience of what other men feel, we can form no idea of the manner in which they are affected, but by conceiving what we ourselves should feel in the like situation" (13). Cavell's conduct of thinking as a difficult homage in *A Pitch of Philosophy* – where he writes about the incomprehension of Derrida for Austin in particular – deploys two divergent uses of Smith's musical metaphor of sympathy's "pitch" and the sympathetically attuned keeping of time: 1) as critical "matters of vocation or trade and tact or pitch" (*Pitch*, 20); 2) and in terms of experiences that give assurance of a "perfect pitch, of evidence of a world I think, at the limit of the world I had conversed with—an experience of music, but one which, though ecstatic, did not lead me to ask for its blessing" (*Pitch*, 48). Yet the perfectly kept pitches of philosophy, literature, conversation, virtuosic performance, and judgments of taste, for Cavell can often and just as meaningfully refer to irresolvable angles and tempest-tossings of pitch that bear no notion of technical knowledge or openings to perfectionist experience. Cavell writes in the expanded edition of *The World Viewed* about the philosophy of film in terms of a particular conversational soundscape of associations that is angled, block, pitched:

> I have in mind not the various ways dialogue can stand at an angle to the life that produces it; nor the times in which the occasion is past when you can say what you did not think to say; nor the times when the occasion for speech is blocked by inappropriateness or fear, or the vessels of speech are pitched by grief or joy. I have rather in mind the pulsing air of incommunicability which may nudge the edge of any experience and placement: the curve of fingers that day, a mouth, the sudden rise of the body's frame as it is caught by the color and scent of flowers, laughing all afternoon

mostly about nothing, the friend gone but somewhere now which starts from here – spools of history that have unwound only to me now, occasions which will not reach words for me now, and if not now, never. I am not asking for more stream-of-consciousness. Stream-of-consciousness does not show the absence of words as the time of actions unwinds; it floats the time of action in order to give space for the words. I am asking for the ground of consciousness, upon which I cannot but move.

But why the sense that words are out of reach, that there will never be the right time for them? From where the sense of the unsayable?—time's answer to the ineffable. Out of my obscurity I reach the wish for total intelligibility, as though my words should form for you but remain part of our breaths. As though poetry were lodged in every cave of memory and locked in every object of thought. For poetry is so out of the ordinary that it could not appear unless the world itself wished for it. Not alone the poetry of poetry, but the poetry of prose—wherever the time of saying and the time of meaning are synchronized. (*The World Viewed*, 148)

The gifted limitation of time grounds critique of the stream of consciousness picture of mind and literary-verbal action. The modernist narration of consciousness as a "float" constructed in art provides occasion, in Cavell's reading, for an ever expandable "space for words." Yet the limited time for a meaningful action of words unwinds incontrovertibly.

"I can attest here sharply to the desire inspired by these connections," Cavell has said of his rich but foreshortened relationships both to Jane Austen and to Michel Foucault (*Little Did I Know*, 479). Finite time and labor, endless passionate exchange. The final sentence of *The Senses of Walden* construes Thoreau's book as "his promise, in anticipation of his going"; from there *Walden* "leaves us in one another's keeping" (*Senses*, 119). By contrast to his morning encounter of Thoreau, Cavell comes late upon these particular and pitched intimacies with Austen and others, which he describes as too close for the thought of forced acquaintance. So he leaves this conversation and the potential for different times for encounter to students and readers, in the provocation and honor of keeping its remarkable company.

Notes

Introduction: On Criticism and Other "Middle Subjects"

1 This is also Austin's local criticism of aspects of ordinary language philosophy from the inside; see "Intelligent Behavior," Austin's review of Gilbert Ryle's *The Concept of Mind*.
2 Are Austin's "philosophical gags" props of a vaudevillian comedy (*CT*, 29)? I think of Austin's schoolboy play with iced ink (I stink).
3 "Home at Grasmere"; *William Wordsworth: The Major Works*, 198.
4 John Locke, *An Essay Concerning Human Understanding*, 109.
5 Austin calls a word such as "real" a *trouser-word*, meaning part of a binary in which it is not the affirmative use but the negative use which is basic (*SS*, 70). "The philosophical tradition," writes Henri Lefebvre from the vantage of the French Marxist critique of the everyday, "has raised half-real, half-fictitious problems"; *Rhythmanalysis: Space, Time, and Everyday Life*, 46.
6 See Austin's note 1, which quotes from Price's *Perception*: "chairs and tables, cats and rocks" – though also water and earth; "physical objects," "(visuo-tactical solids)."
7 P. B. Shelley, *Queen Mab* 4.88–89; *Percy Bysshe Shelley: The Major Works*, 33.
8 Quoted by John Russell in *Henry Green: Nine Novels and an Unpacked Bag*, 26. For an approach to these issues as media, see Yohei Igarashi, *The Connected Condition: Romanticism and the Dream of Communication*.
9 Austin, "Intelligent Behavior," 45. The approach of philosophical satire, distinctive of Austin and Ryle, compares to a surprising extent to the early writings of Marx in the period from his *Notebooks on Epicurean Philosophy* to *The Communist Manifesto* (roughly 1839–1848). Isaiah Berlin records that Austin had once visited the Soviet Union and had at least a "short lived" admiration of Marx and Lenin, one held especially on the basis of their practical-critical prose; "Austin and the Early Beginnings of Oxford Philosophy"; *Essays on J.L. Austin*, 6.
10 Eve Kosofsky Sedgwick, *Touching Feeling: Affect, Pedagogy, Performativity*, 71.
11 Sedgwick, *Touching Feeling*, 8.
12 A passage from Woolf's novel *Jacob's Room* features in Wisdom's Other Minds symposium; *Other Minds*, 228–229. See Dora Zhang, *Strange Likeness: Description and the Modernist Novel*.

13 I. A. Richards, *Practical Criticism: A Study of Literary Judgment*, 5, 7. For more discussion of the medium-sized scale and medial role of critical judgment, see Eric Lindstrom, "Critical Judgment and Free Indirect Style."
14 William Empson, *The Structure of Complex Words*, 254. For more on the ontological dimension of middle beings in Empson's criticism and in his views on literary history, see Paul H. Fry, "Middle Spirits and Empson's chain of being"; in *William Empson: Prophet Against Sacrifice*, 119–146.
15 For the original development of the concept of "affordances," see James J. Gibson, "Notes on Affordances"; in *Reasons for Realism: Selected Essays of James J. Gibson*, 401–418. Gibson indicates his awareness of Austin's *Sense and Sensibilia*. He quotes a remark from the lectures approvingly in his "The Myth of Passive Perception: A Reply to Richards"; *Reasons for Realism*, 397.
16 Graham Harman, *Guerilla Metaphysics: Phenomenology and the Carpentry of Things*, 19.
17 Caroline Levine, *Forms: Whole, Rhythm, Hierarchy, Network*, 6.
18 I refer to the famous directive of Shklovsky's "Art as Technique."
19 Jacques Lezra, *On the Nature of Marx's Things: Translation as Necrophilology*, 178–181.
20 Sandra Laugier, *Why We Need Ordinary Language Philosophy*, 59.
21 Jonathan Kramnick, *Paper Minds: Literature and the Ecology of Consciousness*, 60.
22 But for a distinguished study of modern narrative and the philosophical theories of perception, see Ann Banfield, *The Phantom Table: Woolf, Fry, Russell and the Epistemology of Modernism*. Jesse Matz provides an alternative justification of the language of "impression" to "mitigate[] the sensualism that would have dominated had Pater encouraged his acolytes to devote themselves to 'sensations' alone"; "Cultures of Impression"; in *Bad Modernisms*, 313.
23 Ludwig Wittgenstein, *The Blue and Brown Books: Preliminary Studies for the "Philosophical Investigations,"* 127.
24 Anna Kornbluh, "We Have Never Been Critical: Toward the Novel as Critique," 399.
25 Byrne, *The Real Jane Austen: A Life in Small Things*.
26 This approach to the ordinary as seeking (through something like the relentless critique of the everyday) to recover "the garden of the world in which we live" means not to discount the roles of the entrapping discourses of Lauren Berlant's "cruel optimism," wherein "[i]nstead of the vision of the everyday *organized* by capitalism that we find in Lefebvre and de Certeau, among others, I am interested in the overwhelming ordinary that is *disorganized* by it, and by many other forces besides. [....] This ordinary is an intersecting space where many forces and histories circulate and become 'ready to hand' in the ordinary, as Stanley Cavell would put it, for inventing new rhythms for living, rhythms that could, at any time, congeal into norms, forms, and institutions." *Cruel Optimism*, 8–9.
27 For discussion of the ordinary as a dimension of Austen's vocabulary, see Charlotte Brewer, "'That Reliance on the Ordinary': Jane Austen and the Oxford English Dictionary."

28 George Saintsbury, *The English Novel*, 198. Cited by Brewer, "That Reliance on the Ordinary'," 744.
29 In the Berkeley (February 2002) Howison Lectures version of the chapter, Cavell did not say "renowned surface of containment" as is written in "Philosophy the Day after Tomorrow," but instead (enunciating it with careful energy) "Jane Austen's celebrated surface of lethal calm." Points of Departure: Philosophy the Day After Tomorrow – YouTube
30 Paul Poplawski, ed., *A Jane Austen Encyclopedia*.
31 Cavell's other major American subject, Thoreau, depicts a "restless, nervous, bustling, trivial nineteenth century" that stands in need of the aversive thinker that may produce America's first "heroic book" (*Senses*, 4, 6). Cavell emphasizes "the sense of loss" and "vision of general despair" with which *Walden* opens, but notes that "[d]espair and a sense of loss are not static conditions, but goads to our continuous labor" (*Senses*, 70).
32 Cavell anticipates the simplistic critique of his own outlook as a species of American exceptionalism, and "explore[s] the crux" of mood of Emerson's thinking as "his power of affirmation, or of his weakness for it" (*Senses*, 132).
33 Kathleen Stewart, *Ordinary Affects*, 12, 29.
34 Stanley Cavell, Foreword to Veena Das, *Life and Words: Violence and the Descent into the Ordinary*, xiii. The phrase "the little deaths of everyday life" appears originally in *Philosophy the Day After Tomorrow* in slightly altered form. It is the culmination of a broader discussion of Jane Austen, with specific reference to the character of Elizabeth Bennet as not only experiencing self-knowledge but "*being* known, being acknowledged in her difference" for the first time: "as if until then her existence had been denied, had suffered the polite skepticism—the little deaths—of everyday life" (*P*, 128).
35 See Clara Han and Veena Das, Introduction: A Concept Note; *Living and Dying in the Contemporary World: A Compendium*, 28.
36 Isaiah Berlin, *The Roots of Romanticism*.
37 For more on Cavell's engagement with British Romantic poetry and the re-animation of poetics after Kant, see the essays collected in Eric Lindstrom, ed., *Stanley Cavell and the Event of Romanticism*.
38 Cavell, "Comments on Veena Das's Essay 'Language and Body: Transactions in the Construction of Pain'"; Arthur Kleinman, Veena Das, and Margaret Lock, eds., *Social Suffering*, 98.
39 With respect to this argument, the eighteenth-century British philosopher most compatible to my aims is Thomas Reid, especially as his thought is presented by Richard Moran in *The Exchange of Words: Speech, Testimony, and Intersubjectivity*, 1–5.
40 Developing this aspect of Austin's thought, in *The Exchange of Words* Richard Moran demonstrates the social and intersubjective character of what we might deem purely "epistemic" acts of mind.
41 Toril Moi, *Revolution of the Ordinary: Literary Studies after Wittgenstein, Austin, and Cavell*, 207.

1 Austen and Austin

1 Jane Austen, *Juvenilia*, 477.
2 Bharat Tandon, *Jane Austen and the Morality of Conversation*, may be singled out as an exception to the broad consensus on the secure eighteenth-century philosophical contexts of Austen's fiction.
3 Both Jane "Austins" can be found in Paula Byrne, *The Real Jane Austen*, 289, 307. See Deborah Kaplan, "'There She Is at Last': The Byrne Portrait Controversy."
4 Claudia L. Johnson, *Jane Austen's Cults and Cultures*, 38–43: 41.
5 Johnson, *Jane Austen's Cults and Cultures*, 42.
6 For an argument concerning the anonymous mass eroticism that defines the literary ontology of Austen's characters, especially in *Persuasion*, see David Kurnick, "Jane Austen, Secret Celebrity, and Mass Eroticism."
7 See Christopher Ricks, "Austin's Swink"; *Essays in Appreciation*, 260–279.
8 "It was not, however, what she *knew*, but what she *was*, that distinguished her from others. ... There was, between the front door and the offices, a swing door which creaked when it was opened; but she objected to having this little inconvenience remedied, because it gave her notice when anyone was coming. ... Jane Austen lived in entire seclusion from the literary world: neither by correspondence, nor by personal intercourse was she known to any contemporary authors. It is probable that she was never in company with any person whose talents or whose celebrity equaled her own. ... Few of her readers knew even her name, and none knew more of her than her name." J. E. Austen-Leigh, *A Memoir of Jane Austen*, 72, 90.
9 James Boswell, *The Life of Samuel Johnson*, 351. Quoted by Johnson, *Jane Austen's Cults and Cultures*, 17–18.
10 Johnson, *Jane Austen's Cults and Cultures*, 179.
11 The allusion is to Sarah Austin, noted translator from German, and wife of the legal philosopher, John Austin.
12 Clifford Siskin, *The Work of Writing: Literature and Social Change in Britain, 1700–1830*.
13 In his essay entitled "Style" for the *Oxford Handbook of Philosophy and Literature*, Charles Altieri gestures toward his own "demonstrative" speech-act theory in response to Austin: "The demonstrative is a category describing what can be achieved by foregrounding individual activity within language, and so it contrasts with J. L. Austin's performatives that accomplish something by invoking institutional practices" (422).
14 There is something here of Swift's parodic critique of Defoe's project of recording facts and sense impressions, in the interchange at the start of the novel and process of fictionalization in eighteenth-century Britain. From Swift's viewpoint, Defoe would teach the readers of fiction to normalize "an arrogant, self-serving, even solipsistic way of regarding the world"; J. Paul Hunter, "*Gulliver's Travels* and the Novel"; excerpted in *Gulliver's Travels*, 356.
15 Jenny Davidson, *Reading Style: A Life in Sentences*, 18.

16 Compare Andrew H. Miller in *The Burdens of Perfection: On Ethics and Reading in Nineteenth-Century British Literature*: "(When [D.A.] Miller says that Austen's is a world 'that is nothing if not consistently intelligible,' ... I take him to be describing a threat, the threat that it will become nothing if it is not consistently intelligible)" (87).
17 Cavell, *Little Did I Know*, 200.
18 Cavell, *Little Did I Know*, 202.
19 For a study of the attunement of philosophy and poetry, considered in a more rigorous manner than my use of the word here – and distinguished from ordinary language philosophy – see Maximilian de Gaynesford, *The Rift in the Lute: Attuning Poetry and Philosophy*.
20 Charles Lamb, "Imperfect Sympathies," in *Essays of Elia and Last Essays of Elia*, 69, 70, 71, 74.
21 "Calling things by their right names is the central moral (and aesthetic) project of Austen's fictions," in the words of George Levine in *Darwin and the Novelists: Patterns of Science in Victorian Fiction*, 61.
22 Tim Milnes, *The Testimony of Sense: Empiricism and the Essay from Hume to Hazlitt*; Andrew H. Miller, "Implicative Criticism, or the Display of Thinking."
23 Miller, "Implicative Criticism," 353.
24 Compare Austin on "roughness" of descriptive statement; "it is only a legend that 'true' and 'false' can always be appropriately predicated on constatives; 'France is hexagonal' is a rough description of France, not a true or false one"; J. O. Urmson, "Austin's Philosophy"; K. T. Fann, ed., *Symposium on J.L. Austin*, 28.
25 G. J. Warnock, "John Langshaw Austin: A Biographical Sketch"; *Symposium on J.L. Austin*, 21.
26 Isaiah Berlin, "Austin and the Early Beginnings of Oxford Philosophy"; *Essays on J.L. Austin*, 1, 4. Warnock gives these biographical details in "John Langshaw Austin: A Biographical Sketch," 3.
27 Warnock, "John Langshaw Austin: A Biographical Sketch," 12, 19. Compare Austin in "The Meaning of a Word" (*PP*, 62).
28 Fiona Brideoak, "Sexuality," in Claudia L. Johnson and Clara Tuite, eds., *A Companion to Jane Austen*, 457.
29 Eve Kosofsky Sedgwick, *Epistemology of the Closet*, 29; *Touching Feeling*, 70. Kurnick develops this perspective in terms of media theory and literary ontology, by exploring the non-reproductive mass intimacy experienced by Austen's readers, one that brushes up against her lead characters, at times at the verge of feeling and knowledge that they are "thronged objects of mass attention"; "Jane Austen, Secret Celebrity, and Mass Eroticism," 56.
30 Sedgwick, *Touching Feeling*, 70–71.
31 For a survey of queer Austen up to the millennium, see Claudia Johnson's discussion in "The Divine Miss Jane: Jane Austen, Janeites, and the Discipline of Novel Studies"; in Deidre Lynch, ed., *Janeites: Austen's Disciples and Devotees*.
32 Kurnick, "Jane Austen, Secret Celebrity, and Mass Eroticism," 68.

33 Sedgwick, *Touching Feeling*, 5. By contrast, J. Hillis Miller seeks to disambiguate Austin's performative from ideas of cultural performativity in "Performativity as Performance/ Performativity as Speech Act: Derrida's Special Theory of Performativity."
34 For more detailed overview of scholarship on speech acts, see Mitchell Green, "Speech Acts: An Annotated Bibliography"; *Oxford Bibliographies Online*. Also, Daniel Harris, Daniel Fogal, and Matt Moss, eds., *New Work on Speech Acts*.
35 Sandra Laugier notes an "ironic" reference to Jamesian pragmatism in the title of Austin's lecture series in *Why We Need Ordinary Language Philosophy*, 103.
36 Ferguson, "Jane Austen, *Emma*, and the Impact of Form," 180.
37 In addition to Ferguson, see Trisha Urmi Banerjee, "Austen Equilibrium."
38 For philosophical and historical poetics working together with forms of life, see Jonathan Culler and Ben Glaser, eds., *Critical Rhythm*.
39 Garrett Stewart, *The Deed of Reading: Literature, Writing, Language, Philosophy*, 4.
40 Daniel M. Stout, *Corporate Romanticism: Liberalism, Justice, and the Novel*.
41 Sara Guyer, *Reading with John Clare: Biopoetics, Sovereignty, Romanticism*.
42 Alphonso Lingis, *The Community of Those Who Have Nothing in Common*, 12–13.
43 Franco Moretti, *Graphs, Maps, Trees: Abstract Models for Literary History*, 63–64.
44 Franco Moretti, "The Slaughterhouse of Literature," 211, 225.
45 Amitav Ghosh, *The Great Derangement: Climate Change and the Unthinkable*, 9.
46 Ghosh, *The Great Derangement*, 10; for "uniformitarian expectations," see 35.
47 Ghosh, *The Great Derangement*, 7.
48 Ghosh, *The Great Derangement*, 17. In *The History of Missed Opportunities: British Romanticism and the Emergence of the Everyday*, William Galperin presents the everyday as structurally and not just contingently unavailable to the present.
49 Henri Lefebvre, *Rhythmanalysis*, 24, 53.
50 In *Ugly Feelings*, Ngai underscores the long tradition, going back from Hobbes to Aristotle, in which "[s]pecific kinds of emotion could be said to determine specific 'literary kinds'" (9); her account of the minor non-cathartic kinds of feeling characteristic of affect theory stresses how "affects are *less* formed and structured than emotions, but not lacking form or structure altogether, *less* 'sociolinguistically fixed,' but by no means code-free or meaningless" (27).
51 D. W. Winnicott, *Playing and Reality*, 67.
52 Jennifer D. Carlson and Kathleen C. Stewart, "The Legibilities of Mood Work," 115.
53 Steven Miller and Sara Guyer, eds. *Literature and the Right to Marriage*, 13. Miller and Guyer underline "conditions without which marriage would not be marriage. The primary condition of marriage is tautological: there is no marriage without (actual) marriage; no marriage that does not take place according to certain accepted conventions. But the other conditions are more

specific. There is no marriage without festivity or ceremony; no marriage without the sign or the vow; and no marriage without the ethical sublimation of "natural life." (5)

54 Jonathan Kramnick and Anahid Nersessian propose a constrained and inquiry-specific understanding of form in response to the "elasticity" of all that may go by form in the "millennial reboot of formalism"; "Form and Explanation," 652.

55 Deirdre Le Faye, *Jane Austen: A Family Record*; second edition, 137.

56 Anne-Lise François, "Passing Judgment, Conceding Perfection," ¶ 1. Catching the de-dramatized spirit of exemption in François's analysis, and aligned with Austin's project to make room beyond the "descriptive fallacy," is Christina Rossetti's short lyric poem "Promises Like Piecrust": "Promise me no promises / So will I not promise you; / Keep we both our liberties, / Never false and never true"; *The Complete Poems*, 813.

57 Claire Tomalin, *Jane Austen: A Life*, 181–184.

58 Laura Caponetto outlines the different "undoing" actions of annulment, retraction, and amendment in "Undoing Things with Words."

59 Jonathan Culler, *Literary Theory: A Very Short Introduction*, 26.

60 Queer theory offers multiple different perspectives with regard to this "intelligibility," including the critical project to reject its terms outright. In "Sex in Public," Lauren Berlant and Michael Warner assert the project "to describe what we want to promote as the radical aspirations of queer culture building: not just a safe zone for queer sex, but the changed possibilities of identity, intelligibility, publics, culture, and sex that appeal when the heterosexual couple is no longer the referent or privileged example of sexual culture" (548). Lee Edelman, however, explores a queer subject "who refuses to 'come into being' as 'human'" through his reading of the character of Leonard in Hitchcock's *North by Northwest*. Leonard's refusal of compassion and thus of the coerced logic of the symbolic community "gestures toward [the gap] in intelligibility as such"; *No Future: Queer Theory and the Death Drive*, 104.

61 As Geoffrey Hill remarks in "Our Word is Our Bond"; *The Lords of Limit*, 139. For Hill, "J.L. Austin is himself a writer in the comic tradition" (146).

62 Sarah Beckwith notes that, for ordinary language philosophy and its thinking with criteria, the "problem" of fiction becomes irrelevant. That is because "criteria can only tell us what something is like, not whether or not it exists"; "Are There any Women in Shakespeare's Plays? Fiction, Representation, and Reality in Feminist Criticism," 243–244. Maximilian de Gaynesford has written a set of closely-argued essays on the question of the seriousness of the poetic performative. In one of these, he proposes the phrase *Austin's Claim* for the view that speech acts in poetry are non-serious, instead showing how poetry is not only performative, but can offer commitment-rich language; see "Speech Acts and Poetry." While my own work considers Austen's fiction and prose style, not poetry, I wonder about elevating Austin's classification of poetic utterances as intelligibly non-serious to the singular status of "*Austin's Claim*." My reservation concerns not only the scope and salience given to Austin's

remark on where poetry might fit (or not) within speech-act theory, but also voices my doubt that Austin himself would give "seriousness" such a value. (Isn't "serious" another "trouser word"?) In and beyond *How to Do Things with Words*, Austin elaborates the function of types of utterances that other philosophers had called nonsense or non-serious. So while Austin *is* dismissive of poetry, he has already rescued the whole region of the performative from something like the larger gesture of dismissal for being merely "poetic": not true *or* false, nor even fiction. The critique of the descriptive fallacy already makes Austin a friend to poetry in the Shelleyan sense. (This makes the issue of commitment an important one indeed for the study of the literary performative.) De Gaynesford successfully pursues a version of this argument, concluding that "we need to guard against the temptation to inflate the price" of Austin's remarks on the non-seriousness of poetry; "How Not to Do Things With Words: J.L. Austin on Poetry," 44.

63 Simon Jarvis, "How to Do Things with Tunes," 369–70.
64 Yi-Ping Ong, *The Art of Being: Poetics of the Novel and Existentialist Philosophy*.
65 Though it lacks a single print source, the anecdote about Ryle is in common circulation, and has been cited most recently by Deidre Lynch in *Loving Literature: A Cultural History*, 155.
66 The Derrida is quoted by Simon Gikandi in *Slavery and the Culture of Taste*, 51.
67 Mary Ann O'Farrell, "'Bin Laden a Huge Jane Austen Fan': Jane Austen in Contemporary Political Discourse."
68 For a broader history of English manners, see Keith Thomas, *In Pursuit of Civility: Manners and Civilization in Early Modern England*.
69 O'Farrell, "Bin Laden a Huge Jane Austen Fan," 202.
70 O'Farrell, "Bin Laden a Huge Jane Austen Fan," 203.
71 Gillian Dow and Katie Halsey, "Jane Austen's Reading: The Chawton Years."
72 See, for instance, the essays in E. M. Dadlez, ed., *Jane Austen's* Emma*: Philosophical Perspectives*.
73 Peter Knox-Shaw, *Jane Austen and the Enlightenment*.
74 Knox-Shaw, "Philosophy," 352.
75 Tim Milnes, "Trusting Experiments: Sociability and Transcendence in the Familiar Essay," 1.
76 Slavoj Zizek, *The Sublime Object of Ideology*, 62.
77 Lionel Trilling, *Sincerity and Authenticity*, 76.
78 Ricks, *Essays in Appreciation*, 260.
79 G. J. Warnock, "J.L. Austin: A Biographical Sketch"; *Symposium on J.L. Austin*, 9.
80 Ricks, *Essays in Appreciation*, 260.
81 Margaret Anne Doody, Introduction, *Sense and Sensibility*, xxix.
82 Hina Nazar, *Enlightened Sentiments: Judgment and Autonomy in the Age of Sensibility*.
83 Robert Pippen, *After the Beautiful: Hegel and the Philosophy of Pictorial Modernism*, 10.

84 In the course of this sentence I draw directly from Pippen, *After the Beautiful*, 14, 67, 26.
85 For Hegel in section B of *The Encyclopedia Logic* (1817), empiricism as a moment of thought founders at the point of its inability to distinguish passing perception from abiding, universalizing cognition. In his criticism of the conduct of the empiricist from Locke to Warnock, J. L. Austin of course does not share Hegel's universalism, but on my view he does share Hegel's critique of the empiricist "Second Position" as a hollow double-move enacted in the attempt to secure an incorrigible position on sense certainty.
86 For asyndeton in *Sanditon*, I follow a remark by Kathryn Sutherland in her talk, "Jane Austen's Arrivals." Chawton House, Hampshire; New Directions in Austen Studies Conference, 11 July 2009. Sutherland attributes the "playful comment" to Tony Tanner in her book *Jane Austen's Textual Lives: From Aeschylus to Bollywood*, 196. Miller's *Jane Austen, Or The Secret of Style* also concludes by stressing the erosion of language into "half rock, half sand" (*NA*, 295).
87 Jane Austen, *Later Manuscripts*, 207-208; see 550-552 for the manuscript draft transcript.
88 Marvin Mudrick situates character apart from politics and wittily marks the difference: "of course politics can kill you if it doesn't bore you to death, [but Austen] now has livelier matters to deal with: women and also men"; *Nobody Here but Us Chickens*, 163.
89 Virginia Woolf, *To the Lighthouse*, 209.
90 There is a more circumspect way to make this claim jointly for Austen and Austin, which I forgo in this chapter's exposition of a bolder anti-empiricist disposition. That argument would observe that Austen remains appropriately aware that narrative visuality is always "visuality *in language*" (see Zhang, *Strange Likeness*, 11); and Austin holds the exposition of positivist sense-data philosophy to account for its expression by (more or less) natural language. For the link between Austen and Blake, grounded by intellectual enjoyment, see L. C. Knights's Foreword to D. W. Harding, *Regulated Hatred and Other Essays on Jane Austen*, 3.
91 Jane Austen's inheritor in this regard is Ivy Compton-Burnett, as demonstrated in the classic of biography, Hilary Spurling's *Ivy: The Life of I. Compton-Burnett*.
92 In "Jane Austen, the Prose Shakespeare," Daniel Pollack-Pelzner shows that Austen's free indirect style developed in part (from her reading of the *Tales from Shakespeare* [1807] by Charles and Mary Lamb) as "a means for representing Shakespeare in narrative form" (765). Pollack-Pelzner argues that this strategy links "the ethical concerns over speaking another's words and the narrative strategies that make reading *Emma* or *Mansfield Park* a kind of closet drama" (764).

2 Intelligible Community

1 One can apply to Henry a line of Lefebvre, citing Heidegger: "The philosopher speaks of dialogue, **not of communication**"; *Rhythmanalysis*, 49.
2 As Felman notes, the insight comes via Émile Benveniste.

3 The character Stephen Guest in Eliot's *The Mill on the Floss* (1860) declares to Maggie Tulliver, speaking of Lucy Deane, "God knows, I've been trying to be faithful to tacit engagements" (569).
4 David Hume, "Of the Original Contract"; *Selected Essays*, 288.
5 See E. J. Clery, *Jane Austen: The Banker's Sister*. In *Genres of the Credit Economy: Mediating Value in Eighteenth- and Nineteenth-Century Britain*, Mary Poovey examines the felicitously broken promises at the end of *Pride and Prejudice* in terms of the Bank Restriction Act and its deferral of economic grounds of reference (357–372).
6 Jane Austen, *Later Manuscripts*, 148.
7 Judith Butler, *Excitable Speech: A Politics of the Performative*, 12. Felman also writes of a "force of threat or warning" in Austin's commissives; *Scandal*, 12.
8 Frances Ferguson, "Jane Austen, *Emma*, and the Impact of Form," 170.
9 Margaret Doody, *Jane Austen's Names: Riddles, Persons, Places*, 393.
10 Terry Castle, "On Northanger Abbey"; *Boss Ladies, Watch Out! Essays on Women, Sex, and Writing*, 27, 36, echoing Mary Wollstonecraft's description of her first novel, *Mary, a Fiction* (1788), as pertaining to "the mind of a woman who has thinking powers."
11 The distribution of the fact/fiction divide between economics and literature is the central topic of Poovey's *Genres of the Credit Economy*.
12 Austin famously calls poetry a "hollow or void," "*parasitic*," non-serious, speech act in *How to Do Things*, 22. Rather amazingly, the notion of literary and literary-critical "immodality" that I borrow and elaborate seems to be a misprint for *immorality* – though it remains in the second edition of *How to Do Things with Words*. This moment follows the passage in which Austin cites Euripides' *Hippolytus*: "i.e. 'my tongue swore to, but my heart (or mind or other backstage artiste) did not'" (9–10). It then builds toward his ringing statement on moral responsibility in speech acts: "accuracy and morality alike are on the side of the plain saying that *our word is our bond*" (10). Together this is solid evidence for a misprint. I still take the accidental invitation that *immodality* opens to the rigors and play of aesthetic-conceptual thought.
13 Butler, *Excitable Speech*, 49.
14 On the participatory and promissory nature of happiness, see Sara Ahmed, *The Promise of Happiness*, 13, 27–33.
15 "The New Realistic Novel." *The Oxford Authors: Samuel Johnson*, 176.
16 The novel takes its final twist from a marriage-market version of credit panic later, when it is revealed John Thorpe passed a false rumor greatly inflating Catherine's wealth, then afterward caused a run on her prospects by underselling them. This is the process that forces Catherine – alone and (except for Eleanor's quick thinking) almost without money – out of Northanger onto the dangerous public road.
17 Compare J. L. Austin's preference for "the *cash-value* expression to the 'indirect' metaphor" (*SS*, 18).
18 Even *Emma* begins with the recounting of a significant event: her mother's death in the distant past.

19 Robert Hopkins, "General Tilney and the Affairs of State: The Political Gothic in *Northanger Abbey*."
20 John Wiltshire links Henry's reference to "a neighborhood of voluntary spies" with plausibility to Samuel Johnson's elaboration (in *The Idler* 78 [1759]) of a spa town such as Bath as a place where "each is known to be a spy upon the rest"; *The Hidden Austen*, 22. Austen alludes doubly to Home Office surveillance and to the more everyday policing function of gossip.
21 Knox-Shaw, "Philosophy," 351.
22 D. W. Harding, *The Impulse to Dominate*, 14. Harding's first book, "[t]he bulk of the print run…was destroyed in a warehouse fire during the Blitz. Because of war-time paper restrictions it was never reprinted"; "D.W. Harding: A Biographical Chronology"; *Regulated Hatred and Other Essays on Jane Austen*, 224.
23 Harding, *Regulated Hatred and Other Essays on Jane Austen*.
24 Knox-Shaw, "Philosophy," 351.
25 Claudia Johnson, in her assessment of Catherine's reading of *Udolpho*, points out that Catherine's relation to that book remains responsive to its power over women, and is not governed by Radcliffe's final plot clarifications tending to rationalize paternal power and instead blame women. This level of the gothic is found not in material objects, but in human motivations; *Jane Austen: Women, Politics, and the Novel*.
26 Mary Ann O'Farrell, "'Bin Laden a Huge Jane Austen Fan'," 193.
27 O'Farrell, "'Bin Laden a Huge Jane Austen Fan'," 203.
28 O'Farrell, "'Bin Laden a Huge Jane Austen Fan'," 203.
29 Ivy Compton-Burnett, *The Last and the First*, 4.
30 Joseph Litvak's account of Henry Tilney under the heading of "The Most Charming Young Man in the World" (a phrase applied by the narrator not to Henry but to Eleanor Tilney's fiancé) provides an appropriately wary counter to my reading of negotiations of "intelligibility" in this chapter; *Strange Gourmets: Sophistication, Theory, and the Novel*, 33–54.
31 Laura Mooney White and Carmen Smith, "Discerning Voice Through Austen Said: Free Indirect Discourse, Coding, and Interpretive (Un)Certainty."
32 Compare G. H. Lewes writing of Austen in 1851: "It is only plenitude of power that restrains her from the perils of the form she has chosen – perils, namely of tedium and commonplace. Dealing as she does with every day people and every day life, avoiding all the grander tragic emotions and more impassioned aspects of Life, her art consists in charming us by the fidelity of the picture while relieving it of all the tedium of reality" (*CH* 1, 130).
33 Cavell, "Questions and Answers"; in Morris Eaves and Michael Fischer, eds., *Romanticism and Contemporary Criticism*, 227.
34 Lingis, *The Community of Those Who Have Nothing in Common*, 87.
35 Cavell locates Wittgenstein's very concept of "perspicuous representation" in a "finished" style based on a practice of "breaking off" (*P*, 49).

36 "[W]hat we have loved/Others will love, and we will teach them how"; Wordsworth, *The Fourteen-Book* Prelude, 14. 448–449. "O! if I could only contrive one [a ghost story] which would frighten my reader as I myself was frightened that night!"; Mary Wollstonecraft Shelley, Introduction to the 1831 edition of *Frankenstein*.
37 David Bromwich, *Introduction to Selected Poetry of William Wordsworth*, xvi.
38 Trilling, *Sincerity and Authenticity*.
39 See Rae Langton, *Sexual Solipsism: Philosophical Essays on Pornography and Objectification*, esp. 311–355.
40 Colin Jager, *The Book of God: Secularization and Design in the Romantic Era*.
41 Johnson, "The New Realistic Novel," 175.
42 "For instance Catherine Morland knows nothing; but in *Sense and Sensibility* Marianne Dashwood, another seventeen year old with sparkling eyes, knows everything and won't put up with any nonsense"; Marvin Mudrick, "Honest to Goodness Heroines"; *Nobody Here but Us Chickens*, 167.
43 In his essay about Austen's heroines, Mudrick writes of "[t]he pleasure of their company, the pleasure of their pleasure," and characterizes Catherine Morland in these terms: "Catherine is direct and brimming with curiosity, she never dissembles, she cannot tell a lie: her appetite isn't only for horrors, the whole unexperienced world out there excites her and she hasn't learned not to say so"; *Nobody Here but Us Chickens*, 175.
44 Eric C. Walker, "Austen and Cavell," 6.
45 Mary Hays, *The Victim of Prejudice*, xiii–xiv.
46 Mary Wollstonecraft, *Maria: Or, the Wrongs of Woman*, 11.
47 Carol Jacobs writes in the Preface to *Uncontainable Romanticism: Shelley, Brontë, Kleist*: "Ever since its inception (if such a concept makes sense) Romanticism has denied itself a historically limitable field. [...] What Romanticism has come to mean in recent years, in any case, is a yielding of its own temporal limits to register claims of a much more overwhelming kind" (ix).
48 Timothy Gould, "The Names of Action," 48–78: 50, 49.

3 *Sense and Sensibility* and Suffering

1 Stanley Cavell, *Conditions Handsome and Unhandsome: The Constitution of Emersonian Perfectionism*, 64. A further discussion of Cavell's relation to Wittgenstein and criteria, which by contrast elaborates a sense of dissatisfaction with Cavell's expressive romanticism and prefers "Wittgenstein's wariness" (71) to "imperious authority" (76), is Charles Altieri, "Cavell and Wittgenstein on Morality: The Limits of Acknowledgment."
2 As quoted by Deirdre LeFaye in *Jane Austen: A Family Record*, 112.
3 The "certain" for Wittgenstein is not logical or "transcendent certainty" (8e), but the contingent, accidental, and ostensive ("*This* is" x); see *On Certainty*.
4 John Halperin calls the Marianne of the end of the novel a submissive automaton; *The Life of Jane Austen*, 78.
5 Raymond Williams, *Keywords: A Vocabulary of Culture and Society*; revised edition, 281; excerpted in *S&S*, 333–336. As reviewed by Miranda Fricker, the

central argument of Alice Crary's *Beyond Moral Judgment* and the wide perspective it takes on moral thought is that "moral thinking is not limited to the application of moral concepts in judgement"; for Fricker, though, this expanded sense of the life of moral thought for humans as linguistic beings, activated beyond concepts, raises the counter-assertion that "not all sensibility is moral sensibility" (311, 313).

6   See Aaron Kunin, *Character as Form*.
7   Catherine Malabou has emerged as the foremost contemporary philosopher of radical change in a materialist neurological framework; *Ontology of the Accident: An Essay on Destructive Plasticity*. For more on the conceptual history of sensibility and its relation to the "vehicular" model of mediating sentiment and sympathy from the eighteenth century to the present, see James Chandler, *An Archaeology of Sympathy: The Sentimental Mode of Literature and Cinema*, 176–202.
8   Susan Manning adduces Lear's speech (*King Lear* V.iii. 256–260; 269–272), holding his dead daughter in his arms, as part of her extended genealogy in "Sensibility"; *The Cambridge Companion to English Literature, 1740–1830*, 80.
9   Empson, *The Structure of Complex Words*, 255. More Empson: "*Sensibility* in its new equations treats a reception, in various ways, as a sort of key idea for explaining what a reaction ought to be, and *sense* holds on to a reaction of some kind as a means of interpreting or finding profundity in the mere use of the senses" (259).
10 Empson, *The Structure of Complex Words*, 258. The idea of the senses as spies makes a further allusion to the final act of *King Lear*, turning from tragic loss to market gain.
11 David Hume, "Of the Standard of Taste," in *Selected Essays*, 136–137. From the vantage of the continental philosophical tradition, Jean-Luc Nancy writes of Hegelian "sense" [*Sinn*] in the *Aesthetics* that "[s]ense is a 'wondrous' word that designates 'the organs of immediate apprehension' as well as 'the sense, the thought, the universal underlying the thing.' The two senses of the word must then have, in their distinction and in the opposition that this distinction presents, the same sense. The sense of the word *sense* is thus the passage of each one of the two significations into the other"; *Hegel: The Restlessness of the Negative*, 46.
12 Oren Izenberg, "Poems Out of Our Heads," 219.
13 With gratitude, I owe this sentence to an anonymous reader.
14 The plot is easy to render as a Cavellian allegory, a retelling of "first philosophy" over against (to be claimed at the risk of, or only with the vanquishing of) the threat of "skeptical" madness.
15 In *Failures of Feeling: Insensibility and the Novel*, Wendy Anne Lee adds the metonymic identity of an impersonal "Austen herself … as the insensible of the novel" (125).
16 Adam Smith, *The Theory of Moral Sentiments*, 60. Further citations are given in text. Empson's "hardhearted man" inherits Smith's man of "fortitude," adding a gender component in contrast to the subject of a "good cry," while further playing off Smith's Roman/British ideology of stoicism.

17 It is in contrast to the Stoic ideal that Smith discusses the state of reduction to criminal "insensibility to honor and infamy, to vice and virtue," in *The Theory of Moral Sentiments*, 142.
18 Jill Heydt-Stevenson, *Austen's Unbecoming Conjunctions: Subversive Laughter, Embodied History*.
19 Susan Manning comments that "Elinor Dashwood is a better Smithian than many professional philosophers or economists," because she "understands that truly moral sentiments involve strenuous stoicism as much as a spontaneous expression of feelings"; "Sensibility," 85.
20 Andrew Miller, "Perfectly Helpless," 70.
21 For an account not just of novelistic fiction, but of fictionality as such, see Catherine Gallagher, "The Rise of Fictionality."
22 Compare Richard Moran, *The Exchange of Words*, 5.
23 Recounting Cavell's discovery of a typescript of Wittgenstein's Blue Book in a UCLA philosophy department filing cabinet, K. L. Evans writes that "[f]or Cavell the Blue Book is curious and strange, written in a language dead to him, just as the *Tractatus* had been, as he notes in his essay ["On Wittgenstein I"] or even *Philosophical Investigations*, a book that seemed to him, on his first encounter, 'flat, and arbitrary in its progress'"; "While Reading Wittgenstein"; *Stanley Cavell: Philosophy, Literature and Criticism*, 143.
24 Barbara Johnson, "Nothing Fails Like Success"; *A World of Difference*, 11–16.
25 Jacques Derrida, "Typewriter Ribbon: Limited Inc (2)('within such limits')."
26 Jacques Derrida, *The Animal That Therefore I Am*, 27–28; *The Beast and the Sovereign*, Vol. II, 244.
27 Margaret Anne Doody, Introduction to Austen, *Sense and Sensibility*, xxix.
28 Tobias Menely, *The Animal Claim: Sensibility and the Creaturely Voice*, 17. Stanley Cavell et al., *Philosophy and Animal Life*, 91–126.
29 See Eric Lindstrom, "Cavell's Romanticism and the Autobiographical Animal"; in *Stanley Cavell and the Event of Romanticism*.
30 Laugier, *Why We Need Ordinary Language Philosophy*, 105
31 Hillis Miller, *Speech Acts in Literature*, 160–176. Derrida addresses the (im)possibility of "secret" experience through the performative declarations of love (134–139).
32 In *The Economy of Character: Novels, Market Culture, and the Business of Inner Meaning*, Deidre Shauna Lynch explores the shared cultural space of literary and printed "characters" in eighteenth-century novelistic discourse, and the way in which the relationship between Elinor and Marianne preserves yet complicates the pro forma code. On the question of how to preserve and engage the "early" status of *Sense and Sensibility* outside a teleology of narrative modes, see William H. Galperin's nuanced account of the shift from epistolarity to free indirect discourse in *The Historical Austen*, 109–137. In a comment that footnotes a reference to Alfred Gell's idea of "distributed personhood," while distinguishing his own subject matter and approach from those of Philip Fisher, James Chandler writes: "sentiment is precisely not a 'vehement passion.' Vehement passion draws a line around a human subject, defining an intensifying personal

will, personal limits, a person's strongest emotional attachments. Vehement passion signals our invisible depths. Sentiments, by contrast, might be said to spread us thin. They are the result of a projective imagination across a network or relay of regard"; *An Archaeology of Sympathy*, 12. Also see Amélie Oksenberg Rorty, "Characters, Persons, Selves, Individuals."

33 I am thinking of William Deresiewicz's distinction between an "early" and a "major" phase of Austen's career in *Jane Austen and the Romantic Poets*, 18–55. I depart from the implications of Deresiewicz's book in judging these two periods' relative merits.
34 Eliot's study of the individual consciousness as "cell" or monad in F. H. Bradley's thought (the subject of his undefended doctoral dissertation of 1916) indicates his preoccupation with the problem of other minds.
35 See Galperin, *The Historical Austen*, 110–125.
36 D. A. Miller cites Genette on this narratological distinction between "who sees" and "who speaks"; *Secret of Style*, 27 and 99–100n. But I also open the topic to J. L. Austin: "Uncritical use of the direct object after *know* seems to be one thing that leads to the view that (or to talking as though) sensa, that is, things, colours, noises, and the rest, speak or are labelled by nature, so that I can literally *say* what (that which) I *see*: it pipes up, or I read it off" (*PP*, 97).
37 Brian Boyd, "Does Austen Need Narrators? Does Anyone?"
38 Boyd, "Does Austen Need Narrators? Does Anyone?," 291, 295.
39 Dorrit Cohn, *Transparent Minds: Narrative Modes for Presenting Consciousness in Fiction*.
40 Boyd, "Does Austen Need Narrators? Does Anyone?," 302.
41 My writing on Elinor as a character of "constrained interiority" harkens to Eve Kosofsky Sedgwick's famous account of the novel, in which Elinor's subjectivity is "hollow[ed]" out as an unhappy countenance to Marianne's policed impulses; *Tendencies*, 122.
42 As quoted by Claire Tomalin in *Jane Austen: A Life*, 220–221.
43 I take the final formulation in this sentence from James Wood, *How Fiction Works*, 112.
44 Typically this public emphasis is read to counteract a "romantic" position of isolation. But see Rei Terada, "Philosophical Self-Denial: Wittgenstein and the Fear of Public Language," for the view that Wittgenstein's argument against private language puts yet greater stress on the risks of intelligibility. "[H]ard-core belief in the public nature of language and a terror of isolation may well go together," Terada writes. "The more public language is, the more awful failures of communication must be" (464).
45 But see Cavell, *CT*, 160. In *Puppet: An Essay on Uncanny Life*, Kenneth Gross remarks that Geppetto "has no food in his house, only a picture of a boiling kettle stuck upon his wall" (102).
46 Austen apparently liked the joke about representation. She repeats it with *Persuasion*'s Admiral Croft. Where the Admiral's consternation at the boat in the Bath print shop window stems precisely from his worldly expertise,

however, Mr. Woodhouse's incomprehension is a riff on his fearful apprehensions and cultural illiteracy (*Per*, 119).

47 Hina Nazar, "The Imagination Goes Visiting: Jane Austen, Judgment, and the Social."
48 In "Jane Austen's Friendship," her essay on Emma's insensibility to the merits of Jane Fairfax, Mary Ann O'Farrell comments on the relational dialectics of the Dashwood sisters: "If Openness is enjoined to like Reserve, it is imagined to *want* it, and the apparent complementarity of the friendship one can see in advance of its existence ('those two should be friends') is revealed to be a one-sided supplementarity: the friend urged upon one is perceived as able to complete, to answer, to compensate. If this logic works in reverse—if Reserve lacks Openness—Openness cannot know this, and it seems impossible to see the corrective friend's lack as anything but the recessive form taken by what is in fact an excess and a compensation for what one *has* oneself"; *Janeites*, 49.
49 Compare Richard Eldridge's sense that the conventionalist, naturalist, communitarian, neopragmatist, and neo-Aristotelian views of Wittgenstein's thought are all dogmatic reductions of his "writerliness"; *Leading a Human Life: Wittgenstein, Intentionality, and Romanticism*, 107.
50 In his essay, "Wittgenstein's *Philosophical Investigations* as a War Book," Rupert Read holds that *Philosophical Investigations* "contains a powerful philosophy concerning the pain of others, an ethic of acknowledgment that can found a strong anti-racist stance, a determination to truly *see* the other" (594).
51 Martin Seel, "Letting Oneself Be Determined: A Revised Concept of Self-Determination."
52 Stanley Cavell, "The Availability of Wittgenstein's Later Philosophy"; *Must*, 44–72.
53 *Sense and Sensibility*, directed by John Alexander.
54 Nancy Armstrong claims that "[t]he novel takes it upon itself to solve this contradiction by creating fantastic situations in which one can become a good member of society precisely by risking exclusion from it"; "The Fiction of Bourgeois Morality and the Paradox of Individualism"; in *The Novel, Volume 2: Forms and Themes*, 350.
55 Kramnick, *Paper Minds*, 7.

4 *Pride and Prejudice* and the Comedy of Perfectionism

1 Though there is no hard print citation for this famous sentence, the text of record that demonstrates Ryle's paradigmatic and rich engagement with Austen is the essay "Jane Austen and the Moralists."
2 Zizek, *The Sublime Object of Ideology*, 62.
3 Jane Austen to Cassandra Austen, letter of February 4, 1813; *Jane Austen's Letters*; third edition, 203
4 For another approach to this topic, see Jon Mee, *Conversable Worlds: Literature, Contention, and Community 1762 to 1830*, 201–238.

5 Margaret Anne Doody, *Frances Burney: The Life in the Works*, 169, 175.
6 On the aphoristic unreliability of the novel's opening sentence, see Freya Johnston, "Jane Austen's Universals."
7 Calling it "personal conviction in loud mode, rhetorically inflated into absolute truth," Thomas Keymer cites two instances of the phrase, in a 1756 political pamphlet on the colony of Canada by John Shebbeare and a religious tract from 1792 by Anna Barbauld that calls out impious subjects of prayer; "Narrative"; in *The Cambridge Companion to* Pride and Prejudice, 1. Among other Austen scholars who have done so, Linda Bree points out the appearance of "PRIDE and PREJUDICE" (all caps) as spoken by the character Dr. Lyster in Burney's *Cecilia*. Bree also recalls that a twenty-year-old Jane Austen was among the list of subscribers when *Camilla* was published by subscription "at the substantial cost of one guinea"; "The Literary Context"; in *The Cambridge Companion to* Pride and Prejudice, 63. Amongst eighteenth-century authors Austen would likely have read, the phrase "universally acknowledged" appears in: Addison, Barbauld, Blair, Boswell (both on Johnson and on Mr. Burney, Fanny Burney's father), Fanny Burney herself (in *Evelina* as well as *Cecilia*), George Colman (the playwright), Defoe, Charles Dibdin (in separate volumes on the histories of the English Stage and of the Royal Circus), Francis Gentleman (in a 1770 critical companion to the Dramatic Theater), the sermons of Alexander Gerard, Gibbon, Goldsmith, and Hume.
8 "There is, in other words, an unutterable and indecorous excess to the form of respect Austen imagines as quickening into love"; Nancy Yousef, *Romantic Intimacy*, 104.
9 Fanny Burney, *Cecilia, or Memoires of an Heiress*, 908.
10 John Wiltshire, "Medicine, Illness, and Disease," in *Jane Austen in Context*, 308.
11 Goethe, *Elective Affinities*, is cited in text through the following discussion.
12 Benjamin, "Goethe's *Elective Affinities*"; *Selected Writings, Vol. 1, 1913–1926*, 301. Cavell has written with suggestiveness on Benjamin in "Benjamin and Wittgenstein: Signals and Affinities" and "Remains to be Seen."
13 Linda Bree, "The Literary Context"; *Cambridge Companion to* Pride and Prejudice, 64.
14 See Paula Byrne, *Jane Austen and the Theatre*.
15 Cavell, *The World Viewed* (enlarged edition), 153.
16 On style as language in action, see Garrett Stewart, *The Value of Style in Fiction*.
17 W. K. Wimsatt, Jr., *The Prose Style of Samuel Johnson*, 138–139. George Saintsbury compares Austen's humor – "a certain not inhuman or unamiable cruelty" – to Addison, before he surprisingly adds: "I should put Miss Austen as near to Swift in some ways, as I have put her to Addison in others" (*CH* 2, 216–217).
18 *Jane Austen's Letters*, 335.
19 William Hazlitt, "On Modern Comedy," in *Selected Writings*, 101.
20 Sigmund Freud, "Humour," 162. If comedy is a "classic body genre," the novel, it has been argued, absorbs comic intensities but exiles comedy's full disruptive force from "realist causality"; Lauren Berlant and Sianne Ngai, "Comedy Has Issues," 239.

21 Freud, "Humour," 163. Jillian Heydt-Stevenson discusses Freud's treatise on jokes as an illustration of "the limits of applying male-oriented critiques to women's humor, especially for Austen's bawdy humor"; *Austen's Unbecoming Conjunctions*, 207.
22 Freud, "Humour," 166.
23 See also Kevin Ohi, *Henry James and the Queerness of Style*.
24 The phrase is D. W. Harding's, on Austen, in *Words into Rhythm: English Speech Rhythm in Verse and Prose*, 138.
25 We can see this bourgeois relay-transfer from collective narration to the individual character even in Miller's reading, which locates the perilously social feat of style at the level of a character's language (Elizabeth Bennet's): "from the start Elizabeth's style presumes all the freedom from need, the severance from vulgarity, that it eventually secures her in fact as mistress of Pemberley"; *Secret of Style*, 44.
26 Appearing in his 1849 *Fraser's* essay "Occasional Discourse on the Negro Question," Carlyle's phrase "the dismal science" refers back to Malthus's analysis of population in *An Essay on the Principles of Population* (1798), but also to nineteenth-century economic and political questions of West Indian slavery. For more on Austen's and other women writers' participation in the discussion of political economy, see E. J. Clery, "Conversations on Political Economy in *Sanditon*."
27 In *Utopia, Limited: Romanticism and Adjustment*, Anahid Nersessian argues of Harriet Martineau's *Illustrations of Political Economy*, that "in the *Illustrations*, free indirect discourse turns out to be the voice of a third term between character and narration called political economy, or even just capitalism" (192).
28 Compare Harding in *Words into Rhythm*: "These [rhythmic effects] are modes of energy expenditure (or of preparedness for expending it).... We need not wonder how the rhythm comes to 'express' them; it is part of them" (154).
29 See Austin, "Truth" (*PP*, 117) on the "multifarious" phrasing and application of "is true" in English sentences.
30 Shoshana Felman, "Barbara Johnson's Last Book"; *A Life with Mary Shelley*, 124, citing *The Phenomenology of Spirit*, 288.
31 On the counterfactual plotting of Austen's fictions of marriage in anthropological context, see Elsie B. Michie, "Rich Woman, Poor Woman: Toward an Anthropology of the Nineteenth-Century Marriage Plot."
32 Stanley Cavell, *Cities of Words: Pedagogical Letters on a Register of the Moral Life*, 145.
33 Nancy Yousef comments of *Pride and Prejudice*: "Another way to imagine the disarticulation of gratitude and obligation, of affect and ethics, is as a change of feeling toward the other that is not reducible to a change of mind; emotion is not the cause or prelude or precondition for a new cognition but in itself a mode of judgment"; *Romantic Intimacy*, 108.
34 William Rothman, *Must We Kill the Thing We Love? Emersonian Perfectionism and the Films of Alfred Hitchcock*, 2.
35 Michael Wood, *America in the Movies; or, "Santa Maria, It Had Slipped My Mind,"* 56.

36 Cavell volunteers his suspicion elsewhere that canonical poets are or are in constant danger of being "monsters of fame"; "Remains to be Seen," 262.
37 Edward T. Duffy, *Secular Mysteries: Stanley Cavell and English Romanticism*, is a forerunner to my account of *In Quest of the Ordinary*.
38 Miranda Fricker, *Epistemic Injustice: Power and the Ethics of Knowing*.
39 Compare Cavell's notion of the complicity of meat-eating in "Companionable Thinking"; *Philosophy and Animal Life*, 91–126. In *The Wounded Animal: J.M. Coetzee and the Difficulty of Reality in Literature and Philosophy*, 69–94, Stephen Mulhall discusses this collection of essays on animal ethics and Cavell's role as a contributor.
40 Another quest; John Dewey, *The Quest for Certainty: A Study of the Relation of Knowledge and Action*, 11.
41 Gilles Deleuze, *Cinema 2, The Time-Image*, 229.
42 Compare Zhang, *Strange Likeness*, 3.
43 See also Samuel McCormick, *The Chattering Mind: A Conceptual History of Everyday Talk*.
44 To the extent that Ryle's argument offers a wholescale critique of mind/body dualism, its application to Austen comes with a debt to the tradition of feminist scholarship on Austen. Jillian Heydt-Stevenson argues that "the basis of a happy marriage arises from the affirmation of a woman's physicality and mind – her body-consciousness"; *Austen's Unbecoming Conjunctions*, 203–204.
45 See *CM*, 16, for one instance of Ryle's repeated argument that the mind/body split renders the workings of mind a private space of privileged access, hence "inevitably occult to everyone else." Yet Ryle's position should not be confused with the argument that the mind is simply equal to the body. In his writing on syllepsis, Ryle, and nineteenth-century fiction, Garrett Stewart is shrewd to maintain that though "disembodied Cartesian subjectivity [...] puts otherness in hiding and in doubt," the mind and the body as figured by the two non-dualistic predicates of syllepsis are "neither commensurable nor wholly separate and unavailable to each other. Concerning bodily motion vis-à-vis cognition, there is neither pure disjunction nor pure conjunction between them. But access there is"; *The Deed of Reading*, 122.
46 Contrast Bertrand Russell in "On Denoting." "There seems no reason to believe that we are ever acquainted with other people's minds, seeing that these are not directly perceived; hence what we know about them is obtained through denoting" (480).
47 Alice Crary, *Beyond Moral Judgment*, 138–139. In *Know How*, Jason Stanley argues that thinking and action are not distinct capacities governed by different cognitive states. Compare Jane Austen's skill at spilikins, or cup and ball; J. E. Austen-Leigh, *A Memoir of Jane Austen*, 77.
48 Alice Crary, "Austin and the Ethics of Discourse"; *Reading Cavell*, 3.
49 Crary, *Beyond Moral Judgment*, 139.
50 Daniele Lorenzini focuses on the speech situation of conversation in "From Recognition to Acknowledgment: Rethinking the Perlocutionary."

Notes to pages 119–127   251

51 Barbara Cassin, Emily Apter, Jacques Lezra, and Michael Wood, eds., *Dictionary of Untranslatables: A Philosophical Lexicon*, 769. Cited in text by page. The entry on perfectibility is composed by Bertrand Binoche in the original French edition.
52 John T. Scott in his 2012 translation offers "the faculty of perfecting himself," but suggests "the faculty of self-perfection" as equivalent in a note. Scott, however, also allows the passive "faculty of being perfected"; *The Major Political Writings of Jean-Jacques Rousseau*, 72.
53 Jean-Jacques Rousseau, *Second Discourse* (*Discourse on the Origin and Foundations of Inequality Among Men*); in *The First and Second Discourses*, 114–115. On the relation of perfectibility to sociable life, see 140.
54 Trilling, *Sincerity and Authenticity*, 72–80.
55 Rousseau, *Second Discourse*, 149.
56 Rousseau, *Second Discourse*, 149.
57 Rousseau, *Second Discourse*, 149, 150. Compare Cavell in "Must We Mean What We Say?": "the philosopher who proceeds from ordinary language is concerned less to avenge sensational crimes against the intellect than to avenge civil wrongs; to steady an imbalance, the tiniest usurpation, in the mind" (*Must*, 19).
58 "The Scandal of Style: Jeff Dolven Interviewed by Louis Bury."
59 Austin, "Intelligent Behavior," 51.
60 Phillipe Lacoue-Labarthe and Jean-Luc Nancy, *The Literary Absolute*, 2, 3.
61 Mark Philp, "William Godwin"; *The Stanford Encyclopedia of Philosophy*.
62 Also see *Claim*, 432; Cavell, "Companionable Thinking."
63 Peter Marshall, ed., *Romantic Rationalist: A William Godwin Reader*, xii.
64 For Godwin's "irritation with the bodily accessory" in the context of a transition from Enlightenment materialism to Romantic-era materialism and biopolitical thought, see Andrea Charise, "'The Tyranny of Age: Godwin's *St. Leon* and the Nineteenth Century Longevity Narrative," 910.
65 Raymond Wright, Introduction to Thomas Love Peacock, *Nightmare Abbey and Crotchet Castle*, 13.
66 I take the concern with "soul-blindness" from Part 4 of *The Claim of Reason* (378–380).
67 William Godwin, *Enquiry Concerning Political Justice and Its Influence on Modern Morals and Happiness*, 776.
68 Godwin, *Enquiry Concerning Political Justice*, 770–771.
69 Arguably – given his relentless play with word derivations – the "British Romantic" philosophy that matters to Cavell is not epistemology or meta-ethics but the philosophy of language.
70 I owe this sentence about action in Coleridge's thought to a comment by James Engell.
71 William Godwin, *Fleetwood*, 27.
72 *Fleetwood*, 259.
73 *Fleetwood*, 258.

74 On the icon as a symbolic persona in Roman paternal religious and social rites, see Daniel Heller-Roazen, *Absentees: On Variously Missing Persons*, 77–82.
75 Eric Lindstrom, "Perlocution and the Rights of Desire: Cavell, Nietzsche, and Austen (and Austin)."
76 Compare Rae Langton, "Blocking as Counter-Speech," in *New Work on Speech Acts*, 144–164.
77 According to Austin, it is "out of order" to make statements about how another person feels *in their place* (*PP*, 249).
78 Erving Goffman, "Footing"; *Forms of Talk*, 124–159.

5 Perlocutionary Entailments

1 For an interview with Stillman over his two Austen-inspired movies, see Peter W. Graham, "'I Want to Be a Scavenger': A Conversation with Whit Stillman."
2 Luc Sante, "After the Ball"; *Metropolitan*, dir. Whit Stillman.
3 My approach to entailment is wonderfully anticipated in Clara Tuite's "Decadent Austen Entails: Forster, James, Firbank, and the 'Queer Taste' of *Sanditon* (comp. 1817, publ. 1926)"; *Janeites*, 115–139. Also see Sandra MacPherson, "Rent to Own; or, What's Entailed in *Pride and Prejudice*?"
4 Kurnick, "Jane Austen, Secret Celebrity, and Mass Eroticism," 57–58.
5 The idea that women's slavery is the last form of enslavement in Britain is the main argument of John Stuart Mill and Harriet Taylor in *The Subjection of Women* (1869). For historical context and narrative retellings of the issues at stake in the Mansfield Decision, see Paul Fryer, *Staying Power: The History of Black People in Britain*, 120–130; Paula Byrne, *Belle: The Slave Daughter and the Lord Chief Justice*, 135–150; and David Olusoga, *Black and British: A Forgotten History*, 130–145.
6 In *Loving Literature: A Cultural History*, Deidre Lynch traces this affective relationship throughout the eighteenth and nineteenth centuries.
7 Trilling's "*Mansfield Park*" is cited here from *The Moral Obligation to Be Intelligent: Selected Essays*, 294, 96, 97.
8 Trilling, "*Mansfield Park*," 304.
9 Trilling, "*Mansfield Park*," 294.
10 Trilling, "*Mansfield Park*," 294. Trilling sees *Mansfield Park* as the novel that is "bitterly resented" by men who otherwise respond enthusiastically to Austen. "Yet *Mansfield Park* is a great novel" in Trilling's judgment; "its greatness being commensurate with its power to offend."
11 Trilling, "*Mansfield Park*," 309.
12 Carol Jacobs, *Uncontainable Romanticism: Shelley, Brontë, Kleist*, ix.
13 Andrew Warren, "Incapable of Being Disentangled: On De Quincey's Impassioned Prose," ¶9.
14 July 24, 2013; Jane Austen to appear on £10 note, Bank of England.

15 *Slate*, August 6, 2013; The anger over Jane Austen on a 10-pound note proves people can rage over anything (slate.com).
16 See *The New York Times*, July 26, 2013; Jane Austen Bank Note Earns Huzzahs and Nitpicking – *The New York Times* (nytimes.com).
17 *The New Yorker*, August 6, 2013; Fear of Jane Austen.
18 O'Farrell, "'Bin Laden a Huge Jane Austen Fan'," 193.
19 Eve Kosofsky Sedgwick, "Around the Performative: Periperformative Vicinities in Nineteenth-Century Narrative"; *Touching Feeling*, 71–72.
20 Vivasvan Soni discusses the eighteenth-century marriage plot (though only in novels centering on male protagonists) in relation to trial narrative in *Mourning Happiness: Narrative and the Politics of Modernity*, 267–289.
21 See Tuite, "Decadent Austen Entails," in *Janeites*, 119–120, for more degradation theory and insightful remarks on the English national "romance of degradation."
22 Edmund's first act of kindness to Fanny involves a request to his father on her behalf, to use his standing in parliament to frank a letter from Fanny to her brother William (*MP*, 14).
23 Harding, *The Impulse to Dominate*.
24 Trilling, "*Mansfield Park*," 309.
25 *Slate*, August 6, 2013.
26 Trilling, "*Mansfield Park*," 309.
27 Adam Kirsch, *Why Trilling Matters*, 141.
28 I interpret "improvement" in terms of modern liberalism, not in view of Austen's treatment of the estate as a symbol of Christian tradition; for that approach, see Alistair M. Duckworth's classic study *The Improvement of the Estate: A Study of Jane Austen's Novels*. On agrarian improvement in the previous century, see Paul Slack, *The Invention of Improvement: Information and Material Progress in Seventeenth-Century England*.
29 I take "reading tables" from Wittgenstein's *Brown Book*, where I should make clear it is used to describe not actuarial science but the sort of language game, involving signs, pictures, and behaviors that may be guided by "ostensive definitions" (90). This also is the language game that opens *Philosophical Investigations*. Though writers on statistics such as Augustus de Morgan (b. 1806) still lay in the future when Austen wrote *Mansfield Park*, the growing science of "political arithmetic" beyond Malthus had been well established by 1700 – both as an idea and in the reach of its practical management; Slack, *The Invention of Improvement*, 3. David Kurnick credits Sir John Sinclair with the first use of the term statistics in an anglophone text; "Jane Austen, Secret Celebrity, and Mass Eroticism," 69.
30 *Philosophy the Day after Tomorrow* also presents Emersonian convalescence: "The idea of experience as our allowing the world to become near by mourning it, not grasping it, getting to it, but by letting its distance, its separateness, impress us, is the teaching of the immense essay "Experience" (*P*, 52).
31 Cavell, *Cities of Words*, 164.

32 *Why We Need Ordinary Language Philosophy*, 93. To continue with Laugier: "This shows the proximity of the question of contract—the political question in general—to the question of learning" (94).
33 Stout, *Corporate Romanticism*, 54.
34 Cavell refers to the "unusual latitude of subject and treatment" made possible by such occasions (as a Presidential Address to the America Philosophical Association, the 1996 Shakespeare World Conference, his visiting Spinoza Professorship in Amsterdam two years later, etc.).
35 "The mystery machine Astaire inspires at the end of the second routine, and reveals as concentrating American life, reminds him that he cannot praise black dancing without consenting to, being compromised by, an American scene of mechanical self-praise whose self-forgetfulness the counter-scenes of entertainment deeper within the Arcade have remembered" (*P*, 80).
36 Derrida delivered his text at The University of Virginia in 1976. See J. Hillis Miller, *Speech Acts in Literature*, 112–128.
37 In *The Argonauts*, Maggie Nelson deploys Roland Barthes's evocation of the renaming of the ship Argo as a re-commitment to the speech act "I love you."
38 Both Sedgwick's and Cavell's collections draw from materials published in the decade preceding, but according to the information provided in the authors' acknowledgments pages, the materials I discuss were first published in 2003 and 2005.
39 Sedgwick, *Touching Feeling*, 67. Further citations given in text.
40 Compare Langton, "Blocking as Counter-Speech," in *New Work on Speech Acts*.
41 Priscilla Wald, "Conjunctive Relations," 17.
42 Anne K. Mellor and Alex L. Milsom, "Austen's Fanny Price, Grateful Negroes, and the Stockholm Syndrome."
43 See Simon Critchley, "Cavell's 'Romanticism' and Cavell's Romanticism," in *Contending with Stanley Cavell*, 37–54. Cavell responds in the same volume (164–167). Returning something like that very critique of exceptionalism in other terms, Cavell – observing the contemporaneity of Marx's *Critique of Hegel's Theory of Right* and Emerson's "Experience" – emphasizes the Marxian idea of class history in which "the working class is the inheritor of German philosophy means, let us say, that a certain group of human beings are now, given the conditions of the present developed over the stages of world history, in a position at last to put the ideals of philosophy into practice, and human history will at last begin." By contrast, Cavell says of the idea of America in "Experience," "The very promise of it drives you mad, as with the death of a child." See "Finding as Founding"; in *Emerson's Transcendental Etudes*, 123.
44 Simon Critchley, *Very Little … Almost Nothing: Death, Philosophy, and Literature*; second edition, 150.
45 Critchley, *Very Little … Almost Nothing*, 153.
46 Sarah Beckwith, *Shakespeare and the Grammar of Forgiveness*.
47 Branka Arsic, *On Leaving: A Reading in Emerson*, 7.

48 This is the topic of Cavell's address "Hope against Hope"; *Emerson's Transcendental Etudes*, 171–182. "Is Emerson therefore opposed both to defeat *and* to success?" (186).
49 Cavell, *Conditions Handsome and Unhandsome*, xxi.
50 Cavell, *Cities of Words*, 217.
51 In the UC-Berkeley lecture version of "Philosophy the Day After Tomorrow," Cavell says the words, "No one is entitled in advance to them; they are ours for the taking," in the anti-penultimate sentence of the final paragraph of the printed essay.

6 *Emma* and Other Minds

1 Stuart Hampshire, "'I'm Going to Tamper with Your Beliefs a Little'," 21.
2 Austin follows Hume's *Treatise of Human Nature* in classifying the knowledge we might claim about the future instead as belief.
3 While different modalities and intensities are involved in the performative speech acts "I know" and "I promise," there is not in Austin's thought on speech acts the rift one finds in Paul de Man's absolute division between cognitive (epistemological) and performative (eventual) aspects of language. For de Man, these modes are incommensurate, though precisely for that reason endless rhetorical, cultural, and aesthetic ingenuity goes into the attempt to seal over their divide. See Andrej Warminski's "Postscriptum: On the Superperformative," in *Material Events: Paul de Man and the Afterlife of Theory*, 22–28.
4 John Dewey, "The Live Creature"; *Art as Experience*, 10. Citing Dewey, Eddie S. Glaude argues for a pragmatic dimension to the idea of prophecy as an office in "On Prophecy and Critical Intelligence."
5 John Dewey, "Self-Realization as the Moral Ideal," 659–660. Also see Dewey, *The Quest for Certainty*.
6 John Wisdom, *Other Minds*, unpaginated preface.
7 As Avner Baz holds in *When Words Are Called For: A Defense of Ordinary Language Philosophy*: "Getting us to suppose that it ought to be possible for us just to apply 'know that' or one of its cognates to any pair of person and fact apart from any context of significant use has been the most important move in the skeptic's, but not just the skeptic's, conjuring trick" (200).
8 "The sceptic refuses to back anything, saying that everything may lose except Logic which doesn't. In saying this he appears to back something but he doesn't. For his own statement can't lose and doesn't run." Wisdom, *Other Minds*, 102.
9 Toril Moi, *Revolution of the Ordinary*, 205–210; I cite 207.
10 The notion that authority is transmissible, and that its wagers, speculations, and risks are transmittable through wounding satire, provides a compelling aspect of the autobiographical account of the "*nom de guerre*," Mark Twain, in Twain's *Life on the Mississippi* (1883); *Mississippi Writings*, 520.

11 The passage deserves wider framing: "The fantasy of a private language, I suggested, can be understood as an attempt to account for, and protect, our separateness, our unknowingness, our unwillingness or incapacity either to know or to be known. Accordingly, the failure of the fantasy signifies: that there is no assignable end to the depth of us to which language reaches; that nevertheless there is no end to our separateness. We are endlessly separate, for *no* reason. But then we are answerable for everything that comes between us; if not for causing it then for continuing it; if not for denying it then for affirming it; if not *for* it then *to* it. The idea of privacy expressed in the fantasy of a private language fails to express how private we are, metaphysically and practically." (*Claim*, 369–370)

12 Whereas J. L. Austin serves as guide to my discussion of Austen's *Emma* on the topic of excuses, an alternate deconstructive trajectory famously involves Rousseau and de Man. J. Hillis Miller recounts this complex body of writings and commentary with clarity in *Speech Acts in Literature*, 145–146.

13 Austin's "A Plea for Excuses" shows how we do not know the meaning of "doing an action" as a delimitable event in advance. Thus Laugier: "As Cavell says, 'What does it betoken about human actions that the reticulated constellation of predicates of excuse made for them—that they can be done unintentionally, unwillingly, involuntarily, insincerely, unthinkingly, inadvertently, heedlessly, carelessly, under duress, under the influence, out of contempt, out of pity, by mistake, by accident, and so on? ... It betokens, we might say, the all but unending vulnerability of human action, its openness to the independence of the world and the preoccupation of the mind"; *Why We Need Ordinary Language Philosophy*, 104. See *A Pitch of Philosophy*, 87. "Naming actions is a sensitive occupation," writes Cavell in "Must We Mean What We Say?" (*Must*, 35).

14 For a subtle and productive account of an intersubjective predictive calculus, see William Flesch, "Hyperbolic Discounting and Temporal Bargaining," in *Theory Aside*, 199–217: esp. 213.

15 Like many of the novel's readers, Susan J. Wolfson finds irony in the resonance between the ending of *Emma* and the Box Hill scene: "No wonder that the too-harmonious-by-half close of her novel [...] has struck more than a small band of readers as so patently artificial as to invite a guess at irony. It seems only the latest turn in the novel's larger suspicions about plots of amelioration"; "Boxing Emma; or the Reader's Dilemma at the Box Hill Games," ¶ 19.

16 Anne-Lise François grapples with Cavellian issues of expression and acknowledgment in *Open Secrets: The Literature of Uncounted Experience*. The problem left by Cavell's understanding of skepticism, François explains, "is a function of the impossible roles that the 'process of secularization'—Cavell calls it 'romanticism'—puts humans in the position of playing for one another. For inasmuch as this process accepts Protestantism's antinomian emphasis on inner faith over obedience to external laws, it is now up to me to summon myself before God and determine what is asked of me, shoring up what I can from my own now boundless experience" (212). In *Shakespeare and the Grammar of Forgiveness*, Sarah Beckwith shows how the task of playing God for one another (and ourselves) is historically anchored to the "abandoned sacrament of penance" in the sixteenth century in which the "so-called English Settlement" in matters of state

religion was first drawn up (1, 16). The shift from Catholic rites of penance and the ecclesiological "office of the keys" to Protestant and Calvinist liturgy hollows out the shared social world between the "inner" individual and the confessional state, entailing a "revolution in ritual theory." Beckwith quotes Hannah Arendt's *The Human Condition*: "without being forgiven, released from the consequences of what we have done, our capacity to act, would, as it were, be confined to one single deed from which we would never recover" (2).

17 D. W. Harding, "Civil Falsehood in *Emma*"; *Regulated Hatred and Other Essays on Jane Austen*, 171–189.
18 Mary Russell Mitford, *Our Village* [1824], 1.
19 Sianne Ngai, *Our Aesthetic Categories: Zany, Cute, Interesting*, 135.
20 Sandra Laugier organizes what she has learned from Cavell – and what comprises philosophical learning in Cavell – under the heading of "importance"; "Matter and Mind: Cavell's (Concept of) Importance," 996.
21 "It is a most interesting work. You are fond of that kind of reading?" (*NA*, 74).
22 In *The Great Derangement*, Amitav Ghosh highlights how "serious" modern fiction depends on certain *things not happening*. I would pair his broad critique with the nuance of William Galperin, for whom the "detailism" of Austen's everyday style is not limited to probability and perception, but available to retrospective and subjunctive, historiographically "missed" forms; *The History of Missed Opportunities*, 20.
23 Sianne Ngai, *Ugly Feelings*, 14. For pointed discussion of Ngai's "interesting" and its bearing on the public life of aesthetic judgments, see Michael Clune, "Judgment and Equality."
24 Ngai, *Our Aesthetic Categories*, 233–234.
25 Ngai, *Our Aesthetic Categories*, 132.
26 William James, *The Principles of Psychology*; cited in Ngai, *Our Aesthetic Categories*, 129; Ngai suggestively comments on the time of the "interesting" experience as that of "a feeling of not-yet-knowing" (132).
27 Magdalena Ostas, "Kant with Michael Fried: Feeling, Absorption, and Interiority in the *Critique of Judgment*," 17.
28 See Michel Chaouli, *Thinking with Kant's Critique of Judgment*, 42–75.
29 Giorgio Agamben, *Taste*, 46.
30 Eric Lindstrom, "Critical Judgment and Free Indirect Style."
31 Quoted in *Our Aesthetic Categories*, 276n.
32 Compare Adela Pinch on Coventry Patmore, whose aphorism "'All knowledge worthy of name, is nuptial knowledge' might be best understood not as a statement of confidence in the infallibility of conjugal understanding, but rather as an admission that all knowledge partakes of the uncertainties of love thinking"; *Thinking about Other People in Nineteenth-Century British Writing*, 137.
33 Cavell, *Conditions Handsome and Unhandsome*, 121.
34 Moral Luck (*Stanford Encyclopedia of Philosophy*). See Eva Dadlez, "Jane Austen on Moral Luck." Robert Hopkins, "Moral Luck and Judgment in Jane Austen's *Persuasion*."
35 I quote from the *Stanford Encyclopedia* entry; also see *Jane Austen's Emma: Philosophical Perspectives*.

36 Dewey, *The Quest for Certainty*, 3.
37 Again, see *Pitch*, 87.
38 See Dewey, *The Quest for Certainty*.
39 The generally sanguine Adam Smith characterizes life as such as a void when surveying the Austenian terrain of "all the little occurrences of common life," "in what was said and what was done, in all the little incidents of the present conversation, and in all those frivolous nothings which fill up the void of human life." *The Theory of Moral Sentiments*, 52.
40 Knightley imputes to Emma something like an English version of a quasi-visionary religious enthusiasm, Kant's *Schwärmerei*, in *Dreams of a Spirit-Seer* (1766).
41 Here the protagonist's character alone unites – or "seem[s] to unite" – the combined best attributes of the entire collection of characters banded together in "perfect happiness" at the novel's end.
42 Marshall Brown, "Emma's Depression."
43 Walker, "Austen and Cavell," ¶ 6.
44 Walker, "Austen and Cavell," ¶ 6.
45 Chiara Alfano, "Toward an Ordinary Language Psychoanalysis: On Skepticism and Infancy," 26.
46 I argue throughout this book that Cavell has a precursor in the work of psychologist and literary critic D.W. Harding:

> The inconsistencies [regarding practices of disclosure and reserve at the end of *Emma*], whether or not intended as deliberate ironies by Jane Austen, point to the dilemma of a subtle and sensitive woman who had to come to terms with the moral and intellectual mediocrity of a society on which she was dependent and of friends and relations with whom she had the closest and most affectionate of ties.

"Jane Austen and Moral Judgment"; in *Regulated Hatred and Other Essays on Jane Austen*, 79. Harding comments perceptively on the relation of Austen to British Romanticism:

> The detachment and autonomy of the individual as a centre of self-responsible moral judgment, which [Austen] maintained unswervingly, was in fact another variant of that reaction against submission to ready-made social codes which marks Blake, Shelley, Wordsworth, and even Byron. (79)

47 Quoted by David Rudrum in *Stanley Cavell and the Claim of Literature*, 41.
48 As an anonymous reader has helpfully pointed out, here I underplay how (literally) strict an accounting Thoreau gives of the labor and materials he expended on his house and his bean field, and how much Cavell stresses this feature of Thoreau's writing.
49 Michael Fischer, *Stanley Cavell and Literary Skepticism*, 152n.
50 Walker, "Austen and Cavell," ¶ 7.
51 Langton, "Blocking as Counter-Speech," in *New Work on Speech Acts*.
52 Margaret Anne Doody provides another account of the socially structured "zigzags" of communication in relation to the gendered courtship conventions in fiction of Austen's time, in *Frances Burney: The Life in the Works*, 232. Doody's vivid account of the impasse of courtship transmits its "rules": "The essential paradox of the central action is to be found in the conduct-book views which constitute the two opposing rules. A. Camilla's Rule. A young woman must never allow

her love for a young man to become visible, especially to the object of it, until he has made an unreserved declaration, that is a proposal of marriage" (230). At the other "side of the see-saw—Edgar's rule. B. Edgar's Rule. A man must never propose to a woman unless he is sure her heart is now entirely his own. She must also be capable of loving him devotedly and must never have loved another man" (231). "Rule A ought perhaps to be called Viola's Monument, in memory of "she never told her love." Never telling one's love generates another rule (Rule A2), best formulated as "act naturally" – pretend not to feel what you really feel. The player must seem to go in a direction different from that of the secret objective. Rule A2, if followed for any length of time, will inevitably give rise to strategies called "indifference," "levity," or "coquetry." The subtleties of Rule A2 must lead to what might be called the Moving Toyshop Pattern, or zig-zags" (232).

53 Jeanne M. Britton, "'To Know What You Are All Thinking': Riddles and Minds in Jane Austen's *Emma.*"

54 Hillis Miller does not discuss Cavell in *Speech Acts in Literature*, but a remark in the "Passion Performative" chapter is apposite:

> In the essays I am discussing ["Other Minds" and "Pretending"], as in *How to Do Things With Words*, the highest issues are at stake: no less than the possibility for securing morality, law, and order on a firm foundation. A passion for law and order always lies somewhat covertly behind Austin's jokes about how we can be sure that little bird is a goldfinch or how we can know that man is angry unless he takes a ferocious bite of out the carpet. (173)

"[P]assion for law and order" suggests how Austin himself might understand the relation between "passionate" improvised utterance (perlocution) and "lawful" ritual utterance (illocution).

55 Kathryn Sutherland is wrong to call Harding "a psychologist rather than a literary critic"; as citations throughout the present book indicate, he was both, and his students in literature included Boris Ford; J. E. Austen Leigh, *A Memoir of Jane Austen*, xlv.

56 Harding, *Regulated Hatred and Other Essays on Jane Austen*, 12, 11.

57 Wendy Anne Lee, "Resituating 'Regulated Hatred': D.W. Harding's Jane Austen."

58 Mitford, *Our Village*, v.

59 See Boyd, "Does Austen Need Narrators? Does Anyone?" 296–300.

60 Franco Moretti, *The Bourgeois: Between History and Literature*.

61 Blakey Vermeule, *Why Do We Care about Literary Characters*, 180–181.

62 Mary Poovey, "The True English Style"; *E*, 402.

63 Eve Kosofsky Sedgwick, *The Weather in Proust*, 149. See Alan Richardson, *The Neural Sublime: Cognitive Theories and Romantic Texts*, 79–96, for an account of *Emma* drawing from ToM theory. Richardson follows the behavioral signs of eye movement and body language as a fast-track to solve the mystery plot in *Emma*. My investment in the perlocutionary register – including Austen's as author meaning to affect her reader – takes the dimensions of linguistic behavior less narrowly.

64 Galperin, *The Historical Austen*, 180–213.

65 Pinch seeks "to explain why George Eliot regarded the belief that thinking about someone might make something happen to them as simultaneously

epistemologically irrational and ethically efficacious"; *Thinking about Other People in Nineteenth-Century British Writing*, 144. Pinch mentions the "unrepresented thinking" of Fanny Price in *Mansfield Park*, and contrasts Frank's ploy to access the party's thoughts in the Box Hill scene of *Emma* (151). But she does not draw from *Emma* regarding the more salient comparison of Emma's (exploratory, ultimately negative) "love thinking" about Frank when he returns to Yorkshire, or her later (vulnerable and reflective) thinking about Mr. Knightley while he is away in London. Pinch's characterization of free indirect style borrows from a stunning passage in *Daniel Deronda*: "[t]he unspeakable sentences of free indirect discourse are dark rays doing their work silently in the chatter of broad light" (157).

66 Pinch, *Thinking about Other People*, 15.
67 Austin: "As 'truth' is not a name for a characteristic of assertions, so 'freedom' is not a name for a characteristic of actions, but the name of a dimension in which actions are assessed" (*PP*, 180).
68 Compare Cavell on the excuse as a disclosure "encircled by the present," not perpetually deferred, in *Little Did I Know*, 110.
69 Here is Austin on justifications: "In the one defence, briefly, we accept responsibility but deny that it was bad: in the other, we admit that it was bad but don't accept full, or even any, responsibility" (*PP*, 176).

7 *Persuasion*, Conviction, and Care: Jane Austen's Keeping

1 Aristotle by contrast approaches the persuasive function of language directly. He defines rhetoric as "an ability, in each [particular] case, to see the available means of persuasion"; *On Rhetoric: A Theory of Civic Discourse*, 36.
2 Samuel Weber, *Benjamin's -Abilities*.
3 Joshua Wilner has helped me to see the importance of this passage.
4 Walker, "Austen and Cavell," ¶ 14.
5 Virginia Woolf, *The Common Reader: First Series*, 144.
6 Anne and Wentworth's unsettled condition even in what the novel ultimately calls their "settled life" is witnessed by the identity and interest of their "first visitor," Mrs. Smith, who gains Wentworth's assistance to reclaim property of her late husband in the West Indies (*Per*, 178).
7 For a subtle account of the novel as "historical" and "historicizing," see Emily Rohrbach, *Modernity's Mist: British Romanticism and the Poetics of Anticipation*, 106–133. Reading patterns of anticipated retrojection in *Persuasion*, Rohrbach characterizes Jane Austen as "a theorist of philosophical modernity" (109).
8 Wood, *America in the Movies; or, "Santa Maria, It Had Slipped My Mind,"* 42. The image bears in mind Cavell's own account of the Frank Capra film *It Happened One Night*, and incidentally echoes the memory of Jane Austen's niece of Jane and Cassandra Austen, often seen walking together.
9 In a chapter on *Persuasion* that also shares illuminating remarks on Cavell, Mary Favret writes: "In the end the novel, like Shakespeare's *A Winter's Tale* [sic], reassures us that love can, magically, come back to life"; *War at a Distance: Romanticism and the Making of Modern Wartime*, 146. Favret understands

Cavell's discussion of skepticism and Romanticism as an expression of the "geopolitical situation of England at the turn of the nineteenth century" (158).
10. Walker, "Austen and Cavell," ¶ 14. Walker moves briskly from the foundational reading of Austen's *Persuasion* with Cavell's idea of remarriage, to an application from the field of adoption studies to the idea of Cavell as a *self-adopting* thinker.
11. Cavell places the initial near-encounter with the work of Foucault back further in time: "Yet I am still open to the surprise I expressed nearly twenty years ago in Jerusalem, when Derrida and I both gave talks at a month-long conference there, in asking myself, suddenly (breaking into my essay for the conference that I was preparing on the film *Gaslight*, about a woman being driven mad with self-doubt), who it was I thought I was addressing in the essays in *Must We Mean What We Say?* – written between 1957 and 1968 – in writing about writing and voice and skepticism and madness and inheritance and the modern, throughout questioning philosophy's authority and pressing its relation to literature. The cluster of preoccupations are in some obvious sense closer to those in the rough exchanges in 1963 between Derrida and Foucault on reading Descartes than they are to anything my generation of philosophers was concerned with then in the United States, something it took me a decade or two to discover" (*Little Did I Know*, 537).
12. Daniele Lorenzini, *Éthique et politique de soi: Foucault, Hadot, Cavell et les techniques de l'ordinaire*, 15; 107–199.
13. Persuasion is J. L. Austin's first example of a perlocutionary speech act in *How to Do Things with Words* (102).
14. For the critical/ transcendental distinction on the "Subject's ontological commitment in the act of enunciation," see Michel Foucault, *The Government of Self and Others: Lectures at the Collège de France, 1982–1983*, 379. Also see Daniele Lorenzini, "Performative, Passionate, and Parrhesiastic Utterance: On Cavell, Foucault, and Truth as an Ethical Force."
15. J. S. Mill, "What Is Poetry?"
16. In *The Hidden Jane Austen*, John Wiltshire comments on Anne Elliot's position (both emotional and spatial) within "the theatrical device of overhearing" throughout the novel (152). The circle is brought round, of course, with Wentworth's overhearing of Anne's declaration of constancy in the speech to Captain Harville.
17. See Cavell, *Cities of Words*, 99–100.
18. Aletta J. Norval, "Moral Perfectionism and Democratic Responsiveness: Reading Cavell with Foucault."
19. For a Foucauldian reading of Austen that emphasizes power/ knowledge in the production of regulative culture, see Nancy Armstrong, *Desire and Domestic Fiction: A Political History of the Novel*.
20. I cite from Daniele Lorenzini and Richard Neer, "Introduction: Davidson and his Interlocutors," 257. As David Owen writes, this involves "not simply ... self-knowledge but [...] becoming intelligible to oneself"; "Perfectionism, Parrhesia, and the Care of the Self," 135.
21. In a question and answer session at the 2018 English Institute (New Haven, CT), Heather Love asked the question of whether violence is the bedrock of truth-telling.

22 Again compare Cavell's striking statement on the risks and costs of blood (*P*, 187).
23 See Norval, "Moral Perfectionism and Democratic Responsiveness," 216, for helpful summary.
24 Arnold I. Davidson, ed., *Foucault and His Interlocutors*.
25 I draw the concept of entanglement from the work of Andrew Warren, and cite Warren's essay "Incapable of Being Disentangled: On DeQuincey's Impassioned Prose," ¶1.
26 Warren, "Incapable of Being Disentangled," ¶ 9.
27 Warren, "Incapable of Being Disentangled," ¶ 6.
28 Barbara Cassin, *Sophistical Practice: Toward a Consistent Relativism*, 195. Cited hereafter in text. Cassin dismissively comments that "Foucault ... died a bit too soon" to understand Greek philosophy in depth (9).
29 Compare Sara Ahmed's concept of anticipatory causality in *The Promise of Happiness*, 28ff.
30 Lorenzini, "Performative, Passionate, and Parrhesiastic Utterance," 260.
31 *Foucault and His Interlocutors*, 2.
32 *Foucault and His Interlocutors*, 4.
33 Michel Foucault, "Writing the Self"; *Foucault and his Interlocutors*, 234–247; quoted at 234–235. Also see Roland Barthes, *How to Live Together: Novelistic Simulations of Some Everyday Spaces*.
34 Foucault, "Writing the Self," 237, 247.
35 Another subsequent text in this constellation is Giorgio Agamben's investigation of the practice of "form of life" through the example of monasticism, and the threshold between "rule and life"; *The Highest Poverty*, esp. 62ff.
36 Lorenzini, "Performative, Passionate, and Parrhesiastic Utterance," 266.
37 See, for example, Favret, *War at a Distance*, 145–151, 166–168; Christien Garcia, "Left Hanging: Silence, Suspension, and Desire in Jane Austen's *Persuasion*"; Adela Pinch, *Strange Fits of Passion: Epistemologies of Emotion, Hume to Austen*; Megan Quinn, "The Sensation of Language in Austen's *Persuasion*"; Margaret Russett, "*Persuasion*, Mediation."
38 Deidre Shauna Lynch, Introduction to *Persuasion*, xiv.
39 Barchas points out that the Musgrove family – elevated to the Baronetage in 1611 and a likely source for the Musgroves in the novel – carried the family crest *Sans Changer*; *Matters of Fact in Jane Austen: History, Location, and Celebrity*, 234.
40 Cavell, *Disowning Knowledge in Seven Plays of Shakespeare*; updated edition, 138–139.
41 Leo Bersani, *Thoughts and Things*, 4, ix, 38. Further citations in text.
42 The idiom of "keeping" also applies to "putting up" produce, in home pickling and preservation; see Deidre Lynch's discussion of Q. D. Leavis in "At Home with Jane Austen"; *Cultural Institutions of the Novel*, ed. William B. Warner and Deidre Lynch, 159–192.
43 Mary Shelley, *Frankenstein; 1818 text*, 9. Walton's lament over his misspent education in this letter may echo Orlando in Shakespeare's *As You Like It*: "My brother Jacques he keeps at school, and report speaks goldenly of his

profit. For my part, he keeps me rustically at home or, to speak more properly, stays me here home unkept—for call you that 'keeping' for a gentleman of my birth, that differs not from the stalling of an ox?" (I.i. 4–10). Two instances of a wider use of the "keeping" of Dorlcote Mill occur in the first chapter of George Eliot's *The Mill on the Floss*, 53–55.

44 Kirsten Martin, "In Want of Keeping: Painting and the Sympathetic Imagination of *Frankenstein*."
45 Woolf, *The Common Reader*, 143.
46 Claudia Johnson departs from this critical tradition of viewing *Persuasion* as "autumnal," in *Jane Austen: Women, Politics and the Novel*, 144. Favret remarks on the "various knocks to various heads" in the novel as a matter of "historical substance" in *War at a Distance* (162). She cites John Wiltshire's account of *Persuasion* in *Jane Austen and the Body* as a story of "'broken bones, broken heads and broken hearts'" (167).
47 Woolf, *The Common Reader*, 136; *A Room of One's Own*, 69.
48 For description of several of the Regency-era actors of physical comedy whom Jane Austen saw perform on stage, see Robert Morrison, *The Regency Years: During Which Jane Austen Writes, Napoleon Fights, Byron Makes Love, and Britain Becomes Modern*, 69–73; *Jane Austen's Letters*, 261.
49 I thank Emily Thibodeau for the comparison between the bodies of fallen nuts and soldiers, and for the observation that at some point Wentworth would drop the nut.
50 See Han and Das, *Living and Dying in the Contemporary World: A Compendium*.
51 I draw from David Kurnick's account in "A Few Lies: Queer Theory and Our Method Melodramas."
52 Q. D. Leavis, "A Critical Theory of Jane Austen's Writings, II."
53 Woolf, *The Common Reader*, 140.
54 For the idea of essayism in British Philosophy, see Tim Milnes, *The Testimony of Sense*.
55 As Colin Davis writes in *Critical Excess: Overreading in Derrida, Deleuze, Levinas, Zizek and Cavell*: "Cavell's characteristic speaking position is that of someone who makes claims which appeal for but do not demand assent. This is not to say that he abandons any attempt to persuade his reader of the truth of his claims; but it will be interpretation's aptitude to stick, not its demonstrable validity, which will decide its usefulness" (162).
56 Adam Smith, *Theory of Moral Sentiments*, 27.

Bibliography

Agamben, Giorgio. *Taste*. Trans. Cooper Francis. Chicago: Seagull, 2017.
Agamben, Giorgio. *The Highest Poverty*. Trans. Adam Kotsko. Stanford: Stanford University Press, 2011.
Ahmed, Sara. *The Promise of Happiness*. Durham, NC: Duke University Press, 2010.
Alfano, Chiara. "Toward an Ordinary Language Psychoanalysis: On Skepticism and Infancy." *New Literary History* 49.1 (2018). 23–45.
Altieri, Charles. "Cavell and Wittgenstein on Morality: The Limits of Acknowledgment." *Stanley Cavell and Literary Studies: Consequences of Skepticism*. Ed. Richard Eldridge and Bernard Rhie. New York and London: Continuum, 2011. 62–77.
Altieri, Charles. "Style." *Oxford Handbook of Philosophy and Literature*. Ed. Richard Eldridge. Oxford: Oxford University Press, 2009. 420–439.
Aristotle. *On Rhetoric: A Theory of Civic Discourse*. Trans. George A. Kennedy. New York: Oxford University Press, 1991.
Armstrong, Nancy. *Desire and Domestic Fiction: A Political History of the Novel*. Oxford: Oxford University Press, 1987.
Armstrong, Nancy. "The Fiction of Bourgeois Morality and the Paradox of Individualism." *The Novel, Volume 2: Forms and Themes*. Ed. Franco Moretti. Princeton: Princeton University Press, 2007. 349–388.
Arsic, Branka. *On Leaving: A Reading in Emerson*. Cambridge: Cambridge, MA Harvard University Press, 2010.
Austen, Jane. *Juvenilia*. Ed. Peter Sabor. *The Cambridge Edition of the Works of Jane Austen*. Cambridge: Cambridge University Press, 2006.
Austen, Jane. *Later Manuscripts*. Ed. Janet Todd and Linda Bree. *The Cambridge Edition of the Works of Jane Austen*. Cambridge: Cambridge University Press, 2013.
Austen-Leigh, James Edward. *A Memoir of Jane Austen* [1870]. Oxford: Oxford University Press, 2002.
Austin, John Langshaw. "Intelligent Behavior." *Review of Gilbert Ryle, The Concept of Mind, Ryle*. Ed. Oscar P. Wood and George Pitcher. London and Basingstoke: Macmillan, 1970. 45–51.
Banerjee, Trisha Urmi. "Austen Equilibrium." *Representations* 143.1 (2018). 63–90.
Banfield, Ann. *The Phantom Table: Woolf, Fry, Russell and the Epistemology of Modernism*. Cambridge: Cambridge University Press, 2000.

Barchas, Janine. *Matters of Fact in Jane Austen: History, Location, and Celebrity*. Baltimore, MD: Johns Hopkins University Press, 2012.

Barthes, Roland. *How to Live Together: Novelistic Simulations of Some Everyday Spaces*. Trans. Kate Briggs. New York: Columbia University Press, 2012.

Baz, Avner. *When Words Are Called For: A Defense of Ordinary Language Philosophy*. Cambridge, MA: Harvard University Press, 2012.

Beckwith, Sarah. "Are There Any Women in Shakespeare's Plays? Fiction, Representation, and Reality in Feminist Criticism." *New Literary History* 46.2 (2015). 241–260.

Beckwith, Sarah. *Shakespeare and the Grammar of Forgiveness*. Ithaca, NY: Cornell University Press, 2011.

Benjamin, Walter. "Goethe's *Elective Affinities*." *Selected Writings, Vol. 1, 1913–1926*. Ed. Marcus Bullock and Michael W. Jennings. Cambridge, MA: Harvard University Press, 2004. 297–360.

Berlant, Lauren. *Cruel Optimism*. Durham, NC: Duke University Press, 2011.

Berlant, Lauren, and Michael Warner. "Sex in Public." *Critical Inquiry* 24.2 (Winter 1998). 547–566.

Berlant, Lauren, and Sianne Ngai. "Comedy Has Issues." *Critical Inquiry* 43.2 (Winter 2017). 233–249.

Berlin, Isaiah. Ed. *Essays on J.L. Austin*. Oxford: Oxford University Press, 1973.

Berlin, Isaiah. *The Roots of Romanticism*. Princeton: Princeton University Press, 1999.

Bersani, Leo. *Thoughts and Things*. Chicago: University of Chicago Press, 2015.

Boswell, James. *The Life of Samuel Johnson* [1791]. Oxford: Oxford University Press, 1980.

Boyd, Brian. "Does Austen Need Narrators? Does Anyone?" *New Literary History* 48.2 (2017). 285–308.

Bree, Linda. "The Literary Context." *The Cambridge Companion to* Pride and Prejudice. Ed. Janet Todd. Cambridge: Cambridge University Press, 2013. 56–66.

Brewer, Charlotte. "'That Reliance on the Ordinary': Jane Austen and the Oxford English Dictionary." *Review of English Studies* 66.276 (2015). 744–765.

Britton, Jeanne M. "'To Know What You Are All Thinking': Riddles and Minds in Jane Austen's *Emma*." *Poetics Today* 39.4 (2018). 651–677.

Bromwich, David. "Introduction." *Selected Poetry of William Wordsworth*. Ed. Mark Van Doren. New York: Random House, 2002. xv–xx.

Brown, Marshall. "Emma's Depression." *Studies in Romanticism* 53.1 (2014). 3–29.

Burney, Fanny, *Cecilia, or Memoires of an Heiress* [1782]. New York: Virago Press, 1986.

Butler, Judith. *Excitable Speech: A Politics of the Performative*. New York and London: Routledge, 1997.

Byrne, Paula. *Belle: The Slave Daughter and the Lord Chief Justice*. New York: HarperCollins, 2014.

Byrne, Paula. *Jane Austen and the Theatre*. London: Bloomsbury, 2007.

Byrne, Paula. *The Real Jane Austen: A Life in Small Things*. New York: HarperCollins, 2013.
Caponetto, Laura. "Undoing Things with Words." *Synthese* 197.6 (2018). 2399–2414.
Carlson, Jennifer D., and Kathleen C. Stewart. "The Legibilities of Mood Work." *New Formations: A Journal of Culture/Theory/Politics* 82.1 (2014). 114–133.
Cassin, Barbara. *Sophistical Practice: Toward a Consistent Relativism*. New York: Fordham University Press, 2014.
Cassin, Barbara, Emily Apter, Jacques Lezra, and Michael Wood. Eds. *Dictionary of Untranslatables: A Philosophical Lexicon*. Princeton: Princeton University Press, 2014.
Castle, Terry. *Boss Ladies, Watch Out! Essays on Women, Sex, and Writing*. New York: Routledge, 2002.
Cavell, Stanley. "Benjamin and Wittgenstein: Signals and Affinities." *Critical Inquiry* 25.2 (1999). 245–256.
Cavell, Stanley. *Cities of Words: Pedagogical Letters on a Register of the Moral Life*. Cambridge, MA: Harvard University Press, 2004.
Cavell, Stanley. *Conditions Handsome and Unhandsome: The Constitution of Emersonian Perfectionism*. Chicago: University of Chicago Press, 1990.
Cavell, Stanley. *Disowning Knowledge in Seven Plays of Shakespeare*. Updated edition. Cambridge: Cambridge University Press, 2003.
Cavell, Stanley. *Emerson's Transcendental Etudes*. Stanford: Stanford University Press, 2003.
Cavell, Stanley. et al. *Philosophy and Animal Life*. New York: Columbia University Press, 2008.
Cavell, Stanley. "Remains to be Seen." *Artforum International* 38.8 (2000). 31–35.
Cavell, Stanley. *The World Viewed: Reflections on the Ontology of Film*. Enlarged Edition. Cambridge, MA: Harvard University Press, 1979.
Chandler, James. *An Archaeology of Sympathy: The Sentimental Mode of Literature and Cinema*. Chicago: University of Chicago Press, 2013.
Chaouli, Michel. *Thinking with Kant's Critique of Judgment*. Cambridge, MA: Harvard University Press, 2017.
Charise, Andrea. "'The Tyranny of Age: Godwin's *St. Leon* and the Nineteenth Century Longevity Narrative." *ELH* 79.4 (2012). 905–933.
Clery, Emma J. "Conversations on Political Economy in *Sanditon*." *Persuasions* 38.2 (2018).
Clery, Emma J. *Jane Austen: The Banker's Sister*. London: Biteback, 2017.
Clune, Michael. "Judgment and Equality." *Critical Inquiry* 45.4 (2019). 910–934.
Cohn, Dorrit. *Transparent Minds: Narrative Modes for Presenting Consciousness in Fiction*. Princeton: Princeton University Press, 1984.
Compton-Burnett, Ivy. *The Last and the First*. New York: Knopf, 1971.
Crary, Alice. "Austin and the Ethics of Discourse." *Reading Cavell*. Ed. Alice Crary and Sanford Shieh. Abingdon: Routledge, 2006. 42–67.
Crary, Alice. *Beyond Moral Judgment*. Cambridge, MA: Harvard University Press, 2007.

Critchley, Simon. "Cavell's 'Romanticism' and Cavell's Romanticism." *Contending with Stanley Cavell*. Ed. Russell B. Goodman. New York: Oxford University Press, 2005. 37–54.
Critchley, Simon. *Very Little ... Almost Nothing: Death, Philosophy, and Literature*, second edition. New York: Routledge, 2004.
Culler, Jonathan. *Literary Theory: A Very Short Introduction*. New York: Oxford University Press, 2011.
Culler, Jonathan and Ben Glaser. Eds. *Critical Rhythm*. New York: Fordham University Press, 2019.
Dadlez, Eva M. Ed. *Jane Austen's* Emma: *Philosophical Perspectives*. Oxford: Oxford University Press, 2018.
Dadlez, E. M. "Jane Austen on Moral Luck." *Jane Austen and Philosophy*. Ed. Mimi Marinucci. London: Rowman & Littlefield, 2016. 95–106.
Das, Veena. *Life and Words: Violence and the Descent into the Ordinary*. Berkeley: University of California Press, 2007.
Davidson, Arnold. Ed. *Foucault and His Interlocutors*. Chicago: University of Chicago Press, 1997.
Davidson, Jenny. *Reading Style: A Life in Sentences*. New York: Columbia University Press, 2014.
Davis, Colin. *Critical Excess: Overreading in Derrida, Deleuze, Levinas, Zizek and Cavell*. Stanford: Stanford University Press, 2010.
Deleuze, Gilles. *Cinema 2, The Time-Image*. Trans. Hugh Tomlinson and Robert Galeta. Minneapolis, MN: University of Minnesota Press, 1989.
Deresiewicz, William. *Jane Austen and the Romantic Poets*. New York: Columbia University Press, 2004.
Derrida, Jacques. *The Animal That Therefore I Am*. Ed. Marie-Louise Mallet. Trans. David Wills. New York: Fordham University Press, 2008.
Derrida, Jacques. *The Beast and the Sovereign*, Vol. II. Ed. Michel Lisse et al. Trans. Geoffrey Bennington. Chicago: University of Chicago Press, 2011.
Derrida, Jacques. "Declarations of Independence." Trans. Tom Keenan and Tom Pepper. *New Political Science* 7.1 (1986). 7–15.
Derrida, Jacques. "Typewriter Ribbon: Limited Inc (2)('within such limits')." *Material Events: Paul de Man and the Afterlife of Theory*. Ed. Tom Cohen et al. University of Minnesota Press, 2001. 277–360.
Dewey, John. *Art as Experience* [1934]. New York: Perigree, 1980.
Dewey, John. *The Quest for Certainty: A Study of the Relation of Knowledge and Action*. London: Allen & Unwin, 1930.
Dewey, John. "Self-Realization as the Moral Ideal." *The Philosophical Review* 2.6 (1893). 652–664.
Doody, Margaret Anne. *Frances Burney: The Life in the Works*. New Brunswick, NJ: Rutgers University Press, 1988.
Doody, Margaret Anne. "Introduction." *Sense and Sensibility*. By Jane Austen. Ed. James Kinsley. Oxford: Oxford University Press, 2004. vii–xxxix.
Doody, Margaret Anne. *Jane Austen's Names: Riddles, Persons, Places*. Chicago: University of Chicago Press, 2015.

Dolven, Jeff. "The Scandal of Style: Jeff Dolven Interviewed by Louis Bury." *Bomb* (September 5, 2018).
Dow, Gillian, and Katie Halsey. "Jane Austen's Reading: The Chawton Years." *Persuasions* 30.2 (2010).
Duckworth, Alistair M. *The Improvement of the Estate: A Study of Jane Austen's Novels*. Baltimore, MD: Johns Hopkins University Press, 1972.
Duffy, Edward T. *Secular Mysteries: Stanley Cavell and English Romanticism*. New York and London: Bloomsbury, 2013.
Eaves, Morris, and Michael Fischer. Eds. *Romanticism and Contemporary Criticism*. Ithaca, NY: Cornell University Press, 1986.
Edelman, Lee. *No Future: Queer Theory and the Death Drive*. Durham, NC: Duke University Press, 2005.
Eldridge, Richard. *Leading a Human Life: Wittgenstein, Intentionality, and Romanticism*. Chicago: University of Chicago Press, 1997.
Eliot, George. *The Mill on the Floss* [1860]. Harmondsworth: Penguin, 1979.
Empson, William. *The Structure of Complex Words*. Norfolk, CT: New Directions, 1951.
Evans, K. L. "While Reading Wittgenstein." *Stanley Cavell: Philosophy, Literature and Criticism*. Ed. James Loxley and Andrew Taylor. Manchester and New York: Manchester University Press, 2011. 137–149.
Fann, Kuni T. Ed. *Symposium on J. L. Austin*. London: Routledge and Kegan Paul, 1969.
Favret, Mary A. *War at a Distance: Romanticism and the Making of Modern Wartime*. Princeton: Princeton University Press, 2010.
Felman, Shoshana. "Barbara Johnson's Last Book." *A Life with Mary Shelley*. Stanford: Stanford University Press, 2014. 123–158.
Ferguson, Frances. "Jane Austen, *Emma*, and the Impact of Form." *MLQ* 61.1 (2000). 157–180.
Findlater, Jane, and Mary Findlater. *Crossriggs* [1908]. New York: Penguin, 1986.
Fischer, Michael. *Stanley Cavell and Literary Skepticism*. Chicago: University of Chicago Press, 1989.
Flesch, William. "Hyperbolic Discounting and Temporal Bargaining." *Theory Aside*. Ed. Jason Potts and Daniel Stout. Durham, NC: Duke University Press, 2014. 199–217.
Foucault, Michel. *The Government of Self and Others: Lectures at the Collège de France, 1982–1983*. Ed. Frédéric Gros. Trans. Graham Burchell. Houndmills: Palgrave Macmillan, 2010.
François, Anne-Lise. *Open Secrets: The Literature of Uncounted Experience*. Stanford: Stanford University Press, 2008.
François, Anne-Lise. "Passing Judgement, Conceding Perfection." *Stanley Cavell and the Event of Romanticism*. Ed. Eric Lindstrom. Romantic Circles Praxis Series (2014).
Freud, Sigmund. "Humour." *The Standard Edition of the Complete Psychological Works of Sigmund Freud*, vol. 21. Trans. James Strachey. London: Hogarth Press, 1961.

Fricker, Miranda. *Epistemic Injustice: Power and the Ethics of Knowing*. Oxford: Oxford University Press, 2007.
Fricker, Miranda. "Review of *Beyond Moral Judgment*. By Alice Crary." *European Journal of Philosophy* 18.2 (2010). 311–315.
Fry, Paul H. *William Empson: Prophet against Sacrifice*. London and New York: Routledge, 1991.
Fryer, Paul. *Staying Power: The History of Black People in Britain* [1984]. London: Verso, 2010.
Gallagher, Catherine. "The Rise of Fictionality." *The Novel, Volume 1: History, Geography and Culture*. Ed. Franco Moretti. Princeton: Princeton University Press, 2006. 336–363.
Galperin, William. *The Historical Austen* (Philadelphia: University of Pennsylvania Press, 2003).
Galperin, William. *The History of Missed Opportunities: British Romanticism and the Emergence of the Everyday*. Stanford: Stanford University Press, 2017.
Garcia, Christien. "Left Hanging: Silence, Suspension, and Desire in Jane Austen's *Persuasion*." *The Eighteenth Century* 59.1 (2018). 85–103.
de Gaynesford, Maximilian. "How Not to Do Things with Words: J.L. Austin on Poetry." *British Journal of Aesthetics* 51.1 (2011). 31–49.
de Gaynesford, Maximilian. *The Rift in the Lute: Attuning Poetry and Philosophy*. Oxford: Oxford University Press, 2017.
de Gaynesford, Maximilian. "Speech Acts and Poetry." *Analysis* 70.4 (2010). 644–646.
Ghosh, Amitav. *The Great Derangement: Climate Change and the Unthinkable*. Chicago: University of Chicago Press, 2016.
Gibson, James J. *Reasons for Realism: Selected Essays of James J. Gibson*. Ed. Edward Reed and Rebecca Jones. Hillsdale, NJ: Lawrence Erlbaum, 1982.
Gikandi, Simon. *Slavery and the Culture of Taste*. Princeton: Princeton University Press, 2011.
Glaude, Eddie S. "On Prophecy and Critical Intelligence." *American Journal of Theology and Philosophy* 32.2 (2011). 105–121.
Godwin, William. *Enquiry Concerning Political Justice and Its Influence on Modern Morals and Happiness* [1793]. Harmondsworth: Penguin, 1985.
Godwin, William. *Fleetwood* [1806]. Ed. Gary Handwerk and Arnold A. Markley. Peterborough, ON: Broadview, 2001.
Goethe, Johann Wolfgang von. *Elective Affinities* [1809]. Trans. R. J. Hollingdale. Harmondsworth: Penguin, 1971.
Goffman, Erving. *Forms of Talk*. Philadelphia: University of Pennsylvania Press, 1981.
Gould, Timothy. "The Names of Action." *Stanley Cavell*. Ed. Richard Eldridge. Cambridge: Cambridge University Press, 2003. 48–78.
Graham, Peter W. "'I Want to Be a Scavenger': A Conversation with Whit Stillman." *Persuasions* 38.1 (2017).
Green, Mitchell. "Speech Acts: An Annotated Bibliography." *The Stanford Encyclopedia of Philosophy* (2021). https://plato.stanford.edu/archives/fall2021/entries/speech-acts/.

Gross, Kenneth. *Puppet: An Essay on Uncanny Life*. Chicago: Chicago University Press, 2011.
Guyer, Sara. *Reading with John Clare: Biopoetics, Sovereignty, Romanticism*. New York: Fordham University Press, 2015.
Halperin, John. *The Life of Jane Austen*. Baltimore, MD: Johns Hopkins University Press, 1984.
Hampshire, Stuart, and Isaiah Berlin. "'I'm Going to Tamper with Your Beliefs a Little.'" *The Isaiah Berlin Virtual Library*.
Han, Clara and Veena Das. Eds. *Living and Dying in the Contemporary World: A Compendium*. Oakland: University of California Press, 2016.
Harding, D. W. *The Impulse to Dominate*. London: George Allen, 1941.
Harding, D. W. *Regulated Hatred and Other Essays on Jane Austen*. Ed. Monica Lawlor. Atlantic Highlands, NJ: Athlone Press, 1998.
Harding, D. W. *Words into Rhythm: English Speech Rhythm in Verse and Prose*. Cambridge: Cambridge University Press, 1976.
Harman, Graham. *Guerilla Metaphysics: Phenomenology and the Carpentry of Things*. Chicago: Open Court, 2005.
Harris, Daniel, Daniel Fogal, and Matt Moss. Eds. *New Work on Speech Acts*. New York: Oxford University Press, 2017.
Hays, Mary. *The Victim of Prejudice* [1799]. Ed. Eleanor Ty; second edition. Peterborough, ON: Broadview, 1998.
Hazlitt, William. *Selected Writings*. Ed. Jon Cook. Oxford: Oxford University Press, 1991.
Hegel, Georg Wilhelm Friedrich. *The Phenomenology of Spirit* [1807]. Trans. A. V. Miller. Oxford: Oxford University Press, 1977.
Heller-Roazen, Daniel. *Absentees: On Variously Missing Persons*. New York: Zone, 2021.
Heydt-Stevenson, Jill. *Austen's Unbecoming Conjunctions: Subversive Laughter, Embodied History*. Houndmills: Palgrave, 2008.
Hill, Geoffrey. *The Lords of Limit*. New York: Oxford University Press, 1984.
Hopkins, Robert. "General Tilney and the Affairs of State: The Political Gothic in *Northanger Abbey*." *Philological Quarterly* 57.2 (1978). 213–224.
Hopkins, Robert. "Moral Luck and Judgment in Jane Austen's *Persuasion*." *Nineteenth-Century Literature* 42.2 (1987). 143–158.
Hume, David. *Selected Essays*. Ed. Stephen Copley and Andrew Edgar. Oxford: Oxford University Press, 1996.
Igarashi, Yohei. *The Connected Condition: Romanticism and the Dream of Communication*. Stanford: Stanford University Press, 2019.
Izenberg, Oren. "Poems Out of Our Heads." *PMLA* 123.1 (January 2008): 216–222.
Jacobs, Carol. *Uncontainable Romanticism: Shelley, Brontë, Kleist*. Baltimore, MD: John Hopkins University Press, 1989.
Jager, Colin. *The Book of God: Secularization and Design in the Romantic Era*. Philadelphia: University of Pennsylvania Press, 2006.
Jarvis, Simon. "How to Do Things with Tunes." *ELH* 82.2 (2015). 365–383.
Johnson, Barbara. *A World of Difference*. Baltimore, MD: Johns Hopkins University Press, 1987.

Johnson, Claudia L. *Jane Austen's Cults and Cultures*. Chicago: University of Chicago Press, 2012.
Johnson, Claudia L. *Jane Austen: Women, Politics, and the Novel*. Chicago: University of Chicago Press, 1988.
Johnson, Claudia L. and Clara Tuite. Eds. *A Companion to Jane Austen*. Malden, MA: Wiley-Blackwell, 2009.
Johnson, Samuel. *The Oxford Authors: Samuel Johnson*. Ed. Donald Greene. Oxford: Oxford University Press, 1984.
Johnston, Freya. "Jane Austen's Universals." *Essays in Criticism* 68.2 (2018). 211–233.
Kaplan, Deborah. "'There She Is at Last': The Byrne Portrait Controversy." *Persuasions* 34 (2012). 121–133.
Keymer, Thomas. "Narrative." *The Cambridge Companion to* Pride and Prejudice. Ed. Janet Todd. Cambridge: Cambridge University Press, 2013. 1–14.
Kirsch, Adam. *Why Trilling Matters*. New Haven: Yale University Press, 2011.
Kleinman, Arthur, Veena Das, and Margaret Lock. Eds. *Social Suffering*. Berkeley: University of California Press, 1997.
Knox-Shaw, Peter. *Jane Austen and the Enlightenment*. Cambridge: Cambridge University Press, 2004.
Knox-Shaw, Peter. "Philosophy." *Jane Austen in Context*. Ed. Janet Todd. Cambridge: Cambridge University Press, 2005. 346–356.
Kornbluh, Anna. "We Have Never Been Critical: Toward the Novel as Critique." *Novel: A Forum on Fiction* 50.3 (2017). 397–408.
Kramnick, Jonathan. *Paper Minds: Literature and the Ecology of Consciousness*. Chicago: University of Chicago Press, 2018.
Kramnick, Jonathan, and Anahid Nersessian. "Form and Explanation." *Critical Inquiry* 43.3 (Spring 2017). 650–669.
Kunin, Aaron, *Character as Form*. London: Bloomsbury, 2019.
Kurnick, David. "A Few Lies: Queer Theory and Our Method Melodramas." *ELH* 27.2 (2020). 349–374.
Kurnick, David. "Jane Austen, Secret Celebrity, and Mass Eroticism." *New Literary History* 52.1 (2021). 53–75.
Lacoue-Labarthe, Phillipe, and Jean-Luc Nancy. *The Literary Absolute*. Albany: State University of New York Press, 1988.
Lamb, Charles. *Essays of Elia and Last Essays of Elia* [1823, 1833]. London: Dent, 1962.
Langton, Rae. *Sexual Solipsism: Philosophical Essays on Pornography and Objectification*. Oxford: Oxford University Press, 2009.
Laugier, Sandra. "Matter and Mind: Cavell's (Concept of) Importance." *MLN* 126.5 (2011). 994–1003.
Laugier, Sandra. *Why We Need Ordinary Language Philosophy*. Trans. Daniela Ginsburg. Chicago: University of Chicago Press, 2013.
Leavis, Q. D. "A Critical Theory of Jane Austen's Writings, II." *Scrutiny* (January, 1942). 272–294.
Lee, Wendy Anne. *Failures of Feeling: Insensibility and the Novel*. Stanford: Stanford University Press, 2019.

Lee, Wendy Anne. "Resituating 'Regulated Hatred': D. W. Harding's Jane Austen." *ELH* 77.4 (2010). 995–1014.
LeFaye, Deirdre. *Jane Austen: A Family Record*, second edition. Cambridge: Cambridge University Press, 2003.
LeFaye, Deirdre. Ed. *Jane Austen's Letters*, third edition. Cambridge: Cambridge University Press, 1995.
Lefebvre, Henri. *Rhythmanalysis: Space, Time, and Everyday Life*. Trans. Stuart Elden and Gerald Moore. London: Bloomsbury, 2013.
Levine, Caroline. *Forms: Whole, Rhythm, Hierarchy, Network*. Princeton: Princeton University Press, 2015.
Levine, George. *Darwin and the Novelists: Patterns of Science in Victorian Fiction*. Cambridge, MA: Harvard University Press, 1988.
Lezra, Jacques. *On the Nature of Marx's Things: Translation as Necrophilology*. New York: Fordham University Press, 2018.
Lindstrom, Eric. "Critical Judgment and Free Indirect Style." *Style and Romantic Fiction*. Ed. Anne Toner. Cambridge: Cambridge University Press, forthcoming.
Lindstrom, Eric. "Perlocution and the Rights of Desire: Cavell, Nietzsche, and Austen (and Austin)." *Conversations* 4 (2016). 26–42.
Lindstrom, Eric. Ed. *Stanley Cavell and the Event of Romanticism*. Romantic Circles Praxis Series (2014).
Lingis, Alphonso. *The Community of Those Who Have Nothing in Common*. Bloomington: Indiana University Press, 1994.
Litvak, Joseph. *Strange Gourmets: Sophistication, Theory, and the Novel*. Durham, NC and London: Duke University Press, 1997.
Locke, John. *An Essay Concerning Human Understanding* [1689]. Ed. Roger Woolhouse. London: Penguin, 1997.
Lorenzini, Daniele. *Éthique et politique de soi: Foucault, Hadot, Cavell et les techniques de l'ordinaire*. Paris: Vrin, 2015.
Lorenzini, Daniele. "From Recognition to Acknowledgment: Rethinking the Perlocutionary." *Inquiry* (January, 2020).
Lorenzini, Daniele. "Performative, Passionate, and Parrhesiastic Utterance: On Cavell, Foucault, and Truth as an Ethical Force." *Critical Inquiry* 41.2 (2015). 254–268.
Lorenzini, Daniele, and Richard Neer. "Introduction: Davidson and his Interlocutors." *Critical Inquiry* 45.2 (2019). 255–259.
Lynch, Deidre. *The Economy of Character: Novels, Market Culture, and the Business of Inner Meaning*. Chicago: University of Chicago Press, 1998.
Lynch, Deidre. "Introduction." *Persuasion*. By Jane Austen. Ed. James Kinsley. Oxford: Oxford University Press, 2004. vii–xxxiii.
Lynch, Deidre. Ed. *Janeites: Austen's Disciples and Devotees*. Princeton: Princeton University Press, 2000.
Lynch, Deidre. *Loving Literature: A Cultural History*. Chicago: University of Chicago Press, 2015.
MacPherson, Sandra. "Rent to Own; or, What's Entailed in *Pride and Prejudice*?" *Representations* 82.1 (2003). 1–23.
Malabou, Catherine. *Ontology of the Accident: An Essay on Destructive Plasticity*. Trans. Carolyn Shread. Cambridge and Malden, MA: Polity, 2012.

Manning, Susan. "Sensibility." *The Cambridge Companion to English Literature, 1740–1830*. Eds. Thomas Keymer and Jon Mee. Cambridge: Cambridge University Press, 2004. 80–99.

Marshall, Peter. Ed. *Romantic Rationalist: A William Godwin Reader*. Oakland: PM Press, 2017.

Martin, Kirsten. "In Want of Keeping: Painting and the Sympathetic Imagination of *Frankenstein*." *Eighteenth-Century Fiction*. 32.4 (2020). 599–618.

Matz, Jesse. "Cultures of Impression." *Bad Modernisms*. Ed. Douglas Mao and Rebecca L. Walkowitz (Durham, NC and London: Duke University Press, 2006). 298–330.

McCormick, Samuel. *The Chattering Mind: A Conceptual History of Everyday Talk*. Chicago: University of Chicago Press, 2020.

Mee, Jon. *Conversable Worlds: Literature, Contention, and Community 1762 to 1830*. Oxford: Oxford University Press, 2011.

Mellor, Anne K., and Alex L. Milsom. "Austen's Fanny Price, Grateful Negroes, and the Stockholm Syndrome." *Persuasions* 34 (2012). 222–235.

Menely, Tobias. *The Animal Claim: Sensibility and the Creaturely Voice*. Chicago: University of Chicago Press, 2015.

Michie, Elsie B. "Rich Woman, Poor Woman: Toward an Anthropology of the Nineteenth-Century Marriage Plot." *PMLA* 124.2 (2009). 421–436.

Mill, John Stuart. "What Is Poetry?" *The Monthly Repository* (Jan. 1833). 60–70.

Miller, Andrew H. *The Burdens of Perfection: On Ethics and Reading in Nineteenth-Century British Literature*. Ithaca, NY: Cornell University Press, 2008.

Miller, Andrew H. "Implicative Criticism, or the Display of Thinking." *New Literary History* 44.3 (2013). 345–360.

Miller, Andrew H. "Perfectly Helpless." *Modern Language Quarterly* 63.1 (March 2002) 65–88.

Miller, J. Hillis. "Performativity as Performance/ Performativity as Speech Act: Derrida's Special Theory of Performativity." *South Atlantic Quarterly* 106.2 (Spring 2007). 219–235.

Miller, J. Hillis. *Speech Acts in Literature*. Stanford: Stanford University Press, 2002.

Miller, Steven and Sara Guyer. "Introduction: Literature and the Right to Marriage." *Diacritics* 35.4 (2005). 3–22

Milnes, Tim. *The Testimony of Sense: Empiricism and the Essay from Hume to Hazlitt*. Oxford: Oxford University Press, 2019.

Milnes, Tim. "Trusting Experiments: Sociability and Transcendence in the Familiar Essay." *The Prose of Romanticism*. Ed. Yoon Sun Lee. Romantic Circles Praxis Series (2017).

Mitford, Mary Russell. *Our Village* [1824]. New York: Woodstock Books, 1996.

Moi, Toril. *Revolution of the Ordinary: Literary Studies after Wittgenstein, Austin, and Cavell*. Chicago: University of Chicago Press, 2017.

Mooney White, Laura, and Carmen Smith. "Discerning Voice through Austen Said: Free Indirect Discourse, Coding, and Interpretive (Un)Certainty." *Persuasions* 37.1 (2016).

Moran, Richard. *The Exchange of Words: Speech, Testimony, and Intersubjectivity*. New York: Oxford University Press, 2018.

Moretti, Franco. *The Bourgeois: Between History and Literature*. New York: Verso, 2013.
Moretti, Franco. *Graphs, Maps, Trees: Abstract Models for Literary History*. London: Verso, 2005.
Moretti, Franco. "The Slaughterhouse of Literature." *MLQ* 61.1 (March 2000). 207–227.
Morrison, Robert. *The Regency Years: During Which Jane Austen Writes, Napoleon Fights, Byron Makes Love, and Britain Becomes Modern*. New York: Norton, 2019.
Mudrick, Marvin. *Nobody Here but Us Chickens*. Ticknor & Fields: New Haven and New York, 1981.
Mulhall, Stephen *The Wounded Animal: J.M. Coetzee and the Difficulty of Reality in Literature and Philosophy*. Princeton: Princeton University Press, 2009.
Nancy, Jean-Luc. *Hegel: The Restlessness of the Negative*. Trans. Jason Smith and Steven Miller. Minneapolis, MN: University of Minnesota Press, 2002.
Nazar, Hina. *Enlightened Sentiments: Judgment and Autonomy in the Age of Sensibility*. New York: Fordham University Press, 2012.
Nazar, Hina. "The Imagination Goes Visiting: Jane Austen, Judgment, and the Social." *Nineteenth-Century Literature* 59.2 (2004). 145–78.
Nelson, Maggie. *The Argonauts*. Minneapolis, MN: Graywolf, 2016.
Nersessian, Anahid. *Utopia, Limited: Romanticism and Adjustment*. Cambridge, MA: Harvard University Press, 2015.
Ngai, Sianne. *Our Aesthetic Categories: Zany, Cute, Interesting*. Cambridge, MA: Harvard University Press, 2012.
Ngai, Sianne. *Ugly Feelings*. Cambridge, MA: Harvard University Press, 2005.
Norval, Aletta J. "Moral Perfectionism and Democratic Responsiveness: Reading Cavell with Foucault." *Ethics & Global Politics* 4.4 (2011). 207–229.
O'Farrell, Mary Ann. "'Bin Laden a Huge Jane Austen Fan': Jane Austen in Contemporary Political Discourse." *Uses of Austen: Jane's Afterlives*. Eds. Gillian Dow and Clare Hanson. Houndmills: Palgrave Macmillan, 2012. 192–207.
Ohi, Kevin. *Henry James and the Queerness of Style*. Minneapolis, MN: University of Minnesota Press, 2011.
Oksenberg Rorty, Amélie. "Characters, Persons, Selves, Individuals." *Theory of the Novel: A Historical Approach*. Ed. Michael McKeon. Baltimore, MD: Johns Hopkins University Press, 2000. 537–553.
Olusoga, David. *Black and British: A Forgotten History*. London: Macmillan, 2016.
Ong, Yi-Ping. *The Art of Being: Poetics of the Novel and Existentialist Philosophy*. Cambridge, MA: Harvard University Press, 2018.
Ostas, Magdalena. "Kant with Michael Fried: Feeling, Absorption, and Interiority in the *Critique of Judgment*." *Symploke* 18.1–2 (2010). 15–30.
Owen, David. "Perfectionism, Parrhesia, and the Care of the Self: Foucault and Cavell on Ethics and Politics." *Stanley Cavell and the Claim to Community*. Ed. Andrew Norris. Stanford: Stanford University Press, 2006. 128–155.
Peacock, Thomas Love. *Nightmare Abbey and Crotchet Castle* [1818, 1831]. Harmondsworth: Penguin, 1979.

Philp, Mark. "William Godwin." *The Stanford Encyclopedia of Philosophy* (Summer 2017). Ed. Edward N. Zalta. https://plato.stanford.edu/archives/sum2017/entries/godwin/.
Pinch, Adela. *Strange Fits of Passion: Epistemologies of Emotion, Hume to Austen.* Stanford: Stanford University Press, 1996.
Pinch, Adela. *Thinking About Other People in Nineteenth-Century British Writing.* Cambridge: Cambridge University Press, 2010.
Pippen, Robert. *After the Beautiful: Hegel and the Philosophy of Pictorial Modernism.* Chicago: University of Chicago Press, 2014.
Pollack-Pelzner, Daniel. "Jane Austen, the Prose Shakespeare." *SEL* 53.4 (2013). 763–792.
Poovey, Mary. *Genres of the Credit Economy: Mediating Value in Eighteenth- and Nineteenth-Century Britain.* Chicago: University of Chicago Press, 2008.
Poovey, Mary. "The True English Style." *Persuasions* 5 (1983). 48–51.
Poplawski, Paul. Ed. *A Jane Austen Encyclopedia.* Westport, CT: Greenwood Press, 1998.
Quinn, Megan. "The Sensation of Language in Austen's *Persuasion*." *Eighteenth Century Fiction* 30.2 (2017–18). 243–263.
Richards, Ivor Armstrong. *Practical Criticism: A Study of Literary Judgment.* New York: Harvest, 1929.
Richardson, Alan. *The Neural Sublime: Cognitive Theories and Romantic Texts.* Baltimore, MD: Johns Hopkins University Press, 2010.
Ricks, Christopher. *Essays in Appreciation.* Oxford: Clarendon, 1996.
Read, Rupert. "Wittgenstein's *Philosophical Investigations* as a War Book." *New Literary History* 41.3 (2010). 593–612.
Rohrbach, Emily. *Modernity's Mist: British Romanticism and the Poetics of Anticipation.* New York: Fordham University Press, 2016.
Rossetti, Christina. *The Complete Poems.* Ed. Rebecca W. Crump and Betty S. Flowers. London: Penguin, 2005.
Rothman, William. *Must We Kill the Thing We Love? Emersonian Perfectionism and the Films of Alfred Hitchcock.* New York: Columbia University Press, 2014.
Rousseau, Jean-Jacques. *The First and Second Discourses.* Trans. Roger D. Masters and Judith R. Masters. Boston: Bedford/ St. Martin's, 1964.
Rousseau, Jean-Jacques. *The Major Political Writings of Jean-Jacques Rousseau.* Trans. and Ed. John T. Scott. Chicago: University of Chicago Press, 2012.
Rudrum, David. *Stanley Cavell and the Claim of Literature.* Baltimore, MD: Johns Hopkins University Press, 2013.
Russell, Bertrand. "On Denoting." *Mind* 14.56 (1905). 479–493.
Russell, John. *Henry Green: Nine Novels and an Unpacked Bag.* New Brunswick, NJ: Rutgers University Press, 1960.
Russett, Margaret. "*Persuasion*, Mediation." *Studies in Romanticism* 53.3 (2014). 417–433.
Ryle, Gilbert. "Jane Austen and the Moralists." *Oxford Review* 1 (1966). 5–18.
Saintsbury, George. *The English Novel.* London: J. M. Dent, 1913.
Sedgwick, Eve Kosofsky. *Epistemology of the Closet.* Berkeley: University of California Press, 1990.

Sedgwick, Eve Kosofsky. *Tendencies*. Durham, NC: Duke University Press, 1993.
Sedgwick, Eve Kosofsky. *Touching Feeling: Affect, Pedagogy, Performativity*. Durham, NC: Duke University Press, 2003.
Sedgwick, Eve Kosofsky. *The Weather in Proust*. Ed. Jonathan Goldberg. Durham, NC: Duke University Press, 2011.
Seel, Martin. "Letting Oneself Be Determined: A Revised Concept of Self-Determination." *Philosophical Romanticism*. Ed. Nikolas Kompridis. Abingdon and New York: Routledge, 2006. 81–96.
Shelley, Mary Wollstonecraft. *Frankenstein; 1818 text*. Ed. Marilyn Butler. Oxford: Oxford University Press, 1998.
Shelley, Percy Bysshe. *Percy Bysshe Shelley: The Major Works*. Ed. Zachary Leader and Michael O'Neill. Oxford: Oxford University Press, 2003.
Siskin, Clifford. *The Work of Writing: Literature and Social Change in Britain, 1700–1830*. Baltimore, MD: Johns Hopkins University Press, 1998.
Slack, Paul. *The Invention of Improvement: Information and Material Progress in Seventeenth-Century England*. Oxford: Oxford University Press, 2015.
Smith, Adam. *The Theory of Moral Sentiments* [1759]. Ed. Ryan Patrick Hanley. New York: Penguin, 2010.
Soni, Vivasvan. *Mourning Happiness: Narrative and the Politics of Modernity*. Ithaca, NY: Cornell University Press, 2010.
Spurling, Hilary. *Ivy: The Life of I. Compton-Burnett*. New York: Knopf, 1984.
Stanley, Jason. *Know How*. Oxford: Oxford University Press, 2011.
Stewart, Garrett. *The Deed of Reading: Literature, Writing, Language, Philosophy*. Ithaca, NY: Cornell University Press, 2015.
Stewart, Garrett. *The Value of Style in Fiction*. Cambridge: Cambridge University Press, 2018.
Stewart, Kathleen. *Ordinary Affects*. Durham, NC and London: Duke University Press, 2007.
Stout, Daniel M. *Corporate Romanticism: Liberalism, Justice, and the Novel*. New York: Fordham University Press, 2017.
Sutherland, Kathryn. *Jane Austen's Textual Lives: From Aeschylus to Bollywood*. New York: Oxford University Press, 2005.
Swift, Jonathan. *Gulliver's Travels* [1726]. Ed. Albert J. Rivero. New York: Norton, 2002.
Tandon, Bharat. *Jane Austen and the Morality of Conversation*. London: Anthem, 2003.
Terada, Rei. "Philosophical Self-Denial: Wittgenstein and the Fear of Public Language." *Common Knowledge* 8.3 (2002). 464–81.
Thomas, Keith. *In Pursuit of Civility: Manners and Civilization in Early Modern England*. Waltham, MA: Brandeis University Press, 2018.
Tomalin, Claire. *Jane Austen: A Life*. New York: Vintage, 1999.
Trilling, Lionel. *The Moral Obligation to be Intelligent: Selected Essays*. New York: Farrar, Straus and Giroux, 2000.
Trilling, Lionel. *Sincerity and Authenticity: The Charles Eliot Norton Lectures, 1969–1970*. Cambridge, MA: Harvard University Press, 1971.
Twain, Mark. *Mississippi Writings*. New York: Library of America, 1982.

Vermeule, Blakey. *Why Do We Care about Literary Characters*. Baltimore, MD: Johns Hopkins University Press, 2010.
Wald, Priscilla. "Conjunctive Relations." *J19* 1.1 (2013). 15–19.
Walker, Eric C. "Austen and Cavell." *Stanley Cavell and the Event of Romanticism*. Ed. Eric Lindstrom. Romantic Circles Praxis Series (2014).
Warminski, Andrej. "Postscriptum: On the Super-performative." *Material Events: Paul de Man and the Afterlife of Theory*. Ed. Tom Cohen et. al. Minneapolis, MN: University of Minnesota Press, 2002. 22–28.
Warner, William, and Deidre Lynch. Eds. *Cultural Institutions of the Novel*. Durham, NC: Duke University Press, 1996.
Warren, Andrew. "Incapable of Being Disentangled: On De Quincey's Impassioned Prose." Romantic Circles Praxis Series (2017).
Weber, Samuel. *Benjamin's -Abilities*. Cambridge, MA: Harvard University Press, 2010.
Williams, Raymond. *Keywords: A Vocabulary of Culture and Society*. Revised Ed. New York: Oxford University Press, 1985.
Wiltshire, John. *The Hidden Austen*. Cambridge: Cambridge University Press, 2014.
Wiltshire, John. "Medicine, Illness, and Disease." *Jane Austen in Context*. Ed. Janet Todd. Cambridge: Cambridge University Press, 2005. 306–316.
Wimsatt, Jr. William Kurtz. *The Prose Style of Samuel Johnson*. New Haven: Yale University Press, 1941.
Winnicott, Donald Woods. *Playing and Reality* [1971]. New York: Routledge, 2006.
Wisdom, John. *Other Minds*. Berkeley: University of California Press, 1968.
Wittgenstein, Ludwig. *The Blue and Brown Books: Preliminary Studies for the "Philosophical Investigations."* New York: Harper & Row, 1958.
Wittgenstein, Ludwig. *On Certainty*. Ed. Gertrude Elizabeth Margaret Anscombe and Georg Henrik von Wright. Trans. Denis Paul and Gertrude Elizabeth Margaret Anscombe. Oxford: Blackwell, 1969.
Wolfson, Susan J. "Boxing Emma; or the Reader's Dilemma at the Box Hill Games." *Re-reading Box Hill: Reading the Practice of Reading Everyday Life*. Ed. William Galperin. *Romantic Circle Praxis Series* (2000).
Wollstonecraft, Mary. *Maria: Or, the Wrongs of Woman* [1798]. New York: Norton, 1994.
Wood, James. *How Fiction Works*. New York: Picador, 2018.
Wood, Michael. *America in the Movies; or, "Santa Maria, It Had Slipped My Mind."* New York: Basic Books, 1979.
Wood, Oscar P., and George Pitcher. Eds. *Ryle*. London: Macmillan, 1971.
Woolf, Virginia. *The Common Reader: First Series*. San Diego: Harcourt, 1984.
Woolf, Virginia. *To the Lighthouse* [1927]. San Diego: Harcourt, 1981.
Wordsworth, William. *William Wordsworth: The Major Works*. Ed. Stephen Gill. Oxford: Oxford University Press, 2000.
Yousef, Nancy. *Romantic Intimacy*. Stanford: Stanford University Press, 2013.
Zhang, Dora. *Strange Likeness: Description and the Modernist Novel*. Chicago: University of Chicago Press, 2020.
Zizek, Slavoj. *The Sublime Object of Ideology*. London: Verso, 1989.

Index

acknowledgment, 97–104, 109, 110, 201
  problems of, 26
  skepticism and, 18
  social placement as, 107
aesthetic perfectionism, 217
affordance, concept of, 9
Agamben, Giorgio, 34
Alfano, Chiara, 182
anachronistic conversation, in philosophy, 41
anarchism, rational, 121, 124
Aristotle, 22
Arsic, Branka, 159
art of the sequel, 97–104
Austen Style, 51, 129, 145, 216
  figure of, 216
  impersonal, 106
  post-ironic "late," 218
Austen, Henry, 23, 24, 26
Austen, Jane, 2, 11–16, 22–26, 36, 87–88, 121–123, 138, 150, 160, 231, 252
  acts of exchange in writing of, 27–29
  calm or contained phrases, 144
  censorious narrator, 85
  comic style, 104, 109
  conduct novels, 47
  conjugation, 41, 59–60
  downstage characters, 15
  female-gendered domestic spaces, 91
  fiction of, 1
  free indirect style, 55, 80
  impersonal style, 106
  intellectual solitude, 115
  internal transformation, 103
  keeping, 218–222
  MAD letter, 38, 210–211
  marriage in work of, 29–30
  mitigated skepticism, 17
  narration of cultural desires, 35
  novels associated with constraint, 33
  philosophical account of fiction, questions for, 80–81
  philosophical temperament, 42
  prose fiction, 17, 32–33, 129
  (mis)recognition and acknowledgment, problems of, 26
  rule following behavior, 74
  Shakespeare and, 223–225
  skepticisms, 67
  solitude and solipsism, 67
  and Terror, 134–144
  tormenting problems, 46
  withdrawn consent to marriage, 37–38
  worn-out characters, 14
  written voices, 29
Austen-Leigh, James Edward, 23
Austin, J. L., 12, 17, 18, 22, 25–26, 28, 32, 36, 50, 53, 62, 115, 140, 150, 182
  comic style, 109
  commissives, 52
  debunking of typecast "material things," 9
  descriptive fallacy, 200
  Don Juanism, 32
  familiar objects, 3
  illocutionary speech-act theory, 19
  language of Polonius, 177
  linguistic phenomenology, 6, 12, 167
  and Locke's metaphor of furniture, 3
  mainstream philosophical tradition, 46–47
  marriage in work of, 29–30, 37, 57–58
  The Meaning of a Word, 64, 65
  namesake, 37, 47, 83
  official theory, 43–44
  Other Minds, 39, 59, 80–82, 161–167
  paid tribute to *Sense and Sensibility*, 45
  performative language, 19, 53
  performative utterance, 32, 130
  perlocutionary realm of performative language, 134
  philosophical dispute with Ayer's Foundations, 4–5
  A Plea for Excuses, 6, 7, 15, 19, 65, 166–167, 174, 194–199

Index 279

"Pretending," 19, 194–196
ready-to-hand garden metaphor, 4–5
reliance on adversarial thought, 83
review of Ryle, 123
satire, 6
stylistic satire, 40–41
"Three Ways of Spilling Ink," 3
"Truth," 7
written voices, 29
Austinian performativity, 31
Ayer, Alfred Jules, 2–4
discussion of "argument from illusion," 31

The Bandwagon (film), 152–153
Banfield, Ann, 233n22
Barbauld, Anna, 248n7
Becoming Jane (film), 42
Belle (film), 135
Bemühung, 120
Benjamin, Walter, 102
Bentham, Jeremy, 83
Berlin, Isaiah, 16, 29, 232n9
Bersani, Leo, 218
Bestreben, 120
Bigg-Wither, Harris, 37, 38
Binoche, Bertrand, 120
Blake, William, 126, 128
Bloom, Harold, 48
The Blue and Brown Books (Wittgenstein), 11, 12, 233n23
Boyd, Brian, 87–88
Bree, Linda, 248n7
Brideoak, Fiona, 29
British Romantic-era philosophy, 112, 124, 125
Brontë, Charlotte, 170, 224
Brooks, Cleanth, 118
Brown Book (Wittgenstein), 253n29
Burney, Fanny, 54, 96, 98, 99, 133
rigid Johnsonian sentence style, 103
wise physician account, 101
Butler, Judith, 53, 54
Byrne, Paula, 235n3

The Cambridge Edition of the Works of Jane Austen (Austen), 22
Camilla (Burney), 104
Dr. Marchmont in, 102
capitalism, 103, 108, 114, 116, 146
Capra, Frank, 110
Carlson, Jennifer, 36
Cartesian first philosophy, 87, 218
Cassin, Barbara, 213
Castle, Terry, 54
Cato, 78

Cavell, Stanley, 1–2, 13–15, 22, 31, 34, 39, 41, 46, 70, 109–115, 145–146, 205, 231, *See also The Claim of Reason; Philosophy the Day After Tomorrow*
"Aesthetic Problems in Moral Philosophy," 229
autobiography. *See Little Did I Know*
Cities of Words, 109–110, 145
comments on Austen, 113–114
Disowning Knowledge, 126, 128, 217
economy of horror, 147, 158
Emersonian judgment, 160
epigrammatic language, 150
garden analogy, 5–6
In Quest of the Ordinary, 8, 16, 63, 112–113, 124, 173
Kantian aesthetics, 154
"Knowing and Acknowledging," 5, 42
Little Did I Know, 20, 26, 158, 205, 214–215
"Melodrama of the Unknown Woman," 71, 146, 149, 159
moral perfectionism, 19, 103, 156
Must We Mean What We Say?, 12, 93, 109, 165, 206
ordinary language philosophy, 12, 17
"Othello and the Stake of the Other," 217
passionate utterances, 156, 187–188
perfectionist approach to comedy, 111
perfectionist thinking, 53
performative and passionate utterance, 98, 127
philosophy of Wittgenstein discussed by, 184
A Pitch of Philosophy, 113, 230–231
post-Kantian criticism, 19
and 'private language', 83
problem of praise, 149–156
Pursuits of Happiness, 110–111, 146
rational transformation, 44, 183, 185
The Senses of Walden, 113, 183, 231
skepticism and acknowledgment, 18, 151, 153
unwritten "proper dissertation," 125
vulnerable conformity, 113, 114
The World Viewed, 112, 202, 230–231
writing on Romantic writing, 16
Cavellian perfectionism, 4, 63, 129
Cecilia (Burney), 70, 96, 99, 104
Churchill, Winston, 138
Cities of Words (Cavell), 109–110, 145
The Claim of Reason (Cavell), 6, 16, 49, 53, 63, 72, 90, 95, 109, 124, 128, 166, 229
aesthetic perfectionism, 217
analysis of Rousseau, 148
and *On Certainty*, 188
perfectionist philosophical thought, 124

Cobbett, William, 47–48
Cohn, Dorrit, 53, 88
Colbert, Claudette, 116
Coleridge, Samuel Taylor, 16, 63, 112, 126, 173
comedy, 78
    anti-capitalist theory of, 105
    classic theory of, 102
    dark, 88
    of marriage, 18, 102
    perfectionist approach to, 111
    physical, 21
    of remarriage, 18, 103, 110
    screwball, 115
    and skepticism, 111
    stoic, 105
    and "vulnerable conformity," 104–112
The Comedy of Errors (Shakespeare), 224
The Community of Those Who Have Nothing in Common (Lingis), 34
Compton-Burnett, Ivy, 61, 133
Conditions Handsome and Unhandsome (Cavell), 148, 158
The Concept of Mind (Ryle), 6, 43, 47, 232n1
    Knowing how *vs.* knowing that, 117
conduct novels, 47
consciousness
    individual, 246n34
    modern, 121
    unshareable, 183
consignation, 41
constraint, 37, 145, 146
Contesting Tears (Cavell), 15, 93, 111, 113, 146–147
    and Bette Davis's character in *Now, Voyager*, 148
    feminine voice of philosophy in, 212
    figure of the unknown woman in, 147, 149
    skepticism, 211
conversation, 5, 24, 51, 97–104, 115–117, 131–133
    of aesthetic judgment, 171
    anachronistic, 41
    Cavellian language of, 178
    cultural and critical, speech links, 19
    metaconversation, 98
    as perlocution, 134
    transactional, 128
Cook, John, 5
The Country Wife (play, Wycherly), 222
Cowper, William, 85
Cox, Jo, murder of, 139, 141, 142
Crary, Alice, 117, 244n5
Criado-Perez, Caroline, 139, 142
Critchley, Simon, 158–159
criticism, 134, 151, 154
    affirmative, 153

formalist, 122
literary, 131
New Criticism, 33, 36
ordinary language, 29, 167, 205, 219
philosophical, 171
secondary, 136
Critique of Judgment (Kant), 171, 173–174
Critique of Pure Reason (Kant), 173

Daniel Deronda (Eliot), 157
Darwin, Erasmus, 118
Das, Veena, 16
Davidson, Arnold, 205, 212–215
Davies, Andrew, 94
Davis, Colin, 263n55
de Man, Paul, 82
"Declarations of Independence," 155
Deconstruction and Criticism, 138
deconstructive theory, 31
Deleuze, Gilles, 115
    "half-mad" model of conversation, 116
    screwball comedy, 115
demystification, 198
Derrida, Jacques, 41, 83, 155, 156
    "Typewriter Ribbon," 82
Descartes, 22, 66, 83, 86, 117, 218
    ball of wax, 226
descriptive fallacy, 31, 146, 163, 200
Dewey, John, 163
Dickens, Charles, 157, 186
Dickinson, Emily, 76
The Dictionary of Untranslatables, 119–121
Ding-an-sich, 173
Disowning Knowledge (Cavell), 126, 128, 217
Dolven, Jeff, 122, 123
Don Juanism, 38
Doody, Margaret Anne, 45–46, 258n52
    free indirect style, 53
    Oxford World Classics Introduction to *Sense and Sensibility*, 45

egotism, 66
Elective Affinities (Goethe)
    Benjamin's essay on, 102
    eccentric guest, 101
    of Mittler (or Mediator) in, 101
    obstinate gentleman, 102
elicitation of consent, 114, 132
Eliot, George, 25, 31, 48, 49, 150, 182, 186
    novels of economy, 145
Eliot, T. S., 84–86, 246n34
Éloge de l'amour (film), 159
    false or facile affirmations of America, 160

Emma (Austen), 13, 20, 33, 43, 44, 49, 63, 84, 165–166, 169–177, 210, 220
  banality of, 66
  blandness, 172
  Box Hill episode, 189, 195
  Cavell's interpretation of, 184
  Churchill and Fairfax in, 103
  climactic wounding of Miss Bates, 191
  deficiencies, characters', 167–169
  deserted atmosphere, 180
  disclosure scene, 181
  Eltons in, 187, 189, 192
  Harriet Smith in, 90
  Harriet's proposal from Robert, 165
  intellectual solitude, 182–189
  Knightley and Emma debate, 176
  Knightley and Emma union, 168
  Knightley's conclusion that Emma is "faultless," 174–175
  loss of relationships, 188
  love with Frank, 195–196
  Miss Taylor's marriage, 177–180
  Mr. Woodhouse in, 90, 180, 181
  opening chapter of, 176
  prediction, 167
  protagonist taking interest in her own life, 177–181
  reflecting judgments, 175–176
  sense of Emma's entitlement, 180
Emma Courtney (Hays), 70
empiricism, 13, 16, 240n85
empiricist epistemology, 229
Empson, William, 8, 31, 72, 73, 76
  The Structure of Complex Words, 8
English Dissenting tradition, 124
Enlightenment, 28, 119, 129
  aversion to perfectibility in favor of improvement, 121
  historiography, 121
  Scottish, 229
epistemological program of narrative, 45
epistemological skepticism, 57
essayism (Milnes), 28, 43
Essays of Elia (Lamb), 27–28
Evelina (Burney), 55, 96, 98, 99, 104

O'Farrell, Mary Ann, 41–42, 60–61, 247n48
  ideas about Austenian conjugality, 60–61
Felman, Shoshana, 32, 36–37, 50, 53, 82, 249n30
female-gendered domestic spaces, 91
Ferguson, Frances, 33, 53
Festschrift, 151
fiction, 53–65, 128
  literary, 16, 40, 132, 137, 225

metafiction, 54
prose, 17, 22, 126, 129
Wollstonecraft-haunted, 128
Fielding, Henry, 42
Fischer, Michael, 183
Fleetwood (Godwin), 125–128
Fonda, Henry, 116
foretellings, 163
formalism, 32–40
  New Formalism, 32
  quantitative, 34–35
formalist criticism, 122
Forms: Whole, Rhythm, Hierarchy, Network (Levine), 9, 36
Forster, Edward M., 7
Foucault, Michel, 20, 201, 205, 207–209, 211–215, 218, 231
  asymmetrical couples, 209
  courage to truth, 210
  discussion of democracy, 209
  hermeneutics, 214, 215, 228
  "La Philosophie analytique de la politique," 213–214
  multi-positionality of Austin's theory, 212–213
  ordinary language philosophy, 212
  parrhesia, concept of, 20, 205, 215
  parrhesiastic utterance, 210
  "Writing the Self," 214
The Foundations of Empirical Knowledge (Ayer), 3, 4
François, Anne-Lise, 38
Franklin, Ben, 125
free indirect style, 33, 34, 37, 55, 80, 178–179
Freud, Sigmund, 165, 214
  ego's refusal of suffering, 106
  humor, 105
Fricker, Miranda, 113, 147, 243n5
Fry, Elizabeth, 138
Frye, Northrop, 110

Gable, Clark, 116
Galperin, William, 193
Garden of Eden, 10
Gaslight (film), 147
gender theory, 31
gendered power dynamics, 108
German Idealism, 129
German Romanticism, 124, 171
Gilda (film), 112
Godard, Jean-Luc, 159
Godwin, William, 19, 59, 118, 121, 130, 162
  perfectibility, 122–129
  perfectionist philosophical thought, 124
  political philosophy, 125
  professional writing career, 126

Goethe, Johann Wolfgang von, 101
The Golden Bowl (James), 157
Gould, Timothy, 70
The Government of Self and Others (Foucault), 209, 212
Grant, Cary, 116
The Great Derangement (Ghosh), 35
Green, Henry, 5, 133
Grossman, Allen, 157
Groundwork for a Metaphysics of Morals (Kant), 176
Guyer, Sara, 37

Hadot, Pierre, 205, 214
Hamilton, Emma, 59
Harding, Dennis W., 56, 59, 122, 141–142, 188–189, 258n46
   civil falsehood, 191
   regulated hatred thesis, 189
Harman, Graham, 9
Hays, Mary, 59, 78
Hazlitt, William, 104
   archaic hermaphroditism, 105
   intellectual hermaphroditism, 105
Hegel, Georg Wilhelm Friedrich, 37, 43, 46, 96, 120
Hepburn, Katharine, 115, 116
How to Do Things with Words (Austin), 2, 7, 19, 32, 39, 134
   account of illocution in, 185
   complications of, 166
   descriptive fallacy, 163
   illocution-perlocution distinction, 118
   marriage in, 30, 36
   mock pragmatism of, 200
   ordinary language philosophy, 146
   poetry's immodal status in, 54
Hume, David, 22, 42, 43, 46, 49, 162
   skepticism, 53, 213
   understanding of "sentiment," 76
humor, 105–106, *See also* comedy
   social voice in, 106
hyper-protected cooperative principle, 39

ideal language philosophy, 12
illocution
   Austinian, 212
   in *How to Do Things with Words*, 185
   verbs of, 185
illocutionary speech-act theory, 19
illocutionary verbs, 186
illocution-perlocution distinction, 118, 130
"Imperfect Sympathies" (Lamb), 27–28

In Quest of the Ordinary (Cavell), 8, 16, 63, 112–114, 124, 173
Incidents in the Life of a Slave Girl (Harriet Jacobs), 157
insensibility, 77–79
   Adam Smith, 77–78
   of distraction, 79
   Emma's, 247
   radical, 91
intelligibility, 26, 39, 40
   queer theory and, 31
   zero-degree of, 17
Invade Mecum (Austin), 44–45
It Happened One Night (film), 110
Izenberg, Oren, 76

Jacobs, Carol, 138, 243n47
Jacobs, Harriet, 157
James, Henry, 8, 150, 157
James, William, 172
Johnson, Claudia, 25, 242n25, 263n46
Johnson, R. Brimley, 58, 200, 228
Johnson, Samuel, 42, 55, 67
Johnsonian sentence style, 103–104

Kant, Immanuel, 37, 112, 152, 173, 206, 207
   Ding-an-sich, 173
   philosophy, 86
   purposiveness without purpose, 174
   reflecting judgment, 46, 173–174
keep calm, 222
Keeping, 218–222
   aesthetic idiom for appreciating *Persuasion*, 221
   idiom of, 221, 262n42
   in *Oxford English Dictionary*, 220
The Keepsake (annual gift book), 222
Keymer, Thomas, 248n7
Keywords: A Vocabulary of Culture and Society (Raymond Williams), 74
King Lear (Shakespeare), 92, 128
Kirsch, Adam, 142
Knox-Shaw, Peter, 42, 43, 58, 59
Kramnick, Jonathan, 10–11, 238n54
Kurnick, David, 135

Lacoue-Labarthe, Phillipe, 124, 126
Lady Susan (Austen), 133
Lamb, Charles, 27–28
Laugier, Sandra, 10, 83, 148, 237n35, 257n20
Le Faye, Deirdre, 37
Leavis, Queenie D., 228
Lee, Wendy, 189
   rational anarchism, 121, 124, 128

Lefebvre, Henri, 35
Levine, Caroline, 9, 36
Lewes, George H., 17, 24–25, 42, 48–49, 170, 223
Lezra, Jacques, 10
Limited Inc (Derrida), 82, 118
Lincoln, Abraham, 154–156
Lingis, Alphonso, 34, 64
linguistic habitus, 28
linguistic phenomenology, 6, 12, 167, 177, 197
linguistic virtue, 28
linguistic vulnerability, 53
literary fiction, 16, 40, 132, 137, 225
literary theory, 32
Little Did I Know (Cavell), 20, 27, 158, 205
Litvak, Joseph, 242n30
Locke, John
    social consent, 148
    tabula rasa, 3, 105
Lorenzini, Daniele, 205, 215, 250n50
Love and Friendship (film), 133
Love's Labours Lost (Shakespeare), 224–225
Lynch, Deidre, 252n6

Mackenzie, Henry, 128
Malabou, Catherine, 244n7
Mansfield Decision, 19, 135, 141
Mansfield Park (Austen), 19, 25, 26, 43, 63, 97, 103, 131, 136, 140–141, 146, 170, 211
    catastrophe of, 221
    characters in, 139–140
    conclusion of, 144
    dysphoric affects found in, 139
    liberal progress, notion and function of, 143
    long set-piece scene in wilderness, 225–226
    marriage tie-ups, probability in, 143–144
    modern consciousness, 121
    object lesson, 137
    opening chapter of, 108
    plot of, narrator intervenes in, 143
    preoccupation of, 141
    probabilities, 167
    prose style, 108
    social function of, 149
    Trilling's essay on, 131
Mansfield Park (film), 135
Maria: Or, The Wrongs of Woman (Wollstonecraft), 70
marriage, 36–37
    Austin and Austen work on, 29–30
    illocutionary speech-act theory, role in, 136
    performativity of, 33
Marx, Karl, 11
Mary, a Fiction (Wollstonecraft), 70

Matz, Jesse, 233n22
melodramatic Romanticism, 6
Memoir of Jane Austen (Austen-Leigh), 23
Mendelssohn, Moses, 120
Menely, Tobias, 83
metafiction, 54
metaphor(s)
    entering into (a mind, a place, a marriage) as, 6
    Locke's, 3
    musical, 220
    ready-to-hand garden, 5
    sensus communis, 105
    tabula rasa, 3, 105
Metropolitan (film), 131–134, 136
metropolitan conversation, 131–133
Mill, John Stuart, 43, 206
The Mill on the Floss (Eliot), 205, 241
Miller, Andrew, 28, 79
Miller, D. A., 47, 61, 106–108, 246n36
    criticism of *Persuasion*, 215–217, 219
Miller, J. Hillis, 50, 84, 256n12, 259n54
Miller, Steven, 37
Milnes, Tim, 28, 42
Mind theory, 193, 198
Miss Austen Regrets (film), 38
mitigated skepticism, 17, 45, 46
Moi, Toril, 165
Moore, George E., 187
moral perfectionism, 19, 20, 44, 118, 122–129, 183
    Cavellian, 103, 118, 156, 209
    contemporary version of, 208
    Emersonian, 19, 114, 118, 119, 126, 144
    engagement with, 209
    untimeliness of, 113
    writers, 123
moral theory, 176, 201
Moran, Richard, 234n39
Mullan, John, 139
Murray, John, 210
Must We Mean What We Say? (Cavell), 12, 93, 109, 165, 206

Nancy, Jean-Luc, 124, 126
narcissism, 15, 37, 86
    triumph of, 105
Nazar, Hina, 91
Nersessian, Anahid, 238n54
Neruda, Pablo, 10
New Criticism, 33, 36
"New Realistic Novel," 55
Ngai, Sianne, 35, 139, 171–172
Nichols, Beverley, 4
Nietzsche, Friedrich, 111, 143–146, 150

284 Index

Northanger Abbey (Austen), 17, 38, 49–51, 54–59, 61–63, 81, 99, 210, 221
  Catherine-Henry relationship, 68–69
  forward habits of language in, Catherine's, 61
  good and evil balanced plot, 103
  Henry and Catherine meeting scene, 56–59
  heroine's desire in, 54
  Isabella Thorpe's abuse of the promise, 51
  marriage plots, expectations of, 56
  minor characters, 63
  opening chapter of, 55
  protagonist of, 50
  proto-detective story in, 55–56
  solipsism, 68
  Thorpe's villainy, 61–62
novels of economy, 141, 146
Now, Voyager (film), 148

objective correlative, verbal, 85
object-oriented ontology, 9
Old Comedy, 111
On Certainty (Wittgenstein), 161, 187, 188
The Opposing Self (Trilling), 136, 142
ordinary language, 4, 8, 10–12, 15, 61, 138
  criticism, 29, 167, 205, 219
  notion of promise of happiness, 51
  philosophers, 17, 26, 40, 50, 84, 193
  plurality and multi-sidedness of, 43
  poststructuralism and, 80
  responsiveness, 64–65
ordinary language philosophy, 1, 4, 5, 8, 10, 12, 15, 17, 22, 64, 72, 88, 146, 212
  analytical language, 11
  Austen and, 41
  Cavell as practitioner of, 12
ordinary natural language, 9, 65
ordinary-life genres, 136
other minds philosophy, 88, 89, 193
other minds problem, 4, 16, 18, 29, 37, 66, 80, 91, 193, 196
  anger, 84
  fiction and, 53–65
  Mind theory on, theory of, 193
  Northanger Abbey, 54
  philosophical instantiation of, 117–118
  recognition of, 65
  romanticism and, 53, 63
  solipsistic version of, 87
other minds skepticism, 5, 60
Our Aesthetic Categories (Ngai), 36, 169, 171, 174
Our Village (Mitford), 169, 189

parrhesia, concept of, 20, 205, 215
Peacock, Thomas Love, 133
perfectibilité, 121
perfectibility, 117–122
  concept of, 18–19
  Godwinian, 122–129
  human capacity for, 120
  Romantic-era utopian, 118
  Rousseauian thinking, 120
  versus improvement, 114, 119, 120
perfectionism, 117–122
  aesthetic, 217
  Cavellian, 4, 63, 128–129
  Emersonian, 158, 160, 215, 224
  improvisational dimension of, 112
  moral. *See* moral perfectionism
  philosophical, 121, 182
  Thoreauvian, 215
  Transcendentalist dimension of, 205
Perfektibilität, 120
performative language
  Austinian, 53
  perlocutionary realm of, 19, 134
  types of, 141
performative speech act, 82, 163, 186
performative utterance, 32
performativity, 1, 36–37
  literary, 39
  literary theory and, 32
  of marriage, 33
  social, 7
perlocution, 19, 136, 137, 166, 201, 212, 215
  Austin's neglected terrain of, 186
  Austinian category of, 126
  Cavell's treatment of, 146, 149
  conversation to, 134
  speech actant of, 212
  under-emphasized theory of, 185
perlocutionary responsiveness, 160
perlocutionary verbs, 185–186
persuasion
  care of the self and, 209–210
  and conviction, 205–218
  optative-hypothetical, 208
  self-persuasion, 209
  and symbolic expression, 201
  unfortunate, 203
Persuasion (Austen), 20–21, 63, 131, 228
  account of remarriage, 204
  Anne and Frederick partnership, 202–204
  Anne's emergence into conviction, 209–210
  Cavellian dimension of, 204

climactic scene in, 211
condition of personhood, 217
exquisite delicacy and keeping, 221
figure of Anne Elliot, 211
gendered environment, 207–208
injured body, 228
Keeping, 202, 218–222
last sentence of, 202
Miller's critical account of, 215–217
Musgrove and Benwick in, 103
narrative style, 215–217
persuasion and conviction, 205–218
theme of resolution and wavering, 225
title concept, 201–202
Wentworth and jealousy, 203
Phenomenology of Spirit (Hegel), 43, 97
Philosophical Investigations (Wittgenstein), 64, 72, 77, 84, 90
dialogic approach to public, 89
pain, discussion of, 89, 183
Philosophical Papers (Austin), 29, 32, 146
Philosophy of Right (Hegel), 37
Philosophy the Day After Tomorrow (Cavell), 1, 13, 14, 16, 32, 49, 111–113, 123, 152
aesthetics, criteria, and moral judgments in, 206
Austin-Austen connection, 43–44
charge of American exceptionalism, response to, 158
confinement of women discussed in, 69–70
eponymous essay of, 116
"Fred Astaire Asserts the Right to Praise," 152–153
gender and genre in, 14
Introduction to, 149, 154–155
lecture version of, 13
linguistic responsibility, 64–65
moral perfectionism, 145
"Performative and Passionate Utterance," 115, 149, 156, 166, 185, 201, 207
philosophy of the ordinary, 182
project of praise, 150
remarks on novels by Austen and Eliot, 147
remarks upon Emma in, 182
right to praise, 152
verbs of illocution, 185
Pinch, Adela, 193, 257n32
A Pitch of Philosophy (Cavell), 113, 230–231
Plato, 164
A Plea for Excuses (Austin), 6, 19, 65, 166–167, 174, 194–199
poetry, 11, 16, 33, 39

immodal status in *How to Do Things With Words*, 54
Romantic, 66
Wordsworth's and Coleridge's, 16, 66, 112, 173
Political Justice (Godwin), 125
Poplawski, Paul, 14
poststructuralism, 80
The Prelude (Wordsworth)
rejection of Godwinism in, 125
wishes and fears representation in, 67
Pride and Prejudice (Austen), 18, 25, 43, 49, 63, 97–101, 103, 136, 139, 146, 170, 189
conduct or state of mind, 78
Darcy's comment to Lucas, 121
ebullient style of, 108
Elizabeth and Catherine scene of (Vol. III), 213
Elizabeth and Darcy returned from walk to Oakmount, 110
ideological conservatism, 123
Lady Catherine, 129–130
narrative problem of, 97–98
opening sentence of, 54, 106, 109
persuasion/conviction distinction in, 207
physical energy, 136
preconception of Mrs. Bennet in, 79
rule following behavior, 74
stylistic economy and energy of, 108
truth universally acknowledged, 106
Pride and Prejudice and Zombies (Graham-Smith), 74
private language, 256n11
Cavell and, 83
Wittgenstein's argument against, 147, 246n44
Promethean aspiration, 137
prophecy, 163
prose fiction, 17, 22, 126, 129
prose style, 17, 24, 33, 108, 144
psychoanalytical queer theory, 218
public language, 83, 246n44
Pursuits of Happiness (Cavell), 110–111, 146

qualia (philosophy of mind), 76
quantitative formalism, 34–35
queer theory, 31, 36, 39, 156, 218, 238

Radcliffe, Ann, 54
The Rambler (Samuel Johnson), 55, 67
Rasselas (Samuel Johnson), 67
rational transformation, 44, 176, 183, 185
realism, 54, 84
in artistic production, 12–13
bourgeois, 13
dissociative, 115–116

reflecting judgment, 46, 173–174
  aesthetic, 229
Reid, Thomas, 234n39
responsiveness, 92, 97, 118
  affective, 40
  compulsory, 96
  grammar of, 209
  linguistic, 160
  ordinary language, 64–65
  perlocutionary, 160
  self-critical, 154
rhetoric, 213
Richards, Ivor A., 8, 54
Richardson, Samuel, 133
Ricks, Christopher, 44, 45
Roman Stoics, 78
Romantic Poetry, 16, 66, 113, 115
Romanticism, 12, 17, 43, 53, 69, 114, 124–127, 138, 144, 173, 212
  beginnings of, 65
  Blake's, 128
  canonical, 92
  Cavell's writings on, 183
  garden-variety, 4
  German, 171
  melodramatic, 6
  Raymond Williams's emphasis on, 74
  restive, 212
  restrained, 63
  Wordsworth-Coleridge frame of, 113
Rothman, William, 111
Rousseau, Jean-Jacques, 82, 119, 121–122, 128, 148
Rozema, Patricia, 135
rule following behavior, 74
Russell, Bertrand, 250n46
Russell, John
  Henry Green: Nine Novels and an Unpacked Bag, 232n8
Ryle, Gilbert, 66, 69, 117, 232n1
  category mistake, 6
  Jane Austen and the Moralists, 40, 96–97, 117
  Myth of Descartes, 6
  myth, views on, 117
  praised by Austin, 123
  remark on Austen, 132

Sabor, Peter, 22
Saintsbury, George, 13, 20, 219, 220, 228
  characterization of *Persuasion*, 222–223
Sanditon (Austen), 26, 47, 52, 108
Scandal of the Speaking Body (Felman), 37, 82
Science of Logic (Hegel), 43, 97

Scott, Walter, 35, 169, 186
  review of *Emma*, 13
screwball comedy, 115–116
Second Discourse (Rousseau), 122
Sedgwick, Eve, 7, 31, 140, 147, 156–158
  Touching Feeling: Affect, Pedagogy, Performativity, 30, 31, 156, 232n10
  and perlocutionary "passionate utterances," 156
  weak theory, 7
Seneca, 78
Sense and Sensibilia (Austin), 1, 2, 4, 9, 12, 36, 39, 164, 185
  argument from illusion, 10, 31, 37
  descriptive fallacy, 146
  frames philosophical history, 45
  moderate-sized specimens of dry goods in, use of, 2–3
  reading of, 109
  satirical mode in, 12
  sensibility in, 45
Sense and Sensibility (Austen), 7, 18, 43, 61, 73, 80–81, 84, 221
  Colonel Brandon in, 94
  conduct or state of mind, 78
  contract and promise in, 52
  Elinor after the London ball, 79
  Elinor and Marianne, 73, 86–88, 90–95
  Farrers and Dashwood in, 103
  first readers' offhanded comments on, 89
  Lady Middleton, 77
  linguistic communicability of pain in, 76
  Lucy Steele's actions in, 100
  Marianne and Willoughby, 51, 84, 86, 88
  Mr. Dashwood in, 51–52, 91
  narrative mapping of, 95
  Nazar's conceptual account of, 91
  other minds in, 84, 88
  philosophical resiliency in, 95
  plot of, 51, 88
  tormenting problems of knowledge, 83
Sense and Sensibility and Sea Monsters, 74
The Senses of Walden (Cavell), 113, 183, 231
sensibility, 88
  definition of, 75–76
sensus communis, 105
Shakespeare, William, 21, 48, 63, 141, 152, 184, 200, 208, 223–225
Shelley, Percy B., 118, 159, 232n7
Shklovsky, Viktor, 10
Sincerity and Authenticity (Trilling), 43, 121, 142
Siskin, Clifford, 25
skepticism, 5, 11, 16, 39, 60, 67, 73, 138, 148, 151, 160, 163, 182, 201, 211
  comedic abatement of, 29

comedy and, 111
epistemological, 57
Humean, 53
maneuvers of, 218
mitigated, 17, 45, 46
modern, 117
polite, 65–71
volunteers, 93
Skyfall (film), 59
Smith, Adam, 18, 22, 42, 79, 220, 229, 258n39
disagreements, 230
insensibility, 77–78
physiological concession to "other minds," 117
solipsism, 65–68, 77, 92, 116
Soni, Vivasvan, 253n20
Southam, Brian C., 170
speech act(s), 64, 125, 157
classic, 212
commissive engagement, 38
descriptive, 155
dimension of, 137
explicit, 185
formal, 186
genre, 199
illocutionary, 186
institutional, 157
performative, 82, 162–163, 186, 261
perlocutionary, 28, 97, 134, 138, 149, 151, 261n13
territory of, 115
transition of, 166
typically-ascribed function as, 199
speech actant, 138, 212
speech-act theory, 82
Austinian, 37, 83
demonstrative, 235n13
illocutionary, 2, 19, 136
perlocutionary, 28
St Leon (Godwin), 125, 126
Stanford Encyclopedia of Philosophy, 176
Stanley, Jason, 250n47
Stanwyck, Barbara, 116
Sterne, Laurence, 67
Stevenson, Charles, 205
Stewart, Garrett, 32, 34
Stewart, Kathleen, 15, 97
Stillman, Whit, 131, 133
stoicism, 105, 214
Stout, Daniel, 149
The Structure of Complex Words (Empson), 233n14
stylistic knowledge, 122–123
stylized repetition of acts, 25

The Subjection of Women (Mill and Taylor), 252n5
The Sublime Object of Ideology (Zizek), 43, 96
"Susan" (Austen), 38
syllepsis, 6

tabula rasa, 3, 105
Tandon, Bharat, 235n2
tautology (language), 55
Thackeray, William Makepeace, 186
Theory of Justice (Rawls), 148
Theory of Moral Sentiments (Smith), 77, 117, 230
Things As They Are: or, The Adventures of Caleb Williams (Godwin), 70
Thompson, D'arcy Wentworth, 34
Thomson, Hugh, 219
Thoreau, Henry David, 14, 150, 184, 231
Touching Feeling: Affect, Pedagogy, Performativity (Sedgwick), 30, 31, 156, 232n10
Tracy, Spencer, 116
transactional conversation, 127
transparent minds, 53, 55, 88, 91
Trilling, Lionel, 19, 43, 136, 149, 222
essay on *Mansfield Park*, 131, 142
sentiment of being, 66, 121
sexual objection, 138
Twain, Mark, 137
Twelfth Night (Shakespeare), 224
Ty, Eleanor, 70

Übermensch, 111
Übermorgen, 111
Ugly Feelings (Ngai), 35, 171
Uncontainable Romanticism: Shelley, Brontë, Kleist (Jacobs), 138, 146, 243n47
urbaine haute bourgeoisie (UHB), 133

verbal play, 27, 44
verbal plurality, 19
Vermeule, Blakey, 192
Vermögen, 120
Von Sloneker, Rick, 132
vulnerable conformity, 16, 20, 44, 104–113, 182, 184, 210

Wald, Priscilla, 157
Waldo Emerson, Ralph, 136, 146
Walker, Eric, 69, 201
Austen and Cavell, 184
compared Austen to Nietzsche, 182
views on *Persuasion*, 201, 204
Warnock, Geoffrey J., 29
Warren, Andrew, 212

The Waste Land (T. S. Eliot), 85
Whately, Richard, 223
Whitman, Walt, 221
Williams, Bernard, 175
Williams, Raymond, 74, 84
Wimsatt, William K., 103–104
Winnicott, Donald W., 36
The Winter's Tale (Shakespeare), 63, 92, 126, 128, 203
Wisdom, John, 5, 163
Wittgenstein, Ludwig, 17–18, 69, 80, 84, 89, 91–92, 95, 150, 151, 182, 205
 anti-epistemological standard of knowledge, 188
 The Blue and Brown Books, 12, 233
 Brown Book, 253n29
 contingency, 187
 forms of life, 32, 80
 language-based philosophy of, 77, 88

On Certainty, 161, 187, 188
Philosophical Investigations, 64, 72, 77, 84, 92
private language, 147
Wollstonecraft, Mary, 59, 70, 76, 78, 123, 125, 126, 138
 haunts Godwin's fiction, 128
 moral perfectionism, 118
Wood, Michael, 112, 202
Woolf, Virginia, 8, 133, 202, 220, 224
Words into Rhythm (Harding), 249n28
Wordsworth, William, 16, 63, 66, 72, 80, 232
 poetry and poetic theory, 16, 66, 112, 173
 sentiment of being, 66
The World Viewed (Cavell), 112, 202, 230–231
Wright, Raymond, 251n65

Zizek, Slavoj, 43, 96

CAMBRIDGE STUDIES IN ROMANTICISM

General Editor
James Chandler, *University of Chicago*

1. *Romantic Correspondence: Women, Politics and the Fiction of Letters*
   MARY A. FAVRET

2. *British Romantic Writers and the East: Anxieties of Empire*
   NIGEL LEASK

3. *Poetry as an Occupation and an Art in Britain, 1760–1830*
   PETER MURPHY

4. *Edmund Burke's Aesthetic Ideology: Language, Gender and Political Economy in Revolution*
   TOM FURNISS

5. *In the Theatre of Romanticism: Coleridge, Nationalism, Women*
   JULIE A. CARLSON

6. *Keats, Narrative and Audience*
   ANDREW BENNETT

7. *Romance and Revolution: Shelley and the Politics of a Genre*
   DAVID DUFF

8. *Literature, Education, and Romanticism: Reading as Social Practice, 1780–1832*
   ALAN RICHARDSON

9. *Women Writing about Money: Women's Fiction in England, 1790–1820*
   EDWARD COPELAND

10. *Shelley and the Revolution in Taste: The Body and the Natural World*
    TIMOTHY MORTON

11. *William Cobbett: The Politics of Style*
    LEONORA NATTRASS

12. *The Rise of Supernatural Fiction, 1762–1800*
    E. J. CLERY

13. *Women Travel Writers and the Language of Aesthetics, 1716–1818*
    ELIZABETH A. BOHLS

14. *Napoleon and English Romanticism*
    SIMON BAINBRIDGE

15. *Romantic Vagrancy: Wordsworth and the Simulation of Freedom*
    CELESTE LANGAN

16. *Wordsworth and the Geologists*
    JOHN WYATT

17. *Wordsworth's Pope: A Study in Literary Historiography*
    ROBERT J. GRIFFIN

18. *The Politics of Sensibility: Race, Gender and Commerce in the Sentimental Novel*
    MARKMAN ELLIS

19. *Reading Daughters' Fictions, 1709–1834: Novels and Society from Manley to Edgeworth*
    CAROLINE GONDA

20. *Romantic Identities: Varieties of Subjectivity, 1774–1830*
    ANDREA K. HENDERSON

21. *Print Politics: The Press and Radical Opposition: in Early Nineteenth-Century England*
    KEVIN GILMARTIN

22. *Reinventing Allegory*
    THERESA M. KELLEY

23. *British Satire and the Politics of Style, 1789–1832*
    GARY DYER

24. *The Romantic Reformation: Religious Politics in English Literature, 1789–1824*
    ROBERT M. RYAN

25. *De Quincey's Romanticism: Canonical Minority and the Forms of Transmission*
    MARGARET RUSSETT

26. *Coleridge on Dreaming: Romanticism, Dreams and the Medical Imagination*
    JENNIFER FORD

27. *Romantic Imperialism: Universal Empire and the Culture of Modernity*
    SAREE MAKDISI

28. *Ideology and Utopia in the Poetry of William Blake*
    NICHOLAS M. WILLIAMS

29. *Sexual Politics and the Romantic Author*
    SONIA HOFKOSH

30. *Lyric and Labour in the Romantic Tradition*
    ANNE JANOWITZ

31. *Poetry and Politics in the Cockney School: Keats, Shelley, Hunt and their Circle*
    JEFFREY N. COX

32. *Rousseau, Robespierre and English Romanticism*
    GREGORY DART

33. *Contesting the Gothic: Fiction, Genre and Cultural Conflict, 1764–1832*
    JAMES WATT

34. *Romanticism, Aesthetics, and Nationalism*
    DAVID ARAM KAISER

35. *Romantic Poets and the Culture of Posterity*
    ANDREW BENNETT

36. *The Crisis of Literature in the 1790s: Print Culture and the Public Sphere*
    PAUL KEEN

37. *Romantic Atheism: Poetry and Freethought, 1780–1830*
    MARTIN PRIESTMAN

38. *Romanticism and Slave Narratives: Transatlantic Testimonies*
    HELEN THOMAS

39. *Imagination under Pressure, 1789–1832: Aesthetics, Politics, and Utility*
    JOHN WHALE

40. *Romanticism and the Gothic: Genre, Reception, and Canon Formation, 1790–1820*
    MICHAEL GAMER

41. *Romanticism and the Human Sciences: Poetry, Population, and the Discourse of the Species*
    MAUREEN N. MCLANE

42. *The Poetics of Spice: Romantic Consumerism and the Exotic*
    TIMOTHY MORTON

43. *British Fiction and the Production of Social Order, 1740–1830*
    MIRANDA J. BURGESS

44. *Women Writers and the English Nation in the 1790s*
    ANGELA KEANE

45. *Literary Magazines and British Romanticism*
    MARK PARKER

46. *Women, Nationalism and the Romantic Stage: Theatre and Politics in Britain, 1780–1800*
    BETSY BOLTON

47. *British Romanticism and the Science of the Mind*
    ALAN RICHARDSON

48. *The Anti-Jacobin Novel: British Conservatism and the French Revolution*
    M. O. GRENBY

49. *Romantic Austen: Sexual Politics and the Literary Canon*
    CLARA TUITE

50. *Byron and Romanticism*
    JEROME MCGANN AND JAMES SODERHOLM

51. *The Romantic National Tale and the Question of Ireland*
    INA FERRIS

52. *Byron, Poetics and History*
    JANE STABLER

53. *Religion, Toleration, and British Writing, 1790–1830*
    MARK CANUEL

54. *Fatal Women of Romanticism*
    ADRIANA CRACIUN

55. *Knowledge and Indifference in English Romantic Prose*
    TIM MILNES

56. *Mary Wollstonecraft and the Feminist Imagination*
    BARBARA TAYLOR

57. *Romanticism, Maternity and the Body Politic*
    JULIE KIPP

58. *Romanticism and Animal Rights*
    DAVID PERKINS

59. *Georgic Modernity and British Romanticism: Poetry and the Mediation of History*
    KEVIS GOODMAN

60. *Literature, Science and Exploration in the Romantic Era: Bodies of Knowledge*
    TIMOTHY FULFORD, DEBBIE LEE, AND PETER J. KITSON

61. *Romantic Colonization and British Anti-Slavery*
    DEIRDRE COLEMAN

62. *Anger, Revolution, and Romanticism*
    ANDREW M. STAUFFER

63. *Shelley and the Revolutionary Sublime*
    CIAN DUFFY

64. *Fictions and Fakes: Forging Romantic Authenticity, 1760–1845*
    MARGARET RUSSETT

65. *Early Romanticism and Religious Dissent*
    DANIEL E. WHITE

66. *The Invention of Evening: Perception and Time in Romantic Poetry*
    CHRISTOPHER R. MILLER

67. *Wordsworth's Philosophic Song*
    SIMON JARVIS

68. *Romanticism and the Rise of the Mass Public*
    ANDREW FRANTA

69. *Writing against Revolution: Literary Conservatism in Britain, 1790–1832*
    KEVIN GILMARTIN

70. *Women, Sociability and Theatre in Georgian London*
    GILLIAN RUSSELL

71. *The Lake Poets and Professional Identity*
    BRIAN GOLDBERG

72. *Wordsworth Writing*
    ANDREW BENNETT

73. *Science and Sensation in Romantic Poetry*
    NOEL JACKSON

74. *Advertising and Satirical Culture in the Romantic Period*
    JOHN STRACHAN

75. *Romanticism and the Painful Pleasures of Modern Life*
    ANDREA K. HENDERSON

76. *Balladeering, Minstrelsy, and the Making of British Romantic Poetry*
    MAUREEN N. MCLANE

77. *Romanticism and Improvisation, 1750–1850*
    ANGELA ESTERHAMMER

78. *Scotland and the Fictions of Geography: North Britain, 1760–1830*
    PENNY FIELDING

79. *Wordsworth, Commodification and Social Concern: The Poetics of Modernity*
    DAVID SIMPSON

80. *Sentimental Masculinity and the Rise of History, 1790–1890*
    MIKE GOODE

81. *Fracture and Fragmentation in British Romanticism*
    ALEXANDER REGIER

82. *Romanticism and Music Culture in Britain, 1770–1840: Virtue and Virtuosity*
    GILLEN D'ARCY WOOD

83. *The Truth about Romanticism: Pragmatism and Idealism in Keats, Shelley, Coleridge*
    TIM MILNES

84. *Blake's Gifts: Poetry and the Politics of Exchange*
    SARAH HAGGARTY

85. *Real Money and Romanticism*
    MATTHEW ROWLINSON

86. *Sentimental Literature and Anglo-Scottish Identity, 1745–1820*
    JULIET SHIELDS

87. *Romantic Tragedies: The Dark Employments of Wordsworth, Coleridge, and Shelley*
    REEVE PARKER

88. *Blake, Sexuality and Bourgeois Politeness*
    SUSAN MATTHEWS

89. *Idleness, Contemplation and the Aesthetic*
    RICHARD ADELMAN

90. *Shelley's Visual Imagination*
    NANCY MOORE GOSLEE

91. *A Cultural History of the Irish Novel, 1790–1829*
    CLAIRE CONNOLLY

92. *Literature, Commerce, and the Spectacle of Modernity, 1750–1800*
    PAUL KEEN

93. *Romanticism and Childhood: The Infantilization of British Literary Culture*
    ANN WEIRDA ROWLAND

94. *Metropolitan Art and Literature, 1810–1840: Cockney Adventures*
    GREGORY DART

95. *Wordsworth and the Enlightenment Idea of Pleasure*
    ROWAN BOYSON

96. *John Clare and Community*
    JOHN GOODRIDGE

97. *The Romantic Crowd*
    MARY FAIRCLOUGH

98. *Romantic Women Writers, Revolution and Prophecy*
    ORIANNE SMITH

99. *Britain, France and the Gothic, 1764–1820*
    ANGELA WRIGHT

100. *Transfiguring the Arts and Sciences*
     JON KLANCHER

101. *Shelley and the Apprehension of Life*
     ROSS WILSON

102. *Poetics of Character: Transatlantic Encounters 1700–1900*
     SUSAN MANNING

103. *Romanticism and Caricature*
     IAN HAYWOOD

104. *The Late Poetry of the Lake Poets: Romanticism Revised*
     TIM FULFORD

105. *Forging Romantic China: Sino-British Cultural Exchange 1760–1840*
     PETER J. KITSON

106. *Coleridge and the Philosophy of Poetic Form*
     EWAN JAMES JONES

107. *Romanticism in the Shadow of War: Literary Culture in the Napoleonic War Years*
    JEFFREY N. COX

108. *Slavery and the Politics of Place: Representing the Colonial Caribbean, 1770–1833*
    ELIZABETH A. BOHLS

109. *The Orient and the Young Romantics*
    ANDREW WARREN

110. *Lord Byron and Scandalous Celebrity*
    CLARA TUITE

111. *Radical Orientalism: Rights, Reform, and Romanticism*
    GERARD COHEN-VRIGNAUD

112. *Print, Publicity, and Popular Radicalism in the 1790s*
    JON MEE

113. *Wordsworth and the Art of Philosophical Travel*
    MARK OFFORD

114. *Romanticism, Self-Canonization, and the Business of Poetry*
    MICHAEL GAMER

115. *Women Wanderers and the Writing of Mobility, 1784–1814*
    INGRID HORROCKS

116. *Eighteen Hundred and Eleven: Poetry, Protest and Economic Crisis*
    E. J. CLERY

117. *Urbanization and English Romantic Poetry*
    STEPHEN TEDESCHI

118. *The Poetics of Decline in British Romanticism*
    JONATHAN SACHS

119. *The Caribbean and the Medical Imagination, 1764–1834: Slavery, Disease and Colonial Modernity*
    EMILY SENIOR

120. *Science, Form, and the Problem of Induction in British Romanticism*
    DAHLIA PORTER

121. *Wordsworth and the Poetics of Air*
    THOMAS H. FORD

122. *Romantic Art in Practice: Cultural Work and the Sister Arts, 1760–1820*
    THORA BRYLOWE

123. *European Literatures in Britain, 1815–1832: Romantic Translations*
    DIEGO SIGALIA

124. *Romanticism and Theatrical Experience: Kean, Hazlitt and Keats in the the Age of Theatrical News*
    JONATHAN MULROONEY

125. *The Romantic Tavern: Literature and Conviviality in the Age of Revolution*
    IAN NEWMAN

126. *British Orientalisms, 1759–1835*
    JAMES WATT

127. *Print and Performance in the 1820s: Improvisation, Speculation, Identity*
    ANGELA ESTERHAMMER

128. *The Italian Idea: Anglo-Italian Radical Literary Culture, 1815–1823*
    WILL BOWERS

129. *The Ephemeral Eighteenth Century: Print, Sociability, and the Cultures of Collecting*
    GILLIAN RUSSELL

130. *Physical Disability in British Romantic Literature*
    ESSAKA JOSHUA

131. *William Wordsworth, Second-Generation Romantic: Contesting Poetry after Waterloo*
    JEFFREY COX

132. *Walter Scott and the Greening of Scotland: The Emergent Ecologies of a Nation*
    SUSAN OLIVER

133. *Art, Science, and the Body in Early Romanticism*
    STEPHANIE O'ROURKE

134. *Honor, Romanticism, and the Hidden Value of Modernity*
    JAMISON KANTOR

135. *Romanticism and the Biopolitics of Modern War Writing*
    NEIL RAMSEY

136. *Jane Austen and Other Minds: Ordinary Language Philosophy in Literary Fiction*
    ERIC REID LINDSTROM

For EU product safety concerns, contact us at Calle de José Abascal, 56–1°, 28003 Madrid, Spain or eugpsr@cambridge.org.

www.ingramcontent.com/pod-product-compliance
Lightning Source LLC
LaVergne TN
LVHW020341260326
834688LV00045B/1474